MANCHESTER MEDIEVAL LITERATURE AND CULTURE

CONTEMPORARY CHAUCER
ACROSS THE CENTURIES

Series editors: Anke Bernau, David Matthews and James Paz

Series founded by: J. J. Anderson and Gail Ashton

Advisory board: Ruth Evans, Patricia C. Ingham, Andrew James Johnston, Chris Jones, Catherine Karkov, Nicola McDonald, Sarah Salih, Larry Scanlon and Stephanie Trigg

Manchester Medieval Literature and Culture publishes monographs and essay collections comprising new research informed by current critical methodologies on the literary cultures of the Middle Ages. We are interested in all periods, from the early Middle Ages through to the late, and we include post-medieval engagements with and representations of the medieval period (or 'medievalism'). 'Literature' is taken in a broad sense, to include the many different medieval genres: imaginative, historical, political, scientific, religious. While we welcome contributions on the diverse cultures of medieval Britain and are happy to receive submissions on Anglo-Norman, Anglo-Latin and Celtic writings, we are also open to work on the Middle Ages in Europe more widely, and beyond.

Titles Available in the Series

11. *Reading Robin Hood: Content, form and reception in the outlaw myth*
    Stephen Knight
12. *Annotated Chaucer bibliography: 1997–2010*
    Mark Allen and Stephanie Amsel
13. *Roadworks: Medieval Britain, medieval roads*
    Valerie Allen and Ruth Evans (eds)
14. *Love, history and emotion in Chaucer and Shakespeare:* Troilus and Criseyde *and* Troilus and Cressida
    Andrew James Johnston, Russell West-Pavlov and Elisabeth Kempf (eds)
15. *The* Scottish Legendary: *Towards a poetics of hagiographic narration*
    Eva von Contzen
16. *Nonhuman voices in Anglo-Saxon literature and material culture*
    James Paz
17. *The church as sacred space in Middle English literature and culture*
    Laura Varnam
18. *Aspects of knowledge: Preserving and reinventing traditions of learning in the Middle Ages*
    Marilina Cesario and Hugh Magennis (eds)
19. *Visions and ruins: Cultural memory and the untimely Middle Ages*
    Joshua Davies
20. *Participatory reading in late-medieval England*
    Heather Blatt
21. *Affective medievalism: Love, abjection and discontent*
    Thomas A. Prendergast and Stephanie Trigg
22. *The politics of Middle English parables: Fiction, theology, and social practice*
    Mary Raschko
23. *Performing women: Gender, self, and representation in late-medieval Metz*
    Susannah Crowder
24. *Contemporary Chaucer across the centuries*
    Helen M. Hickey, Anne McKendry and Melissa Raine (eds)

Contemporary Chaucer across the centuries

Essays for Stephanie Trigg

Edited by

HELEN M. HICKEY, ANNE McKENDRY
AND MELISSA RAINE

Manchester University Press

Copyright © Manchester University Press 2018

While copyright in the volume as a whole is vested in Manchester University Press, copyright in individual chapters belongs to their respective authors, and no chapter may be reproduced wholly or in part without the express permission in writing of both author and publisher.

Published by Manchester University Press
Altrincham Street, Manchester M1 7JA

www.manchesteruniversitypress.co.uk

British Library Cataloguing-in-Publication Data

A catalogue record for this book is available from the British Library

ISBN 978 1 5261 2915 4 hardback

First published 2018

The publisher has no responsibility for the persistence or accuracy of URLs for any external or third-party internet websites referred to in this book, and does not guarantee that any content on such websites is, or will remain, accurate or appropriate.

Typeset by
Servis Filmsetting Ltd, Stockport, Cheshire
Printed in Great Britain
by Lightning Source

Contents

List of plates	vii
Notes on contributors	ix
Acknowledgements	xiv

Introduction 1
Helen M. Hickey, Anne McKendry and Melissa Raine

1 Identifying, and identifying *with*, Chaucer 14
  Paul Strohm
2 First encounter: 'snail-horn perception' in Chaucer's
  Troilus and Criseyde 24
  Elizabeth Robertson
3 *Sir Thopas*'s mourning maidens 42
  Helen Cooper
4 Chaucerian rhyme-breaking 56
  Ruth Evans
5 'Have ye nat seyn somtyme a pale face?' 74
  Stephanie Downes
6 Heavy atmosphere 91
  Jeffrey Jerome Cohen
7 Hunting and fortune in the *Book of the Duchess* and *Sir
  Gawain and the Green Knight* 109
  Frank Grady
8 The implausible plausibility of the *Prologue to the Tale
  of Beryn* 125
  Thomas A. Prendergast
9 Caxton in the middle of English 138
  David Matthews
10 'Hail graybeard bard': Chaucer in the nineteenth-
  century popular consciousness 153
  Stephen Knight

11	Chaucer as Catholic child in nineteenth-century English reception *Andrew Lynch*	172
12	Flesh and stone: William Morris's *News from Nowhere* and Chaucer's dream visions *John M. Ganim*	188
13	'In remembrance of his persone': transhistorical empathy and the Chaucerian face *Louise D'Arcens*	201
14	Textual face: cognition as recognition *James Simpson*	218

Bibliography   234
Index   257

Plates

Plates can be found between pages 130 and 131.

1 Brunetto Latini, 'World', *Li Livres dou Tresor*, *c*.1325, London, British Library, MS Yates Thompson 19, fol. 40 (copyright: The British Library Board)
2 Brunetto Latini, 'Four elements', *Li Livres dou Tresor*, *c*.1325, London, British Library, MS Yates Thompson 19, fol. 28, detail (copyright: The British Library Board)
3 Macrobius, 'The five zones of the earth', *Commentarii in somnium Scipionis*, *c*.1150, Copenhagen, Royal Danish Library (Det Kongelige Bibliotek) MS NkS 218 4°, fol. 34*r*, detail (reproduced under a CC BY-NC-ND licence)
4 Prologue to the *Tale of Beryn*, *c*.1450–1500, Alnwick Castle, Northumberland MS 455, fol. 180*r*, detail (copyright: Duke of Northumberland)
5 *Tale of Beryn*, *c*.1450–1500, Alnwick Castle, Northumberland MS 455, fol. 190*r*, detail (copyright: Duke of Northumberland)
6 Thomas Stothard, *The pilgrimage to Canterbury*, 1806–07 (copyright: Tate, London 2018)
7 William Blake, *Chaucer's Canterbury pilgrims*, 1810–20 (copyright: The Trustees of the British Museum)
8 Sir Edwin Landseer, *Queen Victoria and Prince Albert at the Bal Costumé of 12 May 1842*, *c*.1842–46 (copyright: Royal Collection Trust / Her Majesty Queen Elizabeth II 2017)
9 'Ypunctured privilie with sharpe sper ye miller's tyer' from 'Ye Canterburie pilgrymage (ye real thynge)', *Cycling: An Illustrated Weekly* [London], 10 April 1897, pp. 287–8, detail (reproduced by permission of the National Library of Scotland)
10 William Morris, 'Frontispiece', *News from Nowhere*,

Hammersmith: Kelmscott, 1892. London, British Library, Shelfmark: C.43.e.9 (copyright: The British Library Board)

11 Thomas Hoccleve, 'Chaucer', *De Regimine Principum*, c.1411–25, London, British Library, MS Harley 4866, fol. 88r., detail (copyright: The British Library Board)

12 Bill Bailey, 'Pubbe gagge', still from live TV studio version, c.2001, www.youtube.com/watch?v=mNEWatD0viw&t=11s

13 Joseph Jastrow, 'Rabbit duck illusion', *Harper's Weekly*, 19 November 1892, p. 1114, detail (reproduced by permission of the State Library of Victoria)

Contributors

JEFFREY JEROME COHEN is Dean of Humanities at Arizona State University in Tempe and co-president of the Association for the Study of Literature and the Environment. His research examines strange and beautiful things that challenge the imagination, phenomena that seem alien and intimate at once. He is especially interested in what monsters, inhuman forces, and objects and matter that won't stay put reveal about the cultures that dream, fear and desire them. Cohen is widely published in the fields of medieval studies, monster theory, posthumanism and ecocriticism. His book *Stone: An Ecology of the Inhuman* (University of Minnesota Press, 2015) won the René Wellek Prize in Comparative Literature for 2017.

HELEN COOPER is Professor Emeritus of Medieval and Renaissance English at the University of Cambridge, a Life Fellow of Magdalene College, Cambridge, and an Honorary Fellow of University College, Oxford. Her books include *Pastoral: Mediaeval into Renaissance* (D. S. Brewer, 1977); *The Structure of the Canterbury Tales* (Duckworth, 1983); *Oxford Guides to Chaucer: The Canterbury Tales* (Oxford University Press, 1996); *The English Romance in Time* (Oxford University Press, 2004); *Shakespeare and the Medieval World* (Bloomsbury, 2010); and the Oxford World's Classics edition of Malory's *Le Morte Darthur* (Oxford University Press, 1998, 2008). She has also written numerous articles on medieval and early modern topics.

LOUISE D'ARCENS is Professor in the Department of English at Macquarie University. Her publications include the books *Old Songs in the Timeless Land: Medievalism in Australian Literature 1840–1910* (Brepols / University of Western Australia Press, 2011), *Comic Medievalism: Laughing at the Middle Ages* (D. S. Brewer, 2014), and the edited volumes *The Cambridge Companion to Medievalism* (Cambridge University Press, 2016), *International Medievalism and Popular Culture* (Cambria, 2014) and *Maistresse of My Wit: Medieval Women, Modern Scholars* (Brepols, 2004). She is currently writing *World Medievalism: The Middle Ages in Global Textual Cultures* (forthcoming). She has also published chapters on medievalism and articles in journals such as *Representations, Screening the Past, Studies in Medievalism* and *postmedieval*.

STEPHANIE DOWNES is a graduate of the University of Sydney and an honorary research fellow of the University of Melbourne. She has published on aspects of Anglo-French literary culture and its reception from the Middle Ages through to the modern era. Her forthcoming monograph is titled *Reading Christine de Pizan in England, 1399–1929* (Boydell & Brewer). With Stephanie Trigg, she is the co-editor of a special issue of the journal *postmedieval*, 'Facing up to the history of emotions', with Andrew Lynch and Katrina O'Loughlin, *Emotions and War: Medieval to Romantic Literature* (Palgrave, 2015), and with Sally Holloway and Sarah Randles, *Feeling Things: Emotions and Objects through History* (Oxford University Press, 2018).

RUTH EVANS is Dorothy McBride Orthwein Professor of English at Saint Louis University, Missouri, and President (2018–20) of the New Chaucer Society. She works on medieval literature of the period 1300–1580, with particular focuses on gender and sexuality, memory and translation. Her most recent book is a co-edited collection (with Valerie Allen), *Roadworks: Medieval Roads, Medieval Britain* (Manchester University Press, 2016), and she is working on a monograph, *Chaucer and the Forms of Memory*.

JOHN M. GANIM is Distinguished Professor of English at the University of California – Riverside and in 2015–16 served as the 113th President of the Pacific Ancient and Modern Language Association. He has served as President of the New Chaucer Society and has been a Fellow of the John Simon Guggenheim Memorial Foundation. His most recent books are *Medievalism and Orientalism* (Palgrave, 2005), which was translated into Arabic by the Kalima Foundation, and *Cosmopolitanism and the Middle Ages* (Palgrave, 2013). His earlier books, *Style and Consciousness in Middle English Narrative* and *Chaucerian Theatricality*, have just been reprinted in the Princeton University Press Legacy Library series (2014).

Notes on Contributors

FRANK GRADY is Professor and Chair of English at the University of Missouri – St Louis. He is a former editor of *Studies in the Age of Chaucer* (2002–07), author of *Representing Righteous Heathens in Late Medieval England* (Palgrave, 2005), and co-editor of *Answerable Style: The Idea of the Literary in Medieval England* (Ohio State University Press, 2013; with Andrew Galloway) and the revised edition of the MLA's *Approaches to Teaching Chaucer's Canterbury Tales* (MLA, 2014; with Peter Travis). Current projects include essays on *Piers Plowman* and on literacy in fifteenth-century England, and another edited volume, *The Cambridge Companion to the Canterbury Tales* (Cambridge University Press, forthcoming).

HELEN M. HICKEY is a Research Associate at the University of Melbourne. She has published on medieval law, medicine and poetics. Her most recent publications include 'The lexical prison: impairment and confinement in medieval and early modern England' (*Parergon*, 2017) and 'Royal Trauma and Traumatized Subjects in Late Medieval England and France', in *Trauma in Medieval Society*, ed. Wendy J. Turner and Christina Lee (Leiden: Brill, 2018).

STEPHEN KNIGHT is an Honorary Research Professor in Literature at the University of Melbourne, having worked in the universities of Sydney, Melbourne, De Montfort and Cardiff. He has published widely on medieval literature, with a special interest in mythical figures such as King Arthur, Merlin and Robin Hood, and also on popular literature through time, including late medieval forms in ballad and romance as well as more modern crime fiction. Recent books are *Reading Robin Hood* (Manchester University Press, 2015), *Towards Sherlock Holmes* (McFarland, 2017) and *A History of Australian Crime Fiction* (McFarland, 2018).

ANDREW LYNCH is a Professor in English and Cultural Studies at the University of Western Australia, and Director of the Australian Research Council's Centre of Excellence for the History of Emotions, Europe 1100–1800. His recent publications include *Emotions and War: Medieval to Romantic Literature* (Palgrave Macmillan, 2015), with Stephanie Downes and Katrina O'Loughlin, and *Understanding Emotions in Early Europe* (Brepols, 2015), with Michael Champion. He is President of the International Arthurian Society and co-editor of the journal *Emotions: History, Culture, Society*.

DAVID MATTHEWS is Professor of Medieval and Medievalism Studies in the English department at the University of Manchester. He is the author of *The Making of Middle English, 1765–1910* (University of Minnesota Press, 1999), *Writing to the King: Nation, Kingship and Literature in England, 1250–1350* (Cambridge University Press, 2010) and *Medievalism: A Critical History* (D. S. Brewer, 2015). His current work is on the continuities of Middle English literature into the Tudor period.

ANNE McKENDRY teaches and researches medieval and medievalism studies as a Research Associate at the University of Melbourne. She has published on medieval literature and medievalist popular culture, and is currently completing a book, *Medieval Crime Fiction*, to be published by McFarland in 2019.

THOMAS A. PRENDERGAST is Professor of English at the College of Wooster. As well as his book *Poetical Dust: Poet's Corner and the Making of Britain* (University of Pennsylvania Press, 2015), he has co-edited a collection of essays with Jessica Rosenfeld entitled *Chaucer and the Subversion of Form* (Cambridge University Press, 2018) and has completed a monograph with Stephanie Trigg called *Affective Medievalism: Love, Abjection and Discontent* (Manchester University Press, 2018).

MELISSA RAINE is a Research Associate at the University of Melbourne and an Associate Investigator with the Australian Research Council's Centre of Excellence for the History of Emotions for her projects on children's voices in Middle English narrative and contemporary Australia. Her work has been published in *New Medieval Literatures*, *Viator*, Routledge Studies in Social and Political Thought and the *Journal of English and Germanic Philology* (forthcoming).

ELIZABETH ROBERTSON is Professor and Chair of English Language at the University of Glasgow. Co-founder in 1986 of the Society for Medieval Feminist Scholarship, she publishes books, editions, essays and collections of essays on Middle English literature, and especially on gender and religion in Middle English literature from 1190 to 1450, with a primary focus on the *Ancrene Wisse*, the Katherine Group, Chaucer, Langland and Julian of Norwich. She is currently co-directing an international interdisciplinary project funded by the Royal Society of Edinburgh, 'Understanding the senses: past and present'. She is also in the process of completing a book, *Chaucerian Consent: Women, Religion and Subjection in Late Medieval England.*

JAMES SIMPSON is Donald P. and Katherine B. Loker Professor of English at Harvard University (2004–). Educated at the universities of Melbourne and Oxford, he was formerly Professor of Medieval and Renaissance English at the University of Cambridge. He has published *Reform and Cultural Revolution*, being volume 2 in the *Oxford English Literary History* (Oxford University Press, 2002); *Burning to Read: English Fundamentalism and its Reformation Opponents* (Harvard University Press, 2007); and *Under the Hammer: Iconoclasm in the Anglo-American Tradition* (Oxford University Press, 2010). His book *Permanent Revolution: The Reformation and the Illiberal Roots of Liberalism* will appear with Harvard University Press in 2019.

PAUL STROHM is the author of *Social Chaucer* (Harvard University Press, 1989) and various subsequent medieval books and articles. He has also written *Conscience: A Very Short Introduction* (Oxford University Press, 2011) and a micro-biography of Chaucer, published in the US and UK under subtly varying titles (Viking-Penguin and Profile Books, 2014–15), as well as essays and fiction, including *Sportin' Jack: One Hundred Hundred-Word Stories* (CreateSpace, 2012). He has taught at Indiana University, the University of Oxford and Columbia University. Now retired, he writes and lectures, dividing his time between Oxford and Brooklyn.

Acknowledgements

We would like to thank, first and foremost, Redmond Barry Distinguished Professor Stephanie Trigg for her brilliant scholarship, generosity of spirit and inspiring mentorship. We also express our deep appreciation and thanks to all of the contributors to this volume who, without exception, responded with enthusiasm and alacrity to our proposal for a collection of essays that showcases the best of contemporary Chaucer scholarship. Special thanks go to Stephen Knight and David Matthews, who were early champions and advisers for the project.

Sincere appreciation goes to the School of Culture and Communication and the Vice Chancellor's Office at the University of Melbourne for financial assistance, and to the editorial team at Manchester University Press for sympathetic support from the beginning to the end of the publication process.

Helen M. Hickey
Anne McKendry
Melissa Raine

Introduction
Helen M. Hickey, Anne McKendry and Melissa Raine

In *Congenial Souls* (2002), Stephanie Trigg placed Chaucer scholarship at a crossroads, declaring that 'it may be time to refigure both our understanding of the past and our relation to the future of literary studies'.[1] A decade and a half on, this volume evinces the positive and productive response to Trigg's call for change by considering both how that future has come to form the present critical moment, and what the Chaucerian past means to us now.

Central to this exploration of Chaucer's contemporaneity across the centuries is the pioneering research of Trigg herself, whose reputation as an outstanding medieval scholar is closely aligned with her signature concept: the symptomatic long history. As exemplified by *Congenial Souls* and *Shame and Honor* (2012),[2] this critical methodology carefully interrogates moments of reflexivity, as well as instances of heightened tension between past and present within seemingly stable traditions. In *Congenial Souls*, she argues that 'the "Chaucer effect" is not the glorious culmination of continuous and harmonious tradition; rather, it is a negatively structured phenomenon produced by the changing and rival discourses of Chaucer criticism, from which none of us is immune'.[3] Trigg tackles this illusory continuity through close scrutiny of 'the discursive voices of Chaucer criticism' and their construction of traditions, communities and rivalries in relation both to their scholarly predecessors and to their contemporary critical circles, always attentive to how 'new models of hearing Chaucer's voice' reposition seemingly incidental aspects of research as potent enablers of discursive communities.[4]

The methodology established in *Congenial Souls* is similarly integral to Trigg's approach to the mutually distrustful divide between medieval studies and the study of medievalism; a distrust inherited from nineteenth-century pedagogical constructs and entrenched by twentieth-century medieval scholarship's dismissal of medievalism as 'popular culture'. *Shame and Honor* applies sustained pressure to this boundary, in the process shedding the 'secondary' status often assigned to medievalism and its 'derivative' associations.[5] Vexed questions of historical accuracy and factuality are reconceptualised as 'multiple, layered temporalities' and 'mythic capital'.[6] Such challenges to traditionally secure conceptual delineations and the insights afforded by their reevaluation regularly coalesce in Trigg's scholarship.

Trigg's scrupulous unpacking of symptomatic moments underscores her sympathetic yet penetrating understanding of the relationship between scholarly research and contemporary social, political and cultural contexts. An illuminating example of this occurs in *Congenial Souls*: Trigg highlights the historical gender bias of the Chaucerian 'community', arguing that it is 'more like a "club" that polices entry on the basis of the applicant's likeness to Chaucer' and where 'imaginative empathy with Chaucer … often mask[s] a more directly homosocial form of identification'.[7] Arguing that 'For women readers, the implications of this pattern of identification are crucial', Trigg throws these implications into sharp relief by replicating one of the activities that defines this club's membership: she occupies the 'unofficial space in prefaces and introductions' that (mostly male) Chaucerians have long reserved for 'informal, jovial invocations and impersonations of Chaucer'.[8] In the form of a spurious epigram, Trigg writes herself into her own *Canterbury Tales* continuation, in which 'the Pardoner' boasts that he will '"top you all with the tale of a woman who, like myself in a way, made her living by speaking in public, and how she lectured on Chaucer to students at a university in Australia"'.[9] Having stressed the centrality of (an often implicitly English) masculinity to Chaucerian communing, the featuring of herself, an Australian woman, as the subject of a Canterbury pilgrim's tale disrupts the cosy recognition that such playful fragments are intended to invoke, teasing apart the interwoven textual, critical and cultural threads that are symptomatic of her own historical moment. Trigg's treatment of this rhetorical strategy exemplifies her nuanced understanding of the role of the supposedly inconsequential utterance in reinforcing and excluding voices from communities. This awareness extends beyond the context of Chaucerian congeniality into her broader concern with challenging the paradigms of privilege and disenfranchisement in academic criticism.

This commitment to politically engaged research is also apparent in Trigg's consciousness of her participation in a scholarly community based in the southern hemisphere. For instance, when foregrounding the distinctive uses of the gothic and the medieval in Australian culture, she reconceives Australia's geographical and critical distance from the North American and British centres of medieval studies (and anglophone humanities scholarship more broadly) as a strength, rather than a deficit, to interlocution:

> Poised between the traditional ties with Britain, the successive waves of post-war European and Asian migration, a growing affinity with American culture, and an increasing consciousness of indigenous tradition, Australian critics deploy a sophisticated, global awareness of the working of cultural influence and historical tradition, at both an academic and a more popular level.[10]

This privileging of an Australian critical perspective asserts the ethical significance of accommodating difference more generally – insisting, in other words, that diverse voices generate fresh and incisive research perspectives.

Trigg's latest thinking about the politics of research has combined powerfully with her investigation into the history of emotions. In *Affective Medievalism* (2018), Trigg and co-author Thomas A. Prendergast construct a more local, personal and affective historical framework through which to explore the concept of 'medievalism as pretext to the medieval' in a pointed inversion of traditional critical approaches.[11] In their final chapter, the authors call for an end to the 'mutual exclusion' between medieval studies and medievalism studies, arguing that such separateness 'is not only intellectually misleading but also politically damaging',[12] especially considering the current climate in Western universities in which the humanities are increasingly threatened. Trigg and Prendergast argue that both fields

> have every reason to engage with contemporary debates about politics, meaning and culture; to articulate the power of literary and cultural texts, and patterns of historical change; to inform the way we track social change, the way our feelings of and knowledge about the past can change, and the relation between politics, society and the imagination.[13]

This characteristic process of intellectual inquiry also informs Trigg's interest in the relationship between emotions and cultural practices. The history of emotions is a vibrant area of inquiry for the humanities and, as Trigg notes, 'the "affective turn" in the domain of academic study also refers to scholarship that foregrounds the emotional work performed by cultural and social commentary as well as our variable degrees of emotional investment in our chosen objects of study'.[14] Trigg softens an often rigidly held distinction by articulating the significance of emotion to both the object of research and the critical methodology applied to it, generating space for reappraisals of previously unconsidered relationships between research object and method, as well as emotion and cognition. The application of a history of emotions framework to the themes and approaches recurrent in her work productively augments Trigg's critical interrogation of the intersection of ethics, politics and history.

Trigg's scholarship is typically incisive, historically informed, enthusiastic and expansive. Her unflagging commitment to advancing knowledge in her chosen fields is evident in her own publications, as well as in her willing participation in the debates and dialogues taking place within the academy, coupled with a strong desire to foster active and meaningful engagement with the world outside the university. These hallmarks of her critical style attest to her generous, open and inclusive vision of scholarly community. The diverse approaches, debates and inspirations that connect the chapters in this collection with her work all affirm the resonance of her criticism within contemporary medieval scholarship.

In recognition of the methodological strengths of the symptomatic long history, we have arranged the volume's chapters in loosely chronological fashion. However, since the contributions also speak to each other thematically across historical periods, the following discussion describes how their interactions address the shape and concerns of current critical debates. Moreover, we see in these interactions both implicit and explicit dialogue with Trigg's literary criticism, forming intriguing responses to her call to rethink the nature of contemporary scholarship, especially the place of Chaucer within it, and what the medieval past means to us now.

Paul Strohm's thought-provoking meditation on his relationship with Chaucer, as both critic and biographer, opens this collection and engages with one of its major themes: the intellectual and affective experience of communing with Geoffrey Chaucer in the centuries since his death. Strohm wryly admits that his desire 'to have a drink with' Chaucer confirms Trigg's 'worst suspicions of male-to-male complicity' in the futile quest to recover the 'real'

Chaucer from the simulacrum his poetry constructs. However, Strohm goes on to suggest that there may indeed be intellectually 'defensible elements' embedded in the nebulous relations with a revered author such as Chaucer, and he finds these traces in his experience with the poet both as the 'author-in-the-text' and through what he terms the 'biographical encounter'. By engaging with and then complicating the argument in *Congenial Souls*, Strohm reframes the possibility of identification with Chaucer by stepping back from individual texts to consider the poet's literature as a whole – a *gestalt* – through which the reader may discern 'certain recurring traits and dispositions – recurring postures and attitudes' to admire.[15] Furthermore, Strohm's research as a Chaucer biographer prompts him to consider this *gestalt* as a dynamic experience, in an implicit comment upon the vicissitudes of the concept of authorship in critical discourse.

Whereas Strohm has sought an individualised connection with Chaucer-the-man through both his *gestalt* and the historical reality of his day-to-day life as a civil servant and poet, Louise D'Arcens identifies a more generalised pursuit of 'transhistorical empathy' with Chaucer through 'the longstanding preoccupation with Chaucer's face ... [that] forms its own subgenre of reception' (chapter 13). Challenging the tenet that 'transhistorical feeling' is simply a form of naive projection to be eschewed by historians of emotions, D'Arcens draws upon the hermeneutic concept of *Einfühlung* ('feeling into') for her examination of the long 'empathetic afterlife' enjoyed by Chaucer's 'persone'. In the process, she synthesises Chaucer scholarship, medievalism studies and history of emotions research. Drawing from sources as diverse as late-medieval manuscripts, William Blake's engravings, nineteenth-century poetry and, in particular, performance (specifically, Pier Paolo Pasolini's 1972 film, *I Racconti di Canterbury* and comedian Bill Bailey's stand-up routine from 2001), D'Arcens makes a powerful case for an empathetic-experiential paradigm, acknowledging 'Trigg's focus on affective reception in *Congenial Souls*', and deploys that paradigm to demonstrate how the drive to connect emotionally with the subject 'Geoffrey Chaucer' may even displace his writing.

Stephanie Downes also productively engages with Trigg's research on the face as a site of signification, emotion and communication (chapter 5). Downes differentiates between the movement of the speaking face, crucial to conveying its meaning, and facial pallor that 'need not involve any movement at all'. Working from the position that a pale face 'is not something the subject alone can readily perceive', unlike smiling, frowning, blushing or crying, Downes refigures Chaucer's pale faces as offering 'a hermeneutic guide' that asks his readers 'to deploy their own experiential and intertextual face-reading skills'. Downes brings this history of emotions perspective into dialogue with James Simpson's insistence that 'literary cognition is fundamentally a matter of re-cognition' – a stance he reprises in the final chapter of this collection – contributing a fresh perspective to the vibrant discussion of affective experience and the interpretation of textual faces in a specifically Chaucerian context.

Similarly exploiting the rich potential offered by a history-of-emotions – or, more precisely, a history of 'feelings' – approach for reading Chaucer's poetry, Elizabeth Robertson (chapter 2) finds Keats's sensorily evocative concept of 'snail horn perception' apposite for *Troilus and Criseyde*'s snail imagery, whereby extension into and withdrawal from the world, principally through the sense of sight, forms the basis for processing an overwhelming intersubjective encounter. Robertson uncovers the significance of medieval optical theory in Chaucer's 'profound investigation of the nature of emotion [through] an in-depth representation of the complex physiological and psychological processes involved in seeing' in *Troilus and Criseyde*. Her finely calibrated exploration of the sensory force and emotional impact of the first encounter between Criseyde and Troilus elucidates the dialectic between the senses and the mind that informs the overpowering experience of falling in love in this text.

By characterising the intermingling of body and world as 'transcorporeality', Jeffrey Jerome Cohen catapults us into atmosphere, not only into the physical layers of air that surround the earth, but also into the 'heavy atmosphere' of Chaucer's *Reeve's Tale*. In chapter 6, Cohen offers a sophisticated analysis of the relationship between medieval texts, emotions, the environment and the current critical moment; in so doing, he reveals the parallel between the earth's atmosphere and the emotional atmosphere that refuses to be contained by the medieval texts that create it. Furthermore, through examples of transcendence – Troilus, celestial beings, astronauts – Cohen reminds his earth-bound readers that 'weighty atmosphere' is difficult to escape.[16] Cohen's intermingling of premodern and modern transcorporeal modes of being is also suggestive for rethinking concepts of Chaucerian communities, past and present.

Introduction   7

Frank Grady, in chapter 7, considers an atmosphere of a different kind, namely, the psycho-social premodern *zeitgeist* that governs the interplay between literary convention and the construction of a seigneurial self, as expressed in the work of two of the fourteenth century's most significant poets. Trigg's reading of the circular and linear narratives in *Sir Gawain and the Green Knight* is Grady's starting point; he takes Trigg's emphasis on the 'difference in [the] sameness' of *Sir Gawain*'s structure and inverts it, focusing on 'sameness in difference' in order to ascertain parallels between *Sir Gawain* and Chaucer's *Book of the Duchess*.[17] Common to both narratives – albeit unspoken, in the case of *Sir Gawain* – is the overarching significance of Fortune, a force whose continuously turning wheel produces the repetition visible in conventional medieval narratives of aristocratic rise and fall. Despite the texts' differences, Grady argues that their shared 'seigneurial poetics' result in a similarly 'hydraulic' mobilisation of their hunting scenes, allowing Gawain and the Man in Black to eschew temporarily the demands of chivalric action while they experience the non-courtly states of enforced bedrest and overwhelming melancholy. In Grady's memorable assessment, 'Hunting is where the idea of seigneurial agency goes to hide when the narrative of Fortune rears its head' – a formulation that sharpens our awareness of the complicated interface between literary production and the chivalric conventions that structure aristocratic self-image.

In chapter 3, Helen Cooper's discernment of the subtle nuances of Chaucer's parody in *Sir Thopas* combines with a determination to 'hear' Chaucer's voice without 'killing the joke'; a critical framework that illuminates a literary Chaucer who is contemporary across the centuries. Mindful of the tale's dual audiences – the reader or listener who appreciates Chaucer's virtuosity, and the pilgrim audience that does not perceive the parody – Cooper furnishes a nimble and affectionate survey of potential sources for the seemingly minor detail of *Sir Thopas's* 'mourning maidens'. She finds that 'Middle English romance could embrace a plurality of mourning and sleepless maidens', who are generally treated with 'the same kind of light touch that Shakespearean comedy carries'. These depictions form a striking contrast with the psychological flatness and lack of agency displayed by the maidens of *Sir Thopas*, leading Cooper to conclude that Chaucer's suppression of the conventional romance maiden is an overlooked contribution to the parodic intent of his tale. Cooper's approach deftly demonstrates the ongoing potential for enriching the meaning of Chaucer's texts through close attention to contemporary intertextuality.

Where Cooper identifies meaning in overlooked intertextual connections, Ruth Evans's meticulous scrutiny of Chaucer's poetic technique reveals a lacuna in the scholarship and asks why 'rhyme-breaking' – '"where syntax crosses rhyme units"' – has barely registered among Chaucerian critics before now (chapter 4). Evans traces the origins and effect of rhyme-breaking, a little-studied yet powerfully expressive device, arguing that Chaucerian rhyme-breaking warrants closer attention not only for its poetic function, but also for its potential to illuminate Chaucer's position within the multilingual context of late-medieval England.[18] With the exception of Stephen Knight and Thomas Ohlgren, Evans notes, critics have generally overlooked Chaucer's rhyme-breaking, despite its presence in the *Canterbury Tales*, the *Book of the Duchess*, the *Legend of Good Women* and *Troilus and Criseyde*. According to Evans, Chaucer 'exploits the technique to produce a range of narrative effects'; it is especially effective when utilised 'to produce an ironic effect' that gives dynamism to his verse. Moreover, Evans draws attention to the political possibilities of form, and her casting of Chaucer as a European versifier also participates in the growing critical concern with situating Chaucer in a broader global context.

In the late fifteenth century, the overlap between manuscript production and the new technology of printing significantly affected organisational and compositional editing principles.[19] In chapters 8 and 9, Thomas A. Prendergast and David Matthews search for the intent behind two examples of editorial intervention in this period, in both cases situating Chaucer's texts within these broader dynamics. In his examination of the 'Chaucerian' *Prologue* to the *Tale of Beryn*, Prendergast argues that 'th[e] privileging of the author's recuperable intention is more modern than medieval', raising the question of how the *Beryn*-scribe understood his own compositional practice when he acted upon an irresistible desire to complete the pilgrims' journey to Canterbury. Among the relevant conceptual categories of authorship, scribal activity and textual completeness, Prendergast's response to this question attributes agency to the text itself – not supplanting other forms of intervention, but complicating their interactions. Prendergast's case study bypasses the authorially oriented Chaucer*ian* text to alight on something that could be described as "Canterbury Tales*ian*", with compelling implications for both the medieval

Introduction

understanding of the *intentio auctoris*, and the concept of author and text more broadly.

Matthews also identifies substantial discrimination within editorial and discursive modes, this time at work in William Caxton's editing practices. Comparing Caxton's printing of John Trevisa's translation of Ranulph Higden's *Polychronicon* with his treatment of poetical works such as Chaucer's *Canterbury Tales*, Matthews argues that while Caxton 'locates himself as a philological editor where *verse* is concerned', the editor instead 'updates' the language in Trevisa's *Polychronicon* in an effort to achieve 'a modernity-effect'. However, Matthews resists the conclusion that Caxton is 'modernising' Middle English in linguistic terms and instead demonstrates that Caxton was engaged in a self-conscious attempt to render Trevisa's work into 'what the printer thought was good English, and what he wanted to be good English, in his time'. Matthews draws a nuanced distinction between conceiving of philology as a tool for the interpretation of an unfamiliar language, and as a practice that renders texts completely transparent for their own time, affirming in the process the distinctiveness apparent in Caxton's treatment of Chaucer's texts.

Nineteenth-century forms of medievalism intervened vigorously in contemporary debates about national identity, gender, class and the status of medieval literature (including its academic institutionalisation) in ways that still resonate in today's culture, politics and scholarship. The three chapters in this collection that interrogate the significance of Chaucer and the medieval past to nineteenth-century political, academic and cultural concerns do so from distinct yet complementary temporal and thematic perspectives.

Stephen Knight substantially enriches our knowledge of the eccentricities as well as the broader trends apparent in Chaucer's nineteenth-century popular reception through his survey of hitherto little-known Chauceriana, liberated from obscurity by the recent digitisation of archival records (chapter 10). Knight traces in painstaking detail the wide-ranging and at times unexpected contexts in which Chaucer appeared throughout the century, unearthing materials such as cartoons, poems and reviews in publications as diverse as *Cycling: An Illustrated Weekly*, newspapers, ladies' journals, children's books, and examples outside the popular press, including, as Knight happily notes, 'a victorious Victorian racehorse named Chaucer'. His overview tracks instances of symptomatic change in which Chaucer and his works participated in the promotion of national agendas of Englishness (although not limited to England geographically), as well as the establishment of Middle English literature as a respectable field of academic enquiry.

One of the major impediments to the nineteenth-century project of Chaucer's canonisation was the incontrovertible fact of his Catholicism, and this is the focus of Andrew Lynch's analysis in chapter 11. Lynch identifies the strategy employed by nineteenth-century commentators to obscure this unpalatable truth by promoting 'a non-controversial critical discourse in which the poet figured as "Fresh Chaucer", "Simple Chaucer", and "Child Chaucer"'. These deft editorial interventions simultaneously transformed Chaucer into the father of English poetry and infantilised his Catholicism. This reach towards institutional adulthood, Lynch argues, engendered the suppression of certain of his works, such as the 'Retraction', while generating an increased interest in his possible association with John Wyclif. The effect of this combination was to enhance substantially Chaucer's reconfiguration as a proto-Protestant and representative of English nationalism.

The narrator of William Morris's *News from Nowhere* exhibits an elusive relationship with his medieval dream vision counterpart. In chapter 12, John Ganim teases out this shadowy presence by identifying the influence of Chaucer's own dream visions upon Morris's novel. As Ganim argues, the dream vision genre promoted the expression of 'psychological experience and fantasy', generating a 'free space' into which Morris weaves his perverse familial situation. Ganim's exploration of Morris's eroticised but anxious politics in this text also draws upon Trigg's study of the affective history of bluestone in her home state of Victoria.[20] For Ganim, this history of emotions framework illuminates the moment towards the end of the novel when the narrator's guide, Ellen, lays her hand on the wall of a house so that 'stones and emotions meet in an ecstatic union'. Through this encounter, and in an echo of Cohen's transcorporeality, Ganim draws out the implications of the ecosexual erotics of Morris's politics, combined with the masculine subjectivity informed by the medieval dream vision narrator, for the utopian vision of the novel.

In a fitting concluding chapter, James Simpson addresses incisively the concerns with which we introduced this volume: the formation of the critical present, the uses of the past, and the place of the humanities in contemporary academia. For Simpson, the idea of recognition is an essential mode of thinking that is distinctive to humanities scholarship. By tracing interconnections within two pairings of literary texts – Virgil's *Aeneid* with Dante's *Divine Comedy* and Chaucer's *Troilus and Criseyde* with Henryson's *The Testament of Cresseid* – Simpson argues that 'Understanding text is dependent on recognition of the text's long pre-history, compacted into the deep coding of genre'. In other words, meaning in each text is generated by recognising prior experiences, textual or embodied, rendering the 'recovery of truth ... all the more intense for having been known already'. Simpson's paradigm of re-cognition – of how 'recovery [of the already-known] always feels new' – is itself a theory of contemporaneity, and a rallying cry for humanities scholarship to recover the connections he identifies within (or despite) current political and ideological constraints. In this framework, 'recognition' of the Chaucerian text is one example of 'a marvellous uncovering of the immanent and already there' that will generate new, unpredictable interpretations according to the context in which the process occurs; in such a schema, Chaucer – his life and his poetry – represents an ever-rich resource for the simultaneous 'rediscovery' of the past and the practice of innovative scholarship in the present. Simpson thus characterises the work of the humanities as *re*discovery in place of *dis*covery, and the chapters that comprise this collection undertake just such a practice.

The authors collectively strive for innovative methodologies as well as an attentive awareness of the cultural and political implications of their research, while maintaining a determined close focus on the texts themselves and their historical contexts. In the past, these approaches were, at times, considered mutually exclusive. Yet, as Trigg avers, such distinctions are far from stable. The past we think we know is endlessly open to revision according to what the present compels us to search for: the work of cultural, textual and historical rediscovery is never complete. Whatever motivates and shapes this desire to revisit the past, these authors participate in the centuries-long investigation into how and why Geoffrey Chaucer's life, poetry and prose remain intensely affective, intellectual and contemporary.

Notes

1 Stephanie Trigg, *Congenial Souls: Reading Chaucer from Medieval to Postmodern* (Minneapolis: University of Minnesota Press, 2002), p. xxiv.

2 Stephanie Trigg, *Shame and Honor: A Vulgar History of the Order of the Garter* (Philadelphia: University of Pennsylvania Press, 2012).
3 Trigg, *Congenial Souls*, p. 21.
4 Trigg, *Congenial Souls*, p. 197.
5 Trigg, *Shame and Honor*, p. 26.
6 Trigg, *Shame and Honor*, pp. 95, 36.
7 Trigg, *Congenial Souls*, p. 28.
8 Trigg, *Congenial Souls*, pp. 38, 42.
9 Trigg, *Congenial Souls*, p. 40.
10 Stephanie Trigg (ed.), *Medievalism and the Gothic in Australian Culture* (Carlton: Melbourne University Publishing, 2006), p. xiii.
11 Thomas A. Prendergast and Stephanie Trigg, *Affective Medievalism: Love, Abjection and Discontent* (Manchester: Manchester University Press, 2018), p. 5.
12 Prendergast and Trigg, *Affective Medievalism*, p. 120.
13 Prendergast and Trigg, *Affective Medievalism*, p. 121.
14 Stephanie Trigg, 'Introduction: emotional histories – beyond the personalization of the past and the abstraction of affect theory', *Exemplaria*, 26:1 (2014), 3–15 (p. 9).
15 Strohm takes the concept of *gestalt* from Roman Ingarden and Wolfgang Iser. See chapter 1 for detailed references.
16 Cohen's emphasis on atmosphere recalls his collaboration with Trigg on affect and the elements; see Jeffrey Jerome Cohen and Stephanie Trigg, 'Fire', *postmedieval*, 4:1 (2013), 80–92. Trigg continues this line of enquiry in her identification of a shared emotional response to the trauma of the Great Fire of 1666 and Victoria's devastating Black Saturday bushfires in 2012; see 'Vitreous archives: fire and transfigured objects', in Grace Moore (ed.), *On Fire* (Brooklyn: Punctum Books, forthcoming).
17 Stephanie Trigg, 'The romance of exchange: *Sir Gawain and the Green Knight*', *Viator*, 22 (1991), 251–66.
18 On Chaucer's multilingual context, see Ardis Butterfield, *The Familiar Enemy: Chaucer, Language, and Nation in the Hundred Years War* (Oxford: Oxford University Press, 2009); and for a wonderful contemporary collection, see Candace Barrington and Jonathan Hsy, *Global Chaucers: Online Archive and Community for post-1945, non-Anglophone Chauceriana*, https://globalchaucers.wordpress.com, accessed 6 May 2018.
19 Trigg's interest in the politics of editing began with her edition of *Wynnere and Wastoure*, in which she observed that 'The genre of the edition, its characteristic narrative stance, its decorum and its form are objects of study pending investigation in their own right: in the meantime, we are probably right to approach the editorial task with suspicion'; Stephanie Trigg (ed.), *Wynnere and Wastoure*, Early

English Text Society original series 297 (London: Oxford University Press, 1990), p. l.
20 Stephanie Trigg, 'Bluestone and the city: writing an emotional history', *Melbourne Historical Journal*, 44:1 (2017), 41–53. Trigg's article describes the process of writing an affective history of Victoria's signature stone that envelops the countryside and marks the towns and cities with its distinctive colour in the form of laneways, churches and prisons.

1
Identifying, and identifying *with*, Chaucer
Paul Strohm

'I'm just going to start telling people one of my best friends is Chaucer, and we went to high school together and that I have photos of him in my wedding party'.[1]

Well, sure: I feel that way too. This is the mindset that Stephanie Trigg so brilliantly analyses in her *Congenial Souls*,[2] in which she describes those readers (especially but perhaps not exclusively male) who have shared in John Dryden's discovery of 'a soul congenial to his'. Nor do we rest in his sentiment; rather, we elaborate it, imagining his presence in or behind his text and, ourselves, as readers, in privileged communication with him. This is, as she puts it, 'our unspoken ... desire to see and speak with Chaucer, to recapture an elusive, virtually forbidden moment of authorial presence'.[3] And of course, Chaucer abets this inclination when he makes himself into a character in the *Canterbury Tales* – a rather inscrutable character to be sure, but nevertheless one with whom we might imagine ourselves interacting. She describes this illusion as the promise 'of immediate communication with the author, *as if it is we who are speaking with Chaucer*, we who are riding by his side'.[4]

Chaucer's character, both created and implied, is of course a simulacrum, a lure for the unwary, an invitation to make fools of ourselves by mistaking an illusion of presence for presence itself. Trigg's exposure of this process is masterfully conducted. But then how is it that, addressing an audience at the Smithsonian Museum last winter, I found myself blurting out that Chaucer (along with Henry Fielding) was one of the two authors I would most like to have a drink with – a confirmation of her worst suspicions of male-to-male complicity. What were those delusions that led me to suppose that a close reading of Chaucer's works had equipped me with a sufficient knowledge of his real-world personality to be certain that I would enjoy his company in some convenient drinking establishment?

As a supposedly level-headed Chaucer critic and, latterly, Chaucer biographer, I have some explaining to do. My explanations will, following a question well posed in *Congenial Souls*, revolve around the venerable concept of 'identification'. As Trigg poses it, this suspect process – itself based on a questionable fiction of authorial presence – is 'sustained by the possibility of the reader identifying with Chaucer'.[5] She is, of course, quite right in blowing the whistle on this possibility. As already noted, whatever version of the character 'Chaucer' we encounter in his tales, this created character is far too obviously a fabrication to allow any reliable basis for identification. Even if we *wanted* to identify with Chaucer, as a created character or even as a sensibility revealed in his poems, we'd have trouble getting him to stand still long enough to present us with anyone or anything stable enough to identify with.

Chaucer moves his 'poetic I' around, less to inform us about his extra-poetical life than to pursue effects he wants to achieve. That is, his self-representations are more tactical than empirical or biographical. When he deploys the character we call, after Talbot Donaldson, Chaucer the Pilgrim,[6] he assigns characteristics appropriate to whatever he needs from him at the time. For example, the first thing we learn about Chaucer the Pilgrim is how gregarious he is. On chance encounter with the body of pilgrims at the Tabard Inn, he gets around and talks to everybody, and learns many of their secrets too. Stopping here, we might think that Chaucer represents himself as a genial extrovert. But then, when the time comes for his tale, and the necessity is for him to tell an inept one, he becomes an object of derision, a shy introvert. Harry Bailly says he's always staring at the ground as if looking for rabbits, that he's small of stature and plump besides, that he is 'elvyssh' or mysterious, doesn't interact with anybody at all. Then, at yet another moment in the *Tales*, piqued by Harry Bailly and telling his more intellectually ambitious *Tale of Melibee*, he becomes competent again. Chaucer is plainly being tactical, having his persona do anything that best suits the situation at hand.

Another lure, aside from his Pilgrim creation, is that Chaucer frequently deploys a first-person 'I' in his poems, but this 'I' is hardly the poet himself. Much of the agenda for Chaucer's various 'I's is set by generic considerations, the genre of the particular poem he is writing and the customary role of the 'I' in that genre. The 'I' of the dream visions is, for example, hesitant and deferential. Now this may or may not be true of Chaucer in his lifetime (aspects of his biography would argue against it) but it is certainly true for the genre in which he is writing. Many of the traits of Chaucer's narrator are derived from similar figures in poems by Machaut and Froissart, in which a created speaker seeks to ingratiate himself with a lord or patron. And, even if he's not being subservient, this narrator conventionally enters his dream-life in turmoil, with a problem that needs to be solved and in search of a guide to help him solve it. A certain amount of fumbling incompetence is an essential preliminary to the educational process in which he will be involved.

Anyone even trying to identify with so elusive and obviously fabricated a construct as the implied self behind the 'I' of the dream visions, or the Geoffrey who goes on pilgrimage, is going to be grasping at phantom presences, flailing around as aimlessly as Don Quixote among the pig bladders. The end result can only be to end up as much a victim of delusion and imaginary presence as poor Quixote himself.

Nevertheless, as Trigg suggests, there's this constant temptation to imagine ourselves in a special relation to an admired author, and to suppose that all the necessary preconditions of this relation somehow lurk within his or her writings. I'm quite ready to admit that my relation to an admired writer is an imaginary one, and (though sometimes prompted or abetted by authorial strategies) one for which I must take ultimate responsibility. Still, I want to argue that such imaginary relations – relations of 'fandom', as it were – are a frequent if unacknowledged component of literary enjoyment, and I want to think further about whether the formation of such relations might have any defensible elements at all. That is, might one discover an intellectually coherent aspect of this debunked practice? I want to weigh two possible forms of identification with an author: one involving some extremely preliminary thoughts about the author-in-the text and the phenomenology of textual encounter, and the other involving the author-outside-the-text and what might be called the 'biographical encounter'.

The author-in-the-text

Freud imagines two levels of identification, which might for convenience be called 'primary' and 'secondary'.[7] Primary identification occurs in infancy, and involves the abandonment of an object-identification and the 'taking up' of the identification into the child's ego. This process involves a form of participation that amounts to a convergence of self and other, and the elimination of the subject–object distinction. This is, needless to say, an unconscious, or at any rate non-rational, process, occurring in infancy and early childhood, and any bearing it might have on one's attachment to an admired author is too diffuse and preliminary to be of much pertinence here. But Freud also describes what I'm calling a secondary and more potentially self-aware form of identification, in which the distinction between self and other is maintained. This form of identification is expressed in the conviction of a shared ego-ideal; as Freud puts it, 'Social feelings rest on identifications with other people, on the basis of having the same ego ideal'.[8] In the most austere version of Freud's theory, the ego-ideal is enlisted in furtherance of the harsh demands of the super-ego. But the identification founded in the conviction of a shared ego-ideal may be restated (or masked) in a number of homely and ordinary concepts, such as friendship, mutuality, conviviality.

So let us say that I find myself imagining this kind of amicable convergence, involving matters of sensibility and questions of perspective and value, as I read a favourite author – whether it be Geoffrey Chaucer or Jane Austen or Italo Svevo or Raymond Chandler or Margaret Atwood (my personal list). But, rather than treating this convergence as an unexamined fact, let me pose the further and more serious question: on what kinds of access and encounter is it based? How, that is, does one gain access to the attitudes and perspectives of a beloved author, when mediated by the text or written work? The circumstances of literary creation necessarily introduce a host of screens and deflections – a cacophony of voices jostling with the author's own – preventing direct communication between the author and the reader.

I am thinking of reliance on the verbal register itself, with the pre-formed dispositions inherent in literary language; the author's use of previous sources which, however adapted, import a host of influences into the resulting work; the author's adoption of voices and personae other than, or at least incongruent with, his or her own; the additional influences and requirements of literary genre ... all these and more. Chaucer is, for example, an intermediary and relay of a variety of source-texts, in which some views of previous authors clearly remain incompletely assimilated and at large. And an author who – especially in the *Canterbury Tales* – further complicates the matter by ventriloquising the voices and views of invented narrators, withholding his own attitudes or at most co-mingling their attitudes with his own. Even when he speaks as 'I', his first-person voice is itself a literary stylisation, serving a host of objectives other than personal candour or self-revelation.

Identification? Identification, we might ask, *with whom? with what?*

Suppose, though, that, rather than seizing upon a particular utterance or moment, we take the total body of the author's written work as the unit of consideration. Might one not step back from it, and discover in it certain recurring traits and dispositions – recurring postures and attitudes – which one might admire, or even consider a basis for identification, in the secondary – or diluted and homely – sense of the word?

Back in the heyday of phenomenology, Roman Ingarden and Wolfgang Iser advanced the idea of the literary work, or oeuvre, as a *gestalt*, as a totality created, interactively, between the text and the reader.[9] This *gestalt* is not a single, true meaning, but a fragile construct, open to constant revision. It comprises a totality, an entity demanding interpretation, but more in its composite nature than in any of its individual details or particulars. Suppose we regard this totality as a site of various recurring attitudes and dispositions – not necessarily directly expressive of the views of an author, but still authorially 'sponsored', as it were. In the case of Chaucer, the oeuvre itself plays host to noticeable recurrences – sufficiently present as not to seem coincidental – recurring attitudes of bemusement, compliance, deference, critique, appreciative enjoyment, and more. I don't suggest that any of these attitudes is exclusive to Chaucer, but they recur with sufficient frequency to seem like traits, as features of a world view. These attitudes can be bundled and imagined – not individually but collectively – as a loose unity, a *gestalt* providing an approximation of personal encounter.

As I read Chaucer or another beloved author I am aware of such recurrences – ways of viewing situations and handling material – which augment, correct, bolster, or fortify my own ways of viewing the world. I like the fact that Chaucer is, except in the rarest situations, no allegorist, that he means to live in what Bakhtin calls 'the productive horizontal',[10] a world of lateral social relations. I like his inclination for juxtaposition: the fact that, having expressed a strong view or committed to a vivid style, he'll look around for another way of seeing, for its opposite or corrective. I like his capacity for enjoyment, for joy itself, in conjunction with a sense that joy is fleeting and that felicity is all the more precious because it cannot last. I know I'm on thin ice in trying to imagine these dispositions as a personality and in supposing that I can cast my encounters with this personality along the lines of wished-for mutuality or conviviality. Well, so be it; however self-deceived, this loosely identificatory process remains a part of my reading pleasure.

Even as I say this, I realise that I'm in danger of sounding like a complete idiot. I'm aware of every sense in which the encounter I am describing is personally invented, wholly one-sided, objectively unsustainable and incipiently self-delusive. Even if there were such a thing as an authorial sensibility lurking within the totality of the work, it would be probably better elicited with the proven tools of textual explication and analysis, rather than engulfed in a murky and suspect process of identification. I'm not throwing this version of identification overboard because it is most certainly an aspect of my reading experience. But suppose that I bracket it, and proceed to an alternative and more sustainable version of identification: a sympathetic identification with the travail of the author, his or her struggle with circumstance, in the arduous act of getting the book written.

The author-outside-the-text

Contemporary literary criticism pays relatively little attention to the author's life or to questions about the conditions under which a book came to be written. Literary biographies, to be sure, continue to be written and enjoyed, especially in Britain, but are mainly ignored by literary theorists and critics, who, if anything, seem rather embarrassed that their author – or the rather precarious construct they allow to exercise an 'author function'[11] – exists at all. (The analogy here would be the adolescent who is typically embarrassed by any necessity of acknowledging a connection with parents, of having once emerged, in the midst of embarrassing specifics, from a human womb.) The likely reason is that literary critics, so fully focused on the text, as opposed to the worldly conditions within which the text was created, have settled on no legitimate use for biographical details in textual analysis. If anything, an attempt to bring a life-detail to bear in textual analysis or appreciation marks the critic as a fumbling naïf if not a charlatan. After all, knowing the difference between details existing outside the poem and those found within is one of the most rudimentary markers of literary sophistication. Who, in their right mind, would hazard reputation on so elementary a confusion? Would be caught in the embarrassing position of Mr Partridge in *Tom Jones*, who cannot tell the difference between a play and an extra-theatrical experience?

The smartest people among us trip up now and then. Consider the tantalising moment in Chaucer's *House of Fame* when the overbearing eagle shouts 'Awak!' in Geffrey's ear – in voice and volume, Chaucer says, of someone he might (but does not) name ('Ryght in the same vois and stevene / That useth oon I coulde nevene').[12] One influential critic (Skeat) made the plausible suggestion that this was Chaucer's own wife Philippa, waking him up in the morning. And all kinds of other brainy people have gone along with him on this. (I'll refrain from listing them, but they constitute a kind of honour-roll of the recent and even current profession.) But this connection is really entirely suppositional. Speaking as a Chaucer biographer, I would point out that he wasn't even living with his wife Philippa when he was working on his *House of Fame*. She was up in Lincolnshire with her fashionable sister Katherine Swynford and the extended Gaunt household, and Chaucer was perched in his tower room (hardly a suitable accommodation for a classy lady like Philippa anyway) over one of the gates of the City. And then other critics have since suggested that the voice must have belonged to an officious servant, or to Lady Philosophy, or to Christ on Judgment Day. In other words, we'll never know. Perhaps the voice simply belonged to this particular noisy eagle, and Chaucer can't name his source because he invented it.

But let me here propose a different use of authorial biography: less to 'sleuth out' the origins of textual details than to construct the circumstances under which the text was composed. To recognise the life-adjustments and sacrifices the author endured in order to get his or her book written at all. In the course of composing a recent biography,[13] I became increasingly aware of the painful priority decisions, and practical adjustments, and downright risks that Chaucer had to undergo in order to get his poetry written.

No niche like 'court poet' or 'man of letters' – or even, for those writing in English – 'author', even existed. Chaucer had, in effect, to invent himself as *littérateur*, without any apparent external encouragement. Whatever literary endeavours he undertook were founded in personal choice, managed in his own time, and his own time was scarce. His job in Customs was a real job, requiring his presence all or most days of the week and demanding personal inspection of cargoes and record-keeping in his own hand, and regular reports and visits to Exchequer. During those and other years in his life, his evening hours would have been the only available time for writing and he undoubtedly laboured when his neighbours were socialising and sleeping. While I won't claim as direct autobiography the passage in the *House of Fame* about returning home after working hours to devote himself to bookish pursuits,[14] I would certainly argue for its close congruity to the life he seems actually to have lived.

Owing to my increasing sympathy with the labours that his immense literary production entailed, I found myself dwelling – perhaps even over-dwelling – on the rigours of his life. On the more affirmative side of the ledger, he may have enjoyed windfalls through the sale of his family home. Although his stated wages were modest, he seems to have benefited from one substantial reward for a recovered cargo, and may have picked up other perks and fees along the way. His apartment over Aldgate has been so often cited as sought-after accommodation that I may have gone somewhat overboard in describing its cold, cramped and murky character. Philippa was a socialite, living apart and quite caught up in the chic circle surrounding her sister's lover John of Gaunt, but then Chaucer may have preferred not to live with her anyway. I've described him as squeezed out of London in the urban political infighting of 1386, but alternative evidence exists for a voluntary and carefully planned withdrawal; he had recently arranged for a deputy in Customs and may have been electively clearing the decks so he could work on his new project, the *Canterbury Tales*.

All these points being granted, Chaucer lived a demanding life, in which he regularly forfeited opportunities and comforts in order to gain time in which to accomplish the writing for which he is so admired. There's a gain in sympathy, for me at any rate, in dredging up the discomforts of his Aldgate residence, the hard slog of his day job, the probability of lonely nights, the actions against him for petty debts, the apparent lack of a fixed residence in the latter years of his life. I also take note that the ultimate reward of substantial literary recognition was long postponed; his works sketchily circulated in his lifetime and his reputation as a founder of English letters gaining momentum only after his death. He never rested easy, nor was permitted to rest easy, with his accomplishment. At junctures of possible self-congratulation, like the completion of his masterpiece, *Troilus and Criseyde*, he has more to say about self-doubt and misgiving than about crowning himself with imagined laurels. This dedicated servant of letters claimed time when he could, struck deals when he had to, gave the better part of his life not to family or friends or self-advancement but to creating a body of writing that sustains present-day readers with its restless creativity, intellectual acuity, ready sympathy and capacity for mirth.

Perhaps, at this point, I'm talking more about general admiration than about 'identification' as such. But if a sympathetic recognition of an artist's travail can be considered a form of identification, then I am confessing to substantial amounts of it in the case of Geoffrey Chaucer, esquire.

Notes

1. Scott Lear, 15 February 2017 tweet, responding to a Valentine's Day posting by Brantley Bryant ('Chaucer doth tweet', @LeVostreGC).
2. Stephanie Trigg, *Congenial Souls: Reading Chaucer from Medieval to Postmodern* (Minneapolis: University of Minnesota Press, 2002), p. xix.
3. Trigg, *Congenial Souls*, p. xv.
4. Trigg, *Congenial Souls*, p. xvi, emphasis added.
5. Trigg, *Congenial Souls*, p. xviii.
6. E. Talbot Donaldson, *Speaking of Chaucer* (London: Athlone Press, 1979), pp. 1–12.
7. Sigmund Freud, 'The ego and the id', in James Strachey (gen. ed.), *Standard Edition of the Complete Psychological Works of Sigmund Freud*, vol. 19, in collaboration with Anna Freud, assisted by Alix Strachey and Alan Tyson (London: Hogarth Press, 1961), pp. 28–34 and 37–9.
8. Freud, 'The ego and the id', p. 37.
9. Roman Ingarden, *The Literary Work of Art,* trans. George G. Grabowicz (Evanston: Northwestern University Press, 1973); Wolfgang Iser, 'The reading process: a phenomenological approach', in *The Implied Reader: Patterns of Communication in Prose Fiction from Bunyan to Beckett* (Baltimore: Johns Hopkins University Press, 1974), pp. 274–94.
10. M. M. Bakhtin, *The Dialogic Imagination: Four Essays*, ed. Michael Holquist, trans. Caryl Emerson and Michael Holquist (Austin: University of Texas Press, 1981), p. 157.
11. Michel Foucault, 'What is an author? (1969)', in *Essential Works of Foucault 1954–1984, Vol. 2: Aesthetics, Method, and Epistemology*, ed. James D. Faubion, trans. Robert Hurley *et al.* (New York: New Press, 1998), pp. 205–22.

12 Geoffrey Chaucer, *House of Fame*, in *The Riverside Chaucer*, gen. ed. Larry D. Benson (Oxford: Oxford University Press, 3rd edn, 1988), book II, lines 556 and 561–2.
13 Paul Strohm, *The Poet's Tale: Chaucer and the Year that Made the Canterbury Tales* (London: Profile, 2015).
14 Chaucer, *House of Fame*, II.644–60.

2
First encounter: 'snail-horn perception' in Chaucer's *Troilus and Criseyde*

Elizabeth Robertson

'There are two visions, one of perception, one of thought.' (St Augustine)[1]

Why does Geoffrey Chaucer, in his great love poem, *Troilus and Criseyde*, describe Troilus – when he first sees Criseyde – as a startled snail withdrawing into its shell? And why does he recall this same image in his description of Criseyde's first sight of Troilus after which she, too, retreats from what she has seen as she pulls her head quickly inside the window? The image of the snail, I suggest, points us to Chaucer's primary purposes in his descriptions of first sight: to capture the essence of animate behaviour when a living being encounters the world, and especially when it encounters another animate being. Indeed, fundamental to many works of literature is an exploration of the nature of encounter and its consequences. Critics of varying persuasions have focused on these two scenes as charting the moments in which each character falls in love; but, although the passages do present Chaucer's meditation on the relationship between sight, cognition and the formation of attachment, whether these first sights yield an emotion as strong as love is a matter of debate. Whatever the consequences of that first sight, they mark first and foremost the fundamentally wondrous nature of first encounter. As Brian Massumi writes, 'To affect and to be affected is to be in encounter, and to be in encounter is to have already ventured forth. Adventure: far from being enclosed in the interiority of a subject, affect concerns an immediate participation in the events of the world. What is politics made of if not adventures of encounter? It is about intensities of experience. What are encounters, if not adventures of relation?'[2]

As I aim to show, perception – as described by Chaucer – involves processes shared by all animals: seeing involves a complex dialectic between the apprehension of sense data and the cognitive processing of that data in the brain. Perception becomes complicated, however, when a living being sees not just an object, but also one that is a perceiving subject. The poetry I am considering here expresses what can be called intersubjective or social perception.[3] Chaucer captures the complexity of the physiological and phenomenological processes involved in an interchange between self and other, initiated when Troilus first sees Criseyde, and vice versa, in his simple image of a snail engaging in what Keats would later call 'snail-horn perception'.[4] Beginning with a sensual apprehension of the world that is overwhelming – or, as the text puts it, astonishing – snail-horn perception is tentative and the understanding that grows from it is incremental and takes place over time. Falling in love begins simply with snail-horn perception; that is, with a powerful sensory encounter. My purposes here are twofold: to elucidate the ways in which Chaucer first conveys the physiological and phenomenological processes by which an animal cognises the world; and, second, how those processes are complicated when perception becomes social.

My interest in the history of the senses was inspired by the many sessions on the emotions in medieval literature organised by the Australian Research Council's Centre of Excellence for the History of Emotions, of which Stephanie Trigg is one of the chief investigators. These sessions prompted me to wonder how we might further historicise medieval representations of the emotions. According to Thomistic understandings, it is sensation in the five senses, as processed by the faculties of the soul, that triggers the emotions – such as fear, hope, anger – that arise in the concupiscible and irascible appetites. Emotions, then, are linked to the senses and both are products of a soul/body, rather than a mind/body, dialectic. Hugh of St Victor offers a succinct definition of sensation as 'what the soul undergoes in the body as a result of qualities which come to it from without'.[5] As Trigg has pointed out, the terms we use to understand emotion are loaded with ideologically motivated histories: 'feeling, passion, emotion, sentiment and affect ... have trailed also different ideological, physical, humoral, ethical and hermeneutic associations';[6] and I would add to the first list 'sensation'.

Sarah McNamer argues that 'feeling' is a more historically accurate term than emotion for the study of medieval texts since the latter word does not enter the English language until the sixteenth century.[7] The word 'feeling' has a narrower meaning than is generally assumed; however, in its first usages it refers specifically not to emotion, but rather to sensation, and often more narrowly to touch. It is not my purpose here to disentangle these various intertwined concepts and their histories, but rather to historicise just one of them – sight – and to explore how Chaucer, drawing on a variety of contemporary optical theorists, begins his profound investigation of the nature of emotion in *Troilus and Criseyde* with an in-depth representation of the complex physiological and psychological processes involved in seeing.

Theologians in the Middle Ages drew primarily on Aristotle as filtered through Aquinas, as well as new Arabic philosophy, in order to probe how the senses functioned – and poets in turn drew on those theological understandings to shape their representations of sensual interactions and the emotions that arise from them. The literary text, however, should not be, and indeed cannot be, reduced to the theological and philosophical sources upon which it draws, but rather makes its own distinctive contribution to the understanding of the nature and consequences of perception. Indeed, texts are often our only source for recovering the history of perception. As Trigg writes, 'Historically-oriented studies ... must rely on textual and material traces and representations of feelings and passions: the emotions *as they are processed, described and performed by human subjects*'.[8] Chaucer's representation of falling in love, then, begins with his representation of a sensual encounter, seeing; an encounter both shaped by and exceeding his understanding of the latest theological and philosophical understandings of the nature of sight. In fact, the literary text gives us more insight than the philosophical texts by showing us what Sara Ahmed describes as 'the messiness of the experiential, the unfolding of bodies into worlds, and the drama of contingency';[9] it is precisely the body's unfolding into the world that Chaucer encapsulates in his representations of first sight.

The gazes of Troilus and Criseyde have received attention from varying theoretical perspectives, but critics have almost uniformly concluded that both scenes mark the moments in the text when each character's reason is overwhelmed by emotion – the emotion of falling in love. Furthermore, especially in the case of Troilus's gaze, they have drawn strong moral conclusions from their understanding of these moments that shape their view of the poem as a whole. Troilus first sees Criseyde at a festival, which takes place at the Palladium, the temple that houses the household gods of Troy and whose subsequent breach marks the collapse of the city. The narrator states:

> Withinne the temple he wente hym forth pleyinge,
> This Troilus, of every wight aboute,
> On this lady, and now on that, lokynge,
> Wher so she were of town or of withoute;
> And upon cas bifel that thorugh a route
> His eye percede, and so depe it wente,
> Til on Criseyde it smot, and ther it stente.[10]

Despite holding radically opposed critical viewpoints, both patristic and feminist critics conclude that this scene exhibits Troilus's fundamentally sinful nature as one exhibiting a predatory, lustful gaze. The patristic critics, especially D. W. Robertson and John Fleming, argue that Chaucer in this passage represents the first stage of sin as described by St Augustine, *suggestio*, after which develops *delectatio* and *consentio*.[11] Just as Adam and Eve's sin was prompted first by sight of the apple, and completed by Adam's consent to eating it, so Troilus first sees Criseyde and, according to patristic readers, consents to his desire to possess her. How we interpret this first gaze, then, will determine our understanding of the nature of Troilus's desire for Criseyde and indeed our understanding of the poem as a whole.

Troilus's gaze has also been understood as predatory from the point of view of feminist theory. David Aers concludes that, in keeping with the '*cultural* formation of knightly love and the social construction of specific forms of sexuality', Troilus's piercing gaze is 'predatory' and he asserts that Chaucer describes the gaze in 'violent, even sadistic language'.[12] Drawing on feminist discussions of the objectifying nature of the male gaze, he describes Troilus's penetrating gaze as scopophilic, which Laura Mulvey describes as a gaze that 'looks at women in order to objectify them'.[13] The originator of the idea, Otto Fenichel, describes what he calls 'scoptophilia' as 'an "ocular introjection" that takes possession of and assimilates itself into the object' with a look that is 'destructive of its subject'.[14] Feminist and queer theorists alike have criticised the assumption that such a gaze is necessarily masculine, but as E. Ann Kaplan observes, 'The gaze is not necessarily male (literally), but to own and activate the gaze, given our language and the structure of the unconscious is to be in the masculine position'.[15] Some critics might view an analysis based in twentieth-century psychoanalytic theory as anachronistic and therefore inappropriate for the analysis of a medieval text, but as Sarah Stanbury points out in arguing that Troilus's gaze is scopophilic, 'In the social ethos of medieval gender relations the system of taboos and entitlements on gazing seems to have been as firmly fixed in place as it is today'.[16]

The passage, however, may be less morally freighted than either a patristic or a feminist interpretation asserts. It does make use of a common metaphor for sight – piercing – an image that suggests masculine sexual penetration, but the gaze may not necessarily be gendered male. Madeline Caviness has shown, for example, that the image appears just as frequently to describe the female as the male gaze. Chrysostom, for example, writes, 'the eye not only of the wanton but even of the modest woman pierces and disturbs the soul'.[17] In the *Song of Songs*, a woman's look is described as wounding: 'you have wounded my heart by one of your eyes'.[18]

Rather than conclude that this gaze is scopophilic, we might more simply attribute the ray's penetrating character to Chaucer's absorption of Augustine's neoplatonic understanding of the physiology of sight.[19] To Augustine, sight involved extramission in which the rays or *species* emitted from the eye fasten on to the object of sight. The metaphor reinforces an assumption underlying the theory of extramission that vision is an aspect of another sense, touch; to see an object is to touch it with rays from the eye. While Augustine's discussions of the physiology of sight often led to a condemnation of the sin that results from looking, Chaucer's description of Troilus's gaze can be understood simply as physiological in Augustinian terms.

Chaucer not only makes use of Augustine in his description of Troilus's first look, but also draws on newer understandings of the physiological processes involved in seeing that entered the West from Arabic sources. The following passage reveals how Chaucer draws on new Arabic theories of perception to show how Troilus abstracts properties from his observations:

> She nas nat with the leste of hir stature,
> But alle hire lymes so wel answerynge
> Weren to wommanhod, that creature
> Was nevere lasse mannyssh in semynge;
> And ek the pure wise of hire mevynge
> Shewed wel that men myght in hire gesse
> Honour, estat, and wommanly noblesse. (I.281–7)

Hasan Ibn Al-Haythem (Alhazen) explained the *virtus distinctiva*, the discriminative power – what Thomistic theologians called a faculty – that allowed the perceiver to identify twenty-two properties, or *intentiones*, found in visible objects.[20] In this passage, Troilus's gaze determines first what Arabic theologian-philosophers called the 'common sensibles' of size, shape and motion: Criseyde is tall, with a shapely figure and moves well.[21] From these qualities, Troilus determines – or, as the poet puts it, guesses – the abstract qualities of honour, social estate and nobility of character.

While this capacity to abstract seems to move us away from the senses and towards mental activity, Chaucer may understand Troilus here simply to be drawing conclusions based on further sensory observations. Medieval theological guidebooks stressed the significance of gestures: Hugh of St Victor, for example, in his influential work, *De Institutione Novitiorum*, provided one of the most detailed guides to gesture and explained how even the smallest motions on the outside of the body conveyed the inner movements of the soul.[22] Gestures, furthermore, conveyed social status. As John Burrow points out, since 'It was believed that gentlewomen naturally conducted themselves with dignity and restraint, avoiding extravagant *gesticulatio* and hasty or abrupt movements ... bodies spontaneously spoke their status'.[23] Criseyde's movement could in itself convey her honour and nobility. Simply put, something in the way she moves conveys Criseyde's inner moral qualities.

Troilus's seemingly scopophilic Augustinian penetrating ray is complicated by the rays Criseyde herself emits – 'the subtile stremes of hir yen' – that so compel Troilus a few stanzas later:

> Lo, he that leet hymselven so konnynge,
> And scorned hem that Loves peynes dryen,
> Was ful unwar that Love hadde his dwellynge
> Withinne the subtile stremes of hire yen; (I.302–5)

That Chaucer describes the object of sight as emitting rays, 'stremes', raises the question of the degree to which his understanding of vision reflects theories of *perspectiva* current in fourteenth-century England. Heavily indebted to the work of Arabic philosophers, especially Alhazen (whose work I have already shown clearly influenced Chaucer's representation of proper and common *sensibles*), perspectivist optics, taught by theologians such as the influential scholars Robert Grosseteste and Roger Bacon, were well established in the Oxford curriculum by the thirteenth century.[24] While Chaucer may not have known the philosophical details of such debates, their general outlines were readily available to him, as Peter Brown has shown, through the broadly disseminated work of Witelo and Pecham, as well as through the writings of encyclopaedists such as Bartholomeus Anglicus and Vincent of Beauvais. Bacon complicated neoplatonic theories of extramission by arguing that vision also involved intromission; in his argument, not only the viewer, but also the object viewed, emitted *species*.

One might think that Chaucer uses Bacon here to enhance a social reciprocity, one that mitigates the scopophilia of the Augustinian gaze. As Holly A. Crocker writes, Bacon's view 'that both seer and seen are simultaneously active and passive blurs gender distinctions established through medieval vision metaphors'.[25] The streams of Criseyde's eyes might be understood to signify *species* emitted by the object of Troilus's sight – Baconian *species* that interrupt his own penetrating rays. Furthermore, Criseyde not only emits rays from her eyes, but also conveys a look that seems, like Baconian *species*, to have agency. The poet writes:

> And of hire look in him ther gan to quyken
> So gret desir and such affeccioun,
> That in his herte botme gan to stiken
> Of hir his fixe and depe impressioun. (I.295–8)

To Brown, such a representation of impressionability reflects Chaucer's knowledge of Bacon: Bacon's 'insistence that sight is a pro-active process, while the viewer at the same time remains impressionable ... provide a framework for Chaucer's re-creation of the visual and experiential world.'[26] The active viewer here – Troilus – is indeed transformed into the passive recipient of sight. Criseyde's 'look', that is, her image, makes an impression on him as if he were wax that was being imprinted upon. Criseyde's look seems to demonstrate further Baconian influence when the poet writes:

> That sodeynly hym thoughte he felte dyen,
> Right with hire look, the spirit in his herte:
> Blissed be Love, that kan thus folk converte! (I.306–8)

Such attributes of her look need not necessarily reflect Chaucer's interest in Bacon. The idea that sight involves the impression of an object of sight in the viewer was not new to optical theory. Both neoplatonists and Aristotelian writers used the image of a wax impression to describe the action of the sense of sight on the mind. Chaucer may have drawn on other sources for his representation of Troilus's response. Theologians who wrote long before

Alhazen located the common sense in the heart. In addition, medieval medical manuals commonly associated sexual orgasm with a depletion of spirits. By stating that Troilus's spirit has died 'in his herte', the poet suggests that Troilus responds to the way Criseyde looks with *jouissance*.[27] Chaucer, then, draws here on a variety of sources to enhance his representation of a primarily physiological response.

What seems to me of predominant significance in the sequence here is not their Baconian intromitting import, but rather the fact that Criseyde is presented as a subject with rays of her own; that is, her streams might just as readily be described as her own rays of extramission as one who herself is looking. This stanza especially focuses on her status as a subject with a gaze:

> To Troilus right wonder wel with alle
> Gan for to like hire mevynge and hire chere,
> Which somdel deignous was, for she let falle
> Hire look a lite aside in swich manere,
> Ascaunces, 'What, may I nat stonden here?'
> And after that hir lokynge gan she lighte,
> That nevere thoughte hym seen so good a syghte. (I.288–94)

With the exception of Trigg, Stanbury and Burrow, most critics mistakenly assert that Criseyde here either responds to Troilus's look or returns his gaze.[28] To do so underestimates the significance of Criseyde's autonomous look. As Stanbury writes, the poet's description of not one, but several gazes creates 'a complex set of ocular trajectories [that] deflect and restructure the dynamics of control' inherent in the gaze.[29] Troilus's penetrating gaze is deflected by Criseyde's gaze, one that is at an angle to his own, and it is this deflection that intrigues him and inspires him to know more.

The scene would produce quite a different meaning if Criseyde had looked back at Troilus because then they would have been locked into a mutual gaze. In the period, it was considered unacceptable behaviour for a woman to look back at a man. Indeed, she was blamed for bringing unwanted sexual attentions to her if she looked at all.[30] If, on the other hand, Criseyde had looked down in response to Troilus's gaze she would have responded with a humility that the medieval guidebooks considered appropriate to her gender. A downward look would similarly reinforce the idea that Troilus's gaze is predatory since such a downward look was also associated with capitulation to an enemy.[31]

But Criseyde neither returns Troilus's gaze nor responds to it at all. Criseyde's gaze is 'a lite aside … / Ascaunces' (I.291–2). Chaucer's use of the word 'ascaunces' seems to reinforce the idea that Criseyde is looking obliquely. However, as Stephen Barney explains in the notes to *The Riverside Chaucer*, the word 'ascaunces' is most likely simply a translation of Chaucer's Boccaccian source, which at this point says '*quasi dicesse*' ('as if to say').[32] Thus, she looks aside as if to say, 'Why may I not stand here?' If her look is a speaking one, one that expresses her right to stand at the temple door, then, it is one that challenges not only Troilus, but others who look at her.[33] In his analysis of the etymology of the word, which was believed to have originated from the Latin *quam si* and French *quanses*, Leo Spitzer argues that the other, more familiar meaning of the word – to look obliquely – is not as semantically distant from the meaning 'as if' because to look aslant carried the idea that one was looking as if pretending to be someone else or looking with disdain.[34] Trigg also finds it difficult not to hear in Chaucer's use of the phrase more than a simple assertion of a proposed speech act: she writes, 'it is hard not to hear the more modern uses, "obliquely" or even "scornfully, suspiciously, with disapproval, distrust", in Criseyde's stanza, especially since her looks fall "a lite aside" in the indirect gaze that becomes a key feature of her characterization and her "slidyng" heart'.[35] However we translate the word 'ascaunces', Criseyde here has a look of her own and the passage clearly tells us she looks not at Troilus, but a little bit aside.

Troilus's first sight of a person with a sight of her own inspires a powerful reaction, one captured by Chaucer's description of Troilus as a snail withdrawing into its shell. Arrested by this sight, 'And sodeynly he wax therwith astoned' (I.274), he withdraws:

> And though he erst hadde poured up and down,
> He was tho glad his hornes in to shrinke:
> Unnethes wiste he how to loke or wynke. (I.299–301)

Chaucer's representation of Troilus as a snail withdrawing its horns epitomises the nature of a first sensual encounter. Indeed, the moment of this encounter is so powerful that, rather than just comparing Troilus to a snail, Chaucer chooses to represent Troilus *as* a snail; the intensity of this moment is neither because of emotion nor thought, but rather is simply physiological. That sensual response is intensified when the object perceived is itself animate. What he sees in Criseyde, as Trigg and Mann discuss, is the animation of her changing looks, 'a dynamic movement between shifting states'.[36] Through the sense of sight, the animate being reaches out into the world to encounter other animate beings, but then, overcome by the sense data it has gathered – overcome to the point of being able neither to sense further (look) nor to act with intention (wink) – necessarily withdraws into itself to process that data.

In the nineteenth century, it was John Keats who first recognised the efficacy of this image, not as it occurs in Chaucer, but as Shakespeare uses it. Keats pointed to the image in *Venus and Adonis* as a prime example of Shakespeare's extraordinary poetic skill.[37] Shakespeare compares Venus's horrified recoil at the sight of Adonis's gored body to a snail withdrawing into its shell:

> Or as the snail, whose tender horns being hit,
> Shrinks backward in his shelly cave with pain,
> And there, all smoth'red up, in shade doth sit,
> Long after fearing to creep forth again;
>   So at his bloody view her eyes are fled
>   Into the deep-dark cabins of her head.[38]

In a passage where he compares a female rather than a male viewer to a snail, Shakespeare uses the image to describe the processes by which information gathered by the senses enters the mind, as well as to reinforce the idea that Venus is in sensory overload and must withdraw, just as a snail withdraws the antennae that allow it to sense. Shakespeare's use of this image could well have been inspired by his intimate knowledge of Chaucer. Troilus, too, is overwhelmed by what he has seen. He, like Venus, is 'astoned' by the sight and withdraws into himself.

Keats turned to the image of the snail yet again in another letter of 8 April 1818, when he expressed his inability to describe adequately what had happened to him in the presence of a painting because of 'The innumerable compositions and decompositions which take place between the intellect and its thousand materials before it arrives at that trembling, delicate and snail-horn perception of Beauty'.[39] Keats's discussion of snail-horn perception captures the physiological and mental processes that occur as Troilus looks at Criseyde. Stunned by what he has seen, his senses are overwhelmed and he must pull back and retreat into his mind. The image of the snail aptly conveys both the fear that the unknown inspires and the courage it takes to seek to understand an object or being outside the self. Augustine's famous description of those who look at God, as doing so with a 'trembling glance', captures a similar dialectic about the activity of the sight as something that involves both desire and hesitation, longing and fear.[40] The image of the snail epitomises the processes by which all living beings encounter the world – a world that is desirable but potentially dangerous.

When Chaucer describes how Troilus processes the image he has seen in his mind, he turns away from optical theory and instead to Aristotelian understandings of the workings of the mind or soul. After Troilus returns home, he considers what he has seen:

> Thus gan he make a mirour of his mynde
> In which he saugh al holly hire figure,
> And that he wel koude in his herte fynde.
> It was to hym a right good aventure
> To love swich oon, and if he dede his cure
> To serven hir, yet myghte he falle in grace,
> Or ellis for oon of hire servauntz pace. (I.365–71)

Arguing against the view that Chaucer represents Troilus as governed by scopophilic desire, Mary Carruthers writes: 'He behaves in a manner considered at the time to be ordinary rational behavior, and far from self-indulgence, "making a mirror of [one's] mind" was a standard medieval procedure of analytical thought prior to making informed judgments.'[41] For the patristic and feminist reader, this stanza portrays the moment when Troilus consents to selfish desire. For Carruthers, Chaucer here describes the medieval understandings of rational thought processes required in decision-making. The passage does indeed reflect Aristotelian understandings of the processes by which an image is stored in the memory and brought forward before the mind's eye for consideration and judgment. As Carruthers argues, we observe here the *intentio animi*, the motion of Troilus's soul, as he makes a plan.[42] But while I agree with Carruthers that this passage focuses on the mental processes that result in decision-making, the scene emphasises desire as much as it does reason. Indeed, the passage represents decision-making as the result not only of rational 'argument', but also of the activity of the will, for Troilus's decision is found both in the mind and, as we are told, in 'his herte'. Although both of the primary faculties of the soul, reason and the will, are operating here, the passage leaves open whether or not Troilus consents to sin – that is, whether or not his understanding is governed by sensual lust or the beginnings of a higher love.[43]

Chaucer's representation of the mind's activity here does not provide us with the detailed map of the brain's different behaviour when someone falls in love or lust that modern neurology can provide us with today. However, Chaucer represents the growth of Troilus's love over time in an array of mental and emotional events that show his movement away from the merely sensory appreciation of Criseyde that we are given in these opening scenes and towards a richer and more stable feeling of love – one sustained despite the absence of the lover. It would take a longer chapter than this to chart the incremental development of Troilus's love and the minute and ever-shifting negotiations of power between Troilus and Criseyde that take place over the course of the poem. One's interpretation of the poem as a tragedy of lust or love, however, depends on whether one views this first look as the processing of sense data that can be the first step towards a deeper love, or merely Troilus's predatory and possessive gaze.

Even within an Augustinian framework, a sensual encounter does not necessarily lead to a destructive lust. According to Augustine, sensory apprehension can be the first step to understanding, if the experience of the senses is reoriented to an appreciation of the world rather than a desire to possess it. In her analysis of Augustine's discussion of vision in *De Trinitate*, Margaret Miles (quoting Augustine) explains that 'Images of sensible objects, either experienced, or retained in the memory, "do not harm *if one does not seek after them passionately* if they cause pleasure, or *flee them like a coward* if they are unpleasant"'.[44] Augustine intuits the power dynamics that sensation can induce: sensation produces desire, especially the desire to possess. In his view, desire needs to be transmuted instead into acknowledgement and appreciation, and uneven power hierarchies must be balanced. In Massumi's terms, sensual encounter needs to be directed to a politics of democratic intersubjectivity rather than to one that involves domination. Troilus's capacity for love depends on his ability to process the significance of the autonomy of the lively figure of Criseyde that first arrests his attention. As Augustine argues, according to Miles, seeing 'truly' involves both the body and soul: 'Physical vision which fails to recognise the spiritual aspect of its *own* functioning fails also to "see" its object accurately in that it fails to take into account an essential feature of the object – its life, that is, the spiritual quality which informs or creates it'.[45] While the degree to which Troilus's first sight of Criseyde rises above cupidinous desire is debatable, the first quality he sees is Criseyde's movement – that is, her life force, the animation that exudes from her body and especially from the streams in her eyes. What the literary text does is capture and celebrate that life force.

Is Criseyde's first sight of Troilus also snail-like? Discerning critics such as Stanbury and Trigg have discussed this scene in depth, so I will make only a few comments here.[46] Criseyde's gaze is not described in any way as scopophilic nor is it described in terms of Augustinian extramission or Baconian intromission and extramission. The features the narrator tells us Criseyde observes are closely linked to the emotion she has expressed already in relationship to the war – the fear Criseyde has already told Pandarus she feels is answered by the signs of violence on Troilus in the blood and dents on his armour. His triumphant entry into the city answers her overarching desire for a protector:

> This Troilus sat on his baye steede,
> Al armed, save his hed, ful richely;
> And wownded was his hors, and gan to blede,
> On which he rood a pas ful softely.
> But swich a knyghtly sighte trewely
> As was on hym, was nought, withouten faille,
> To loke on Mars, that god is of bataille. (II.624–30)

Like Troilus and the snail, she is overwhelmed by what she sees:

> When he the peple upon hym herde cryen,
> That to byholde it was a noble game
> How sobrelich he caste down his yën.
> Criseÿda gan al his chere aspien,
> And leet it so softe in hir herte synke,
> That to hireself she seyde, 'Who yaf me drynke?' (II.646–51)

Many read Criseyde's query 'Who yaf me drynke?' as an indication that she has fallen in love. But I understand this moment as an expression of a physiological rather than a psychological response; her exclamation marks her astonishment, inspired by a powerful sensual apprehension in a first encounter. Even the narrator dispels the idea that this is love at first sight: this is just a 'gynnyng' (II.671). Like Troilus and the snail, she has tentatively reached out into the world and 'she gan enclyne / To like hym first' (II.674–5). The sense data she takes in 'in hire herte synke' (II.650), overwhelming her reason to the point that she exclaims 'Who yaf me drynke?' Engulfed by sensation, she 'Gan in hire hed to pulle' (II.657); like Troilus, she becomes snail-like and pulls her head into the window, withdrawing from the exterior world into the private interior world. Then, in this interior space, she, again like Troilus, ponders what she has seen:

> And gan to caste and rollen up and down
> Withinne hire thought his excellent prowesse,
> And his estat, and also his renown,
> His wit, his shap, and ek his gentilesse;
> But moost hire favour was, for his distresse
> Was al for hire, and thoughte it was a routhe
> To sleen swich oon, if that he mente trouthe. (II.659–65)

Like Troilus, she considers the *proper* and *common sensibles* of her sight. Her assessment of his desirable attributes, however, becomes complicated by her acknowledgment of Troilus not just as an object of her gaze, but also as a subject who feels – and significantly feels – for her.[47] Perception, then, is presented as a dialectic between the experience of sense data that can overwhelm and assessment of the same sense data in the mind or soul; a dialectic that inevitably involves power dynamics, but that yields meaning incrementally.

To conclude, the Chaucerian literary examples I have discussed here draw on medieval philosophical traditions concerning the complex interchanges between the soul/mind and the body that take place in perception. They add to these rich philosophical traditions a consideration of the complexity of the mind–body – or, in medieval terms, the soul–body – dialectic when the object perceived turns out to be a living subject with perceptions of his or her own. Seeing God is particularly wondrous and involves special activities of the mind to produce understanding. All perception, however, is wondrous in its way, and takes place, as the philosopher A. Mark Smith has suggested, in 'a coherent succession of stages through which we forge a mental passage to objective reality'.[48] The ineffability of this incremental process is particularly well signified by the image of snail-horn perception. Hugh of St Victor describes perception as snail-like when he writes of vision, 'in order to get the "traces of corporeal objects" necessary for cognition, the soul "rushes out toward the visible forms of bodies and draws them into itself through imagination"'.[49] Poetry also invites the viewer or reader to engage first in a trembling, delicate and snail-horn encounter and then to withdraw in order to transmute whatever has been perceived into the strength of understanding. As we learned from Augustine, however, the purpose of such dialectical engagement is ultimately to learn how to love the world and to love each other.[50]

Notes

1 Suzanne Conklin Akbari also uses this quotation from Augustine's *De Trinitate* 11.9.16 as an epigraph to her book *Seeing Through the Veil: Optical Theory and Medieval Allegory* (Toronto: University of Toronto Press, 2004).
2 Brian Massumi, *Politics of Affect* (Cambridge: Polity Press, 2015), back cover.
3 Chaucer's fascination with the nature of the social has been powerfully illuminated by the work of Paul Strohm, beginning with his book *Social Chaucer* (Cambridge MA: Harvard University Press, 1989).
4 John Keats, 'To B. R. Haydon, 8 April 1818', in *The Letters of John Keats: 1814–1818*, vol. 1, ed. Hyder Edward Rollins (Cambridge: Cambridge University Press, 1958), pp. 264–6.
5 Hugh of St Victor, *Didascalicon*, trans. Jerome Taylor, quoted in A. Mark Smith, 'Perception', in Robert Pasnau and Christina Van Dyke (eds), *The Cambridge History of Medieval Philosophy* (Cambridge: Cambridge University Press, 2014), pp. 334–45 (p. 334).
6 Stephanie Trigg, 'Introduction: emotional histories – beyond the personalization of the past and the abstraction of affect theory', *Exemplaria*, 26:1 (2014), 3–15 (p. 7).
7 Sarah McNamer, 'Feeling', in Paul Strohm (ed.), *Oxford Twenty-First Century Approaches to Literature: Middle English* (Oxford: Oxford University Press, 2007), pp. 241–57. Discussed by Trigg, 'Introduction', p. 6.
8 Trigg, 'Introduction', p. 7 (emphasis in original).
9 Sara Ahmed, 'Happy objects', in Melissa Gregg and Gregory J. Seigworth (eds), *The Affect Theory Reader* (Durham NC: Duke University Press, 2010), pp. 29–51 (p. 30). Discussed by Trigg, 'Introduction', p. 6.
10 Geoffrey Chaucer, *Troilus and Criseyde*, in *The Riverside Chaucer*, gen. ed. Larry D. Benson (Boston: Houghton Mifflin, 3rd edn, 1987, 2008), I.267–73. Further quotations from *Troilus and Criseyde* are cited in-text by book and line number.
11 See D. W. Robertson, 'Chaucerian tragedy', *English Literary History*, 19 (1952), 1–37; and John Fleming, 'Deiphoebus betrayed: Virgilian decorum, Chaucerian feminism', *Chaucer Review*, 21:2 (1986), 182–99.
12 David Aers, 'Masculine identity in the courtly community: the self loving in *Troilus and Criseyde*', in *Community, Gender and Individual Identity: English Writing, 1360–1430* (London: Routledge, 1988), pp. 117–52 (pp. 121, 120 (emphasis in original)).

13 Quoted in Madeline Caviness, *Visualizing Women in the Middle Ages: Sight, Spectacle, and Scopic Economy* (Philadelphia: University of Pennsylvania Press, 2001), p. 25. See also Laura Mulvey, 'Visual pleasure and narrative cinema', *Screen*, 16 (1975), 6–18.
14 Quoted in Caviness, *Visualizing Women*, pp. 27–8.
15 Quoted in Sarah Stanbury, 'The voyeur and the private life in *Troilus and Criseyde*', *Studies in the Age of Chaucer*, 13 (1991), 141–58 (p. 148). This chapter is much indebted to Stanbury's astute work on the nature of the gaze and voyeurism in medieval literature. See also her earlier essay, 'The lover's gaze in *Troilus and Criseyde*', in R. A. Shoaf (ed.), *Chaucer's Troilus and Criseyde, 'Subgit to alle Poesye': Essays in Criticism* (Binghamton: Medieval and Renaissance Texts and Studies, 1992), pp. 224–38; and her study of the gaze in the *Gawain*-poet, *Seeing the Gawain Poet: Description and the Art of Perception* (Philadelphia: University of Pennsylvania Press, 1991). A. C. Spearing has also perceptively analysed voyeurism in medieval literature: see his *The Poet as Voyeur: Looking and Listening in Medieval Love-Narratives* (Cambridge: Cambridge University Press, 1993).
16 Stanbury, 'The voyeur', p. 148.
17 John Chrysostom, *De Sacerdotio* 6.8, trans. Blake Leyerle in 'John Chrysostom on the gaze', *Journal of Early Christian Studies*, 1:2 (1993), 159–74 (p. 163), quoted in Caviness, *Visualizing Women*, p. 21.
18 Caviness, *Visualizing Women*, p. 21, quoting *Song of Songs* iv.9 [not v.9].
19 Augustine outlines his view of optics in *De Trinitate*. Numerous critics discuss his optical views, including David C. Lindberg, *Theories of Vision from al-Kindi to Kepler* (Chicago: University of Chicago Press, 1976); see also the wide-ranging study of optical theory in medieval literature by Akbari, *Seeing Through the Veil*.
20 Peter Brown, *Chaucer and the Making of Optical Space* (Bern: Peter Lang, 2007), p. 56.
21 Smith, 'Perception', p. 337. Dominik Perler also discusses the medieval understanding of the Aristotelian 'common sensibles' in 'Perception in medieval philosophy', in Mohan Matthen (ed.), *The Oxford Handbook of Philosophy of Perception* (Oxford: Oxford University Press, 2015), pp. 51–65 (pp. 51–5).
22 J. A. Burrow, *Gestures and Looks in Medieval Narrative* (Cambridge: Cambridge University Press, 2002), p. 110.
23 Burrow, *Gestures and Looks*, p. 128. See also Barry Windeatt, 'Gesture in Chaucer', in Paul Maurice Clogan (ed.), *Medievalia et Humanistica 9: Studies in Medieval and Renaissance Culture* (Cambridge: Cambridge University Press, 1979), pp. 143–62.
24 See the discussion of the dissemination of optical theory in Brown, *Chaucer and the Making of Optical Space*, pp. 13–110.

25 Holly A. Crocker, *Chaucer's Visions of Manhood* (New York: Palgrave Macmillan, 2007), p. 21. See also Stanbury's discussion of the blurring of subject and object in these multiple gazes in 'The lover's gaze'.
26 Brown, *Chaucer and the Making of Optical Space*, p. 68.
27 *Jouissance* is a common term for sexual pleasure in the writings of Jacques Lacan, Julia Kristeva and Luce Irigaray.
28 Jill Mann assumes that Criseyde's look – especially the fact that her look lightens – implies she responds to Troilus's gaze. See her 'Shakespeare and Chaucer: "what is Criseyde worth?"', *Cambridge Quarterly*, 18:2 (1989), 109–28 (p. 112). For those who conclude that Criseyde is unaware of Troilus's gaze, see Stanbury, 'The voyeur'; Stephanie Trigg, '"Language in her eye": the expressive face of Criseyde/Cressida', in Andrew James Johnston, Russell West-Pavlov and Elisabeth Kempf (eds), *Love, History and Emotion in Chaucer and Shakespeare:* Troilus and Criseyde *and* Troilus and Cressida (Manchester: Manchester University Press, 2016), pp. 94–108; and Burrow, who discusses both Troilus's and Criseyde's first looks in *Gestures and Looks*, pp. 127–33.
29 Stanbury, 'The lover's gaze', p. 237.
30 See, for example, the discussion of Dinah, who was blamed for her own rape because of her looking, in *Ancrene Wisse*, ed. Bella Millett, EETS o.s. 325 (Oxford: Oxford University Press, 2005), part two, pp. 20–3.
31 C. M. Woolgar, *The Senses in Late Medieval England* (New Haven: Yale University Press, 2006), p. 148.
32 Stephen Barney, 'Explanatory notes', in Chaucer, *The Riverside Chaucer*, gen. ed. Benson, p. 1026.
33 Trigg discusses Criseyde's speaking face in detail in '"Language in her eye"' and in her 2016 biannual Chaucer lecture, 'Chaucer's silent discourse', *Studies in the Age of Chaucer*, 39 (2017), 33–56, both of which came out after I had composed this discussion.
34 Leo Spitzer, 'Anglo-French etymologies', *Philological Quarterly*, 24 (1945), 20–32 (pp. 20–3).
35 Trigg, '"Language in her eye"', p. 99.
36 Trigg, '"Language in her eye"', p. 101. See also Mann, 'Shakespeare and Chaucer', pp. 109–17.
37 Keats, 'To J. H. Reynolds, 22 November 1817', in *Letters*, ed. Rollins, p. 189.
38 William Shakespeare, 'Venus and Adonis', in John Roe (ed.), *The Poems* (Cambridge: Cambridge University Press, 1992), lines 1033–8.
39 Keats, 'To B. R. Haydon', in *Letters*, ed. Rollins, pp. 264–5.
40 Augustine, *Confessions*, 7.17.23. For a discussion of seeing God, see Barbara Newman, 'What did it mean to say "I saw"? The clash between theory and practice in medieval visionary culture', *Speculum*, 80:1 (2005), 1–43.

41 Mary Carruthers, 'Virtue, intention and the mind's eye in *Troilus and Criseyde*', in Charlotte Brewer and Barry Windeatt (eds), *Traditions and Innovations in the Study of Middle English Literature: The Influence of Derek Brewer* (Cambridge: D. S. Brewer, 2013), pp. 73–87 (p. 74).
42 Carruthers, 'Virtue, intention and the mind's eye', pp. 82ff.
43 Distinguishing the activities of mind that yield love, rather than mere lust, poses a challenge not only to literary criticism but also to contemporary neuroscience. Recent work in neuroscience has discovered that falling in love stimulates a different part of the brain than does lust. See Dean Burnett, 'Why do relationship breakups hurt so much?', *Guardian* (16 February 2016). See also Andreas Bartels and Semir Zeki, 'The neural basis of romantic love', *NeuroReport*, 11:17 (2000), 3829–34.
44 Margaret Miles, 'Vision: the eye of the body and the eye of the mind in Saint Augustine's "De Trinitate" and "Confessions"', *Journal of Religion*, 63:2 (1983), 125–42 (p. 132). The passage is taken from Augustine's *De Trinitate* 11.5.8 and the emphasis is that of Miles.
45 Miles, 'Vision: the eye of the body', p. 139 (emphasis in original).
46 Stanbury, 'The lover's gaze'; Trigg, '"Language in her eye"'.
47 Stanbury discusses in detail the complexity of the subject–object relations in 'The lover's gaze', pp. 234–8.
48 A. Mark Smith, 'Getting the big picture in perspectivist optics', *Isis: A Journal of the History of Science*, 72 (1981), 568–89 (p. 569).
49 Smith, 'Perception', p. 334.
50 I am indebted to Robert Pasnau who carefully discussed the Chaucerian lines with me in terms of medieval optical theory. I also thank James Simpson and Paul Strohm for perspicacious readings of the chapter. Jeffrey Robinson, my most constant interlocutor, deserves special acknowledgement. This chapter is part of a longer plenary talk I gave at the gracious invitation of Carrie Griffin in Dublin in March 2016 on 'Seeing is believing: veridical perception in medieval art and literature' for the interdisciplinary conference, *The Senses in Medieval and Renaissance Europe: Sight and Visual Perception*. I also gave a shorter version of this paper for a roundtable that Stephanie Trigg organised for the International Medieval Institute Meetings in Kalamazoo, Michigan in May 2017 on 'Why do we read fiction?'

3
Sir Thopas's mourning maidens

Helen Cooper

> Ful many a mayde, bright in bour,
> They moorne for hym paramour,
>   Whan hem were bet to slepe;
> But he was chaast and no lechour.[1]

The tale of *Sir Thopas* that the pilgrim Chaucer tells on the road to Canterbury was designed to delight the widest possible range of readers or listeners. The romances that it parodies, adventure stories written in the stanzaic form of tail-rhyme, were widely known across England, and to a broad social range.[2] Chaucer's imitation is an apparently unsophisticated tale written for a sophisticated audience; its closest literary descendant is the interlude of Pyramus and Thisbe in *A Midsummer Night's Dream*, a play that bases its main plot on the *Knight's Tale* and its fairy monarchs on the *Merchant's*.[3] Like 'Pyramus', *Sir Thopas* is presented to a fictional audience who fail to get the joke, who see only doggerel (a word Chaucer apparently invented) where the real audience can see a virtuoso performance. The direct appeal of both to a popular audience, or at least to an audience familiar with popular culture, aligns with Stephanie Trigg's own delight in extending her learning out to the world.

Of the many parodic elements in Chaucer's tale, *Sir Thopas*'s mourning maidens look as if they should be the one element that is most accessible to modern readers. There are minimal problems of vocabulary (nothing comparable with the *payndemayn*, *syklatoun* or *cetewale* found elsewhere in the poem), and the idea of all those amorous and pretty young women being taken to task for not getting enough sleep is gently ludicrous. Even that, however, deserves more unpacking. '"Hearing" Chaucer speak', as Trigg puts it, 'is a learned activity',[4] and knowing more about the literary context for *Sir Thopas* can sharpen that 'hearing' without, I hope, killing the joke. The accuracy of Chaucer's parody has long been recognised, but there is a lot more to be said about these maidens.[5] To have so many falling for the hero looks as if it should cater for the most unsophisticated male fantasy; but the narrating voice glosses them with a moral that sounds as if it might come from a disapproving parent advising on bedtimes, one that kills both desire and fantasy stone dead.

The idea that a romance hero might be *chaast* is another element in the parody, though probably for rather different reasons for modern and medieval audiences: heroism now is more often associated with being highly sexed, especially now that chastity is often misunderstood as meaning celibacy or virginity. At the very least, chastity is not a masculine attribute that any modern writer is likely to pick out for celebration. Even for Middle English writers, who as a group are much more likely to note their heroes' sexual restraint, there is some cross-gendering going on. Gawain's behaviour at Hautdesert is nothing unusual in an English text, in contrast to his French counterpart; but it is women for whom chastity is the pre-eminent virtue, often the first one to be praised, and the fact that instead it is Thopas's chastity that is praised calls attention to the omission of any mention of the maidens' chastity.

Familiarity with medieval and early modern ideas of lovers' sleeplessness can also make it seem as if the sexes have got confused somewhere, though that too is more complex than it at first appears. Sleeplessness is a recurrent state of male lovers in the Petrarchan tradition, and before that in medieval French romance. Likewise in the *General Prologue*, we are introduced to the Squire by being informed that

> So hoote he lovede that by nyghtertale
> He sleep namoore than dooth a nyghtyngale (I.97–8)

as if the fact of his sleeplessness mattered far more than the identity of his lady. The lover's inability to sleep is typified again by Troilus after his first sight of Criseyde, when 'tho refte hym love his slep' (*Troilus and Criseyde* I.484). Absolon of the *Miller's Tale* is likewise familiar enough with the expectation that lovers should be sleepless for him to make a point of staying awake 'for paramours', to show just how 'amorous' he is (I.3354–5). Arcite and Aurelius, in the Knight's and Franklin's tales, both pine away when their love is unrequited, a pining that includes sleeplessness; and the 'I' of the *Book of the Duchess* is so sorrowful on account of what seems to be unrequited love that he believes that lack of sleep is driving him close to death. Before love-sleeplessness becomes morbid, however, it is presented as simply natural – witness those 'smale foweles' of the *General Prologue*:

> That slepen al the nyght with open ye
> (So priketh hem nature in hir corages). (I.10–11)

'Corage', in this context, is good Middle English for what we would term sexual desire. When the sleepless Squire is compared to a nightingale, he is not doing anything unnatural; and the small fowls are implicitly of both sexes, as they are in the *Parliament of Fowls*. That women too can naturally feel desire is a recurrent element in romance, and it often carries no more condemnation by the author in a human than in an ornithological context. The heroines in question are much more likely to blame themselves for their desire, or at least to debate their culpability, than the authors are likely to condemn them. The women, that is, are familiar with all the social and moral requirements of maidenly chastity, and are typically shocked when they find themselves emotionally compromised.

The lines from *Sir Thopas* therefore go wrong in two ways. That the moralising is attached to the wrong thing is one of these. Preachers and secular moralists alike condemned sexual desire, and especially in women; the romances that make an exception of their heroines, to allow them an approved sexuality, stand out from the background not just of the more virulent kinds of antifeminism but of the accepted norms of good female behaviour. To blame these maidens most for losing out on sleep, however, is a distinct aberration from any homiletic norms. Then there is the sheer number of the young women, 'ful many a mayde', who fall for Sir Thopas. Such love-longing is more typically reserved for the heroine alone, marking her out as something special. Usually it is only elf-queens who are allowed to express sexual desire openly and without shame, but here the elf-queen does not even do that: taking her as a lover is presented as entirely Thopas's own idea, and we are told nothing about her own feelings (that has to wait for the fairy's declaration of love in Spenser's *Faerie Queene*, in a passage based on *Sir Thopas* but without the parody).[6] What is *not* parodic, contrary to what we might assume, is that the maidens fall in love first: that is, the priority given to the heroine in falling in love and being unable to sleep is a widespread feature of many Middle English romances. The heroine, furthermore, is not always the only maiden to suffer such love-sickness: there are sometimes two or three, even four, though the stories give them space as individuals rather than lumping them together into a generalised plural.

Not every romance heroine is given such predominance, but when they are, they typically respond actively, interrogating their hearts in soliloquy and taking the lead in courting. Such figures appear in a number of early French and Anglo-Norman romances down to around 1200, but it was in Middle English that they maintained their popularity.[7] Resistant or disdainful maidens do exist, and are generally now thought of as the more typical kind of heroine (again, Petrarch has something to do with the perception), but mourning maidens are sufficiently widespread to call for a survey of them and their habits. The obvious place to start looking is in the romances that are listed in Chaucer's text:

> Men speken of romances of prys,
> Of Horn child and of Ypotys,
> Of Beves and sir Gy,
> Of sir Lybeux and Pleyndamour. (VII.897–900)

'Sir Percyvell', of *Sir Percyvell of Gales*, is added later (VII.916). Of these, two can be ruled out instantly. *Ypotis* certainly does not contain any lovesick maidens: its eponymous hero is the instructor in Christian faith (among much else) in a long didactic work. Its qualifications for appearing here might be that it was just occasionally copied alongside romances; that its setting is far away and long ago, in classical Rome; and that Ypotis appears to be mis-associated with Horn as a 'child', though he was so in a different sense – he was supposedly just three years old, whereas the term as used in 'Horn child' carries the chivalric meaning now most familiar from 'child Roland'. Pleyndamour has never been identified, and is probably an invention of Chaucer's to match the many romance heroes (and indeed heroines) whose names likewise end in '-amour', such as Eglamour. Both Pleyndamour and Ypotis, along with the misunderstanding of 'child', are signs of the inadequacy of that fictional author of the 'rym' that the pilgrim Chaucer claims to have 'lerned longe agoon' (VII.709).

The other romances cited all have some claim to plausibility as inspiration for *Sir Thopas*. The one whose relevance for the 'mourning maidens' passage is picked out in *Sources and Analogues of the Canterbury Tales* is *Guy of Warwick*, specifically for the lines early in the romance when Guy is commanded by the heroine's father to serve her and her maidens at a meal in her chamber:

> Þat day Gij dede his miȝt
> To serue þritti maidens briȝt;
> Al an-amourd on him þai were,
> & loued Gij for his feir chere.[8]

This has the multiplicity of maidens, though they are not mourning (or not visibly), and the principal heroine, Felice, remains impervious to Guy's attraction for much longer. His reaction to seeing her, in this same scene, is the more familiar one of the love-struck hero: he sighs and weeps, retreats to bed unable to sleep, and generally pines away while 'euer his song is wo & wi'.[9] Despite this, he later comes within minutes of marrying the daughter of a monarch he has helped (something of a professional hazard for these knights), leaving her in her own state of weeping and hand-wringing: 'Neuer woman wers nas'.[10] The romance is, however, one of those that offers the most parallels to *Sir Thopas*, and it is a safe assumption that Chaucer was familiar with it: it was one of the most widely known of all the Middle English metrical romances, and it is included in the Auchinleck manuscript, which may or may not have been known to Chaucer but which represents the kind of manuscript anthology in which he and his contemporaries might have read a range of such romances.[11]

Bevis of Hamtoun is the romance of another distinctively English hero, and was similarly widely known. Here there is a more likely model of a mourning maiden, in the shape of Josiane, daughter of the pagan king Ermin, though the laconic and action-focused style of the work does not allow her much space to express herself. She does, however, like many of the heroines in the other romances Chaucer names, fall in love with the hero before he falls for her, and takes the initiative in persuading him to respond. She falls for him first when she sees him fighting a fierce boar, declaring to herself that she would give the whole world to marry him, for 'loue-longing me haþ be-couȝt'[12] – one of the earliest uses of the term 'love-longing', a phrase frequently associated with women in love.[13] Later, after Bevis has killed an enemy of her father's, Ermin orders Josiane to serve him in her chamber while he eats – the opposite situation to Guy's serving of Felice – and after doing so, and having seated him on her bed, she declares,

> 'Beues, lemman, þin ore!
> Ichaue loued þe ful ȝore,

> Sikerli can I no rede,
> Boute þow me loue, icham dede,
> And boute þow wiþ me do þe wille.'[14]

When Bevis reacts with horror at the thought of doing anything that would show ingratitude towards her father, Josiane moves further into an explicit declaration of sexual desire, and then into mourning mode:

> 'Merci,' ȝhe seide, 'ȝet wiþ þan
> Ichauede þe leuer to me lemman,
> Þe bodi in þe scherte naked,
> Þan al þe gold, þat Crist haþ maked,
> And þow wost wiþ me do þe wille!'
> 'For gode,' queþ he, 'þat I do nelle!'
> Ȝhe fel adoun and wep riȝt sore.[15]

When he again resists, she dismisses him angrily, but later goes to her chamber weeping, wakes him (though he is in fact already awake and pretending to snore)[16] and promises that she will become a Christian for his sake – at which point Bevis kisses her, and they remain true to each other throughout all their ensuing trials. Despite her open declaration of desire, they both remain chaste until they are married: a particular problem for Josiane, who is forced into marrying someone else along the way and has to dispose of her new husband by hanging him from the bed-rail on their wedding night. This is altogether not quite the behaviour expected from a Christian virgin, but Josiane's Saracen upbringing allows a degree of freedom to her that might incur rather more disapprobation in a more home-grown heroine.[17]

Guy and *Bevis* are written only partly in tail-rhyme, but the other romances listed in *Sir Thopas* offer a more precise metrical parallel. 'Horn child' is the fourteenth-century *Horn Childe and Maiden Rimnild*, the tail-rhyme Auchinleck version of the Anglo-Norman *Romance of Horn* that had earlier been given a Middle English couplet adaptation as *King Horn*. The Rimenhild of *King Horn* is drawn on the same model as Josiane, though without the excuse of being pagan. She falls for Horn and suffers accordingly:

> Heo lovede so Horn child
> That negh heo gan wexe wild
> ...
> Hire soreghe ne hire pine
> Ne mighte nevre fine.
> In heorte heo hadde wo.[18]

When she manages to get him into her chamber (after a false start, when her steward sends along the wrong man), she embraces him, kisses him and offers herself to him as his wife – at least a more modest offer than Josiane's. When Horn insists that he must prove himself worthy of knighthood before he will even be considered as her suitor, she faints, but at least she has a promise from him for the future. The Rimnild of *Horn Childe* is similarly forward; but the greatest extent of her demonstration of love-longing is sleeplessness, in that she does not let him out of her mind 'bi day no bi niȝt'.[19] Further on in this version another maiden appears who does rather more in the way of mourning: Acula, daughter of the King of Ireland, almost breaks her heart for Horn and falls sick for him – or at least pretends to, in order to make a declaration of her love to him.[20] If this is indeed the version that Chaucer knew, he may have been able to fill in the gaps in its more summary version of Horn's wooing women by extrapolation from similar stories, even if he did not know the older *King Horn*. In all its versions, including the Anglo-Norman, Horn is another hero who, like Sir Thopas, 'was chaast and no lechour', though the women who offer themselves to him make no secret of their desires.

Most of these women have marriage as their aim, a wish that brings them more closely into line with socially approved practice, or would do if they were not so determined to choose their own husbands: none of them considers consulting her father, or her council if she is a ruler in her own right. The Dame d'Amore, a comparatively minor character in *Lybeaus Desconus*, is a rare exception to this aim of marriage, and comes close to being a villainess; and Lybeaus himself, Chaucer's Sir Lybeux, is similarly unusual in his readiness to be seduced by her beauty, helped along by her sorcery – 'Alas he ne hadde y-be chast!', as the narrating voice exclaims.[21] He misspends a year with her when he ought to be pursuing his quest to aid the lady of Synadoune, and has to be recalled to his duties by Eleyne, the lady's maiden who is escorting him to her castle. When he encounters the lady herself, she again makes the first move, rushing at him to kiss him on the mouth; but the circumstances here put her far outside the normal range of forward heroines, since she has been metamorphosed by enchantment into the shape of a serpent, and it is only by kissing Gawain or one of his kin (Lybeaus is his son) that she can be changed back into a woman's form. She offers him fifteen castles and herself as his wife, which he accepts with enthusiasm. Although it is not one of the Auchinleck romances – or not in the manuscript as it now survives – its tail-rhyme brings it into the same metrical group as many of those, and of *Sir Thopas* itself.

Of the romances Chaucer names, there remains *Sir Percyvell of Gales*, a very loose adaptation of Chrétien's *Conte du Graal*. Like *Lybeaus*, it is not an Auchinleck romance, though it too is written in tail-rhyme – in the case of *Percyvell*, a particularly elaborate version of the form.[22] The English version is interested in the development of its hero from his infancy in the forest through his naive misunderstanding of chivalry to his growth into mature knighthood, with his winning of a maiden and his rescue of his mother as part of that. The Grail, and anything spiritual or mystical, is of no interest, and neither is the notion introduced into the later French prose versions of the story that Perceval remained a virgin. Chrétien's heroine – if she deserves such an epithet, given the small part she plays in his story – comes to the hero's bed, wearing very little, to beg him to fight for her in her hour of need, and Perceval (still unnamed) takes her under the covers with him, where they sleep mouth to mouth; but both his sexual innocence and his anxiety for his mother prevent him from going any further, even though, we are told, she would have been willing, and in this incomplete version we never hear the end of their story.[23] The English Percyvell goes to the rescue of the lady Lufamour of Maidenland and performs notable feats of martial prowess against the soldiers of the Sultan who is besieging her, while she watches her champion from her castle walls. She accordingly promises him marriage if he will also kill the Sultan himself, and when in due course he does so they are indeed married. She does not, however, show any signs of either mourning or sleeplessness: any emotions other than Percyvell's and his mother's barely figure in this romance. In the final stanza, we are told that Percyvell dies fighting in the Holy Land, but by that time Lufamour has disappeared from the story.

In addition to the romances cited by name in *Sir Thopas*, there is one other that gives a special predominance to mourning maidens in a way that more than justifies its place in the received list of sources and analogues. This is *Ipomadon*, as found in the earliest of three Middle English versions of the Anglo-Norman *Ipomedon* of Hue de Rotelande.[24] Like *Sir Thopas*, it is written in tail-rhyme, and although it is very free as a translation, it is closer to Hue's original in both length and narrative detail (including the space it gives to its mourning maidens – three of them, plus a wife) than the later couplet and prose versions. Its hero is presented as being as irresistible to women as Sir Thopas is. The first to fall for him is the heroine, the young queen of Calabria known simply as the Fere – La Fière, 'the proud lady', in the Anglo-Norman; it may contribute towards the more sympathetic treatment of her in the English than in Hue's original that Middle English 'fere' means companion, fellow or mate, with much more positive connotations. When Ipomadon arrives anonymously at her court, everyone who looks at him loves him, we are told, 'bothe lord and lady shene';[25] but the one who gazes at him most, and who is overwhelmed with love for him, is the Fere herself. Embarrassed by her own feelings, she retreats to her chamber and tumbles down on her bed with 'wrythyng and wyth woo':

> No thynge sche slepyd all the nyght,
> But ofte tymes turnyd and sadely syte,

and agonises over her love in a soliloquy of over a hundred lines: 'her mynde was not but for to morne', and she continues to mourn 'for sorowe' for a long time.[26] 'Mourning' is indeed the word most often associated with her feelings as well as being expressed in her actions.[27] Ipomadon is likewise smitten, but he is given rather less space, and his feelings are regularly subordinated to hers in both position and length. His love for her does not in any case prevent him from flirting with other women. When the King of Sicily asks him to stay at his court, he agrees on the condition that he should serve the queen at meals and kiss her on each occasion. He continues to insist on anonymity, so he is given the byname Drew-le-reyne, the queen's lover. When he first kisses her,

> She louyd hym wondur wele þerfore;
> And he had axed her any more
> I hope he myght haue bene.[28]
> But of foly he ne roughte;
> Another loue was in his thoughte.[29]

Her chastity is preserved, in other words, more by his being (like Sir Thopas) 'no lechour' than by her own restraint. She is careful to hide her feelings both from him and from everyone else, however, though she regrets missing the opportunity to have taken more advantage of him, and she too has her turn at 'makyng her moone' when her heart almost breaks when he leaves.[30] Like Guy, Ipomadon later must make a quick getaway to avoid marrying another princess, who is likewise left mourning.[31] Through all this, he makes himself out to be a knight of no standing or prowess; and that is taken to an extreme in the case of the next woman to fall for him. This is Ymayne, the Fere's cousin and confidante, who goes to find a champion for her mistress against an enemy who wishes to marry her. Ipomadon this time disguises himself as a fool, and there follows an episode rather like Malory's story of Gareth and Lynette (which may be based on the Ipomedon story), in which she scorns the man who has volunteered himself for her mistress's rescue despite his repeated acts of prowess. Here, however, Ymayne is overtaken by desire for him when they are staying at a small wayside inn and he disarms, exchanging his armour for a silk shirt – and, by implication, showing off his manly physique, in the equivalent of a wet-shirt moment. Lying awake 'waltryng on a woofull wyse' with passion in the inn's only bedroom,[32] she finally goes over to his bed, where he is pretending to be asleep, and offers herself to him. His reaction is to take hold of her hand and bite it, as if to confirm his role as fool – a response that does not help her to get to sleep, this night or the next;[33] and she stays in a state of grief until she is finally given an appropriate alternative husband several hundred lines later.

Given its multiplication of mourning maidens (and a wife too), it would be gratifying to think that Chaucer knew *Ipomadon*, but there are problems over its dating. The one surviving manuscript dates from the later fifteenth century; dates for the composition of the text have generally ranged from 1390 to the early fifteenth century; Rhiannon Purdie favours 1390 to 1400.[34] Chaucer was working most intensively on the *Canterbury Tales* in the 1390s, so it is not impossible that he knew it; it is written in the North Midland dialect, most likely from the West Riding of Yorkshire, and although the text made its way southward at some point, there is no evidence for its presence there in the fourteenth century beyond any wishful thinking that may attach to *Sir Thopas* itself.[35] The story underlying the work does, however, seem to have been fairly widely known. Quite apart from the two later adaptations and the possibility that it was known to Malory, the fourteenth-century *Parlement of the Thre Ages* includes 'Sir Ypomadonn de Poele' and the 'faire Fere de Calabre' in its list of lovers who are now dead.[36] It is impossible to know whether the *Parlement* author knew the story in its Anglo-Norman form, in an earlier and now lost English version, or (if the *Parlement* itself were composed at the very end of the century, later than its generally received dating) *Ipomadon* itself; or indeed whether he knew of the story by reputation and hearsay rather than direct knowledge of any text at all. The same range of options might be applicable to Chaucer too. *Ipomadon* is therefore more safely classified as an analogue for *Sir Thopas* rather than a source; but it is an analogue that is a useful reminder of how easily Middle English romance could embrace a plurality of mourning and sleepless maidens, and how generously it could treat them if they were given space to express themselves. Chaucer's parody may relate, not to their widespread presence in such romances, but to his absolute refusal to take them seriously. *Ipomadon* does not share the misogyny-tinged irony of Hue's original, but it is not too serious either: it treats its lovers with the same kind of light touch that Shakespearean comedy carries, as indeed do many Middle English romances. Rimenhild and the Fere, even Ymayne, could be joined by the Melior of the alliterative *William of Palerne* and other such lovesick heroines for the psychological sympathy of their portrayal. They are never taken as seriously as they take themselves, but they are neither mocked nor condemned, and the space given to them allows them to become agents rather than objects.

The women of *Sir Thopas*, maidens and fairy alike, are very different. The romance is as uninterested in the psychology of its sleepless women as it is in the psychology of its elf-queen. They are all devoid of agency: the maidens are ascribed the simplest of reactions to their sight of Sir Thopas, with neither any further insight into their minds nor any attempt on their part to take the initiative in putting their love-longing into practice. Elf-queens in medieval romance do not mourn, but – or because – they do take action themselves, instigating an affair with the hero: *Sir Launfal* is a leading example, another tail-rhyme romance recognised as an analogue and that could have been known to Chaucer, though it is not one that he mentions by name. The elf-queen of *Sir Thopas*, by contrast, is merely the subject of his dream, and we only know she exists because the giant says so. We know even less about her state of mind, or what her feelings towards her suitor might be. She is furthermore merely 'an' elf-queen, without even the distinction of the definite article (VII.788, VII.790, VII.795, VII.799). Romance fairies are typically the strongest female presence in secular literature, not least because they are unconstrained by normal female standards of chastity or modesty. When the pilgrim Chaucer is prevented by the Host from continuing with his romance, he changes to a prose homily of which the central character is emphatically a woman, the Prudence of *Melibee*. There it is the man who spends his time lamenting, while she works to stiffen his resolve in all the best moral directions. She does not have much of an individual psychology beyond what her name, with its strong suggestions of personification, would suggest; but that is still enough to make her an active player in the larger debate across the *Canterbury Tales* about the role and nature of women. *Sir Thopas*'s mourning maidens, even its elf-queen, are not normally thought about in the context of that debate; however, the maidens' very failure to contribute anything whatsoever is another marker of *Sir Thopas*'s parody in its refusal to live up to the literary standards it invokes.

Notes

1 Geoffrey Chaucer, *Sir Thopas*, in *The Riverside Chaucer*, gen. ed. Larry D. Benson (Boston: Houghton Mifflin, 3rd edn, 1987; Oxford: Oxford University Press, 1988), VII.742–5. All quotations from Chaucer are taken from this edition and cited by fragment or book and line number.

2 For a survey of these romances, including dates of composition, regional provenance and dialect features, see Rhiannon Purdie, *Anglicising Romance: Tail-rhyme and Genre in Medieval English Literature* (Cambridge: D. S. Brewer, 2008).

3 See, for instance, Peter Holland's account of the play's sources in his edition, *A Midsummer Night's Dream*, ed. Holland (Oxford: Oxford University Press, 1995); for discussion and further bibliography, see Helen Cooper, *Shakespeare and the Medieval World* (London: Methuen, 2010), pp. 211–19.

4 Stephanie Trigg, *Congenial Souls: Reading Chaucer from Medieval to Postmodern* (Minneapolis: University of Minnesota Press, 2002), p. 234.

5 The latest collection of echoes is by Joanne A. Charbonneau in Robert M. Correale and Mary Hamel (eds), *Sources and Analogues of the Canterbury Tales*, vol. 2 (Cambridge: D. S. Brewer, 2005), pp. 649–714. She gives three brief entries for these lines (nos. 44–6 at pp. 671–2), discussed here further below.

6 Edmund Spenser, *The Faerie Queene*, ed. A. C. Hamilton (Harlow: Longman, 2nd edn, 2001), I.ix.13–14.

7 See further Helen Cooper, 'Passionate, eloquent and determined: heroines' tales and feminine poetics', Sir Israel Gollancz Memorial Lecture, *Journal of the British Academy*, 4 (2016), 221–44, www.britac.ac.uk/publications/passionate-eloquent-and-determined-heroines-tales-and-feminine-poetics, accessed 1 May 2018.

8 *The Romance of Guy of Warwick: From the Auchinleck ms. in the Advocates' Libr., Edinburgh and from ms. 107 in Caius College,*

Cambridge, ed. Julius Zupitza, EETS e.s. 42 (London: Oxford University Press, 1883, repr. 1966), Auchinleck text lines 237–40; Correale and Hamel (eds), *Sources and Analogues*, p. 671.

9 *Guy of Warwick*, ed. Zupitza, Auchinleck lines 247, 261, 320.

10 *Guy of Warwick*, ed. Zupitza, Auchinleck line 4232.

11 For a recent discussion, see Helen Phillips, 'Auchinleck and Chaucer', in Susanna Fein (ed.), *The Auchinleck Manuscript: New Perspectives* (Woodbridge: Boydell & Brewer for York Medieval Press, 2016), pp. 139–55.

12 *The Romance of Sir Beues of Hamtoun*, ed. Eugen Kölbing, EETS e.s. 46 (London: Trübner, 1885; Millwood: Kraus Reprint, 1978), lines 893–7. This edition uses the Auchinleck MS, which may have been known to Chaucer. Jennifer Fellows's recent edition uses later MSS; compare her *Sir Bevis of Hampton*, EETS o.s. 349–50 (Oxford: Oxford University Press, 2017), lines 990–4.

13 Around half the citations in the *Middle English Dictionary* relate to women's emotions, both secular and devotional (s.v. 'love', 4d). The line from *Bevis* is one of the earliest.

14 *Sir Beues of Hamtoun*, ed. Kölbing, lines 1093–7. Compare *Sir Bevis*, ed. Fellows, lines 1226–30.

15 *Sir Beues of Hamtoun*, ed. Kölbing, lines 1105–11. Compare *Sir Bevis*, ed. Fellows, lines 1240–6; the omission of this passage in the Cambridge MS is ascribed by Fellows to eyeskip rather than bowdlerisation.

16 *Sir Beues of Hamtoun*, ed. Kölbing, line 1180. Compare *Sir Bevis*, ed. Fellows, line 1321.

17 See further Judith Weiss, 'The wooing woman in Anglo-Norman romance', in Maldwyn Mills, Jennifer Fellows and Carol Meale (eds), *Romance in Medieval England* (Cambridge: D. S. Brewer, 1991), pp. 149–61.

18 *King Horn*, in Jennifer Fellows (ed.), *Of Love and Chivalry: An Anthology of Middle English Romance* (London: J. M. Dent, 1993), lines 251–2, 261–3. On the relationships between the versions, see pp. viii–xi.

19 *Horn Childe and Maiden Rimnild*, ed. Maldwyn Mills (Heidelberg: Carl Winter, 1988), line 309.

20 *Horn Childe*, ed. Mills, lines 817–23.

21 *Lybeaus Descomus*, ed. Maldwyn Mills, EETS o.s. 261 (London and New York: Oxford University Press, 1969), line 1414.

22 *Sir Percyvell of Gales* in *Ywain and Gawain, Sir Percyvell of Gales, The Anturs of Arther*, ed. Maldwyn Mills (London: J. M. Dent, 1992). Probably written in the early fourteenth century, it survives only in the fifteenth-century Thornton manuscript.

23 Chrétien de Troyes, *Le conte du Graal (Perceval)*, in *Les romans de Chrétien de Troyes*, vol. V, ed. Félix Lecoy (Paris: Honoré Champion, 1972–75), lines 1962–77, 2056–67, 2912–14.

24 *Ipomadon*, ed. Rhiannon Purdie, EETS o.s. 316 (Oxford: Oxford University Press, 2001); Hue's original is *Ipomedon: poème de Hue de Rotelande (fin du XIIe siècle)*, ed. A. J. Holden (Paris: Klincksieck, 1979). 'Rotelande' is Rhuddlan, in North Wales.
25 *Ipomadon*, ed. Purdie, line 381.
26 *Ipomadon*, ed. Purdie, lines 904, 908–9, 1046, 1381.
27 *Ipomadon*, ed. Purdie, lines 1382–477, 3405–13, 4685–706, 5249.
28 That is, 'I believe he might have been [successful]' or 'been more to her' (glossed by Purdie in *Ipomadon*).
29 *Ipomadon*, ed. Purdie, lines 2792–6.
30 *Ipomadon*, ed. Purdie, lines 5316–19.
31 *Ipomadon*, ed. Purdie, lines 6073–9.
32 *Ipomadon*, ed. Purdie, line 7125.
33 *Ipomadon*, ed. Purdie, lines 7191–2, 7223, 7358–63.
34 *Ipomadon*, ed. Purdie, pp. xi, xlviii, liv–lx; in *Anglicising Romance* Purdie qualifies this slightly by noting that it cannot be earlier than 'the last quarter of the 14c' (p. 200).
35 *Ipomadon*, ed. Purdie, pp. xxxvii–xlvii.
36 *The Parlement of the Thre Ages*, ed. M. Y. Offord, EETS o.s. 246 (London: Oxford University Press, 1959), lines 618–19; discussed in *Ipomadon*, ed. Purdie, pp. lix–lx.

4
Chaucerian rhyme-breaking
Ruth Evans

In this chapter I discuss a characteristic of Chaucer's handling of rhyming couplets that has been almost entirely neglected in Chaucer scholarship, namely his use of a technique known as rhyme-breaking: in Stephen Knight and Thomas Ohlgren's definition, 'where syntax crosses rhyme units'.[1] Chrétien de Troyes is widely regarded as the most systematic and adept practitioner of rhyme-breaking in European vernacular poetry in the later Middle Ages; the technique is also used extensively in twelfth- and thirteenth-century Old French (OF) narrative poetry in couplets, in the twelfth-century Middle High German (MHG) romances of Gottfried von Strassburg and Hartmann von Aue, and in Pfaffe Lamprecht's Early MHG Alexander-romance, the *Alexanderlied* (*c*.1130).[2] The practice is likewise found in Middle English romances in couplets, such as *Richard Coeur de Lion* (*c*.1300), in Anglo-French narrative poetry and chronicles, such as Geoffrei Gaimar's *Estoire des Engleis* (*c*.1136–50) and Robert Wace's *Roman de Brut* (1155), in Middle Dutch *chansons de geste*, and, less frequently, in medieval Castilian and Italian poetry.[3] Though much overlooked, rhyme-breaking is a central feature of Chaucer's versification, and one that is not confined to couplets.[4] My aim in this chapter is threefold: to draw attention to the striking disparity between the extensive discussion of rhyme-breaking by OF and MHG prosodists and the near-total neglect by Chaucerians of this aspect of Chaucer's verse; to consider how he exploits the technique to produce a range of narrative effects; and to ask how an awareness of his use of the technique deepens our understanding of Chaucer's relation to other medieval vernacular poets, and to the English poets of the 1590s who consciously imitated Chaucer's rhyming couplets.[5]

Chaucer's deployment of rhyme-breaking looks at first blush to be very specific and on a very small scale. Yet it has large implications. Chaucer was clearly aware of the technique in couplet poetry in other European vernaculars, something that would have been noticed sooner if anglophone critics were less insulated from French and German scholarship. His use of it also raises questions about the relationship between politics and form, questions that are only belatedly coming to the attention of modern scholarship. For example, Caroline Levine's project, which is to link formalism to historicism and literature to politics, opens up the possibility of understanding how rhyme-breaking as an aesthetic form might also be understood, in Levine's words, as doing 'political work in particular historical contexts'.[6] Levine focuses almost exclusively on the novel, but her discussion of rhythm offers suggestive comments about how medieval temporal rhythms (such as monastic time) impose themselves as formal structures, as 'repetition and difference, memory and anticipation'.[7]

Did Chaucer develop the technique of rhyme-breaking independently, or had he noticed it in Chrétien, and/or earlier Middle English writers, and/or Anglo-French writers, such as Wace? As Ardis Butterfield argues, Chaucer's achievements need to be set 'in a wider and more detailed French context than before', because '[t]his setting ... better represents the multilingual literary perspective of the time than our own retrospective isolation of English'.[8] And not just a literary perspective: a formal one as well. When we talk about multilingualism in late medieval England, we need to talk about versification and metre and syntax as much as about vocabulary and genres. Why did Chaucer's postmedieval editors not notice his use of rhyme-breaking? Given Thomas Tyrwhitt's investment in the unity of the Augustan heroic couplet, is it not odd that his lengthy essay on versification in Chaucer does not once refer to Chaucer's rhyme-breaking?[9] Rhyme-breaking has long been a feature of the handling of couplets in European vernacular poetry, but how can we move beyond what Eric Weiskott calls 'ahistorical formalism' to consider rhyme-breaking's changes over time? And how can we represent Chaucer's practice of rhyme-breaking in a way that answers Weiskott's argument that not only does formalism need to be historicist but that 'historicism needs to be formalist'?[10]

The most compact definition of rhyme-breaking is, as noted above, Knight and Ohlgren's: 'where syntax crosses rhyme units'. But what does this mean? A more explanatory definition is provided by the German-Austrian philologist Jakob Schipper, in his *History of English Versification* (1910):

> Another metrical licence connected with the line-end ... is rhyme-breaking. This occurs chiefly in rhyming couplets, and consists in ending the sentence with the first line of the couplet, instead of continuing it (as is usually done) till the end of the second line. Thus the close connexion of the two lines of the couplet effected by the rhyme is broken up by the logical or syntactic pause occurring at the end of the first line. This is used rarely, and so to say unconsciously, by the earlier Middle English poets, but is frequently applied, and undoubtedly with artistic intention, by Chaucer and his successors.[11]

Schipper makes three salient points: that the syntactic or logical (semantic) break occurs midway through the couplet, rupturing the expected 'close connexion' of the two lines of the couplet; that Middle English poets before Chaucer employed rhyme-breaking 'unconsciously'; and that Chaucer deliberately employed it for artistic effect. Schipper's comment about the unconscious use of the technique in Middle English poets before Chaucer begs the question, and could no doubt be argued against. Perhaps Schipper means that in earlier poetry the practice arose spontaneously and with no detectible aesthetic rationale. Evert van den Berg's definition also illustrates some of the problems of providing an elegant and clearly graspable explanation of the technique:

> La brisure du couplet désigne une rupture entre le couplet, c'est-à-dire deux vers accouplés par la rime, et la fin d'une phrase ou d'un groupe de mots unis par le sens. Ou en d'autres termes: la brisure du couplet signifie la rupture entre le couplet de rimes plates et la structure syntaxique et/ou le sens de la phrase, ou tout simplement l'absence de coïncidence entre la fin de la phrase et la seconde rime.[12]

> (Couplet-breaking denotes a break between the couplet [that is to say, two lines linked by rhyme] and the completion of a phrase or group of words linked by sense. Or, to put it another way, couplet-breaking refers to the break between the rhyming couplet and the syntactic structure and/or the sense of the phrase, or more simply the lack of coincidence between the end of the phrase and the second rhyming word of the couplet.)

Van den Berg's three stabs at a definition tend to complicate, rather than clarify, the meaning, but like many prosodic terms rhyme-breaking is best understood through illustration. This is a well-known example from the *General Prologue* to the *Canterbury Tales*:

> A YEMAN hadde he and servantz namo
> At that tyme, for hym liste ride so,
> And he was clad in cote and hood of grene.
> A sheef of pecok arwes, bright and kene,
> Under his belt he bar ful thriftily (I.101–5)[13]

The first sentence concludes at the end of the first line of the couplet – 'clad in cote and hood of grene' (103), that is, halfway through the couplet – and offers not only a 'logical or syntactic pause' (Schipper) but also a respiratory pause, one that would have been emphasised in performance. A new sentence – more properly, a new syntactic unit – begins in the next line, and that line completes the rhyme of the couplet that the ear expects ('grene' / 'kene') but does not complete the syntactic unit, which extends beyond the couplet into the following lines.

It's not just the pull of rhyme against syntax that's at stake; it's also the form of the couplet itself, namely its unity, which is usually powerfully allied to the seduction of rhyme, with its promise of closure. In rhyme-breaking, the couplet reveals itself to be capable of being interrupted at its midpoint, suspending the resolution of the rhyme aa. Our expectation is that the second rhyme will clinch the couplet, and that the couplet will coincide with the end of a sentence. Rhyme-breaking violates a formal principle that we are familiar with in the Petrarchan sonnet, namely the *volta*, the underlying principle of which is, in Nelson Miller's much-quoted definition, that 'a change from one rhyme group to another signifies a change in subject matter'.[14] In rhyming couplets, there are two systems or linguistic structures in operation – rhyme and syntax – and they sometimes coincide (the syntactic structure coincides with the rhyming structure) and sometimes diverge (rhyme-breaking). In the latter case, we might think of it as two walkers out of step with each other. The effects, as I aim to show, are various.

The English phrase 'rhyme-breaking' is a calque of the German term *Reimbrechung*, less commonly *Reimpaarbrechung*, which becomes current in studies of German prosody from around 1848 (and probably earlier), but which has a history that stretches a long way back before that.[15] The term is still widely used by German prosodists today.[16] The earliest reference to the technique (although not itself an example of it) is at the end of Book 6 of Wolfram von Eschenbach's *Parzival*:

> ze machen nem diz maere ein man,
> der âventiure prüeven kan
> unde rîme künne sprechen,
> beidiu samnen unde brechen[17]

(To make this tale, let some man take it up who knows how to assess adventure and can recite rhymes, both linking and breaking them)

The corresponding term for *Reimbrechung* in French is *la brisure du couplet* (couplet-breaking), which seems to have been first used by Paul Meyer in 1894, and then given wide currency by Jean Frappier's 1965 article on versification in Chrétien de Troyes's *Érec et Énide*.[18] 'Couplet-breaking' is not, of course, precisely analogous to 'rhyme-breaking'. The former assumes that the verse that is 'broken' is a couplet; the latter is broader. Somewhat surprisingly, Meyer does not discuss MHG poetry, and it is not clear if he knew the German term *Reimbrechung*.[19]

Scholarship on rhyme-breaking in the German and French prosodic traditions, and the respective terms *Reimbrechung* and *la brisure du couplet*, appear to have developed independently of each other. Alice Colby's 1965 study of Chrétien's poetry, which offers extensive analysis of his use of what she calls 'breaking of the couplet', is indebted to Meyer's 1894 article; Frappier's seminal article coincidentally appeared in 1965, but Colby did not know it.[20] Meyer's article, however, was known by the American Romanist Frederick Morris Warren in 1907, and by at least one German editor of a French romance in 1909.[21] In discussions of Middle English versification, there is, to the best of my knowledge, no awareness of rhyme-breaking in German and French prosody, with the exception of recent work by Weiskott on Old and Middle English alliterative verse.[22] In the case of German prosody, this lack of awareness may be related to James Schultz's observation (allowing for some exaggeration) that 'the German tradition [of MHG texts] … has received little attention from scholars writing outside Germany'.[23] The same cannot of course be said of the French tradition of courtly romances and chronicles. But scholars of Middle English, Old French and Anglo-French need to acknowledge that rhyme-breaking is a prominent feature of the MHG romance corpus. There is no entry for 'rhyme-breaking' (or any of its cognate terms) in the *Princeton Encyclopedia of Poetry and*

Poetics, and no entry for it in the *Oxford English Dictionary*, and the term is only sporadically used by anglophone literary critics.[24]

The exception is Stephen Knight. In *The Poetry of the Canterbury Tales*, Knight defines rhyme-breaking as 'the effect created when the rhyme and the syntax do not coincide', and he discusses the contribution of rhyme-breaking to irony in the portrait of the Prioress in the *General Prologue*.[25] He also briefly discusses the technique in *Rymyng Craftily: Meaning in Chaucer's Poetry*, but does not use the term 'rhyme-breaking' itself: in a discussion of rhyme-breaking in the *Franklin's Tale*, lines 820–8, Knight argues that the completion of the sentence in the ninth line 'does not give the even rhythms we might expect because the two-line syntax units are exactly at odds with the two-line rhyme units', contending that '[c]onsequently, the passage has a disturbing effect'.[26] Knight tells me that his interest in this effect probably came out of the practice at the University of Sydney of reading Chaucer aloud onto tapes for school students in the distant regions to use because they were unable to get to the city to hear sessions there, which is when he noticed the irony-enhancing sequences in the description of the Prioress. It is also, he argues, a way of varying the otherwise rather leaden and monotonous fall of rhyming couplets, which is especially emphasised if the material is read aloud. Knight thinks he may have learnt the term from George Russell or Bernie Martin, New Zealand medievalists at Sydney, both of whom knew the German material very well.[27]

But what of Chaucer's 'artistic intention', to invoke Schipper's problematically anachronistic formulation (problematic because it assumes a post-Romantic notion of aesthetics)? The rhyme-breaking in the Yeoman's portrait may not at first seem especially remarkable, but in drawing attention to details of the pilgrim's dress it may serve to make the audience especially alert to sartorial markers of social degree. The *General Prologue* contains numerous examples of rhyme-breaking that play even more dynamically with the formal and aural effects of the arrest of one syntactic unit midway through a rhyming couplet and the launch of another. Its use is particularly insistent in the Prioress's portrait. Here are three examples in the portrait where the syntactic structure crosses the rhyme structure, with deliberate ironic effect:

> And peyned hire to countrefete cheere
> Of court, and to been estatlich of manere,
> And to ben holden digne of reverence.
> But for to speken of hire conscience, (I.139–42)

> She wolde wepe, if that she saugh a mous
> Kaught in a trappe, if it were deed or bledde.
> Of smale houndes hadde she that she fedde (I.144–6)
>
> Ful fetys was hir cloke, as I was war.
> Of small coral aboute hire arm she bar
> A peire of bedes, (I.157–9)

The non-coincidence of the rhyme unit with the syntactic unit lends liveliness, movement and unpredictability to the verse, and in turn draws attention to the carefully calibrated irony of the portrait. All three of these examples, like the earlier one from the Yeoman's portrait, involve substantial enjambment before or after the rhyme-breaking, and this is a pattern in Chaucer's use of the technique. The disrupted rhythm enacts the disjunction between, on the one hand, the pilgrim Chaucer's naively appreciative assessment of the Prioress as a woman of fastidious manners who is compassionate towards small animals, and, on the other hand, the audience's uneasy sense that a female religious should not display such worldly behaviour or care so much how genteel she appears to others.[28] Rhyme-breaking is one of the formal devices employed in the portrait that makes the audience question Chaucer the pilgrim's approbatory judgment. This renders the portrait less an exercise in ironic ekphrasis or rhetorical *descriptio* – composed of *effictio* (external characteristics) and *notatio* (moral characteristics) – which would focus our attention purely on the presentation of the stereotype of the worldly nun, than an exercise in the presentation of the narrator's persona. That is, rhyme-breaking draws attention to his rhetorical command of ethos, pathos and logos, and what that reveals – or conceals – about him as a subject. Rhyme-breaking alone does not of course do that, but it considerably adds to the ironic effect.

In the first example above, from the Prioress's portrait, rhyme-breaking reinforces the use of the adversative conjunction 'but' to alert the audience to the irony of 'Chaucer's' speaking of her inner 'conscience' after the praise of her outward, courtly manners. That reversal has already been anticipated by the suggestion that her courtliness is dissembling, a performance that lacks authenticity because it is striven for and self-regarding: '*peyned hire* to *countrefete* cheere'; '[peyned hire] *to ben holden digne* of reverence' (I.139 and 141). Rhyme-breaking, grammar and lexis combine to produce scepticism in the audience: *does* the Prioress have a conscience? Should she have a conscience? In the second example, rhyme-breaking invites us to question her response to animal suffering (does a mouse caught in a trap merit weeping? In certain situations, yes, but in this context?) and the propriety of a woman religious keeping small dogs as pets. In the third example, we are invited to consider the relationship between her neat cloak (neatness of dress being a signifier of aristocratic secularity) and the rosary (a signifier of religious devotion) that she wears on her arm. The rhythmic disjunction – the non-coincidence between syntactic and rhyme units – echoes and enacts the disjunction between the secular values she espouses and the religious values she purports to live by. It also invites us to consider the reliability of our moral judgments of others: how should we judge the Prioress? Is Chaucer the pilgrim right in his assessment of her character? Are we judging her, or judging 'Chaucer'? Or both?

Further examples of rhyme-breaking in the *General Prologue* do not necessarily produce irony. For example, there are striking instances of rhyme-breaking that occur across the boundaries between the portraits; for example, where the Yeoman's portrait ends and the Prioress's begins:

> A forster was he, soothly, as I gesse.
> Ther was also a Nonne, a PRIORESSE, (I.117–18)

Or the boundary between the Monk's and the Friar's portraits:

> His palfrey was as broun as is a berye.
> A FRERE ther was, a wantowne and a merye, (I.207–8)

These instances pick up on a familiar late medieval use of rhyme-breaking – found in Chrétien de Troyes – to demarcate boundaries of sections within long narrative description. Douglas Kelly insists that Chrétien's versification serves the 'story-telling side of his art', illustrating 'the adaptation of the couplet to *brisure* ... so as to enhance story-telling, especially for reading out loud', and thus 'completing a major development in the evolution of French versification'.[29] The effect in the *General Prologue*, however, is not so much to enhance story-telling as to suggest both the connections and the differences between the pilgrims, who are separated by the syntactic structure, but closely united by, and within, the rhyming couplet. A similar trick of Chaucer's is to end a lengthy verse paragraph with a single-line piece of syntax that does not usually rhyme with the previous line. Examples abound in the *Wife of Bath's Prologue*. While there are several instances of a verse-paragraph being clinched with a couplet – 'The dart is set up for virginitee; / Cacche whoso may, who renneth best lat see'

(III.75–6); 'Freletee clepe I, but if that he and she / Wolde leden al hir lyf in chastitee' (III.93–4) – there are others in which the single-line piece of syntax ends the paragraph but does not rhyme with the previous line:

> They were ful glad whan I spak to hem faire,
> For, God it woot, I chidde hem spitously.
> Now herkneth hou I baar me proprely, (III.222–4)

The effect is to drive the reader on to the next paragraph, rather than giving a confident 'that's it' effect at the end of the verse-paragraph. The *Wife of Bath's Prologue* exploits the contrast between the Wife's triumphant, argument-clinching couplets, where rhyme and syntax coincide – most strikingly in 'I wol bistowe the flour of al myn age / In the actes and in fruyt of mariage' (III.113–14) – and the dynamic, forward-driving, narrative effects of rhyme-breaking. Moreover, rhyme-breaking's lack of synchronisation of the two systems of syntax and rhyme, in Kristin Lynn Cole's words, 'keeps the ear entertained'.[30]

Rhyme-breaking is also common in the individual tales, and with various effects. For example:

> 'Spek, sweete bryd, I noot nat where thou art.'
> This Nicholas anon leet fle a fart (*Miller's Tale*, I.3805–6)

or

> Wommen may go saufly up and doun.
> In every bussh or under every tree
> Ther is noon oother incubus but he,
> And he ne wol doon hem but dishonour.
>   And so bifel that this kyng Arthour (*Wife of Bath's Tale*,
> III.878–82)

The former example, from the *Miller's Tale*, uses the breaking of the couplet to serve, as Joseph Duggan puts it in his discussion of Chrétien's technique, as 'the passage between individual events in a sequence of actions'.[31] But the rhyme-breaking in Chaucer does more than this: by marking a boundary between syntactic units, it sharply divides the characters' purposes: what Absolon is about is very different from what Nicholas and Alison are about, and this discrepancy is comic. The rhyme, on the other hand, proposes that lofty, courtly expression is merely the equivalent of a fart, recalling the comment by the lord in the *Summoner's Tale* that the 'rumblynge of a fart' and 'every soun' are 'but of eir

[air] reverberacioun' (III.2233–4): all expression is broken air. Absolon's pretensions are thus brought down to the level of a fart, and the fart is correspondingly elevated, as a signifier that delivers poetic justice.

Rhyme-breaking is not an innovation of Chaucer's mature period as a writer. He uses it almost from the start of his career, and in metrical forms other than the five-beat couplet, for example in the octosyllables/tetrameter of his early poem the *Book of the Duchess*:

> For sorwful ymagynacioun
> Ys alway hooly in my mynde.
>   And wel ye woot, agaynes kynde (14–16)

> Our first mater is good to kepe.
>   So whan I saw I might not slepe (43–4)

Here the see-sawing rhythms of rhyme-breaking contribute to our sense of the malaise and restlessness that the insomniac narrator experiences at the beginning of the poem. Interestingly, there is no rhyme-breaking in Chaucer's immediate sources for the above lines, Jean Froissart's *Paradis d'amour*, 1–12 (for 14–16), and Guillaume de Machaut's first *Complainte* (for 16, although Machaut's poem is not in rhyming couplets) and *Dit dou lyon*, 67–8, which is in rhyming couplets (for 43–4).[32] G. L. Kittredge's discussion of Chaucer's indebtedness to Froissart and Machaut does not touch on Chaucer's rhyme-breaking, but Kittredge refers to the 'trite transitional turn in *B. Duch.*, 41, 43, and *Dit dou Lyon*, 67–68', which shows that he reads Chaucer's (and Machaut's) abrupt change of topic as an aesthetic failure, and does not hear the rhyme-breaking that contributes to the deliberate – and far from trite – enactment, on the level of the rhyming form, of the narrator's dis-eased state of mind.[33]

Rhyme-breaking is also found in the *House of Fame*, another poem in octosyllabic couplets, where it is used to mark the borders between description and action, or between sections of description in a long narrative sequence:

> That in his face was ful broun.
>   But as I romed up and doun, (139–40)

It is also found in the *Legend of Good Women*, and in the closing couplet of rhyme royal stanzas, used here to drive forward the narrative:

> This see clepe I the tempestous matere
> Of disespeir that Troilus was inne;
> But now of hope the kalendes bygynne. (*Troilus and Criseyde*, II.5–7)

It is also used, more often than not, in the penultimate couplet of rhyme royal:

> O Alma redemptoris everemo.
> The swetnesse his herte perced so (*Prioress's Tale*, VII.554–5)

Here the effect is to anticipate and enact, at the level of both rhyme and syntax, a narrative reversal.

Another effect of rhyme-breaking in rhyme royal is to bring together speakers who would otherwise be differentiated by the metrical form of the stanza, as in the following exchange between Troilus and Pandarus in *Troilus and Criseyde*:

> 'We han naught elles for to don, ywis.
> And Pandarus, now woltow trowen me?
> Have here my trouthe, I se hire! Yond she is!
> Heve up thyn eyen, man! Maistow nat se?'
> Pandare answerde, 'Nay, so mote I the!
> Al wrong, by God! what saistow, man? Where arte?
> That I se yond nys but a fare-carte.' (V.1156–62)

As Eleanor Johnson notes, 'the enclosure of Troilus within the quatrain of the stanza and of Pandarus in the tercet is partially frustrated by the fact that the switch in their voicing ruptures a rhymed couplet – the bb of lines four and five', yet 'the metrical form still facilitates the reading of dialogue'.[34] Johnson argues that 'The effect of this split couplet is to create the sense of closeness between Pandarus and Troilus – quite literally, the sounds of their speech echo each other in rhyme', concluding that 'the space between stanzas typically serves to aestheticise differentiation between speakers; the space between stanzas, while keeping Pandarus and Troilus distinct, also serves to draw them together'.[35]

Conclusion

A great deal of work has been done on the relationship between poetic form and irony, yet very little has been done, with the exception of the work by Knight, on Chaucer's use of rhyme-breaking to produce an ironic effect. The cumulative effect of rhyme-breaking in the *General Prologue* is to emphasise irony and to give dynamism to Chaucer's verse. The closeness of the paired rhymes in a rhyming couplet works to bring together disparate entities, to the ear, eye and brain, while the syntax works to separate or individuate those entities. The resulting tension gives rise to a number of different effects, depending on the context. Chaucer may have been innovating here, but it would require a great deal of comparative work to claim that he is doing something that is distinctly different from twelfth-century MHG and OF writers, and from the writers of Anglo-French and Middle English romances. Contemporary critical analysis of Chaucer's versification needs to attend more centrally to the use and effects of rhyme-breaking, and to consider it comparatively, in the light of OF, MHG and Anglo-French practices, especially since the *brisure du couplet* is more often noted as a phenomenon of twelfth-century French verse than of other medieval and later vernacular verse, probably because of Frappier's influential essay.

If, for Roman Jakobson, 'The poetic function projects the principle of equivalence from the axis of selection into the axis of combination', namely, that 'Equivalence is promoted to the constitutive device of the sequence' (in other words, the poetic function consists of the 'regular reiteration of equivalent units': syllables, stresses, rhymes, syntactic pauses and so on), then rhyme-breaking audaciously proposes that while there may be equivalence between individual units (syntactic boundary equals syntactic boundary; rhyme equals rhyme), it is nevertheless possible to produce non-equivalence by having one unit out of lockstep with another.[36] The effect is not that of antithesis, which is of course a form of equivalence. Rather, rhyme-breaking sets up a notion of the line as a unit while also disrupting it. And this notion lies somewhere between the formal and the syntactic.

Notes

I would like to thank Ardis Butterfield, Megan Gilge, Antony Hasler, Stephen Knight, Evelyn Meyer, Jonathan Sawday, Sebastian Sobecki and Eric Weiskott. This chapter pays homage to Stephanie Trigg's ground-breaking work on the critical reception of Chaucer's poetry. In her book *Congenial Souls*, Stephanie delineates beautifully the 'special Chaucerian community' that editors and critics have constructed over the centuries since Chaucer's death. I offer this chapter by way of including myself in the modern Chaucerian community that Stephanie has done so much to create and foster, both on the page and in real life.

1 Stephen Knight and Thomas Ohlgren, 'Introduction', *The Tale of Gamelyn*, in Knight and Ohlgren (eds), *Robin Hood and Other Outlaw Tales*, TEAMS Middle English Texts Series (Kalamazoo: Medieval Institute Publications, 1997), pp. 184–91: 'the "rhyme-breaking" characteristic of Chaucer, where syntax crosses rhyme units, is almost unknown in *Gamelyn*, which tends to march steadily on with two- and four-line statements, all squarely mapped onto rhyme' (p. 187). As Rebecca M. Rush observes, the term 'couplet' did not become widespread until the seventeenth century; couplets were disdained by Elizabethan theorists, such as George Puttenham in *The Arte of English Poesie* (London, 1589), who associated them with the 'light and bawdy narrative verse' of Chaucer and his imitators; see R. M. Rush, 'Licentious rhymers: John Donne and the late-Elizabethan couplet revival', *ELH*, 84:3 (2017), 529–58 (p. 534).

2 In Frappier's words, 'nul avant Chrétien n'avait brisé le couplet aussi fréquemment que lui, et, ajoutons-le, aussi adroitement', Jean Frappier, 'La brisure du couplet dans Érec et Énide', *Romania*, 86:341 (1965), 1–21 (p. 3), that is, 'no-one before Chrétien had broken the couplet as often as he, and none, moreover, as skilfully' (translation mine); Alice M. Colby, *The Portrait in Twelfth-Century French Literature: An Example of the Stylistic Originality of Chrétien de Troyes* (Geneva: Droz, 1965); Otto Glöde, 'Die Reimbrechung in Gottfried von Straßburgs Tristan und den Werken seiner hervorragendsten Schüler', *Germania*, 33 (1888), 357–70; Karl Stahl, 'Die Reimbrechung bei Hartmann von Aue' (PhD dissertation, Rostock, 1888); Joris Vorstius, 'Die Reimbrechung im frühmittelhochdeutschen Alexanderliede' (PhD dissertation, Marburg, 1917); Paul Meyer, 'Le couplet de deux vers', *Romania*, 23 (1894), 1–35. On the emergence of rhyme-breaking in Early MHG, see Friedrich Maurer, 'Über Langzeilen und Langzeilenstrophen in der ältesten deutschen Dichtung', in Karl Friedrich Müller (ed.), *Beiträge zur Sprachwissenschaft und Volkskunde: Festschrift für Ernst Ochs zum 60 Geburtstag* (Lahr: Schauenburg, 1951), pp. 31–52; and Cola Minis, 'Zum Problem der frühmittelhochdeutschen Langzeilen', in *Zur Vergegenwärtigung vergangener philologischer Nächte* (Amsterdam: Rodopi, 1981), pp. 310–32.

3 See www.middleenglishromance.org.uk/mer/45, accessed 2 May 2018; Frappier, 'La brisure du couplet'; Joseph J. Duggan, *The Romances of Chrétien de Troyes* (New Haven: Yale University Press, 2001), p. 284; Evert van den Berg, 'Évolution de la versification des adaptations des chansons de geste en moyen néerlandais', in *Au Carrefour des routes d'Europe: la chanson de geste*, vol. 2 (Aix-en-Provence: Presses universitaires de Provence, 1987), pp. 1075–88; and Meyer, 'Le couplet de deux vers', pp. 33–5.

4 See Jakob Schipper, *A History of English Versification* (Oxford: Clarendon Press, 1910), p. xx. This work is Schipper's translation of

his *Grundriss der englischen Metrik* (1895), an abridged version of his original two-volume *Englische Metrik in historischer und systematischer Entwickelung dargestellt*, 2 vols (Bonn: Strauss,1881–88). As Schipper observes, rhyme-breaking in English poetry also occurs in metres other than decasyllabic or five-stress lines, for example, in four-foot iambic verses, examples of which occur in the poetry of Henry Howard, Earl of Surrey (*History of English Versification*, p. 148).

5 According to Rush, Puttenham saw the Chaucerian couplet as characterised by 'enjambment, loose placement of the caesura, and slant rhyme' ('Licentious rhymers', p. 533), but Chaucer's rhyme-breaking seems to have escaped his notice, as it also has Rush's. One of the poems by John Donne that Rush discusses – 'Elegy XVIII: Love's Progress' – uses rhyme-breaking once (lines 3–4), but she makes only one passing reference to the technique, in a discussion of 'Satire III': 'Donne ... breaks syntactical units across lines and couplets' ('Licentious rhymers', p. 551).

6 Caroline Levine, *Forms: Whole, Rhythm, Hierarchy, Network* (Princeton: Princeton University Press, 2015), pp. 3–5.

7 Levine, *Forms*, p. 53. See also Rush, who draws attention to recent criticism by early modernists that discusses 'the ideological implications of forms' ('Licentious rhymers', p. 530); she situates her discussion of Donne's use of the couplet in relation to what she identifies in early modern poetics as three different types of formal analysis (p. 531). Contra Levine, see Simon Jarvis, 'For a poetics of verse', *PMLA*, 125:4 (2010), 931–5; and 'The melodics of long poems', *Textual Practice*, 24:4 (2010), 607–21. Jarvis takes critics to task for assuming an obvious correspondence between poetic and political forms: 'The historical force of verse thinking may at a particular juncture depend upon rendering the metacommunications of verse less immediately legible – that is, upon preventing verse effects from shrinking to no more than a series of mere badges of belonging, of social, political, cultural, or poetical affiliation – so that verse can be reanimated as a repertoire of historically and affectively saturated paralinguistic gestures.... The formula *politics of style*, as usually wielded, empties both the terms it glues together. It diminishes politics to its least complex moment, that of wearing a badge, and then makes style be that badge' ('For a poetics of verse', p. 932).

8 Ardis Butterfield, *The Familiar Enemy: Chaucer, Language, and Nation in the Hundred Years War* (Oxford: Oxford University Press, 2009), p. xxii. Chaucer would have been familiar with rhyme-breaking from French poetry, but did he also know the MHG works that use rhyme-breaking? I think it is likely that he did. Although it has been argued that there is no evidence that Chaucer 'knew German, was familiar with German literature, or traveled in Germany', to quote Peter G. Beidler, 'The *Reeve's Tale*', in Robert M. Correale and

Mary Hamel (eds), *Sources and Analogues of the Canterbury Tales*, vol. 1 (Woodbridge: D. S. Brewer, 2002), pp. 23–74 (p. 24), Beidler's modern terminology is misleading; what medieval Germanists call 'low German' is a wide category that comprises Dutch, Flemish, some German dialects and combination dialects, such as Swiss-German and Limburgish (Dutch/German). Chaucer may well have known German via his Flemish connections and via the fact that Edward III's queen, Philippa, was from Hainault, although this knowledge might be spoken and quotidian, rather than literary: see Butterfield, *Familiar Enemy*, p. 118.

9   Thomas Tyrwhitt, *The Canterbury Tales of Chaucer, to which are added an essay upon his language and versification; an introductory discourse; and notes*, vol. 1 (London: T. Payne & Son, 1775).

10 Eric Weiskott, 'Real formalism, real historicism', unpublished paper delivered at the MLA Annual Convention, Vancouver, January 2015, pp. 2 and 1.

11 Schipper, *History of English Versification*, pp. 148–9.

12 Van den Berg, 'Évolution de la versification', p. 1075 (translation mine).

13 All quotations from Chaucer are cited by fragment or book (where relevant) and line number, taken from Geoffrey Chaucer, *The Riverside Chaucer*, gen. ed. Larry D. Benson (Boston: Houghton Mifflin, 3rd edn, 1987).

14 Nelson Miller, 'Basic sonnet forms', www.sonnets.org/basicforms.htm, accessed 2 May 2018.

15 Wolfram von Eschenbach's phrase 'rîme ... brechen' shows an awareness of the technique in twelfth-century MHG epic poetry. In the early nineteenth century, Jakob and Wilhelm Grimm acknowledge the practice in their *Altdeutsche Wälder*, 3 vols (Cassel: Thurneissen, 1813–16): 'es sind zwei sich gegenseitig kreuzende und nur ausnahmsweise sich berührende Strukturen' (vol. I, p. 193), that is, 'they [sense and metre] are two structures that mutually cross each other and only rarely touch'. I cannot locate a precise date for the appearance of *Reimbrechung*; it is used, but evidently not as a neologism, in Wilhelm Wackernagel, *Geschichte der deutschen Literatur* (Basel: Schweighauser, 1848), p. 466. See also Max Rachel, *Reimbrechung und Dreireim im Drama des Hans Sachs und andrer gleichzeitiger Dramatiker* (Freiberg: Gerlach, 1870), title and p. 28. The Duden German dictionary, widely considered to be the German authority on the German language and currently in its twenty-sixth edition (2013), has no entry in its online edition for either *Reimbrechung* or *Reimpaarbrechung* (see www.duden.de/woerterbuch). But the German *Wikipedia* entry for 'Brechung (Verslehre)' has the following definition: 'Bei der *Reimpaar-Brechung* gehört der erste Vers eines Reimpaars zur gleichen syntaktischen Einheit wie der vorhergehende

Vers und der zweite Vers zur syntaktischen Einheit des folgenden Verses', https://de.wikipedia.org/wiki/Brechung (Verslehre), accessed 2 May 2018, that is, 'In rhyme-breaking, the first line of a couplet belongs to the same syntactic unit as the previous line [i.e. the second line of the previous couplet] and the second line [of the couplet] is part of the syntactic unit of the following line [and therefore of the next couplet]' (translation mine).

16 For example, Heinz Sieburg, *Literatur des Mittelalters* (Berlin: Akademie Verlag, 2010), pp. 113–14.

17 Wolfram von Eschenbach, *Parzival*, ed. Karl Lachmann (Berlin: Walter de Gruyter, 6th edn, 1926), p. 337, lines 23–6. Translation by Cyril Edwards: see Wolfram von Eschenbach, Parzival, *with* Titurel *and the Love-lyrics*, trans. Cyril Edwards (Cambridge: D. S. Brewer, 2004), p. 108. For the reference in *Parzival*, see Reinhold Bechstein, '*Der Heliand* und seine künstlerische Form', *Jahrbuch des Vereins für Niederdeutsche Sprachforschung*, 10 (1885), 133–48 (p. 139).

18 Meyer, 'Le couplet de deux vers', p. 21; Frappier, 'La brisure du couplet'.

19 Knowledge of Meyer is widespread among German and anglophone scholars: see, for example, Karl Warnke (ed.), *Die Fabeln der Marie de France* (Halle: Niemeyer, 1898). There are other pre-1909 German references: Lewis Freeman Mott, *The System of Courtly Love Studied as an Introduction to the* Vita Nuova *of Dante* (Boston and London: Athenaeum, 1896), p. 99, n.2; Albert Eugene Curdy (ed.), *La Folie Tristan: An Anglo-Norman Poem* (Baltimore: John Murphy, 1903). See also Georges Lote, *Histoire du vers français, Tome 1, Première partie: Le Moyen Âge* (Paris: Boivin, 1949), pp. 282–3, and Tony Hunt, *Miraculous Rhymes: The Writing of Gautier de Coinci* (Cambridge: D. S. Brewer, 2007), who notes the use of 'breaking of the couplet' in his discussion of *rime suspendu* in Gautier (p. 165).

20 Colby, *The Portrait in Twelfth-Century French Literature*; Frappier, 'La brisure du couplet'.

21 See F. M. Warren 'Some features of style in early French narrative poetry (1150–70) – (Concluded)', *Modern Philology*, 4:4 (1907), 655–75 (see the section 'The broken couplet', pp. 662–75), and Raoul de Houdenc, *La Vengeance Raguidel*, ed. Matthias Friedwagner (Halle: Niemeyer, 1909), pp. xcvii and civ.

22 I am grateful to Eric Weiskott for pointing out that Old and Middle English alliterative verse has its own version of rhyme-breaking: when syntax crosses line units, the result is what the Germans call *Hakenstil* (a stylistic tradition that features a great deal of enjambment and frequent mid-line syntactic breaks, as opposed to *Zeilenstil*, a style characterised by end-stopped lines). It's very common in Old English verse, where sentences or paragraphs often begin in the second half of the line (b-verse). *Hakenstil* is rather uncommon in Middle English alliterative

verse, though, where poets prefer to vary the metre/syntax relationship through enjambment, which is less directly analogous to rhyme-breaking in rhyming verse. Rachel notes that *Reimbrechung* goes back to alliterative beginnings (Rachel, *Reimbrechung und Dreireim*, p. 11). See also David Lawton, 'Larger patterns of syntax in Middle English unrhymed alliterative verse', *Neophilologus*, 64:4 (1980), 604–18. In Early Middle English poetry written in couplets, it is usual for the couplet to be self-contained: see Carolynn VanDyke Friedlander, 'Early Middle English accentual verse', *Modern Philology*, 76:3 (1979), 219–30, especially pp. 224 and 229. See also Evert van den Berg and Bart Besamusca, 'Middle Dutch Charlemagne romances and the oral tradition of the *chansons de geste*', in Erik Kooper (ed.), *Medieval Dutch Literature in its European Context* (Cambridge: Cambridge University Press, 1994), pp. 81–95 (p. 84).
23 James A. Schultz, *Courtly Love, the Love of Courtliness, and the History of Sexuality* (Chicago: University of Chicago Press, 2006), p. xix.
24 Stephen Cushman et al. (eds), *The Princeton Encyclopedia of Poetry and Poetics* (Princeton: Princeton University Press, 4th edn, 2012); the entry 'Broken rhyme' refers to another phenomenon altogether. The German critic Max Kaluza's *A Short History of English Versification from the Earliest Times to the Present Day*, trans. A. C. Dunstan (London: George Allen & Co., 1911), which is heavily indebted to Schipper's work, briefly discusses Chaucer's use of rhyme-breaking (e.g. pp. 234 and 255). Roger S. Loomis alludes to it in his review of Karl Brunner's edition of the Middle English romance *Richard Coeur de Lion* and its Anglo-Norman source, but calls it, after Brunner, *Reimbrechung*, or (his translation) 'the split couplet' (or 'split couplet'), never 'rhyme-breaking': 'Review of *Der Mittelenglische Versroman über Richard Löwenherz, vol. XLII*, ed. Karl Brunner', *Journal of English and Germanic Philology*, 15:3 (1916), 455–66 (p. 458). Loomis seems to be encountering the technique for the first time: 'We gather from pp. 35 f. that Dr. Brunner means by Reimbrechung a couplet where there is a sharp break in the sense after the first line (indicated usually by colon or period) and where either one line or both are closely connected by the sense with what precedes or follows the couplet' (p. 458). In contemporary poetics, the term 'split couplet' means something very different from rhyme-breaking, namely a 'rhymed two line form with the first line in iambic pentameter and the second in iambic dimeter', http://poetscollective.org/poetryforms/split-couplet/, accessed 2 May 2018. A search for 'rhyme-breaking' in the poetry collection of the Princeton Prosody Archive, http://prosody.princeton.edu, accessed 2 May 2018, yields 242 hits; of these, all except three are passages that contain the separate terms 'rhyme' and/or 'breaking'. The exceptions, significantly, are three prosodists trained or working in Germany: Schipper, *History of English Versification*; Kaluza, *A Short History*

of English Versification; and Harry Sharp Cannon, *Sudermann's Treatment of Verse* (Tübingen: Laupp, 1922), p. 55. On John Gower's use of rhyme-breaking in rime riche, see Masayoshi Ito, 'Gower's use of *rime riche* in *Confessio Amantis*: as compared with his practice in *Mirour de l'Omme* and with the case of Chaucer', *Studies in English Literature* (English Literature Society of Japan), 46 (1969), 29–44. Eleanor Johnson discusses rhyme-breaking in *Troilus and Criseyde*, but calls it 'the split couplet'; see Johnson, *Practicing Literary Theory in the Middle Ages: Ethics and the Mixed Form in Chaucer, Gower, Usk, and Hoccleve* (Chicago: University of Chicago Press, 2013), pp. 82–3.

25 Stephen Knight, *The Poetry of the Canterbury Tales* (Sydney: Angus & Robertson, 1973), pp. x and 10.
26 Stephen Knight, *Rymyng Craftily: Meaning in Chaucer's Poetry* (Sydney: Angus & Robertson, 1973), pp. 131 and 190.
27 Stephen Knight, private email to Ruth Evans, 2017.
28 Of course, my perception of irony in the portrait owes a great deal to earlier critics, such as Jill Mann, *Chaucer and Medieval Estates Satire* (Cambridge: Cambridge University Press, 1973), pp. 128–36. My point is not that rhyme-breaking questions previous interpretations, but rather that it reinforces or extends them.
29 Douglas Kelly, 'The art of description', in Norris J. Lacy, Kelly Busby and Keith Busby (eds), *The Legacy of Chrétien de Troyes*, vol. 1 (Amsterdam: Rodopi, 1987), pp. 191–223 (pp. 199 and 191).
30 See Kristin Lynn Cole's discussion of tension within metre: 'Chaucer's metrical landscape', in Clíodhna Carney and Frances McCormack (eds), *Chaucer's Poetry: Words, Authority and Ethics* (Dublin: Four Courts Press, 2013), pp. 92–106 (p. 106).
31 Duggan, *The Romances of Chrétien de Troyes*, p. 284.
32 Jean Froissart, *Le Paradis d'amour; L'Orloge amoureus*, ed. Peter F. Dembowski, Textes littéraires français 339 (Geneva: Droz, 1986); Guillaume de Machaut, *Poésies lyriques*, vol. 1, ed. V. Chichmaref (Paris: Champion, 1909, repr. Geneva: Droz, 1973), p. 241 (for the first *Complaint*); Guillaume de Machaut, *Les œuvres de Guillaume de Machaut*, ed. P. Tarbé, Collection des poètes de Champagne antérieurs au XVIe siècle 3 (Reims: Regnier, 1849), pp. 40–4 (for the *Dit du lyoun*).
33 G. L. Kittredge, 'Guillaume de Machaut and *The Book of the Duchess*', *PMLA*, 30:1 (1915), 1–24 (p. 4).
34 Johnson, *Practicing Literary Theory*, p. 83.
35 Johnson, *Practicing Literary Theory*, p. 83.
36 Roman Jakobson, 'Closing statement: linguistics and poetics', in Thomas A. Sebeok (ed.), *Style in Language* (Cambridge MA: MIT Press, 1960), pp. 350–77 (p. 358).

5
'Have ye nat seyn somtyme a pale face?'

Stephanie Downes

To be or to become pale is a unique form of facial expressivity. Facial pallor is not something the subject can readily perceive for him or herself, like the sensation of grinning, grimacing, crying or blushing. Instead, it is an outward sign which is perceived primarily by others ('you look pale'), the significance of which tends to reveal itself only in context ('are you okay?'). For the pale-faced individual, the subjective experience of pallor is channelled through other sensorial or emotional means, such as feeling cold or weak, shocked or frightened. Literature, as Stephanie Trigg has observed, repeatedly explores the complex relationship between words and the face, including its aspects, movements and general appearance.[1] Trigg's work in the field of the history of emotions has shown how literary texts both encode and decode the unsayability of emotion, and how, in a wide variety of narrative forms and cultural temporalities – from Chaucer to Jane Austen – the expressive human face is a crucial hermeneutic sign.[2] Within the expressive range of the face, facial pallor is almost always a marker of some essential absence or lack, whether of colour, feeling, reason, health, vitality or any combination of these; its exceptionality is further compounded by this sense of deviation from a facial 'norm'. Rarely, if ever, do we encounter a crowd of pale faces in Middle English literature. It is perhaps precisely because of the atypicality of the pale face that it insists on being interpreted and understood. Such faces come to represent and to induce a variety of affects and emotions in (and around) the texts in which they appear. In Chaucer's works especially, pale faces exemplify processes of textual interpretation that are highly attuned to feeling, functioning as hermeneutic guides to reading non-gestural, narratological expressions of emotion effectively and appropriately. In this chapter, I examine various discursive constructions of facial pallor in Chaucer's works, with a special focus on the *Canterbury Tales*.

Shades of pale

Chaucerians have often singled out the pale face of the unlucky heroine, Custance, in the *Man of Law's Tale*, for special scrutiny,[3] and the pallid hues of Troilus, in *Troilus and Criseyde,* have long been taken for granted as a – if not the – defining aspect of the lovesick hero.[4] Both characters tend to pale at moments of heightened dramatic tension, involving a level of such individual distress that life itself either is – or seems to be – at stake.

Throughout the *Tales*, it is frequently difficult to pinpoint which emotional condition(s) or physical state(s) a pale face signifies: in the *Knight's Tale*, Arcite questions his love-struck cousin, Palamon: 'what eyleth thee, / That art so pale and deedly on to see?' (I.1081–2).[5] In the *Tales* alone, facial pallor variously accompanies expressions of shock, grief, melancholy, anxiety, dread, ill-health, exhaustion, drunkenness and death. Griselda reacts 'with ful pale face' to her first sighting of her future husband in the *Clerk's Tale* (IV.340); Dorigen, in the *Franklin's Tale*, begins her suicidal lament 'With face pale and with ful sorweful cheere' (V.1353); and the mother in the *Prioress's Tale* searches for her lost child 'With face pale of drede and bisy thoght' (VII.1779). In these examples, facial pallor is not so much a sign as a symptom which accompanies the other physical and cognitive behaviours associated with a specific subject in a particular narrative moment. Taken alongside Troilus, one could be forgiven for thinking that the pale face in Chaucer was reserved specially for male lovers and women experiencing emotional duress. Yet in the *Pardoner's Tale*, the old man, eluded by youth and Death alike, sums up his fate by conjuring the image of his pale and worn visage: 'For which ful pale and welked is my face' (VI.738); while in the prologue to the *Manciple's Tale*, the Manciple wryly excuses the inebriated Cook from speaking as the Host has asked: 'I wol as now excuse thee of thy tale. / For, in good feith, thy visage is ful pale' (IX.29–30). The Manciple vows he will not misinterpret the metaphorical text of Cook's pale face, sunken eyes and foul breath – 'thou shalt nat been yglosed' (IX.34) – while the Cook himself claims to have fallen suddenly into a 'hevynesse' that he cannot explain – 'Noot I nat why' (IX.22–3). Empathic or derisive, sober or comic, in the *Tales* – as elsewhere in Chaucer's works – the pale face invites further scrutiny from witness and reader alike.

In thinking through the narratological 'affects' of Chaucerian pale faces, I have been influenced by Trigg's work on what she calls 'Chaucer's silent discourse'; a broadening and deepening of our understanding of the gestural face in Chaucer's works, and a sub-category of what J. A. Burrow describes as 'speaking looks'.[6] Trigg's Biennial Lecture at the New Chaucer Society Congress in London in 2016 explored the trope of the 'speaking face' in Chaucer's poetry: the face that communicates a subjective and often emotional truth without making any sound. Trigg's reading of the affective primacy of the face in Chaucer recalled to my mind the lecture given by Carolyn Dinshaw, in the same city, in the year 2000: 'Pale faces: race, religion and affect in Chaucer's texts and their readers'. Dinshaw argued that by paying attention to and juxtaposing pale faces in both Chaucer's works and Chaucer studies, we might more effectively 'engage the challenging heterogeneity of our times'.[7]

Since the publication of these comments, the field of Middle English studies has rapidly developed its prior investment in affective states and conditions – both in general and more specifically in association with the history of emotions – through which it has found new ways of embracing diversity and appreciating difference in both the field and its objects.[8] The role of compassionate feeling has often been emphasised within this new discourse, especially in relation to spiritual works.[9] But secular literary contexts are increasingly of interest: in 2015, Trigg's TEDx talk at the Opera House in Sydney, 'What does normal look like?', explored the intersections of empathy, mental health and Middle English literature in relation to both medieval and modern stigma.[10] Although I do not, in this chapter, consider the specific implications of race or religion for pale (white) faces in Chaucer's works, I do wish to explore Chaucer's narratological representation of the non-normative exemplarity of facial pallor, according to which the pale face often invites compassion for the other; if not explicitly for the Other. Michael Edward Moore mounts the case for a familiarly Levinasian construction of humanism in medieval spiritual and secular conceptions of the face.[11] The pale faces of Chaucer's characters similarly require that readers recognise the script of the face-to-face textual encounter. At the same time as they acknowledge the fundamental difference of another face from their own, they are encouraged to find in that face the broader mark of a humanity for, or with, which they might feel.

Pale and interesting

While references to facial pallor recur throughout the telling of the pilgrims' tales, the Middle English word 'pale' is used only once in Chaucer's *General Prologue*, where it describes an individual who is anything but. Of the Monk, 'a manly man' (I.167), the narrator declares: 'He was *nat* pale as a forpyned goost' (I.205, my emphasis). The Monk's litotical pallor is the first-half of a couplet which concludes with reference to his pleasure in eating a good roast dinner: pallor is so familiar a sign as to be worth conjuring for ironic effect. Far from wasting away in body, mind and spirit, like the figurative 'forpyned goost', the Monk is brought into being before us, healthful and vigorous, with an appetite for food that matches his appetite for life. The general absence of facial pallor in the *General Prologue* is worth pausing briefly to consider. Throughout the twentieth century the vast majority of critical interpretations of Chaucer's interest in faces focused on the *General Prologue*: scholars have long characterised Chaucer's descriptions of the pilgrims as 'portraits', interpreting faciality according to late medieval humoral and physiognomic theories as signs of fixed character. A plausible explanation for the lack of examples (or, for that matter, counter-examples) of pallor among the descriptions of facial features in the *General Prologue* may be that the pilgrims are, by and large, a vigorous group.

Contemporary scientists and anthropologists researching facial expression tend overwhelmingly to focus on static images of faces rather than faces (and bodies) in motion; that is, on the manipulation of facial muscles into various culturally – and sometimes, it is claimed, universally – recognisable signs of specific emotional states.[12] They are especially interested in facial gestures: in how smiles, frowns and raised eyebrows are produced and interpreted by others. In the premodern era, however, as Philippa Maddern has observed, scientific discourses were equally if not more interested in the face's movements, colours and aspects as spontaneous, reliable evidence of the sensations of the heart.[13] Pallor in particular, Maddern argues (where it was not a sign of disease), was considered a sincere manifestation of emotional trauma, whether of 'sorrow', 'sudden fright' or 'shock'.[14] Like certain forms of facial redness, facial pallor was believed to generate spontaneously from within the body. As Bartholomeus Anglicus wrote in *On the Properties of Things*:

> the chekes schewith not onliche the diuersite of complexiouns but also the qualite and affeccioun and wil of herte; for by effecciouns of herte, by sodeyne drede othir ioye, he waxith sodeynliche pale othir red.[15]

Bartholomeus draws a distinction between facial colouring (which is most obviously visible on the 'chekes') as a legible sign of various physiognomic or humoral conditions, and facial colouring as external evidence of 'effecciouns', which rise uncontrollably from the heart. Such experiences produce a sudden, corresponding response on the body: a pale face denotes 'drede'; a red face signifies 'joye'.

In the *Book of the Duchess*, the Man in Black recalls his hesitant wooing of White: 'Ful ofte I wex bothe pale and red' (l.1215). Both Bartholomeus and the Man in Black present pallor as part of a fast-moving narrative of facial display, in which the face's appearance changes rapidly ('sodeynliche'), depending on the will of the heart. In Chaucer's works, facial pallor, when it is humorally induced, is sometimes described as an inverse redness – such as, for example, the drunken Cook, 'that was ful pale and no thyng reed' (*Manciple's Prologue*, IX.20). A red face, however, whatever its source, is rarely figured as an absence of pallor: the Monk's lack of ghostly pallor in the *General Prologue* is a rare exception. It is relatively easy to understand how the Monk might know if his face is flushed while eating; or how the Man in Black knows when he has blushed – but how does he know when he has turned pale?

To grow pale is a physical or somatic action of which the pale-faced person may not be physically aware. Pallor provokes no muscle memory, and no cognitive sense of how to arrange one's facial features to convey whatever meaning the pale face conveys. The sensation of becoming pale is closely linked to a cognitive perception of what the pale individual *feels* – emotionally or physically – and how such pallor might (unbidden) appear outwardly. The Man in Black, for example, both pales and blushes specifically when he is in his lady's company. Like blushing, growing pale has a social significance, of which Chaucer's characters are fully cognisant: although Troilus pales when he is alone in his room (IV.235), he worries especially that his paleness might be seen by others and recognised as the mark of his love for Criseyde (V.536).

Guillemette Bolens argues that Chaucer's representations of embodied emotions – shame in particular – launch an 'interpretative challenge' to both medieval and modern readers of his fiction.[16] Where facial pallor is concerned, the reader must first perceive the pale face, and then exercise their mental faculties in understanding what the mind and body it represents is experiencing – or has experienced. And yet Chaucer makes this task easy for his readers by narrating the pale face in such a way that it becomes a lesson in how to proceed hermeneutically. It is in narrative settings that the various 'pale faces' in Chaucer's writing are most meaningful, not always or only as indices of a specific humour or disposition, but as highly variable manifestations of the complex and inconstant social and emotional life of the individual.[17]

Although facial pallor may indicate or accompany a change in facial expression, it is not itself, strictly speaking, a gesture. One of the most noteworthy features of the 'speaking face' in Chaucer is its gestural nature – the fact that it is usually accompanied by some form of facial manipulation.[18] When Troilus, mocking his lovestruck companions in Book I of *Troilus and Criseyde*, 'gan caste up the browe', the Anglo-French composite 'ascaunces' ('as if to say') articulates rhetorically how his brow-raising might best be understood: 'Loo! is this naught wisely spoken?' (I.204–5). Criseyde, less than a hundred lines later, in a reversal of Troilus's confidence, 'let falle / Hire look a lite aside ... / Ascaunces, "What, may I nat stonden here?"' (I.290–2). In these and other examples, the face 'seems' to speak through the subject's moving gaze, as Chaucer unpacks the narratological significance of facial gesture – a single glance – with words. As a rhetorical feature, facial pallor need not involve any movement at all, voluntary or involuntary, of individual muscles or the whole head and neck. Indeed, in its most acute form, the pale face may be a prelude to the swoon, in which all forms of feeling dissipate and the body is suddenly still. And yet, on closer examination, pale faces rarely conform to our assumptions about the passivity of the pale-faced individual: even when the body is stunned or stilled – when it is metaphorically 'astoned' like Griselda's – Chaucer's pale faces are often actively engaged in the act of looking all about or around, whether with fear, shock or doubt, or attempting to appraise a particular situation or scene. While it is being singled out and looked at, the pale face appears, with its active looking, as if it might be about to look back: it seems to seek the reader's own gaze. By associating facial pallor with facial gesture, Chaucer's pale faces stage a potential encounter with a Levinasian 'other' face. They look beyond the narrative frame, asking the reader to deploy their own experiential and intertextual face-reading skills.

Pale in comparison

The most famous example of such an extra-textual appeal occurs in the *Man of Law's Tale*, when Custance has been publicly accused of the murder of the woman she loved 'as hir lyf' (II.625). At this moment, the narrator abruptly breaks from the narrative action to prompt his audience:

> Have ye nat seyn somtyme a pale face,
> Among a prees, of hym that hath be lad
> Toward his deeth, wher as hym gat no grace,
> And swich a colour in his face hath had
> Men myghte knowe his face that was bistad
> Amonges alle the faces in that route? (II.645–50)

This long and frequently discussed rhetorical question appeals directly to a subjective understanding of what facial pallor looks like. The Man of Law conjures an image of the 'ultimate' pale face, at least in his view: that of the condemned man, facing imminent death. The verb 'knowe' insists on the listener or reader's engagement of their cognitive faculties, but a cognitive leap must still be made in order to grasp the emotional relevance of the scene to Custance's story: what sort of feeling is being expressed by the pale face of the man who is going to die? How is his pallor to be interpreted by a witness? There is no 'emotion word' in this passage – no reference, here, to fear or despair. Instead, the narrator's question targets the reader's own memory of such moments, real or textual, to 'knowe' *which* man in the crowd is marked and destined to die, rather than to identify what the man might have been feeling. And yet despite this lack of overtly emotional language, this is (and has often been described as) a highly emotive scene, the intensity of which is generated precisely through the narrator's insistence that the reader recognise the face of the condemned man as one which is familiar.

As James Simpson explains, 'Literary cognition is fundamentally a matter of re-cognition':

> Contrary to the way critics talk about what kind of new liberatory truths literature expresses, our actual reading practice is grounded in long-standing forms of recognition. Every time we interpret we

recall deep-seated, ingrained, and circular protocols that give us access to truths immanent within the separate realms of literary experience.[19]

The Man of Law's question reveals this process in action, encouraging the listener to participate actively in the construction of meaning and the attribution of emotional, personal significance to Custance's pale face: 'So stant Custance, and looketh hire aboute' (II.651). In this swift return to the story, we find Custance standing still, at the same time as she gestures with her face, looking all around. William McClellan suggests that Custance's behaviour here echoes that of Griselda in the *Clerk's Tale*. On first seeing her future husband, Griselda is 'astoned / To seen so greet a gest come in that place; / ... / For which she looked with ful pale face' (IV.337–40). Despite the stillness of their bodies (Custance 'stant', while Griselda is 'astoned'), both women actively 'look', taking in and attempting to process their surrounds. McClellan describes Griselda's looking as taking place in a state of innocent 'wondre', which appears five lines earlier in the text – 'But outrely Grisildis wondre myghte' (IV.335)[20] – and Custance's looking as 'distracted' and 'aimless'.[21] And yet, as they look about themselves, each woman potentially looks back at those observing her, including the reader, while Custance's own fixed looking occurs at precisely the moment in which the text most powerfully evokes pathos for her situation.

Indeed, in the very next stanza, the Man of Law again diverts from his tale to appeal to his audience – here, specifically, an audience of elite courtly women:

> O queenes, lyvynge in prosperitee,
> Duchesses, and ye ladyes everichone,
> Haveth som routhe on hire adversitee!
> An Emperoures doghter stant allone;
> She hath no wight to whom to make hir mone.
> O blood roial, that stondest in this drede,
> Fer been thy freendes at thy grete nede! (II.652–8)

And yet this is not simply a call for female witnesses to empathise with the suffering of Custance, but an appeal to a specifically gendered form of Christian compassion, a mode that Sarah McNamer calls 'feeling like a woman' in medieval religious lyric.[22] V. A. Kolve proposes that, though the face of the condemned man may call to mind any face in a crowd of prisoners on the way to Newgate for execution, the face of Christ on the road to Calvary has a powerful resonance with that of Custance.[23] Abandoned and alone in her moment of 'grete nede' (II.658), the suffering of Custance – 'an Emperoures doghter' – takes on a comparatively Christian frame of reference, recalling the passion of Christ – the son of God – before the Virgin and Mary Magdalene. Unlike the condemned Christ, however, who 'gat no grace', Custance's pale face – the visualisation of which the narrator has lingered over now for fourteen lines – will succeed in bringing her God's succour in this narrative moment. King Alla serves in this scene as model for the reader's empathy: he has 'swich compassioun' on seeing her that 'his gentil herte is fulfild of pitee' and 'from his eyen ran the water doun' (II.659–61). A complexly gendered emotional dynamic underpins the scene: Custance 'suffers' metaphorically, like a man; while Alla 'feels' compassion, like a woman. This figurative association of Custance with Christ, who embodies all humanity, and Alla's empathetic response to her suffering, suggests facial pallor is a universal sign for which compassion is an appropriately Christian response. Alla's spontaneous practice of Christian piety precipitates his own conversion to Christianity. He subsequently orders that Custance's accuser swear to her guilt on a 'book', which turns out to be the Gospels (II.662–6): the accuser is instantly struck dead by the hand of God, and Custance's innocence declared (II.666–79).

Later, when Alla's pagan mother, Donegild, orders Custance's exile, Custance moves toward to the ship 'with a deedly pale face' (II.822). Custance prays first to Christ, and then, after comforting her crying babe, to Mary, raising her face to the heavens.[24] McClellan has argued that, when Custance prays, a 'discrepancy' is revealed 'between what the phrase "deadly pale face" portrays of her inner crisis and the rational, rhetorical substance of her prayer'.[25] And yet, as elsewhere in Chaucer's works, the pale face is here an entirely appropriate prelude to a prayer of sufferance. As both classical and medieval manuals of rhetoric and poetry remind us, facial expression is a crucial aspect of the orator's repertoire. There is, in other words, an appropriate expressive register for the *literally* speaking face: to convey and elicit emotion, and to represent emotion sincerely, it is not sufficient for a speaker simply to speak. As Geoffrey of Vinsauf writes in the *Poetria Nova*, a good poet must mould his facial expression or *vultus* to his tongue during a performance of the text;[26] in the opening stanzas of *Troilus and Criseyde*, the narrator acknowledges that he must match 'to a sorwful tale, a sory chere' (I.14). Facial pallor is the ultimate

'Have ye nat seyn somtyme a pale face?' 83

index of sincerely felt speech: Dorigen thus begins her lament in the *Franklin's Tale*, 'With face pale and with ful sorweful cheere' (V.1353); at the start of the *Nun's Priest's Tale*, Chauntecleer recounts the story of the ghost who visits his friend in a dream, having 'tolde hym every point how he was slayn / With a ful pitous face, pale of hewe' (VII.4212–13). In the *Prioress's Tale*, the pale, dreadful face of the mother correlates to her 'bisy thought' rather than her prayer or speech – her mind active as she searches for her missing son. Rather than a gendered 'discrepancy' between a feeling woman and her reasoned speech or thought, Custance here presents the face most appropriate to her recitation, that which both models Christian compassion and is most likely to elicit compassion or pity in a witness or reader. In this sense, the pale face is indeed a 'gestural' face, which performs, textually, the affective register most appropriate to her prayer.

'with face deed and pale'

The *Knight's Tale* demonstrates the pathetic effects of the pale face and of pale-faced speech in a secular and romantic rather than a spiritual context. Part two opens on Arcite as the embodiment of Petrarchan lovesickness, 'His hewe falow and pale as asshen colde' (I.1364). Following a dream in which Mercury commands him to go to Athens to see his lady, he takes up a mirror and sees for himself that 'chaunged was al his colour / And ... his visage al in another kynde' (I.1400–1). Some years later, singing joyfully of spring in a grove outside Athens, he falls suddenly into melancholy, as lovers do: 'Whan that Arcite had songe, he gan to sike' (I.1540). Arcite sits down and begins his lament, unaware that Palamon, concealed, is listening. Having overheard Arcite's passion for the lady Emelye, Palamon feels as if his heart has been struck through with a cold blade, and he shakes 'For ire' (I.1574–6). Stirred in this way to action, he jumps up from the bushes and prepares to confront Arcite's treachery, 'As he were wood, with face deed and pale' (I.1578). Palamon's actions rather than his pallor elicit this comparison to madness; but his pallor serves to underscore the effect of Arcite's speech, which was itself delivered in a moment of lovesick contemplation. The reference to his 'deed and pale' face reprises Palamon's appearance in part one, when he was first struck with love for Emelye (I.1082). Here, however, Palamon's deathly pallor is triggered by his emotional reaction to his cousin's speech – his jealousy and anger, rather than his love.

Deathly pale faces in Chaucer tend to converge with intensely physical and involuntary emotional reactions (Palamon shakes with anger), which generate dramatic action (he leaps from the bushes). In *Anelida and Arcite*, deathly pallor, of a specifically greenish hue, precedes another dramatic event – the faint: 'With face ded, betwixe pale and grene, / She fel a-swowe' (353–4). As a state, the swoon mimics death, and yet it is the drama of the fall that tends most frequently to characterise the faint's narrative intensity. The pale-faced subject may be intensely death-like, and yet is still very much alive: in the *Book of the Duchess*, the dreamer marvels that the Man in Black can suffer so, and yet 'be *not* deed' (468–70, my emphasis). Here, as in the *Tales*, facial pallor accompanies an expression of personal grief which, by being 'pitous', suggests that it should provoke the witness's/reader's compassion: 'Ful pitous, pale, and nothyng red, / He sayd a lay, a maner song' (470–1). Deathly pallor abounds in the final two books of *Troilus and Criseyde*, as the lovers' romance starts to unravel. Chaucer has Troilus appear twice with a deadly pale face: once as he retreats to his room after he has heard that Criseyde is to be exchanged – 'Upon his beddes syde adown hym sette, / Full lik a ded ymage, pale and wan' (IV.234–5); and again in book V, when he paces back and forth outside Criseyde's empty palace, 'with chaunged dedlich pale face' (V.536). In the first instance, Troilus's pallor anticipates an outburst of lover's madness, in which he hurls himself about the chamber, before beginning his seventy-seven-line lament to Fortune; while, in the second, he reacts to the sight of the closed doors and windows of Criseyde's home by riding so quickly back and forth in front of them that no man might see – and guess the true reason for – his dramatically changed appearance (V.539). Troilus and the Man in Black both possess a lover's intuition, through which they are (remarkably, I would argue) sensitive to the social manifestation of their pallor.

Occasionally, a deathly pale face follows drama, provoking an onlooker to compassion even in extreme circumstances. Phebus, in the *Manciple's Tale*, grieves over the body of the wife he has just murdered:

> O deere wyf! O gemme of lustiheed!
> That were to me so sad and eek so trewe,
> Now listow deed, with face pale of hewe,
> Ful giltelees, that dorste I swere, ywys!
> O rakel hand, to doon so foule amys!

O trouble wit, O ire recchelees,
That unavysed smyteth gilteles!
O wantrust, ful of fals suspecion,
Where was thy wit and thy discrecion? (IX.274–82)

The sight of his unfaithful wife's dead body and pale face triggers the murdering husband's pity and remorse. Phebus responds to the affective text of her corpse, reading his wife's facial pallor as a sign of her purity: in death, she is become 'gilteles' in life. Chaucer added the pale face to his version of the story: in Gower's *Confessio Amantis*, Phebus reacts to his wife's death with 'wo ynowh' and 'full gret repentance', but not directly to her dead body.[27] The transformation of the crow's feathers – from white to black – takes on the full significance of the wife's murder. The reader knows that her unfaithful white body is also metaphorically tarnished – turned black, like the crow's – and that she, too, has been forcefully deprived of life through Phebus's violence, as the crow has been stripped of its feathers and deprived of song.

Beyond the pale

Pallor reemerges throughout Chaucer's poetry as an appropriate facial marker for a virtuous woman – a Custance or a Griselda, or a Dorigen – an inverse of the blush of shame, and a hue complementary to the maiden blush of modesty.[28] While all three women are either threatened with or accused of shame (and all three fear it), none finds herself in a justified or enduring shameful state. Their non-normative facial pallor in these moments, when their potential 'loss of face' is at stake, underscores for the reader not so much the innate virtue of the character, but the exemplary nature of her actions.[29] Phebus's blatant misreading of his wife's deathly pallor, however, suggests the problem of interpreting the pale face out of context. Appearances, after all, are not always in truth as they appear to be. In the *Romaunce of the Rose*, the image of Poope-Holy, painted on the garden wall, 'maketh hir outward precious, / With pale visage and pitous' (A.419–20). Chaucer inserts this image of facial pallor into his translation of the *Roman de la Rose*, where it functions – as elsewhere – as a conveniently alliterative symptom of piteousness: a hallmark of the face which asks to be pitied. Wearing a cope of *'papelardie'* (C.6796; from the French, *paper* – eat, and *lard* – bacon), the hypocritical Poope-Holy is pure false-seeming – a personification of *faus semblant*, her 'vis simple et piteus' (simple and pitiful expression) an elaborate façade.[30] Where Envy and Avarice are depicted as inherently pale-faced and thin with disease (A.306; A.311), Poope-Holy, that *'semede* lyk an ipocrite' (A.414, my emphasis) makes her face 'pale and pitous' purely for outward display. The Garden's ekphrastic representation of the real Poope-Holy is ironically accurate – 'Ful lyk to hir was that ymage, / That makid was lyk hir semblaunce' (A.424–5) – in being all about contrivance. 'Ne, certis', the narrator concludes,

> she was fatt nothing,
> But *semed* wery for fasting;
> Of colour pale and deed was she. (A.439–41, my emphasis)

The narrator's description of Poope-Holy's 'seeming' ends with the image of her 'pale and deed' reflection. For the reader of the *Manciple's Tale*, the pale face of Phebus's dead wife reflects Phebus's own hypocrisy.

While Chaucer's lovers and his virtuous women have a common tendency toward pallor, the majority of male characters in the *Tales*, like Phebus, do not pale, even at moments of heightened emotional intensity. And yet to conclude that the pale face is a feminine or feminising trait in Chaucer's works is to oversimplify its narrative condition. The emotional significance of paleness extends beyond the individual concerned, whether biologically male or female, to those charged with the task of reading the pale face, and responding to it appropriately: Phebus's wife, for example, feels nothing in death; instead, her pale face is a mirror which reflects his own emotional turmoil and remorse. Similarly, it is not the emotions of Custance as she is about to stand trial which are of greatest hermeneutic significance in the *Man of Law's Tale*, but those of Alla, who bears witness to her paleness and responds with compassionate tears. Later, when Custance is banished with her child, her witnesses' ability to read empathy in the text of her pale face is again called into play. Having received the King's order for her exile, the people all weep in a scene which anticipates the pathos and compassion that Custance's 'deedly pale face' should provoke anew for the poem's auditors (II.820, II.822). The Man of Law's original invitation that his audience visualise Custance's pale face, and contextualise it among all the other faces in an imagined crowd, encourages us to think more openly about both the cognitive and affective functions of facial pallor in literary narrative. The pale face is one that is worth interrogating – as Chaucer does repeatedly – whether rhetorically engaging the readers in their own understanding and experience, or offering various models of compassionate response in his characters. As a form of expressivity which is characterised precisely by its idiosyncrasy – its deviation from a facial norm – the pale face is nonetheless normalised through a sense of both intertextual and experiential familiarity as a face which has been seen before. By writing with the 'blank' page of the pale face, Chaucer proves once more to be an exemplary teacher, instructing his readers in how to read feeling in fiction.

Notes

1 Stephanie Trigg, 'Chaucer's silent discourse', *Studies in the Age of Chaucer*, 39 (2017), 33–56.
2 In addition to 'Chaucer's silent discourse', see also: Stephanie Trigg, 'Langland's tears: poetry, emotion and mouvance', *Yearbook of Langland Studies*, 26 (2012), 27–48; Trigg, '"Language in her eye": the expressive face of Criseyde/Cressida', in Andrew James Johnston, Elizabeth Kempf and Russell West-Pavlov (eds), *Love, History and Emotion in Chaucer and Shakespeare:* Troilus and Criseyde *and* Troilus and Cressida (Manchester: Manchester University Press, 2016), pp. 94–108; and Trigg, 'Faces that speak: a little emotion machine in the novels of Jane Austen', in Susan Broomhall (ed.), *Spaces for Feeling: Emotions and Sociabilities in Britain, 1650–1850* (London and New York: Routledge, 2015), pp. 185–201.
3 The most recent example is Ethan Knapp, 'Faciality and ekphrasis in late medieval England', in Andrew James Johnston, Knapp and Margitta Rouse (eds), *The Art of Vision: Ekphrasis in Medieval Literature and Culture* (Columbus: Ohio State University Press, 2015), pp. 209–23 (pp. 213–17). See also William McClellan, *Reading Chaucer After Auschwitz: Sovereign Power and Bare Life* (New York: Palgrave Macmillan, 2016), especially 'Chapter 3: marriage and exile', pp. 41–59; and Carolyn Dinshaw's important essay, based on the text of her Biennial Chaucer Lecture at the twelfth International Congress of the New Chaucer Society, 'Pale faces: race, religion and affect in Chaucer's texts and their readers', *Studies in the Age of Chaucer*, 23 (2001), 19–41.
4 See, for example, Mary F. Wack, 'Lovesickness in "Troilus"', *Pacific Coast Philology*, 19 (1984), 55–61; Carol F. Heffernan, 'Chaucer's *Troilus and Criseyde*: the disease of love and courtly love', *Neophilologus*, 74:2 (1990), 294–309; and Sealy Gilles, 'Love and disease in Chaucer's *Troilus and Criseyde*', *Studies in the Age of Chaucer*, 25 (2003), 157–97. For a more general treatment of this theme in Chaucer, see Rebecca F. McNamara, 'Wearing your heart on your face: reading lovesickness

and the suicidal impulse in Chaucer', *Literature and Medicine*, 33:2 (2015), 258–78.
5 All quotations of Chaucer's poetry refer to Geoffrey Chaucer, *The Riverside Chaucer*, gen. ed. Larry D. Benson (Oxford: Oxford University Press, 3rd edn, 1988) and are cited by fragment or book (where appropriate) and line number.
6 Trigg, 'Chaucer's silent discourse', pp. 33–56; J. A. Burrow, *Gestures and Looks in Medieval Narrative* (Cambridge: Cambridge University Press, 2002), pp. 69–113.
7 Dinshaw, 'Pale faces', p. 39.
8 Stephanie Downes and Rebecca F. McNamara, 'Middle English literature and the history of emotions', *Literature Compass*, 13:6 (2016), 444–56; for a summary and review of very recent scholarship on the emotions among medievalists, especially Middle English scholars, see Holly A. Crocker, 'Medieval affects now', *Exemplaria*, 29:1 (2017), 82–98.
9 Sarah McNamer, *Affective Meditation and the Invention of Medieval Compassion* (Philadelphia: University of Pennsylvania Press, 2010); Fiona Somerset, *Feeling Like Saints: Lollard Writings After Wyclif* (Ithaca: Cornell University Press, 2015).
10 Stephanie Trigg, 'What does normal look like?', *TEDxSydney*, 21 May 2015, www.youtube.com/watch?v=tHlh5v5erWA, accessed 5 May 2018.
11 Michael Edward Moore, 'Meditations on the face in the Middle Ages (with Levinas and Picard)', *Literature and Theology*, 41:1 (2010), 19–37.
12 See Stephanie Downes and Stephanie Trigg, 'Editors' introduction: facing up to the history of emotions', *postmedieval*, 8:1 (2017), 3–11 (pp. 5–6), in which we summarise briefly the oft-referenced, highly influential and frequently controversial studies of Paul Ekman on the universality of facial expression. For a perspective from the sciences, see D. T. Cordaro, *et al.*, 'The great expressions debate', *Emotion Researcher: The Official Newsletter of the International Society for Research on Emotion*, Special Issue (2015), http://emotionresearcher.com/the-great-expressions-debate/, accessed 24 April 2018. At the time of writing, a new volume has just appeared, which I have not yet been able to consult: José-Miguel Fernández-Dols and James A. Russell (eds), *The Science of Facial Expression* (Oxford: Oxford University Press, 2017), and which appears to include several chapters exploring facial expression from historical and linguistic perspectives.
13 Philippa Maddern, 'Reading faces: how did late medieval Europeans interpret emotions in faces?', *postmedieval*, 8:1 (2017), 12–34 (pp. 19–21).
14 Maddern, 'Reading faces', p. 20. Andrew Lynch discusses Lydgate's association of pale faces with melancholy violence in '"With face

pale"': melancholy violence in John Lydgate's Troy and Thebes', in Joanna Bellis and Laura Slater (eds), *Representing War and Violence: 1250–1600* (Woodbridge: Boydell & Brewer, 2016), pp. 79–94.

15 Quoted in Maddern, 'Reading faces', p. 19, my emphasis.

16 I quote, in translation, Bolens, who wrote: 'L'ecrivain Chaucer, quant il met en récit l'expression coorporelle d'une emotion, lance un defi interpretatif a ses destinataires', Guillemette Bolens, 'La narration des émotions et la réactivité du destinataire dans les *Contes de Canterbury*', *Médiévales*, 61 (2011), 97–118 (p. 97). My analysis differs from Bolens' in that, rather than focusing on kinesic intelligence, I am interested in Chaucer's uses of corporeal signs in the text to trigger affective – often specifically compassionate – responses in the reader. The larger project to which this work belongs investigates the wider reading contexts of such signs, juxtaposing textual and visual representations of human faces in medieval manuscripts.

17 Knapp briefly adumbrates Chaucer's 'narratologically significant use of [pale] faces' in the *Man of Law's Tale* and *Troilus and Criseyde*. I here extend this argument about the importance of facial pallor in a range of Chaucerian texts ('Faciality and ekphrasis', p. 214).

18 Trigg, 'Chaucer's silent discourse', pp. 33–56.

19 James Simpson, 'Cognition is recognition: literary knowledge and textual "face"', *New Literary History*, 44 (2013), 25–44 (p. 25). See also Simpson's contribution to this volume, p. 218.

20 William McClellan, 'Full pale face: Agamben's biopolitical theory and the sovereign subject in Chaucer's *Clerk's Tale*', *Exemplaria*, 17 (2005), 103–34 (p. 111).

21 McClellan, *Reading Chaucer After Auschwitz*, p. 64.

22 McNamer, *Affective Meditation*, p. 119.

23 V. A. Kolve, *Chaucer and the Imagery of Narrative: The First Five Canterbury Tales* (Stanford: Stanford University Press, 1984), p. 304.

24 McClellan, *Reading Chaucer After Auschwitz*, pp. 69–74. For an earlier reading of Custance's association with Mary in this scene, see Hope Phyllis Weissman, 'Late gothic pathos in the *Man of Law's Tale*', *Journal of Medieval and Renaissance Studies*, 9 (1979), 133–54 (pp. 149–51).

25 McClellan, *Reading Chaucer After Auschwitz*, p. 68.

26 Geoffrey of Vinsauf, *Poetria Nova*, in E. Faral (ed.), *Les arts poétiques du XIIe et du XIIIe siècle* (Paris, 1924), p. 259, lines 2031–2. On Geoffrey and on the practice of co-ordinating speech and facial expression, see 'Looks', in Burrow, *Gestures and Looks*, pp. 69–113.

27 John Gower, *Confessio Amantis: Volume 2*, ed. Russell A. Peck, trans. Andrew Galloway (Kalamazoo: Medieval Institute Publications, 2013), book 3, lines 802–3.

28 See Valerie Allen, 'Waxing red: shame and the body, shame and the soul', in Lisa Perfetti (ed.), *The Representation of Women's Emotions in*

Medieval and Early Modern Culture (Gainsville: University of Florida Press, 2005), pp. 191–210; and Mary C. Flannery, 'A bloody shame: Chaucer's honourable women', *Review of English Studies*, 62 (2011), 337–57 and 'The concept of shame in late medieval English literature', *Literature Compass*, 9:2 (2012), 166–82.

29 On shame and 'loss of face' in medieval English literature, see Bolens, 'La narration des émotions', and Flannery, 'A bloody shame'.

30 Guillaume de Lorris and Jean de Meun, *Le Roman de la Rose*, ed. and trans. Armand Strubel, Lettres Gothiques (Paris: Le Livre de Poche, 1992), p. 62, line 414.

6
Heavy atmosphere
Jeffrey Jerome Cohen

Air is substance, affect and story. In all three forms it offers an abiding archive.

The roiled substantiality within which human lives unfold, air was understood in the Middle Ages as volatile matter that hugged the Earth in two or three perispheric layers. Pure only in its upper reaches (the *caelum aetherium*, outer edge of the atmosphere), air at the Earth's surface had trouble staying put, eager in its embrace of sibling elements. John Gower described air's work as *environing*: 'Air / ... / environeth bothe tuo, / The water and the lond also' (7.369–74).[1] As its French and Latin etymology suggests, *envirounen* means surround, encircle, fill, attend, enclose, beset. *Air* is matter, action, place and mood. It is turbulent, mixing land and sea and human emotion into storm and tempest. Thunder, lightning and gale find their forceful habitat in the air. So do birds, insects and angels, filling the element with song. That cheerfulness can infect life, so that air raises emotive states and refreshes. The Middle English phrase 'to take the eire' means to stroll outdoors and allow the element healthfully to permeate the skin.[2] When air is 'infect', 'ivel' or 'thik', however, its heavy impress will contaminate both temperament and body. 'Kyndely mevable and chaungeable' (in Trevisa's words), air is climate in its dynamic relation to embodiment.[3] *Weder* (weather) possessed for medieval people the same affective and meteorological connotations that *atmosphere* does for us. Setting is never still.

Air is the enmeshment of environment with life – even indoors.

Inner atmosphere

Chaucer frequently suggests that environmental narratives are for humans always also economic (that is, *household*) stories, in which violence and mood are interconnected in ways that trouble the walls between home and world. The *Reeve's Tale* is a fabliau known for its heavy atmosphere – a mood, most certainly, but also an embodied mode of contemplating environmentality. Whereas the preceding *Miller's Tale* is full of hymns, love songs and musical instruments, this story offers an aerial ecosystem of dissonant, nonverbal signifying: the 'rowtyng' and 'fnortyng' of Symkyn the miller and his sleeping family; the 'wehee' of the escaping stallions, released to chase mares in the fens; the whistles and shouts ('Keep! Stand! Jossa!') used by the clerks to call back their wayward horses. Every word that John and Aleyn speak at the beginning of the tale threatens to break from linguistic signification and hang in the air as mere sonority, so thick are their Northern accents: 'Swa werkes ay the wanges in his heed' (I.4030).[4] Sound is a vibration that travels through air to implant itself in flesh. But its force ripples far beyond merely human environs. Sound saturates, renders air thick with narrative.

Tobias Menely has written eloquently of how 'atmosphere – the Earth's gaseous envelope, an aerial surround' is usually figured as an insubstantial and ahistorical exterior, and is thereby dismissed as 'impervious to the impress of human action'.[5] The Anthropocene atmosphere, weighty with the material accumulations of our industrial history, tells a different story. So does Chaucer, for whom air likewise offers a suspended repository of human history, stories that resonate longer and travel farther than expected. In the *House of Fame* Chaucer describes sound (of which speech is a special type) as 'air ybroke' (770), a reverberation that moves 'with violence' (775), as when 'thow / Throwe on water now a stoon' (788–9). Sonic vibrations ripple and intensify, drenching the air with 'speche ... / Or voys, or noyse, or word, or soun' (818–19) – speech or voice or noise or word or sound – a dense repository of human and nonhuman tales in whirring motion. With its snores, cries, shouts, pleas, poems and prayers, the *Reeve's Tale* noisily foregrounds the penetrability and porousness of flesh within a similarly saturating, story-laden atmosphere.

The miller and his family snore because their bodies are humoral environments out of balance. As Chaucer explains in the *Squire's Tale*, excessive drinking engenders a superfluity of blood, which in turn triggers a profound need for restorative slumber. The sleep that follows inebriation is restless, though, since a drunken head is filled with 'fumositee' (V.358), alcohol-induced fumes that burden the mind with meaningless signification. The intoxicated body well illustrates the fluidity of medieval embodiment. The four humours do their work within skin that offers a permeable membrane rather than a barrier.[6] This open, fleshly system enmeshes the gravity of the moon, the impress of place, the agency of matter and the density and humidity of atmosphere, creating what Gail Paster has called 'an ecology of passions' and 'the body's weather', which may be both shared with the environment and heavy.[7] The human form is a dynamic ecology easily thrown into crisis, a 'conviviality of animate and inanimate matters' as J. Allan Mitchell describes it, that makes clear 'anthropocentrism has not always been an inevitable mode of self-understanding'.[8]

Yet the plot of the *Reeve's Tale* is in the end all too human, all too masculine, and not at all humane. The narrative culminates in two acts of sexualised revenge, messages sent by the clerks to the miller through the bodies of his wife and daughter. Horses, cakes, wheat, beds, sex and blows are exchanged, with little regard for the lived consequences that such equivalence entails. Interpenetrability is subject to constant economic recapture. The *Reeve's Tale* is the story of a miller who fleeces his customers. The clerks believe the proper payment for such abuse is to be made through the sexual enjoyment of the women in his household. Once Aleyn and John sleep with the miller's wife and daughter, the tale becomes a heavy account of what happens when a wide ecology is reduced to a constricted economy of sale, substitution and revenge, wheat to pie to profits, all things (even virginity) rendered vendible. No wonder the fabliau ends with screams, blows, blood. Women's bodies are used by men to send stories to other men. That these women have their own narratives is hinted at but never with much attention explored. The atmosphere is heavy on many accounts, and the *Reeve's Tale* is therefore one many choose not to teach. Yet the tale's perturbing weightiness also makes it worth examining closely, with all the burdens its ambiance carries, especially in its insistence that gender and other embodied differences matter profoundly to the climatic stories that we tell.

Economic and environmental violence might be complex and enmeshed, but that does not mean that some specifically embodied human agents are not culpable, that economic and environmental suffering is never evenly distributed or felt. Medieval writers knew well that climate is affect as well as thing, and human narratives persist much longer than we intend, resonating over vaster distances of space and time. Heavy atmosphere endures.

Life in the sea of air

As Chaucer knew well, earth dwellers are intimate to an atmosphere too often dismissed as mere background. Skin is a permeable membrane caressed and battered by a lively element. Air's invisibility obscures its heft and dynamism. The stories we tell to convey its activity are limited by the fact that we perceive the element mainly through aftermath. We cannot see aerial motion, though we behold trees that bend and clouds that scud as a result of its swift transit. Our skin prickles and our emotions rise and fall with its ambiance. Air can seem like nothing at all. Because of its volatility air might appear to be, as Steve Mentz writes, 'history's opposite, sheer unintegrated force, roaring through our planet and our bodies', sound and fury that does not signify.[9] But medieval writers knew that the element is thick with enduring history. Air engulfs us, acts on us and with us; it is storied matter that conveys and jars.

Air is intimate to affect.[10] Fresh breezes invigorate, dense atmosphere dispirits, the cloy of humidity enervates, the scent of spring rain lightens the mood. Such feelings may effloresce in a breezy moment but they connect us to longer durations (as 'petrichor' – the redolence of rain upon stone – does after a drought). As a classical and medieval inheritance, terms like *air, climate* and *atmosphere* name the porosity between ecology and mood. 'Hevinesse' designates in Middle English a weightiness that may be material or emotional, or both. People can, like the elements, be cold, warm, volatile, even 'stormy' (as Chaucer labels the changeable populace of Saluzzo in the *Clerk's Tale*).[11] Medieval science found in this similitude an environmental interface, a crossing of place and flesh, cognition and mood. Today we might describe the intermingling of body and world as transcorporeality (to invoke Stacy Alaimo's apt description of environmental penetrability).[12] Medievalists and early modernists label a similar phenomenon 'geohumoralism', designating the physical-material-psychological intimacy of individual and communal bodies to clime and place.[13] Physical and mental states are entangled within both native and immediate ecosystems. Medieval bodies therefore carried raced and gendered specificities to be examined within at least two contexts, historical (stories of origin) and contemporary (stories of present flourishing). This is not to say that medieval writers did not abstract and generalise bodies in ways that we would today describe as racist and sexist. They did, and with gusto. Yet all eleven bodies within the geohumoral model are changeable as ecological circumstance shifts, since all are by nature ecologically entangled.[14]

Most contemporary scholarship on environmental entanglement looks for its examples to the Anthropocene, finding in this epoch when carbon and nuclear isotopes are embedded by human industry into the geological record the termination of air's invisibility. Recognising air's weight as historical marker, Jesse Oak Taylor argues that the neologism 'smog' (1905) conveys a climatic interface that only the industrial revolution could engender: through a pea-soup swirl of coal particles mixed with fog, climate comes to be understood as 'suffused with the accumulated residue of an artifact and understandable only within the cultural and historical conditions that led to its production'.[15] This becoming-visible of human/nature indistinction in suffocating form leads Taylor to posit that atmosphere is a 'material property inhering in the air shared by the world, the text, and the critic'.[16] Yet medieval writers upped that aerial burden to argue that atmosphere is so formative that all bodies carry environmental imprint indelibly in their flesh, a lasting spur to thought, feeling and action.[17] Taylor conveys well this medieval conception of both climate and atmosphere when he writes of life in the Anthropocene that 'the environment ceases to exist as such: no mere passive backdrop or container, climate no longer hovers outside, surrounding us (as indicated by the root enviro) but rather strikes within'.[18] Climate is the impress of an environing. Such entangled agency is made evident through narrative, which offers both a repository and 'a kind of forecasting', since storytelling is our best technology for speeding time up and slowing history down, for manifesting atmospheric force.[19]

Weighty atmosphere is not a phenomenon only of the Anthropocene, when the air we breathe is heavy with carbon emissions and the geological record replete with industrial registers of altered climate. Air holds lasting stories, only some of which revolve around hearths, bombs and factories. Medieval writers like Chaucer knew that air is a noisy archive of tales, only some of which centre upon humans – and that heavy atmospheres can sometimes engender congenial communities in their wake.[20] Climate become affect as well as object conveys how human histories persist much longer than we intend, resonating over vast spatial and temporal distances – tales of human and nonhuman entanglement, violence and the possibility of better worlds. *Heavy atmosphere* is therefore at once: the density of an enveloping element; weighty emotion that can hang in the air and suffuse bodies; and the feel of a particular narrative. All three atmospheres (elemental, affective, diegetic) resound with stories about human industry, unequally distributed suffering, and responsibility.

In the *Confessio Amantis* Gower stresses the continuity between humans and their world, with human bodies functioning as ecological interfaces as well as miniature versions of the cosmic order. Environmental turbulence is inextricable from the human inclination to disorder. Gower deploys the word 'climat' to designate specifically an earthly zone of habitation in the Macrobian sense, but his noun is already becoming *climate* in our mixed contemporary sense, as barometer of the effects of human actions as well as thick conveyor of affect. Gowerian bodies are dynamically enmeshed in climate, bound within a cosmos that reaches all the way to weather in the 'welkin' and the distant stars. The human form in turn offers a reduced version of that universe, microcosm and macrocosm as the same order at different scales. In the Prologue, Gower cites Pope Gregory's *Moralia in Job* for this moody and material analogousness:

> Forthi Gregoire in his *Moral*
> Seith that a man in special
> The lasse world is properly:
> And that he proeveth redely; (Pr. 945–8)

Man is 'lasse world' (microcosm) because he is midway on the ladder of Nature. Above him are angels, whom he resembles with his 'soule resonable'. Just below are beasts, which likewise possess the ability to feel. On the next rung down are plants, exerting their strength through growth. The ladder's base is stone, which like everything higher on the steps can at least be said to exist ('The stones ben and so is he' [Pr. 953]). This *scala naturae* is not built upon transcendence but continuity. Humans are made of rock, plant, animal, angel. Mitchell writes that the 'medieval environmental imaginary' is composed of cross-ontological entanglements in which 'complicated ecologies underpin even the tidiest of cosmologies'.[21] Nature's ladder has a tendency to intermix what it only seems to compartmentalise. The human at its middle is much to blame. 'The man' writes Gower, is 'as a world' – but not a self-enclosed one:

> And whan this litel world mistorneth,
> The grete world al overtorneth.
> The Lond, the See, the firmament,
> Thei axen alle jugement
> Ayein the man and make him were. (Pr. 957–61)

When human society is divided against itself, turbulent and divisive, the world likewise becomes unstable, stormy. Humans trigger ecological upheaval through their actions: 'The man is cause of alle wo, / Why this world is divided so' (Pr. 965–6). Gower, it seems, postulated anthropogenic climate change centuries ago: 'The purest Eir for Senne alofte / Hath ben and is corrupt fulofte' (Pr. 921–2).

As Gower makes clear, even though he is using this figuration politically, it is in fact a story 'as telleth the clergie', a tale of divine rebuke for humanity's earthly sins, a tale of ecocatastrophe based on the narrative of Noah's flood. Before we dismiss this entanglement of politics with theology as too symptomatically medieval, however, it is worth bearing in mind that we hardly separate our politics from our theology at this moment, when we expect the Earth to act against us as a punishing deity for having thrown the environment out of balance. Our world is an intensified version of the ecology of disarray that Gower describes. He writes that our earthly habitation as full of 'hyhe wyndes', overflowing seas, deluge and drought, land that erodes, vanishing plants, storms – and at the centre of 'al the worldes werk' is 'man and his condicioun' (Pr. 923–44). As Mitchell puts it so well in his reading of Gower's 'ecocentric and epigenetic' cosmology:

> there is no neutral background or foreground for individuals in this universe – all the elements are equally 'there'.... Anthropogenic change affords a much-needed view of the total catastrophe. And it is a medieval view.[22]

How then to escape this endemic terrestrial turbulence, a 'dedly werre' (Pr. 904), of all mundane things, so profound that it catches up the very elements? We could adopt the point of view ascribed by Gower to the celestial angels, high above humans on the ladder of being, creatures for whom the Earth is a small world. But, as Chaucer knew well, weighty atmosphere is likely to prove difficult to leave behind.

Elemental foundations

According to an elemental physics articulated by the early Greek philosopher Empedocles and subtending materialist thinking throughout the Middle Ages, four restless substances form all matter and give the cosmos its curving topologies, spheres within spinning spheres. Earth, air, water and fire name lively matter as well as dynamic expanses. Tempestuous admixtures of cold, hot, dry and moist, each element possesses particular velocities and attributes that enter into whatever forms they compose. Pulled towards embrace by gravity (or *philia*, 'love') and pushed apart by entropy (*neikos*, 'strife'), the elements never stop moving, and yet each tends towards a natural place within the universe, an enduring home. Ponderous earth sinks downwards and forms the orb of land upon which we erect our fragile habitations. Water is next in heft, lapping the edges of dense shorelines while churning tempestuously into its sibling substance air, the element that whirls between surface and firmament. Celestial fire rises high, the stuff of planets and stars. This structure of concentric environs is apprehensible only by imagining a radically exterior perspective, as if observers could leave the confines of their terrestrial home and behold the world from its outside. Medieval manuscript illustrations depict these four elements in their native ecologies as expanding rings, brown to green to blue to red, often with a building or person at centre, emphasising that macrocosms and microcosms are nested intimacies. This quadricameral arrangement, diagrammed as circles within spinning circles, suggests a medieval origin for modern diagrams of the Earth's layered atmosphere.

Now held in the British Library, an early fourteenth-century manuscript (Yates Thompson MS 19) of Brunetto Latini's French compendium of classical learning (originally compiled in the 1260s), *Li Livres dou Tresor* is elegantly illustrated with two elemental diagrams of this concentric type (see plates 1 and 2).[23] In one arresting image, a globe of golden earth is clasped by a ring of verdant water through which fish merrily swim (see plate 1).[24] The green ocean is banded in turn by stormy blue air, embraced next by a ring of celestial flame, domain of the blazing stars. Beyond that crimson fire lie two pale bands of blue, the Aristotelian fifth element of ether, outer stability for a world of insistent motion. A golden sun and a moon with a dubious face rotate through these distant limits, heavenly bodies traversing the edges of an ethereal eggshell that keeps the inner circles environed but not stilled. The gleaming Earth at the illustration's centre is dominated by a stone building that declares human inhabitance. The cosmos rotates around an anthropocentric ecology, even if its components may act without humane regard. The four elements are ecological agents. Their nested spheres seem stable but constant movement roils them into a generative restlessness.

Latini's discussion of air ranges over the entire hydrologic cycle of evaporation and precipitation: storm systems, prevailing winds, the formation of clouds. To express atmospheric substantiality he offers an oceanic metaphor: 'Man and the other animals live in the air, and they breathe it, and they are like fish in water, and they would not be able to do this if it were not moist and thick.'[25] If air is marinal and we humans are creatures treading the bottom of another kind of sea, then the element thickens into sudden presence, as a substance we could suffocate within were we not well adapted to its embrace.[26] When lungs become gills and air 'moist and thick', then the invisible matter that we take into our bodies through mouth, nose and skin is no longer something out there at some exterior distance, swirling the distant heavens, but a weather system of embodied climate. Skin is a drenched interface.

In a second elemental illustration from the same manuscript of *Li Livres dou Tresor*,[27] the four elements encircle a physician attending a bedridden man (see plate 2). Dense earth again forms the world's spherical centre, embraced by roiling water full of fish, girdled next by gusty air and illuminated at last by a ring of blazing, sky-bound fire. Air is a halo of blue, mottled light and dark to emphasise its liveliness. The universe is again depicted as bounded, stable, a machine of concentric spheres in motion.[28] The doctor at the illustration's centre attempts to discern the relation between cosmic and bodily balance, hoping to restore a disharmonised body to equilibrium. The phial which he holds is likely what Chaucer called an 'urynal'. Familiar from the *Physician's* and *Canon's Yeoman's Tales* (VI.305, VIII.792), such bottles were used to collect bodily efflux and discern the story of health that such fluid conveys. The Greek physician Galen medicalised earth, air, fire and water through their innate properties of heat, cold, moisture and aridity so that the four elements are always to the medieval mind intimates of the humours. A healthy body, animal or human, is a balanced one, no quality in excess. The physician's charge is to study his patient as enmeshed ecosystem. Bile, blood and phlegm are in this medical-environmental model the very matter of psychology: feeling materialised, affect in substantial form.

We can put on airs of superiority, or bring everyone down by having a sombre atmosphere. The dual signification of climatic nouns like these is a humoral inheritance. They signal a thing as well as mood, environment as public affect. Chaucer's *Troilus and Criseyde* contains a powerful vision of Earth as *place* and *feeling* at once. When the poem's hero is slain in battle his soul ascends heavenward. Freed from his body, Troilus rises through the four elemental spheres and wandering planets to view the cosmos from its very edge, a stable expanse of music, harmony, stability and levity from which the spinning world is glimpsed as distant home:

> And whan that he was slayn in this manere,
> His lighte goost ful blisfully is went
> Up to the holughnesse of the eighthe spere,
> In convers letyng everich element;
> And ther he saugh with ful avysement
> The erratik sterres, herkening armonye
> With sownes fulle of hevenyssh melodie.
>
> And down from thennes faste he gan avyse
> This litel spot of erthe that with the se
> Embraced is, and fully gan despise
> This wrecched world, and held al vanite. (V.1807–17)

The Earth and its volatile stories recede so far that they are reduced to a 'litel spot', an embrace of sea and land in which swift-moving humans become unremarkable. Permeated by the lightness of the heavens and granted a vision of the world's order almost from its outside, Troilus laughs at the heaviness he has abandoned along with his body (V.1821). What had seemed all-consuming becomes a dwindled and 'wrecched world' – albeit, from this distance, a resplendent one.[29]

The impulse to imagine a perspective from outside and above the Earth in order to escape the tumultuous vicissitudes of being human is an ancient one. For as long as humans have understood the Earth as round (which is to say, pretty much throughout Western recorded history), we have also imagined a point of view that can apprehend our home from far above the surface on which we dwell. Medieval authors like Chaucer inherited one possible frame for that perspective from the *Dream of Scipio*, narrated by Cicero in the sixth book of his *De re publica*. In the Middle Ages this classical text was available only within the detailed commentary composed around it by Macrobius, who used the dream to articulate more precisely the contours of the cosmos.[30]

The Roman general Scipio is visited in slumber by his adoptive grandfather, a famous military man, who gives his young relative a view of Rome from the heavens. To the melodious soundtrack of the planetary spheres, Scipio the Younger peers down from the ether, surrounded by the Milky Way, at the Earth become a small spot, his city almost nothing upon its surface. The various climates of the globe resolve into five bands: two polar ice fields, two temperate and habitable zones on either side of the equator, and a torrid desert dividing each from each. In medieval manuscript illustrations this Earth resembles a small version of Jupiter, vivid in its planetary stripes (see plate 3).[31] When Scipio awakens from this dream of shimmering stars that offer a lasting home for the souls of the great, he is fortified with Stoic contempt for all things terrestrial and small. The world is beautiful from space, perhaps, but its human and climatic dynamism is just bustle. More lasting things reside at the system's exterior. Scipio the Younger rises above it all to gain new perspective. He beholds a Striped Marble rather than what the Apollo astronauts called a Blue Marble. NASA realises dreams that have long haunted us – or, better, imagination offers a means of propulsion out of human boundedness that was realised first through the technology of narrative and then through space flight.

Where Scipio goes, Chaucer follows. His narration of the backwards glance of Troilus upon a globe become 'This litel spot of erthe that with the se / Embraced is' (V.1815–16) derives directly from Boccaccio, but ultimately from the *Dream of Scipio*. Macrobius's five climates were sometimes multiplied to seven, each one dominated by a particular planet, stressing the intimacy of the atmospheric to the mundane. Our desire to be less Earthbound, at least during the space of a dream or a science fiction film or a narrative poem about the last days of Troy, is a desire to escape our entanglement in a world that exceeds us and yet remains intimate to our thoughts and deeds. We never quite manage that liberation, at least not for long. Though the price of its achievement is death, Troilus attains a critical distance from the elements' incessant imbroglios that few other Chaucerian characters attain, aspire as they might. Only the soaring eagle of the *House of Fame* comes close, declaring to a perplexed Chaucer that climate and inclination are the same thing.[32] The elemental composition of matter induces every 'kyndely thyng' to move towards its 'kyndely stede' (730–1). 'Kyndely' here means natural, so that all matter is imbued with a substantial 'enclynyng':

> Thorgh his kyndely enclynyng
> Moveth for to come to
> Whan that hyt is awey therfro;
> And thus: loo, thou maist alday se
> That any thing that hevy be,

> As stoon, or led, or thyng of wighte,
> And bere hyt never so hye on highte,
> Lat goo thyn hand, hit falleth doun.
> Ryght so seye I be fyr or soun,
> Or smoke or other thynges lyghte;
> Alwey they seke upward on highte. (734–44)

From his lofty perspective above the heavy things of this world, the eagle knows that *kynde* (nature) means being *enclyned*, moving in sympathy towards a space that is heavy or light. Just as elements are inclined towards certain climates, so whatever they compose moves towards a home: 'every ryver to the see / Enclyned ys to goo by kynde' (748–9). With this macrocosmic view in which all things incline towards their natural place, the eagle attempts to lighten the mood of the heavy-hearted poet. Yet heavy atmosphere is not easy to transcend.

On not leaving Earth behind

A failed attempt at dispassionate abstraction from this world's confluences of matter and mood is staged in the *Knight's Tale*, when Duke Theseus strives to lighten the mood of his court after Arcite's unexpected death just after his moment of victory. Using language adapted from Boethius's *Consolation of Philosophy*, Theseus attempts to demonstrate how a world that seems full of chance is undergirded by deep bonds and a universal structure of meaning, visible from a heavenly perspective. A First Mover bequeaths to all matter proper and meaningful duration, a chain of love that joins the elements, at least for while: 'For with that faire cheyne of love he bond / The fyr, the eyr, the water, and the lond, / In certeyn boundes, that they may nat flee' (I.2991–3). The First Mover is eternal, but all created things exist in time, so that after 'Certeyne dayes and duracioun' elemental bonds dissolve and matter reasserts its restless motion (I.2996). Theseus's attempt at mood change through changed perspective offers a narrative version of Brunetto Latini's concentric cosmic rings in motion, whirring so that anything made by the elements is never at rest, always moving towards becoming something else. Whether Theseus succeeds in lightening the post-funeral feeling of the court remains an open question, especially after he concludes his oration with an incongruous observation that it is probably best to die young and leave a beautiful corpse. Yet the world he describes, where oaks grow too slowly for humans to perceive and stone is daily incised by the erosive force of human footsteps, stresses that the world is never stable when viewed from the middle of things, when narrated from lived experience.[33] The cosmos in motion can be difficult to comprehend, but when thought from sufficient remoteness and within a proper scale then perturbations that seem senseless and local become intimate to larger, more meaningful environings.

The *Knight's Tale* also takes perverse delight in sabotaging all such attempts to imagine the universe from its outside. Readers are made to inhabit the knight Arcite's subjectivity as he feels his body undergo the process of death. His swollen breast clots with blood so that no 'lechecraft' can restore health. A medicalised and coldly technical vocabulary clusters around the description of his perishing flesh ('ventusinge', 'vertu expulsif'), but unlike the illustration in Latini's *Li Livres dou Tresor*, we abide here not with the physician but the patient in bed. The focus and mood remain personal. Cures are attempted but crushed lungs and infected blood resist treatment. Hope dies before the body starts to yield: 'Fare wel physik! Go ber the man to chirche!' (I.2760). Arcite imagines the solitude of his 'colde' grave: 'Allone, withouten any compaignye', as if he will be trapped inside its small space like a soul that cannot leave dead flesh (I.2779). As his speech fails, he senses 'the cool of deeth' creep 'from his feet up to his brest' (I.2798–800). His 'vital strengthe' drains while his 'intellect' clings to 'his herte syk and soore' (I.2804). He knows that the end is coming, knows that this heart must stop beating ... and as his breathing ceases and his eyes 'dusked' we who have been trapped within his dying frame want some moment of comfort, an escape to a larger perspective from which that death makes better sense.

At this point in Boccaccio's *Il Teseida*, Chaucer's source for the *Knight's Tale*, Arcite's soul rises from his body to ascend above the Earth and view, Scipio-like, the spheres of the universe in their orderly rotations.[34] Chaucer loved this episode so much that he gave it to Troilus in the passage with which we lingered earlier, the one with the 'litel spot of erthe'. In the *Knight's Tale*, however, we are granted no transcendence. Arcite dies and the narrator states coolly 'His spirit chaunged hous and wente ther, / As I cam nevere, I kan nat tellen wher' (I.2809–10). Chaucer stops here ('I stynte') because he is no 'divinistre', no theologian, no confident articulator of heavenly perspectives. And yet we know that he is fully capable of such cosmic views – his source materials contain the very thing he refuses to provide. Why trap readers on this 'litel', messy and fraught Earth?

The *Knight's Tale* is a narrative of failed encompassings, with its ardour for order sometimes aligned with a tendency towards tyranny. To materialise his authority over what seems to him lawlessness, Theseus has the clearing where Palamon and Arcite are discovered brawling overlaid with a 'noble theatre' so vast that 'The circuit a myle was aboute' (I.1885, I.1887). Shaped 'in manere of compas' (I.1889), this monumental architecture rises to great heights, spreads across a vast terrain and offers a veritable cosmos of unobstructed views of its centre space: 'whan a man was set on o degree, / He letted nat his felawe for to see' (I.1891–2).[35] Theseus attempts, in other words, to render in stone the kind of all-encompassing perspective that inheres in elemental diagrams or Troilus's perspective from the stars, a point of view from which the world's turmoil resolves into neat circles. Yet rings have a way of moving, undermining desired stability. Theseus's colossal stadium houses a temple of Mars on the walls of which is illustrated a cart-maker crushed by the wheels of his own vehicle: 'The cartere overryden with his carte' (I.2022). The gods to whom the theatre's three temples are dedicated (Mars, Venus, Diana) function not as classical deities but planetary climates, exerting a mundane gravity that connects atmosphere to inclination to body to history to feeling. Like the cart-maker's wheel, the compass-like structure that Theseus has built cannot help becoming a metaphor: the arena is destined to become a funeral grove. Though the vast stadium aspires to materialise cosmic order, with Theseus set at a window 'Arrayed right as he were a god in trone' (I.2529), its circuit will become Fortune's ever-spinning wheel, crushing Arcite beneath it at his moment of victory. Arcite, with whom the audience will experience what it is to die. Arcite, whose soul does not flee from the body, whose destiny remains earthbound. Through an inept yet strangely beautiful metaphor, Theseus's father Egeus expresses this failed transcendence best, offering that on this earth 'we been pilgrymes, passynge to and fro' (I.2848). Egeus cannot be right. If we are metaphorical pilgrims we pass *to* somewhere else, not *from*. Death is permanent abstraction. But what if we never escape this whirling middle space – at least, not during the space of the *Knight's Tale*, which ends with the marriage of Palamon and Emilye, and life lived fully below the celestial spheres?

Heavy atmosphere endures, but as a constant movement. So in fact does life.

Notes

1 All references to Gower's poetry are cited by book and line number: John Gower, *Confessio Amantis*, in *The Complete Works of John Gower*, ed. G. C. Macaulay (Oxford: Clarendon Press, 1899–1902), Oxford Text Archive and Corpus of Middle English Prose and Verse (1993), http://name.umdl.umich.edu/Confessio, accessed 6 May 2018.
2 'Air' (n. (1)), *Middle English Dictionary*, 3b, https://quod.lib.umich.edu/cgi/m/mec/med-idx?type=id&id=MED939, accessed 6 May 2018.
3 *On the Properties of Things, John Trevisa's Translation of Bartholomaeus Anglicus De Proprietatibus Rerum, a Critical Text*, 3 vols, ed. M. C. Seymour et al. (Oxford: Clarendon, 1975–88), p. 133a/b. Cited in 'Air', *Middle English Dictionary*, 3c.
4 All references to Chaucer's work are from *The Riverside Chaucer*, gen. ed. Larry D. Benson (New York: Houghton Mifflin, 3rd edn, 1987) and are cited by fragment or book (where appropriate) and line number.
5 Tobias Menely, 'Anthropocene air', *Minnesota Review*, 83 (2014), 93–101 (p. 100).
6 For a thorough discussion of embodiment as a material process in the Middle Ages see Joan Cadden, *Meanings of Sex Difference in the Middle Ages: Medicine, Science, and Culture* (Cambridge: Cambridge University Press, 1993).
7 See Gail Kern Paster, *Humoring the Body: Emotions and the Shakespearean Stage* (Chicago: University of Chicago Press, 2004), pp. 42 and 139. For more on materiality and humoral psychology, see also Paster, *The Body Embarrassed: Drama and the Disciplines of Shame in Early Modern England* (Ithaca: Cornell University Press, 1993). Suzanne Conklin Akbari explicates well the place-bound environmentality of the medieval body in *Idols in the East: European Representations of Islam and the Orient, 1100–1450* (Ithaca: Cornell University Press, 2009).
8 J. Allan Mitchell, *Becoming Human: The Matter of the Medieval Child* (Minneapolis: University of Minnesota Press, 2014), pp. xix and xviii.
9 See his excellent essay: Steve Mentz, 'A poetics of nothing: air in the early modern imagination', *postmedieval*, 4.1 (2013), 30–41 (p. 32).
10 On the confused taxonomies of emotion versus affect – and a strong argument for not retaining a difference between the two terms – see Stephanie Trigg, 'Introduction: emotional histories – beyond the personalization of the past and the abstraction of affect theory', *Exemplaria*, 26:1 (2014), 3–15; and Trigg, 'Affect theory', in Susan Broomhall (ed.), *Early Modern Emotions: An Introduction* (New York: Routledge, 2017), pp. 10–13.

11 'O stormy peple! Unsad and evere untrewe!' (Chaucer, *Clerk's Tale*, IV.995).
12 Stacy Alaimo, *Bodily Natures: Science, Environment, and the Material Self* (Bloomington: Indiana University Press, 2010).
13 Although derived from classical models, geohumoralism has been most deeply explored by early modernists; see especially Mary Floyd-Wilson, *English Ethnicity and Race in Early Modern Drama* (Cambridge: Cambridge University Press, 2003). Among medievalists, Suzanne Conklin Akbari's work is indispensable; see *Idols in the East*.
14 The literature on medieval race is too vast to reduce to a pithy footnote, but for an excellent overview of the state of the field see the special journal issue, edited by Cord Whitaker, 'Making race matter in the Middle Ages', *postmedieval*, 6:1 (2015).
15 Jesse Oak Taylor, *The Sky of Our Manufacture: The London Fog in British Fiction from Dickens to Woolf* (Charlottesville: University of Virginia Press, 2016), p. 1. Smog, in other words, 'does not simply emerge at the intersection of nature and culture, it emerges *as* that intersection' (p. 3).
16 Taylor, *The Sky of Our Manufacture*, p. 7. On human 'indistinction' see Jean Feerick and Vin Nardizzi (eds), *The Indistinct Human in Renaissance Literature* (New York: Palgrave Macmillan, 2012).
17 Taylor separates the latter, more abstract perspective into climate – which conveys 'ideas, politics, cultural forms, bioregions and weather patterns' (*The Sky of Our Manufacture*, p. 8; see also p. 14) – but medieval geohumoralism enmeshed these spheres. On the long history of climate from classical Greece onwards, emphasising its descriptive non-neutrality, see Taylor, *The Sky of Our Manufacture*, pp. 12–13.
18 Taylor, *The Sky of Our Manufacture*, p. 99.
19 Taylor, *The Sky of Our Manufacture*, p. 14.
20 I am inspired here by the work of Stephanie Trigg on community-making (and community-feeling) in the long wake of Chaucer's work, and here attempt to extend a possibility for community (congenial and otherwise) to nonhumans. See Trigg's magisterial *Congenial Souls: Reading Chaucer from Medieval to Postmodern* (Minneapolis: University of Minnesota Press, 2002).
21 Mitchell, *Becoming Human*, pp. xii and 175. See also Kellie Robertson, 'Exemplary rocks', in Jeffrey Jerome Cohen (ed.), *Animal, Vegetable, Mineral: Ethics and Objects* (Washington DC: Oliphaunt, 2011), pp. 91–121.
22 Mitchell, *Becoming Human*, pp. 42–3. Mitchell continues: 'Gower's thought is consequently ecological, not despite the hierarchical and holistic cosmos, but owing to the strength of the contingent bonds between upper and lower elements. Gower highlights the

ligatures, joints, and connective tissues of the organized whole, as does Macrobius when he says that people and planetary bodies share in *animus*. No micro or macro view has a monopoly over the whole complex system of interrelations, then' (p. 43).

23 See plates 1 and 2. A digitised copy of some of the manuscript – including the two illustrations I discuss – is available at www.bl.uk/catalogues/illuminatedmanuscripts/record.asp?MSID=8128, accessed 6 May 2018.
24 *Li Livres dou Tresor*, London, British Library MS Yates Thompson 19, fol. 40. See plate 1.
25 Brunetto Latini, *The Book of the Treasure* (*Li Livres dou Tresor*), trans. Paul Barrette and Spurgeon Baldwin (New York: Routledge, 2013), p. 106. Cf. 'The air supports birds with its thickness' (p. 104).
26 On medieval envisionings of the atmosphere as ocean, see my essay, 'The sea above' in Cohen and Lowell Duckert (eds), *Elemental Ecocriticism: Thinking with Earth, Air, Water, and Fire* (Minneapolis: University of Minnesota Press, 2015), pp. 105–33.
27 *Li Livres dou Tresor*, fol. 28. See plate 2.
28 On the 'machine of the world', thinking the spherical cosmos, and elemental ordering, see Robert Bartlett, *The Natural and the Supernatural in the Middle Ages* (Cambridge: Cambridge University Press, 2008), pp. 35–52.
29 On this powerful moment, see John W. Conlee, 'The meaning of Troilus' ascension to the eighth sphere', *Chaucer Review*, 7 (1972–73), 27–36; and John M. Steadman, *Disembodied Laughter:* Troilus *and the Apotheosis Tradition – A Reexamination of Narrative and Thematic Contexts* (Berkeley and Los Angeles: University of California Press, 1972). Lindy Elkins-Tanton and I have contemplated the stakes and risks of apprehending the Earth as a celestial object in *Earth* (London: Bloomsbury, 2017).
30 Macrobius, *Commentarii in somnium Scipionis*, ed. James Willis (Leipzig: B. G. Teubner, 1970). The best recent treatment of the *Dream of Scipio* in the Middle Ages is Karma Lochrie, *Nowhere in the Middle Ages* (Philadelphia: University of Pennsylvania Press, 2016), pp. 15–33.
31 My favourite of these banded Earths is an illustration in a twelfth-century copy of the *Commentarii in somnium Scipionis*, now held by the Royal Danish Library (Det Kongelige Bibliotek, Copenhagen), MS NkS 218 4°, fol. 34*r*. See plate 3.
32 On the intimacy of Chaucer's eagle (as well as sound) to the intermediate element of air, see Reginald Berry, 'Chaucer's eagle and the element air', *University of Toronto Quarterly*, 43:3 (1974), 285–97.
33 The First Mover who is itself unmoved is an Aristotelian concept well known in the late Middle Ages; like Boethius, whose entire *Consolation of Philosophy* he translated, Chaucer associates that Mover with God.

See *Boece*, II, m.8 for the binding of the four elements through love. With the map from Brunetto in mind here, we have entered the realm of ether, beyond the whirling elements and circuits of the planets.

34 *Il Teseida*, 11.1–3 narrates the heavenward flight of Arcite's soul.

35 In foregrounding the making visible of faces and the consequent ability to read what might be shared, or collective affective states, I am also thinking of the work collected in the special issue, 'Facing up to the history of emotions', *postmedieval*, 8:1 (2017); especially the editors' introduction by Stephanie Downes and Stephanie Trigg (pp. 3–11).

7
Hunting and fortune in the *Book of the Duchess* and *Sir Gawain and the Green Knight*

Frank Grady

Near the end of 'The romance of exchange: *Sir Gawain and the Green Knight*', Stephanie Trigg writes:

> The poem does its best to knot itself up again in the closing moments with its verbal echoes of the opening lines about Brutus, affirming historical continuity with the present. Yet in these final moments, as we realize the embedded structure of the whole, we appreciate the difference in this sameness, just as the linear plot of Gawain's fortunes and development is set against the cycle of his departure and return.[1]

Certainly the poem is structured by repetitions – the multiple feasts and hunts and seductions, the two beheading scenes and, as noted, the framing references to the fall of Troy – and making meaning out of these recurrences is the goal of critic and casual reader alike. But *Sir Gawain* is also a poem in which the apparently linear plot mapping Gawain's fortunes can be seen as itself a kind of repetition of a conventional medieval story, one whose meaning derives from sameness in difference. This is the story of Fortune, whose ceaseless turning of her wheel produces narratives of aristocratic rise and fall across generations, languages, and empires, stories experienced by their protagonists as linear, but which are often represented by their narrators as analogous instances in a repeating historical series. In what follows, I propose to explore the way that Gawain's fortunes can be seen as depending on that cyclical plot of Fortune, and what our recognition of that relationship can reveal to us about the poem's structuring principles. Those principles stand out in still sharper relief when we set *Sir Gawain* beside Chaucer's *Book of the Duchess*, a poem with its own peculiar connection to Fortune, and one with which *Sir Gawain* shares a number of formal and thematic ambitions, despite their differences in region, dialect and genre.

A number of secular fictions in the later Middle English period incorporate both representations of hunting and stories of aristocratic loss. Some are of course explicitly allegorical and hortatory, like the esoteric hunting-as-confession allegory in Henry of Lancaster's *Livre de seynts medecines*, or the explicitly moralised hunts of the Three Living and the Three Dead tradition, where to go out hunting literally means confronting one's own mortality.[2] But *Sir Gawain and the Green Knight* belongs to another set of vernacular texts in which any moralisation is implied rather than stated. In these texts, writers make sure that the two elements – hunting and aristocratic loss – are not contiguous; moreover, these elements typically occur in non-consecutive if sometimes tantalisingly analogous episodes or precipitate into frame and dream or prologue and tale. What seems to be the rule in such texts is a kind of formal parataxis: in the *Parlement of the Thre Ages* the hunt is prologue, and the *ubi sunt* moralising takes place in a dream. In the case of Chaucer's Monk, hunting is so constitutive of his character as to induce the Ellesmere illustrator to represent him accompanied by a pair of iconographic hounds, but his lugubrious tragedies of Fortune are never explicitly connected to his pastime, and he pointedly rejects the Host's later request that he 'sey somwhat of hunting'. In *The Siege of Jerusalem*, hunting is a Roman holiday interlude in the poem's remorselessly grim and grinding history of the fall and rise of empires. Finally, in *Sir Gawain and the Green Knight*, the hunts are confined to one fitt, and the puzzling explanation of Gawain's failure occurs at the end of another, while in the *Book of the Duchess*, Octovyen's hunt frames the conversation between the Dreamer and the Man in Black about the latter's betrayal by Fortune, but does not apparently influence it (though the ingenuity of Chaucer critics has long been devoted to removing that 'apparently').

These instances are various enough that we might resist calling them a topos or a motif, but numerous enough to suggest that the pairing represents a shared compositional resource for writers whose work exemplifies the era's 'seigneurial poetics'. In a 2013 essay, I argued that the nature of the literary hunt – its formal elaboration in terms of process, ritual and diction – makes it a useful and flexible mechanism for the redirection of anxieties about the apparent precariousness of lordly advantage, as well as anxieties about the construction of vernacular fictions in the shadow of more authoritative Latin and clerical traditions. The literary hunt and the reductive tragic plot of the fall of Fortune work analogously to impose manageable form on contingent phenomena and bring a formally satisfying if temporary sense of order to narratives that, in appealing to aristocratic tastes, apparently cannot avoid triggering aristocratic unease.[3]

In the *Book of the Duchess* and *Sir Gawain* we find two members of this hunting-and-Fortune group that are particularly valuable for what they reveal about the nature of the compositional reflex that seems to govern the formal disposition of those elements – that is, the paratactic, non-moralising juxtaposition of hunting scenes and *de casibus* rhetoric. They are, of course, very different poems, despite the fact that each features a pair of upper-class men, one of whom has an appearance strongly marked by colour, standing around in a forest not far from a castle discussing the influence of absent women on how badly one of them is feeling. What they share on a deeper formal level – in an architectonic way – is a similar disposition of hunting scenes to channel aristocratic energies away from their protagonists, thus more fully enabling those characters' attitudes (respectively melancholy and self-accusing) towards their predicaments.

The claim that Chaucer's poem belongs to this group is straightforward: the hunt of 'Octovyen', in which the narrator somewhat half-heartedly and confusedly takes part,[4] brackets the encounter between the Dreamer and the Man in Black, while at the centre of the latter's speech, at about the midpoint of the poem, lies the unhappy chess match with false Fortune, whose apparent treachery has left him so wretched as to claim that 'I am sorwe and sorwe is I'.[5] The passages concerning Fortune are, notoriously, dependent upon or derivative from Chaucer's sources, Machaut and the *Roman de la Rose*; they are thus 'conventional', an adjective that can either call into question Chaucer's originality, or confirm the degree to which he is participating in European traditions of courtly fiction-making.[6] Chaucer obscures the identity of most of his sources, and in obscuring might also be altering their genre; his account of Ceyx and Alcyone is attributed not to Ovid or Machaut but to a volume that sounds rather like a *de casibus* collection, 'a repository of stories about illustrious men and women': 'This book ne spake but of swiche thinges, / Of quenes lyves and of kings / And many other thinges smale' (57–9).[7]

Though it does feature a king and a queen, *Sir Gawain and the Green Knight* is perhaps a harder sell: a personified Fortune appears nowhere in the text, and the word itself occurs only once, very early on, to describe the contingent outcome of a hypothetical knightly combat. Among the options that might satisfy Arthur's desire to see a wonder before he tucks into his Christmas feast would be the possibility that 'sum segg hym biso3t of sum siker kny3t / To joyne wyth hym in justyng, in jopardé to lay, / Lede, lif for lyf, leue vchon oþer, / As fortune wolde fulsun hom, þe fayrer to haue'.[8] Certainly these lines can be read as foreshadowing Gawain's confrontation with the Green Knight, in a somewhat unusual form of 'justyng' – be careful what you wish for! But while fortune can help ('fulsun') one or the other of these two imaginary knights, there is no sense in the passage that the one who ends up losing should necessarily be seen as Fortune's victim, crushed beneath her wheel.

And anyway, isn't *Sir Gawain* a fundamentally comic poem, or at worst an ironic review of the chivalric enterprise? Well, of course, yes and no; the poet's stance may be essentially ironic, and Bertilak and Camelot do take the lenient view of Gawain's fault, but Gawain himself is not so indulgent, as we learn in the speech that we tend to call his 'misogynistic outburst':

> Bot hit is no ferly þa3 a fole madde
> And þur3 wyles of wymmen be wonen to sor3e,
> For so watz Adam in erde with one bygyled,
> And Salamon with fele sere, and Samson eftsonez –
> Dalyda dalt hym hys wyrde – and Dauyth, þerafter,
> Watz blended with Barsabe, þat much bale þoled.
> Now þese were wrathed wyth her wyles, hit were a wynne huge
> To luf hom wel, and leue hem not, a leude þat couþe.
> For þes wer forne þe freest, þat fol3ed alle þe sele
> Exellently of alle þyse oþer vnder heuenryche
>   þat mused;
> And alle þay were biwyled
> With wymmen þat þay vsed.
> Þa3 I be now bigyled,
> Me þink me burde be excused. (2414–28)

In availing himself here of what Mark Miller has recently called 'the comfort of self-aggrandisement' in the face of his adventure's anticlimactic conclusion,[9] Gawain is undoubtedly allying himself with a deeply rooted tradition of medieval misogyny (and also, as the criticism has frequently noted, exposing some of the incoherency in that tradition, with his perversely exculpatory account of David and Bathsheba). But this passage also clearly evokes *de casibus* writing as well, which is the governing genre here; Gawain's examples are 'þe freest, þat fol3ed alle þe sele / Exellently of alle þyse oþer vnder heuenryche / þat mused' (2422–4) – princes and worthies, in the vocabulary of that tradition (including David, one of the Nine). Adam and Samson regularly appear in *de casibus* collections, and they reprise their clichéd roles not only in Chaucer's *Monk's Tale,* but also in Boccaccio and his inheritors, Premierfait and Lydgate.[10] The passage even offers up a perspective that, in a slightly different context, we might read as tending towards Boethian detachment: 'hit were a wynne huge / To luf hom wel, and leue hem not, a leude þat couþe' (2420–1).

Certainly *Sir Gawain and the Green Knight* has invested in the ethos of this familiar rise-and-fall model – 'blysse and blunder' – from its opening lines. Gawain's claim may be self-aggrandising, but no more than the *Gawain*-poet's sweeping gesture at the beginning of the poem, conventionally but ambitiously linking his tale to the fall of Troy, that foundational episode in the history of the West that connotes, in Vance Smith's words, 'both the potency of cultural capital and its instability'.[11] Far from being 'an outtrage awenture of Arthurez wonderez' (29) – an extraordinary episode in the history of chivalry – *Sir Gawain* here threatens to reveal itself, and Gawain's own blunder, as a simple and conventional iteration of a very familiar story indeed. Gawain's brief attempt to excuse himself from blame – as it turns out, only a short hiatus from his preferred stance of self-accusation – suggests that his story might be as easily assimilated into a dreary *de casibus* collection as into 'þe best boke of romaunce' (2521). Fortunately, Bertilak is on hand to direct things back into the romance mode. His surprising assignment of responsibility to Morgan, while on the one hand consistent with Gawain's apparent misogyny, also has the effect of turning Gawain back into the victim of a plot as opposed to a structure; that is, Morgan's absurd plan 'to haf greued Gaynour and gart hir to dyȝe' (2460). The knights' encounter can then safely be read not as emblematic of the inevitable end of all aristocratic activity, as Gawain perhaps inadvertently suggests, but as a simple contingency with its causes in a particular woman's intention and nature – like many another romance.

Of course, the basic *de casibus* narrative also trades in gender stereotypes: men are betrayed by the fickle goddess Fortune, something that Chaucer's Man in Black makes clear in his own misogynistic outburst, decrying 'The traiteresse fals and ful of gyle' who has stolen his *fers* (620).[12] Thus, another way to make the case for the relevance of this 'fall of Fortune' motif to *Sir Gawain* would be to see the role of Fortune as not concentrated in one allegorical personification, but distributed between Hautdesert's women, whose actions and appearance we are invited to read figuratively as well as literally. The conventional role of Fortune is dispersed in the poem, visible in the roles played by Morgan – 'the goddess' identified by Bertilak as the one responsible for the plot that has brought Gawain low – and the Lady, who literally bears gifts that sustain life and promise worldly success and survival, even triumph, in the context of a competitive aristocratic hierarchy.[13] The two ladies' initial appearance in the poem as contrasting avatars of youth and age, one very attractive to Gawain and the other not so much, recalls the Janus-like representation of Fortune in the *Book of the Duchess*, where the Man in Black describes her as walking upright but limping, squinting but looking 'faire', acting both disdainfully and courteously, and laughing with one eye while weeping with the other. From this perspective, then, we might add another layer to the meaning of the scenes of temptation Gawain faces in fitt three; he is tempted to climb onto Fortune's wheel – that is, to take up the proffer of a female figure who promises success in worldly activity. Note that the end result for Gawain, in each of the three seduction scenes, is his literal rise from recumbency and passivity at the lady's behest, after he agrees to embrace her will (1309–14, 1558, 1872–5).

The nested structure of *Sir Gawain*'s narrative episodes is well-known – the poem's formal *emboîtement* and *dilatio* – and as Trigg notes, at the centre of this structure is the encounter between Gawain and the Lady: 'at the heart of the poem is revealed a female bargain.... The poem itself delivers a judgment on the wiliness and deceit of women, but it is less a piece of antifeminist abuse than it is testimony to their power'.[14] What I am describing here by suggesting that the poem can be read as a romance enclosing a fall-of-Fortune narrative is one more aspect of that embedding. And Bertilak, as noted, rescues the poem for romance; instead of letting Gawain's outburst stand as the poem's moral, in the style of one of Lydgate's *Fall of Princes* envoys, his revelation – however clumsy some have found it – plugs the story back into the Arthurian circuit.

The opportunity to make the events at the Green Chapel into a cautionary lesson does theoretically arise with Gawain's return to Camelot, but there the choice is made to treat his adventure as a success rather than a monitory episode, *pace* his own protestations. I say 'choice' – and much *Gawain* criticism grounds itself in the assumption that Camelot's denizens elect to hear only what they want to hear when they listen to Gawain's tale – but of course their reaction too is conventional from the *de casibus* perspective. What Gawain brings back to the court cannot be, as it were, actionable intelligence: no lord ever really learns the lesson of Fortune in advance, but only when it's too late to change the course of his worldly life. This is true for Boethius, and for Chaucer's Troilus, and for the Arthur of the *Alliterative Morte*. There is no narrative pattern available to the *Gawain*-poet to tell the story of aristocratic enlightenment – no secular pattern, anyway; there is only the possibility of withdrawal from worldly engagement, and in the Arthurian context that takes place only at the end of the story when, Camelot having fallen, Malory's Guenevere takes the veil and his Lancelot the tonsure. The capacity to treat Fortune's changeability as something that could be managed by policy, as opposed to penitential retreat, was essentially a development of the fifteenth century, as Paul Strohm has shown, and its province was not romance.[15]

What there is at the end of the poem is more displacement. *Sir Gawain and the Green Knight* teases us with an explicit reference to the rise-and-fall model in its opening lines, offers us an intricately detailed version of how that process can play out in an individual story, and then refuses to draw any future-oriented lesson from that story. As Trigg notes, the cyclic structure that *Sir Gawain* wants us to attend to is that of departure and return, not – as in *de casibus* writing – a rise-and-fall story potentially repeated *ad infinitum*. The knowledge that Gawain thinks that he brings, knowledge that Camelot in its first age simply cannot process – the knowledge of knightly 'losse' and 'vntrawthe' and harms that can never be erased, and the potential consequences of such failures – flows instead into a well-worn channel, into a place where it can be safely contained and processed: back into the past, specifically into the history of Troy that frames the whole narrative, rounding out the poem's famous ring-like structure. Though rings, of course, have the same shape as wheels.

If the *Book of the Duchess* and *Sir Gawain and the Green Knight* both exemplify this hunting-and-fortune collocation – the former quite explicitly and the latter in slightly more oblique fashion – we are left to consider the effect of the pairing. And here it can be noted that one thing that distinguishes these poems from some of the others in this tradition is the fact that in neither of them does the protagonist take part in the hunt. Gawain's host orders him 'to lenge in youre lofte and lyȝe in your ese' (1096), while in response to the Dreamer's opening conversational gambit about Octovyen's hunt having foundered, the Man in Black says 'Y do no fors therof ... / My thought ys theron never a del' (542–3).

The answer to the question 'why *don't* they hunt?' lies, I think, in the generic demands of the *de casibus* model, which typically enjoins a certain passivity in its subjects: whatever their worthy, worldly accomplishments, they are all in the end subject to Fortune. In this context, the aristocratic relation to Fortune only allows for two narrative positions: one can be Fortune's beneficiary, or Fortune's victim. Indeed, the essence of the *de casibus* tale is precisely the transition from being one to being the other. But why don't they *hunt*? Whatever their sources, the plots of both poems are still contrivances – in order to convey their passivity, gentlefolk could just as easily not hawk, or not ride, or not joust, as not hunt.[16] So why is their passivity specifically registered in their not hunting?

Three reasons suggest themselves. The first is quite patent: the hunt is already an accessible and fully packaged literary tradition in courtly writing, with well-developed forms, narrative sequences, and a technical vocabulary whose use is typically a sign of poetic virtuosity. Secondly, hunting involves mortal stakes, which makes it appropriate for the main plots of these poems, both of which involve death or the threat of it.[17] This is made most clear during the second day's pursuit of the boar in *Sir Gawain*. The fierceness of the prey is well established throughout that portion of the hunt, such that even at the end of the episode Bertilak's companions fear for his safety: 'so hetterly [the boar] fnast / Þat fele ferde for þe freke, lest felle hym þe worre' (1587–8). The 'worre' is not difficult to imagine: a fatal tusking, of which literary and historical examples abound: Adonis, Robert de Vere, Robert Baratheon. Finally, not only does hunting demonstrate agency and express lordly vigour and purpose – the kind of activity that would tend to undermine the representation of characters weighed down by melancholy or ignorance – it is also directly analogous to the *de casibus* plot, which, like the hunt, puts an end to the careers of noble creatures. In the hunt aristocratic males take on the role of Fortune, pursuing their quarry to an unhappy (if still ostensibly contingent) end. But they can't be agents of Fortune and victims of Fortune at the same time; hence, in these two poems, the hunting scenes are separated from the elevated lamentations. Hunting is where the idea of seigneurial agency goes to hide when the narrative of Fortune rears its head.

What I wish to claim, then, is that scenes of hunting are strategically deployed in the *Book of the Duchess* and *Sir Gawain and the Green Knight* to siphon off purposive aristocratic energies from their protagonists, so as to make available the positions of victimisation that are occupied by the Man in Black and Sir Gawain, to purify those states and drain them of potentially troublesome ideological content. In Gawain's case it's fairly obvious that his enforced lolling about in fitt three is meant to be read in contrast to Bertilak's frantic expeditions; what's surprising – certainly surprising to Gawain – is that at the end of the poem, it is exactly that contrast that turns out to have been at the centre of things. What Gawain is moved to lament in the closing scene is not any failure in the beheading game, but rather what happened when he wasn't hunting and instead deviated from the 'larges and lewte ... þat longez to kny3tez' (2381).

Turning to the *Book of the Duchess*, the argument about passivity renders the question of whether or not the hunt is successful – an abiding topic in the criticism – essentially moot; the important thing is that the Man in Black refrains from taking part. Indeed, the poem goes to some lengths to strip him of any signs of conventional, non-melancholy courtly activity, even those conventionally associated with *fin'amor*. The Man in Black specifies that White 'ne used no swich knakkes smale' (1033) as to make her suitors undertake romantic quests to Alexandria or Tartary: unlike the three tercels in the *Parliament of Fowls*, each of whom is admonished to 'peyne him in his degree / For to do wel' (662–3) during the gap year of their courtship of the formel, White's potential mate 'did my besynesse / To make songes, as I best coude' (1156–7).

In fact, the effort to maintain the impression of passivity in a figure so self-evidently full of *gentilesse* as the Man in Black turns out to require constant vigilance on the part of the poet, and extends even to the stories the Man himself tells. Consider, for example, the role that Troy plays in the poem. As noted, the fall of that city is a type-scene of noble disaster that the *Gawain*-poet keeps carefully at the margins of his story. At first this seems like Chaucer's plan, too; though images of the story are 'y-wrought' in the stained glass of the Dreamer's chamber – the first thing he notices – the tale is merely mentioned, not narrated; it's just a collection of names that stretches from Lamedoun to Lavyne. But when it comes up again, in the Man in Black's list of the worthies whose virtues he doesn't possess, the Troy story's memorialisation of aristocratic self-destruction tries to re-assert itself. Though he had the beauty of Alcibiades, the strength of Hercules, the worthiness of Alexander,

> And therto also hardy be
> As was Ector, so have I joye,
> That Achilles slough at Troye –
> And therfore was he slayn alsoo
> In a temple, for bothe twoo
> Were slayne, he and Antylegyus
> (And so seyth Dares Frygius),
> For love of Polixena –
> Or ben as wis as Mynerva,
> I wolde ever, withoute drede,
> Have loved hir, for I moste nede. (1064–74)

The passage is probably rooted in a similar claim in Machaut's *Remede de fortune*, where Alexander and Hector also appear (and where beauty is the attribute of Absalom, not Alcibiades). The mention of Hector here, though, provokes the reference to his slaying by Achilles, and that elicits the story of Achilles being slain in revenge, for love of Polixena – and all of a sudden the poignant loss-of-love story of the Man in Black is threatened by its family relation to a far bloodier tale. The passage threatens to wander off down the rabbit hole of *de casibus* histories, so it is quickly closed off with a striking *non sequitur*, the reference to Minerva – a goddess hauled in from a different pantheon – to close off a list of male worthies. The rhetorical gesture is all the more striking for the fact that Chaucer apparently introduces the name to Middle English here; the *Book of the Duchess* is the earliest citation that the *Middle English Dictionary* supplies for its use in a vernacular context. However, closing off this valve only redirects the pressure elsewhere. When the Man in Black describes his sorrow at receiving White's first refusal of his suit, he claims that his woe was greater than that of Cassandra at the 'destruccioun / Of Troy and of Ilioun' (1247–8), acknowledging in his hyperbole that all species of aristocratic loss, even the temporary kinds, are fundamentally analogous.[18]

I have argued that the hunting scenes in these two poems serve a kind of hydraulic function, by means of which potentially disruptive chivalric energies are re-purposed and made apparently recreative, so as to relieve the pressure on the poems' protagonists to act instead of suffer. By safely and conventionally embodying one set of aristocratic motifs, the hunting scenes enable the exploration of others, permitting – to adopt another scientific metaphor – a general conservation of seigneurial values. One particular courtly individual seized by melancholy, or made a virtual prisoner in the bedroom, may represent a disturbance in the force for the noble ethos, but the hunting scenes mean that courtly idealisations are still functioning smoothly overall.

Making this structural claim has meant ignoring to this point the several moral/topological readings these hunting passages have generated, readings which for the most part try to import or adapt the sententiousness of the 'mortality tradition' to a pair of texts that stand at a certain remove from it. That no single interpretation of this sort has been universally embraced is not surprising, and David Lawton, though referring specifically to the hunting prologue of *The Parlement of the Thre Ages,* could be describing this practice at large when he characterises that episode as a sequence 'that readers have often felt to be emblematic but whose detail defeats allegorical exegesis'.[19] Bridging the gap between emblem and allegory is the hard part: it is easy enough to construe a hunting scene as 'an emblem of secular courtly life and indulgence',[20] but having made that designation we still have to figure out exactly what relationship towards that life a particular poem endorses, for its characters and for its readers.

The formal approach taken here helps reveal one reason why making that judgment can be so difficult. Consider that, in addition to being an *emblem* of courtly activity, the hunt is also an *instance* of it: the relationship is not so much metaphorical as synecdochic, in which one aspect of the lordly life stands in for the whole. But this is potentially the case for many aristocratic undertakings. For example, the Man in Black's account of the chess game with Fortune in the *Book of the Duchess* prompts a strangely literal-minded reaction from the narrator: surely the loss of a single game piece shouldn't make someone suicidal? 'There is noon alyve here / Wolde for a fers make this wo!' (740–1), the narrator opines. His obtuseness here has elicited considerable commentary, starting with the Man in Black's own refrain, 'Thow woste ful litel what thou menest' (743). But on one level, at least, the narrator's impulse to read this scene literally makes sense, for lords and ladies did play chess together, in life and in literature: Tristan and Isolde, Lancelot and Guenevere, Edward III and the Duchess of Salisbury. Like hunting, chess can figurally represent amorous intrigue and also literally enable it, because it is an actual aristocratic pastime.[21] A game of chess does more than simply add a note of verisimilitude to depictions of noble characters; it helps to make them legible as noble characters in the first place.

Likewise, and like the hunt,[22] 'luf-talkyng' is both expressive and formative of chivalric subjectivity on the page. In speaking the language of courtly love, both the Man in Black and Sir Gawain enact conventional paradigms, but they are also made courtly by means of their participation in these conventions. The former goes from neophyte – ready 'as a whyt wal or a table / ... to cacche and take' the correct impression of love as his 'firste crafte' (780–1, 791) – to successful courtly lover of White, before her untimely death. Gawain, 'þat fine fader of nurture', is welcomed to Hautdesert as the embodiment of courtliness and the master of 'þe teccheles terms of talking noble' (919, 917); in the course of his noble talk with the Lady, he eventually becomes the Gawain that she playfully suggests he might not be.[23] But if courtship works in the same way as hunting and chess in this regard, it should be just as susceptible to emblematic readings as these other textual representations of the lordly life. When readings of *Sir Gawain* argue that the three hunts offer metaphorical comment upon the bedroom scenes, they necessarily treat the former as vehicle and the latter as tenor. But what are the grounds for such a distinction when both undertakings are equally rooted in literary tradition? Rather, it seems that all these courtly motifs are essentially interchangeable modules that can stand in for a way of life.

Thus it is not surprising that we find ourselves sliding from one to another, from hunting to 'luf-talkyng' or from chess to courtship, rediscovering the sameness in these different seigneurial exercises. They are spokes on the same wheel; a wheel that, in these two poems, is evidently turned by Fortune. The real focus of Chaucer's consolation, and the source of Gawain's disappointment, is the aristocratic subject's recurrent encounter with helplessness and irreparability,[24] the struggle between noble designs and Fortune's utterly predictable (if always untimely) predations. This is, of course, a melancholy conclusion, but an elegy delivered in the guise of a celebration of courtly virtues and practices can evidently have an apotropaic effect, provided those elements are arranged with a certain degree of tact.

Notes

1 Stephanie Trigg, 'The romance of exchange: *Sir Gawain and the Green Knight*', *Viator*, 22 (1991), 251–66 (p. 264).
2 Anne Rooney, *Hunting in Middle English Literature* (Cambridge: D. S. Brewer, 1993), describes this 'alliterative mortality tradition' (p. 188); she and William Marvin conveniently and thoroughly survey the extensive critical literature on the literary hunt in Middle English writing. See William Perry Marvin, *Hunting Law and Ritual in Medieval English Literature* (Cambridge: D. S. Brewer, 2006).
3 Frank Grady, 'Seigneurial poetics, or the poacher, the *prikasour*, the hunt and its oeuvre', in Grady and Andrew Galloway (eds), *Answerable Style: The Idea of the Literary in Medieval England* (Columbus: Ohio State University Press, 2013), pp. 195–213.
4 David Scott-McNabb, 'A re-examination of Octovyen's hunt in *The Book of the Duchess*', *Medium Ævum*, 56 (1987), 183–99.
5 Quotations from Chaucer — henceforth cited in the text — are drawn from *The Riverside Chaucer*, gen. ed. Larry D. Benson, 3rd ed. (Boston: Houghton Mifflin, 1987), here *Book of the Duchess* 597.
6 The chess game appears in Machaut's *Remede de fortune*, though some of the iconography is also found in *Le jugement dou roy de Behaingne*. See Barry Windeatt, *Chaucer's Dream Poetry: Sources and Analogues* (Cambridge: D. S. Brewer, 1982); and for a broader consideration of the literary relations, James Wimsatt, *Chaucer and the French Love Poets: The Literary Background of the Book of the Duchess* (Chapel Hill: University of North Carolina Press, 1968). Ardis Butterfield, *The Familiar Enemy: Chaucer, Language, and Nation in the Hundred Years War* (Oxford: Oxford University Press, 2009), pp. 271ff. provides a critical review of the 'originality' issue. The hunt seems to lack a specific direct source, though Colin Wilcockson, in *The Riverside Chaucer*'s explanatory notes, connects the beginning of the hunt in the *Book of the Duchess* with the hare-hunting in Machaut's *Le jugement dou roy de Navarre*, a suggestion endorsed by A. J. Minnis, with V. J. Scattergood and J. J. Smith, *Oxford Guides to Chaucer: The Shorter Poems* (Oxford: Clarendon, 1995), p. 118.
7 Minnis suggests that the lines might illustrate how Chaucer thought about the *Ovide moralisé*, another likely source for the tale (*Oxford Guides to Chaucer*, p. 95). They may possibly allude to Machaut's *Dit de la fontienne amoreuse*, whose anonymous aristocrats turn out to be the Duke and Duchess de Berry – not exactly a king and queen, but pretty close. This passage (lines 31–96) does not appear in the three extant MSS of *Duchess*, but only in Thynne's 1532 edition; their genuineness has thus occasionally been questioned. Elizabeth Scala provides a critical summary of this controversy in *Absent Narratives:*

Manuscript, Textuality, and Literary Structure in Late Medieval England (New York: Palgrave, 2002), pp. 27–33.

8 *Sir Gawain and the Green Knight,* lines 96–9. All quotations for *Sir Gawain and the Green Knight* are from Malcolm Andrew and Ronald Waldron (eds), *The Poems of the Pearl Manuscript* (Berkeley: University of California Press, 1978), and cited in-text by line number.

9 Mark Miller, 'The ends of excitement in *Sir Gawain the Green Knight*: teleology, ethics, and the death drive', *Studies in the Age of Chaucer*, 32 (2010), 215–56 (p. 233).

10 In *The Fall of Princes*, Samson's story is followed by 'A chapitle of Bochas discryuyng þe malis of women', which Lydgate spends almost two hundred lines translating and then disavowing, reminding us again of the intersection of the two traditions. See John Lydgate, *The Fall of Princes*, 4 vols, ed. Henry Bergen, EETS e.s. 121–4 (London: Oxford University Press, 1924), 1.184–9.

11 D. Vance Smith, 'Plague, panic space, and the tragic medieval household', *South Atlantic Quarterly*, 98:3 (1999), 367–414 (p. 375).

12 In this passage (618–709), the Man in Black curses Fortune in recognisably antifeminist language focusing on her contrasting physical traits and habits. It is, again, all quite conventional stuff, so it is not surprising – though it is somewhat gratifying for the argument I am making – to find the Man in Black rhyming with two of the keywords from Gawain's own speech: 'For Fortune can so many a *wyle*, / Ther be but fewe can hir *begyle*' (673–4). Much of Chaucer's iconography derives from Machaut here – see note 6, above – but Helen Phillips notes how Chaucer's Fortune differs from Machaut's: she is not an abstract or impersonal force, but 'above all, a person, a woman, and one with whom his Knight is painfully engaged'; see Phillips, 'Fortune and the lady: Machaut, Chaucer, and the intertextual "dit"', *Nottingham French Studies*, 38:2 (1999), 120–36 (p. 132).

13 Randy Schiff explores the connection between Fortune and Morgan, ultimately putting that structural echo into the service of a historicist reading of the poem's gender politics in the context of 'the rich material culture of the militarized Midlands'; see R. Schiff, *Revivalist Fantasy: Alliterative Verse and Nationalist Literary History* (Columbus: Ohio State University Press, 2011), p. 99. He also highlights the other conventional stories to which *Sir Gawain* is linked by virtue of its cast: a Youth / Medill / Elde tale like *The Parlement of the Thre Ages*, or a loathly lady story like Florent's or the *Wife of Bath's Tale*. It is kind of charming to imagine the plot of *Sir Gawain* as something that the linked avatars of the loathly lady tale – hag, knight, lady – might cook up for the second season of their show.

14 Trigg, 'Romance of exchange', p. 262.

15 Paul Strohm, *Politique: Languages of Statecraft between Chaucer and Shakespeare* (Notre Dame: Notre Dame University Press, 2005), pp. 1–4, 90–104.
16 Consider, in reviewing this list, the entertainments conjured up for Aurelius by the clerk of Orleans in Chaucer's *Franklin's Tale*: hunting, hawking, jousting and dancing (V.1193–1201).
17 Miller's 'The ends of excitement' takes up this issue, along with the relationship between the poem's deep structure and its deployment of 'the topos of the body's capacity to be slit open' (p. 226); see also Susan Crane, *The Performance of Self: Ritual, Clothing, and Identity During the Hundred Years War* (Philadelphia: University of Pennsylvania Press, 2002), pp. 172–3; and Marie Borroff, '*Sir Gawain and the Green Knight*: the passing of judgment', in Christopher Baswell and William Sharpe (eds), *The Passing of Arthur: New Essays in Arthurian Tradition* (New York: Garland, 1988), pp. 105–28.
18 Chaucer's other uses of 'Minerva' are all associated with the city, two in the *Troilus* and one in the 'Legend of Dido' – which of course begins after the siege and the assault have ceased at Troy: 'Whan Troye brought was to destruccioun / By Grekes sleyghte, and namely by Synoun, / Feynynge the hors offered unto Mynerve' (*Legend of Good Women*, lines 930–3). On Chaucer's suppression of Troy in the *Book of the Duchess*, see also Smith, 'Plague, panic space', pp. 388–90; and for a different symptomatic reading of this catalogue, L. O. Aranye Fradenburg, *Sacrifice Your Love: Psychoanalysis, Historicism, Chaucer* (Minneapolis: University of Minnesota Press, 2002), pp. 109–10.
19 David Lawton, 'Titus goes hunting and hawking: the poetics of recreation and revenge in *The Siege of Jerusalem*', in O. S. Pickering (ed.), *Individuality and Achievement in Middle English Poetry* (Woodbridge: D. S. Brewer, 1997), pp. 105–17 (p. 111).
20 Anne Rooney, 'The hunts in *Sir Gawain the Green Knight*', in Derek Brewer and Jonathan Gibson (eds), *A Companion to the Gawain-poet* (Woodbridge: Boydell & Brewer, 1997), pp. 157–64 (p. 161).
21 Froissart's account of the Duchess of Salisbury's chess game with the king is translated in Edith Rickert (comp.), *Chaucer's World*, ed. Clair C. Olson and Martin M. Crow (New York: Columbia University Press, 1948), pp. 228–31. Francis Ingledew explores the relevance of chronicle accounts of this relationship to *Sir Gawain and the Green Knight* in *Sir Gawain and the Green Knight and the Order of the Garter* (Notre Dame: University of Notre Dame Press, 2006); see also the commentary by Stephanie Trigg, *Shame and Honor: A Vulgar History of the Order of the Garter* (Philadelphia: University of Pennsylvania Press, 2012), pp. 57–71. On the literary role of the game, see Jenny Adams, *Power Play: The Literature and Politics of Chess in the Late Middle Ages* (Philadelphia: University of Pennsylvania Press, 2006).

For an account of the *Book of the Duchess* that connects the chess scene's 'semiotic confusion' to the specific lexical history of the word 'fers', see Peter W. Travis, 'White', *Studies in the Age of Chaucer*, 22 (2000), 1–66 (pp. 9–13).
22 Trevor Dodman, 'Hunting to teach: class, pedagogy, and maleness in *The Master of Game* and *Sir Gawain and the Green Knight*', *Exemplaria*, 17:2 (2005), 413–44.
23 On the process of Gawain's 'becoming' in these scenes see Geraldine Heng, 'A woman wants: the lady, *Gawain*, and the forms of seduction', *Yale Journal of Criticism*, 5:3 (1992), 101–34 (pp. 113–17).
24 Fradenburg, *Sacrifice Your Love*, p. 79.

8
The implausible plausibility of the *Prologue to the Tale of Beryn*

Thomas A. Prendergast

The 'Chaucerian' *Prologue to the Tale of Beryn* would appear to provide what is missing from the *Canterbury Tales*, Canterbury itself. It narrates the pilgrims' adventures when they arrive at Becket's shrine, tour the town and retire to Canterbury's most famous inn, The Checker of the Hoop. The piece focuses most especially on the night-time peregrinations of one character, the Pardoner, who (in something of a departure from his character in the *General Prologue*) attempts to spend the evening with a tapster, Kit, and is beaten for his efforts by her boyfriend. The *Prologue* was part of a larger fifteenth-century scribal project in which the *Canterbury Tales* was reordered to offer a more complete version of Chaucer's work that included both the arrival in Canterbury and the trip back to Southwark. But if the *Prologue*'s inclusion in Alnwick Castle, Northumberland MS 455 (Nl) was meant to convince readers that it was by Chaucer, its first appearance outside its manuscript context was inauspicious.

In the preface to John Urry's posthumous *The Works of Geoffrey Chaucer*, Timothy Thomas wrote 'it may (perhaps with some shew of reason) be suspected that Chaucer was not the author ... but a later Writer'.[1] The *Prologue* had been included (so Thomas claimed) because Urry had believed it to be genuine. But had Urry lived, it would have been surprising if he had maintained his belief that the *Prologue* was by Chaucer.[2] The manuscript in which it appears has what can only be called an unusual ordering of the *Canterbury Tales*. The *Prologue* is itself followed by another obviously spurious work, the *Tale of Beryn* (a loose translation and adaptation of part of the fourteenth-century French prose romance *Bérinus* that is assigned to the Merchant). Finally, the metre is unlike anything attributed to Chaucer except for the *Tale of Gamelyn*. Some later editions would include it, but its placement suggested that editors had doubts about its authenticity. In fact, one pronounced it not only un-Chaucerian but 'ludicrous'.[3]

Yet over a hundred and fifty years after Urry's edition, F. J. Furnivall, while admitting that it was from a 'poorer hand', still decided to publish a version of the text for the Chaucer Society. His reasons were twofold. First, he asserted 'that Chaucer intended to have given us such an account himself, we can hardly doubt. The scenes at the "Cheker of the Hope", in the Cathedral and the town, must have afforded him so many a chance for a happy line, a humorous touch, that he *must* have thought of sketching his companions in their fresh surroundings'; and second, even if the *Beryn*-writer is inferior, nonetheless the later verser has 'a good bit of the Master's humour and lifelikeness … in his Prologue'.[4] The desideratum for the text is based on Furnivall's recuperation of Chaucer's intention which, if unfulfilled, is happily realised by someone who is a lot like Chaucer.

As Stephanie Trigg has demonstrated, Furnivall's attribution of Chaucerian-ness to the writer of the *Prologue* was only an extension of his own belief in *his* affinity with/for Chaucer.[5] He, in fact, enacts this affinity by putting much of the *Prologue* under correction, emending and padding out lines and in one case confecting a 'Chaucerian' line that playfully draws attention to its non-Chaucerian-ness (hence making Furnivall more like Chaucer).[6] Furnivall's governing, if unstated, assumption in thinking about the author of the *Prologue* (and himself) is resolutely romantic – he collapses writing like Chaucer with being like Chaucer. But as Trigg suggests, this analogy was probably false. The 'possibility of recuperating Chaucer as a congenial soul' wasn't available to fifteenth-century writers both because they hadn't experienced the 'greater sense of cultural distance from Chaucer' that later writers did, and because, as I aim to show, this privileging of the author's recuperable intention is more modern than medieval.

But Furnivall's analogical thinking raises some interesting questions. What was the *Beryn*-writer thinking when he wrote the *Prologue*? And, equally important, what was the *Beryn*-scribe thinking when he included it in the Northumberland manuscript? The first question is difficult to answer for, as we will see, we lack the historical context for the original production of the work. But the manuscript context of the copied *Prologue* (and the *Tale* that follows) can shed light on how the scribe would have interpreted the *Prologue* even as he repurposed it in his work. There is no doubt, for instance, that the scribe knew that the *Prologue* and the *Tale* were not Chaucer's. Though this might seem to suggest that the inclusion of the *Prologue* in Northumberland MS 455 was simply a cynical attempt to create out of whole cloth what the scribe knew he did not have – a more complete version of the Canterbury journey – the truth is a bit more complicated. I argue that he believed his inclusion of the *Beryn*-writer's invention was sanctioned by a kind of occulted authority that by its very nature remains shadowy and ill-defined: the agency of the text itself.

We are extremely limited in our knowledge surrounding the *Prologue*. We don't know when or why it was written (though there's been some speculation that it could have been produced for Canterbury's 1420 jubilee).[7] We don't know who wrote it (Manly and Rickert have said that it almost certainly was not the scribe, and most speculation centres on a monk at Canterbury).[8] We don't really know much about the relationship between the *Prologue to the Tale of Beryn* and the *Tale* itself. The governing assumption is that they were written by the same person, but it's not clear that the *Prologue* and the *Tale* were written at the same time.[9] Most importantly for this chapter, it's not clear what the scribe expected his audience to think about either the *Prologue* or the *Tale*.

What we know is that the scribe of Northumberland 455 (often referred to as the *Beryn*-scribe) was partly or wholly responsible for at least nine other manuscripts, including half a dozen copies of the *Brut*, a work by Lydgate, a *Prick of Conscience*, the *Parliament of Fowls* and, most relevant for our purposes, another copy of the *Canterbury Tales*.[10] The evidence suggests both that he was responsible for the ordering of the tales and that he knew that Chaucer's original design for the pilgrimage was in all likelihood never realised. The first part of the Northumberland manuscript follows the ordering of what Manly and Rickert have called the *b* group of manuscripts until the *Second Nun's Tale*. We then get six more tales (drastically reordered), the *Prologue*, *Beryn* and the end of the *Summoner's Tale* (see below), after which the manuscript returns to the ordering of a *b* manuscript. Unfortunately, lost leaves at the end make it impossible to know whether the manuscript returned the pilgrims to the Tabard Inn.

Part of the eccentricity of Northumberland 455 clearly has to do with the scribe's access to his exemplars. For instance, the *Summoner's Tale* is initially copied only up to line 2158.[11] The scribe apparently found a complete version of the tale only after he had already copied the *Prologue* and the *Tale of Beryn* as he includes lines 2159–94 (the lesson on arsmetrick) after *Beryn* with the *incipit* 'Here endith the tale of the Sompnour within the boke Wryten'.¹² It would, however, be a mistake to think that the tale order is the result of the scribe simply copying texts as they came to him. He clearly makes the choice to move the *Canon's Yeoman's Prologue* and *Tale* to just before the *Beryn* prologue in order to square the geographical reference to Boughton under Blee in line 556 (just five miles outside Canterbury) with the pilgrims' arrival at the shrine.¹³ And he must have had it in mind to include the *Prologue to the Tale of Beryn* very early as he alters the famous comment about the Pardoner in the *General Prologue* ('I trow he were a geldying or a mare' to 'I trow he *had* a geldyng or a mare') in order better to fit the portrait of the Pardoner that we get in the *Prologue* to *Beryn*.

Did he know that he was doing something that in all probability was not realised in any extant manuscripts? Linne Mooney and Daniel Mosser argue that it's likely that he had produced Princeton, Firestone Library MS 100 (often referred to as the Helmingham MS or He) before he put together the Northumberland manuscript.¹⁴ The close relationship between the two manuscripts and the *b*-ordering through to the *Second Nun's Tale* in Northumberland together tell us that the scribe had encountered at least one relatively 'complete' version of the *Tales* before he produced the manuscript. In addition, in producing the Northumberland manuscript, the scribe used at least three sources that would have looked nothing like the Northumberland manuscript, so it's more than likely that he knew he was producing something that was, as Mosser and Mooney put it, 'adventurous'.¹⁵

Although it might seem counter-intuitive, the scribe probably thought he was producing a work that, while audaciously different from what could be found in extant manuscripts, inhered in the idea (or, more accurately, ideas) of the work itself. In thinking about where these textual ideas might come from, it's important to remember that the *Canterbury Tales* is notoriously reluctant to articulate its own form. In the *General Prologue* the Host calls for two tales from each pilgrim each way, later it's 'a tale or two', and later still 'tales too or three'.¹⁶ By the time we get to the final tale the form has again changed as Harry Bailey turns to the Parson and asks him to 'knytte up wel a greet mateere' because 'every man … hath toold his tale'.¹⁷ This revision of the plan for the work would seem to be reflected in the manuscript tradition. Most manuscripts, including He, explicitly link the *Parson's Prologue* to the *Manciple's Tale* (with its reference to Harbledown), making it a one-way journey in which each pilgrim tells one tale. Were the scribe interested in replicating the intentions of the author (at least insofar as they could be divined), it would make sense to end the journey in Canterbury. But recent scholarship on medieval ideas about authorial intention and the notion of the 'work' suggests that scribes didn't think about the *intentio auctoris* in the same way that post-Romantic writers did.

It's not that medieval readers didn't respect some notion of intention as being formative in terms of the work. But as Mary Carruthers has shown, texts in the Middle Ages were conceived to have 'considerable agency separate from the human, historical author'.[18] The intention of the human author was available, but only insofar 'as it [was] displaced into the work' and the '*intentio auctoris* refers most often to the intention of the work'.[19] Its intention is made manifest in the manner in which it leads its reader to its end. This '*ductus* [as they called it] models an artefact as *iter*, a journey, with an overall intention or *tenor* towards its end'.[20] Of course, in any thinking about *intentio auctoris*, the *Canterbury Tales* did and does present a particular problem. Its ultimate form remained unrealised and the portions that were finished seemed to suggest different 'journeys'.

This might help explain why there was, for many scribes, a desire to provide a complete, or more complete, version of the text than what they found in their exemplars.[21] British Library Lansdowne MS 851 is one of the more obvious examples of this phenomenon. It has four spurious links between tales that have been created in order to facilitate its ordering of the tales. At the end of the *Squire's Tale,* for instance, which many manuscripts leave unfinished (and even acknowledge the unfinished nature of the tale with some variation of 'squyers tale for Chawser made no more'), the Lansdowne editor inserts eight lines in which the Squire promises to continue his tale later (the first two of which read, 'Bot I wil here nowe maake a knotte / To þe time it come next to my lotte'), at which point the Wife of Bath begins her tale.[22] Scribes and editors not only created their own links, but would repurpose already existing links in order to smooth out their own tale order. The editors of Bodleian Library MS Arch. Selden B. 14, for instance, having obtained access to the Lansdowne link, altered it slightly and used it to join the *Squire's Tale* with the *Man of Law's Tale*.[23] Even if we believe (as Simon Horobin has argued) that versions of the links, perhaps authored by Chaucer himself, circulated separately from the tales, it's clear that the scribes often felt no compunction about rewriting them in order to suppress troubling signs of incompleteness (like the Cook's and Squire's fragmentary tales).[24]

But as the text was fragmentary, so too was the *intentio auctoris*, and the scribes had to reconstruct the *intentio auctoris* in order to provide a text that would lead the reader 'both through the different stages of the way and (perhaps after delightful delays) towards the journey's ultimate destination'.[25] This circular process (the scribes are led to reconstruct the *intentio auctoris* from the fragmentary text in order to complete the text so that the *intentio auctoris* is manifest) would seem to confirm what most contemporary scholars believe: that Chaucerian inventions, continuations and even repurposed links tell us a lot more about fifteenth-century readers and scribes than they do about the text of the *Canterbury Tales*. But it's not clear that this is how scribes and fifteenth-century readers of the tales thought. What Daniel Wakelin has suggested about another scribe is relevant here: 'he is not seeking an authorial original, nor any historical reconstruction of the text at one point in its transmission. ... his corrections seem to express not a textual idealism necessarily but a rejection of materialism, or to be specific, of the material forms of the text he inherits'.[26] Medieval ideas about the immanent form of the text suggest that if 'the act of accessing the work ... is hidden, radically absent perhaps, covered up in any case, obfuscated by the visibility of the book', then the job of the scribe is not necessarily to hew to the material appearance of his exemplar, but to exhibit formal fidelity to something that might not be physically present.[27]

It might well seem that the creation of a new tale, as well as a substantial addition to the frame narrative, might be of a different order of magnitude than the repurposing of links or the invention of a few lines to fill in gaps. Indeed, Wakelin distinguishes between 'wilful, knowing, creative acts of new authorship' like the creation of the *Tale of Beryn* and its *Prologue* and 'kinds of scribal copying' that might include minor accommodations to produce a 'faithful' text.[28] But it's important to remember that the *Beryn*-scribe didn't create either the *Prologue* or the *Tale* – instead he dutifully copied them in order to realise (though incompletely) the *intentio auctoris* of the text. This doesn't mean that the scribe believed that the *Prologue* or the *Tale* were written by Chaucer. Their profoundly un-Chaucerian metre would have told against them, and, in any case, the scribe had already produced a manuscript that not only lacked the *Prologue* and the *Tale*, but lacked a place to put them.[29]

Finally, the unique alteration of the description of the Pardoner in Northumberland 455 suggests that the scribe knew that he was dealing with non-Chaucerian Chauceriana and needed to alter the text in order to realise this particular *iter*.

This kind of *bricolage* would suggest that scribal fidelity to the idea of a work could lead to the complete suppression of what we think of as the intent of the author, and there are instances, as we will see, of precisely this phenomenon. But here the scribe enacts a Solomonic solution to do justice to competing agencies of the two works. A colophon follows the end of the *Tale of Beryn* ('Nomen autoris presentis Chronica Rome / Et translatoris Filius ecclesie Thome') which roughly translates to 'the name of the present author is a chronicle of Rome and the name of the translator is son of the Church of Thomas'.[30] Manly and Rickert assert (correctly I think) that this colophon was copied by the scribe from his exemplar. The second half of this distich makes sense and long ago it was speculated that it meant a monk from the Cathedral translated *Bérinus*. But, as John Burrow points out, the first half of the distich is strange: it would be appropriate to call the *Tale of Beryn* a chronicle of Rome and in fact the English writer refers to his source as a chronicle, but the author seems to engage in what Burrow calls the 'the boldest of metonymies' in identifying that chronicle with the author of the *Tale of Beryn*. At least it would be strange, if we didn't already understand that *auctor* here has a much more slippery quality than traditional conceptions of the author. At the same time, divining the *intentio auctoris* depends on our understanding that whoever we think the *translatour* is ('son of the Church of Thomas'), it's pretty certainly not Chaucer. The colophon thus calls attention to its own making by someone other than Chaucer even as it offers 'Chaucerian' texts. It doesn't quite put up front the fact that it is non-Chaucerian Chauceriana, since the colophon follows the *Tale,* but it radically separates textual authority from Chaucerian making.

The closest analogue to this strange state of affairs seems to be another 'Canterbury Tale' that draws attention to the fact that it was by someone other than Chaucer. John Lydgate's *The Siege of Thebes* was included in four Chaucer manuscripts that have complete versions of the *Tales*.[31] It's connected to the *Tales* in three of the manuscripts where it's appended to the end. All three of the manuscripts contain *incipits* before the *Siege* that identify Lydgate as the poet. British Library MS Egerton 2864, for instance, reads 'Heer begynneth the laste tale of Cauntirbury talis tolde homeward and maad by daun John Lidgate monk of Bury'.³² As Trigg has argued, these 'rubrics show how seriously the scribes took the internal signature of Lydgate in his prologue'.³³ In fact, it's clear that they revelled in the authorial playfulness of the fictive addition as scribes referred to it even in manuscripts that did not contain the *Tales*. British Library Royal MS 18 D II, for instance, prefaces the *Siege* with a reference to its intertextual nature: 'In this preamble shortly is comprihendid A Mery conseyte of John Lydgate Monke of Bury declarynge how he aionyde þe sege of Thebes to the mery tallys of Caunterburye.'³⁴ Lydgate is understood as engaging in *imitatio* in which what is striven for is similitude not sameness – the imitation, as Francesco Petrarch famously noted, is like that of a son to a father, advertising 'its consciousness of difference from the imitated text'.³⁵

There are, of course, things that differentiate the *Prologue* and the *Tale of Beryn* from a straightforward imitation like *The Siege of Thebes*. There is no *incipit* in Northumberland 455 announcing authorship. Also, the colophon in the Northumberland manuscript not only manifests a different notion of the *nomen auctoris*, but, as it refers to the author or source as 'a chronicle of Rome', can only refer to the *Tale of Beryn* and not to the *Prologue* itself. It's quite possible that the scribe understood the *Tale* as distinct from the *Prologue*.³⁶ And the presentation of the two texts might suggest as much. Elizabeth Allen observes that the *Prologue* 'is visually set off, not completely integrated into the *Tales*: it is introduced and concluded on separate folios and with more elaborate colophons'.³⁷ Following most critical thinking here, Allen understands the colophon following the *Tale* as applying to the *Prologue* as well. But both the *Prologue* and the *Tale of Beryn* seem to be set off not only from the other tales, but also from each other. They both begin and end on separate folios. And while the opening of the *Prologue* is more elaborately decorated than the various beginnings of the tales (see plate 4), the decoration at the beginning of the *Tale of Beryn* itself is a close match (see plate 5). There is no *explicit* at the end of the *Prologue* but there is, in fact, a visual indication that the *Prologue* is over – an instruction '[Be]gynnyth the [March]ant his tale' and though the *incipit* for the *Tale of Beryn* is missing, room was left to execute it. The *Prologue*, then, stands in a kind of strange twilight both in relation to the 'authentic' Chaucer in Northumberland 455 and the *Tale of Beryn* it precedes. The scribe links the authentic tale of the Canon's Yeoman and the demonstrably false second tale of the

Merchant with what he understood was a non-Chaucerian stretch of text as would be evident from its metre – yet he seemingly represents it as Chaucer's.

This strange similitude – asserting itself even as it remains different – manifests itself in other non-Chaucerian Chauceriana. For instance, those involved in the compilation of Bodleian Library MS Bodley 686 – a manuscript that has 'little concern to maintain distinctions between individual authors or to ascribe authorship correctly' – padded out the incomplete *Cook's Tale* with what John Bowers characterises as verses that 'owe less to Chaucer ... [than] to Langland, with longer four-stress lines, heavy alliteration, and the introduction of allegorical personifications':[38]

> He loved bet the taverne than he dede the shoppe,
> For when ther was eny rydyng in Chepe,
> Out of the shoppe theder wolde he lepe,
> Til that he hedde al the sight y-seyn,
> And daunced wel – he *nold* not come agayn –
> And gadered hym a mayny of his sort
> To hoppe and synge and make such disport.
> *With Rech-never and Recheles this lessoun he lerys*
> *With Waste and with Wranglere, his owne pley-ferys,*
> *With Lyght-honde and with Likorouse-mowth, with Unschamfast;*
> *With Drynke-more and with Drawe-abak, her thryst is y-past,*
> *With Malaperte and with Mysseavysed – such meyny they hight,*
> *That wolle do but a lytull tylle her dyner be dyght.*
> *Thus* they stevyn *whan they myght* mete
> To pley at the dyse in suche a *prevey* strete,
> For in *Londoun* ther was none apprentyse
> That feirer couth caste a *scharpe* peir of dyse
> Than couthe Perkyn, and therto he was free,
> *Large* of his dispence in place of prevytee
> *With Magot and with Mylsent, whan that he mette.*[39]

The impulse governing the *Beryn*-scribe could be seen as similar to those responsible for Bodley 686. They perceive absence and produce or adapt texts that, in their metrical unlikeness to that which they supplement, draw attention to difference. Of course, not all scribes were so fastidious in their pursuit of a more complete *Canterbury Tales*. For instance, the scribes responsible for Oxford, Christ Church MS 152 assign Hoccleve's 'Item de Beata Virgine' (along with a five-stanza prologue) to the Plowman, but fail to signal either with a signature, or metrical irregularity, or any other means that the tale is by someone other than Chaucer.

Though all of these writers attempt to realise the *intentio auctoris* of the *Canterbury Tales* and thus might be seen to produce (in their minds at least) a faithful text, their methods and maybe their very notions of fidelity vary.

So, to rephrase our initial question, what did the *Beryn*-scribe think he was doing? It's possible that the scribe was engaging in, as Andrew Higl has claimed, a form of play, that reveals '[a] writerly reader playing with the *Canterbury Tales*'.[40] In writing about the genre of romance, D. H. Green has claimed that there is a 'knowing collusion between author and audience. The latter undertake imaginatively to believe what they know to be fictive, so that the author and audience are both playing a double game of belief and disbelief.'[41] As an approach to thinking about the making of Northumberland 455, this ludic notion has a good deal to recommend it. Plausibility then renders the narrative 'true' only in a kind of approach to fiction that is necessarily fictional, as the audience makes believe 'that a fictional statement is true, while knowing it is not'.[42] But I'd like to make the claim that while the binaries of true/false, belief/disbelief are operative here (the scribe did not believe, for instance, that everything in Northumberland 455 was truly by Chaucer), the scribe's larger concern was informed by the agency of the work – in this case the *Canterbury Tales*. Other manuscripts by this scribe suggest that he was especially interested in providing versions of works that were informed by fairly radical 'ideas' about the *intentio auctoris*, but I don't think he thought of his additions, alterations and non-authorial interventions in Northumberland 455 as false; rather, he was faithful to an idea of the *Canterbury Tales* that some would say is immaterial.[43]

Notes

1 John Urry, *The works of Geoffrey Chaucer, compared with the former editions, and many valuable mss. out of which, three tales are added which were never before printed; by John Urry, student of Christ-Church, Oxon. deceased: together with a glossary by a student of the same college* (London, 1721), sig. K2v.

2 Even at its discovery Urry seems to be discomfited by the fact that it exists in only one manuscript. See his letter to Lord Harley quoted in Caroline Spurgeon, *Five Hundred Years of Chaucer Criticism and Allusion: 1357–1900*, 3 vols (Cambridge: Cambridge University Press, 1925), vol. 1, p. 325.

3 See Simone Celine Marshall, 'The 1807 edition of the poetical works of Geoffrey Chaucer', *Notes and Queries*, 57:2 (2011), 183–6 (p. 184);

and Geoffrey Chaucer, *The Canterbury Tales of Geoffrey Chaucer*, ed. Thomas Wright (London and Glasgow: R. Griffith, 1880), p. vi.
4 F. J. Furnivall and W. G. Stone (eds), *The Tale of Beryn, with a prologue of the merry adventure of the pardoner with a tapster at Canterbury* (London: N. Trübner & Co. for the Chaucer Society, 1887), p. vii (emphasis in original).
5 Stephanie Trigg, *Congenial Souls: Reading Chaucer from Medieval to Postmodern* (Minneapolis: University of Minnesota Press, 2002), pp. 103–4. This, in turn, was a symptom of a much larger modern desire to 'be the true inheritors of his spirit or members of that best, most sophisticated audience of his confreres, the "congenial souls" of the Chaucerian community' (p. 38).
6 Trigg, *Congenial Souls*, pp. 103–4.
7 Peter Brown, 'Journey's end: the prologue to *The Tale of Beryn*', in Julia Boffey and Janet Cowen (eds), *Chaucer and Fifteenth-Century Poetry* (London: King's College Centre for Late Antique and Medieval Studies, 1991), pp. 143–74 (pp. 152–3).
8 J. M. Manly and E. Rickert (eds), *The Text of the Canterbury Tales*, vol. 1 (Chicago: Chicago University Press, 1940), p. 392. Matthew Irvin believes that both the *Tale* and *Prologue* are a London tale, in the milieu of the London Mercers and John Carpenter (private communication). See his essay, 'The Merchant's Tale: *Beryn* and the London Company of Mercers' (forthcoming in *Studies in the Age of Chaucer*).
9 The *Prologue* and the *Tale of Beryn*, in John M. Bowers (ed.), *The Canterbury Tales: Fifteenth-Century Continuations and Additions*, TEAMS Middle English Text Series (Kalamazoo: Western Michigan University, 1992), p. 57.
10 See the list from Daniel W. Mosser and Linne R. Mooney, who also identify fragments and other manuscripts associated with the *Beryn*-scribe in 'More manuscripts by the Beryn scribe and his cohort', *Chaucer Review*, 49 (2014), 39–76.
11 Alnwick Castle, Northumberland MS 455 [Nl], fol. 116r.
12 Northumberland MS 455, fol. 240r.
13 The geographical reference to Harbledown (two miles outside Canterbury) in the *Manciple's Prologue*, which seems to confirm the one-way nature of the pilgrimage (if one believes fragments IX and X are linked), is absent from the manuscript as the *Prologue* is not included within Nl.
14 Mosser and Mooney, 'More manuscripts by the Beryn scribe', p. 53.
15 Manly and Rickert (eds), *The Text of the Canterbury Tales*, p. 389; Mosser and Mooney, 'More manuscripts by the Beryn scribe', p. 53.
16 Derek Pearsall, *The Canterbury Tales* (Winchester: Allen & Unwin, 1985), p. 26.

17 Geoffrey Chaucer, the *Parson's Prologue*, in *The Riverside Chaucer*, gen. ed. Larry D. Benson (Boston: Houghton Mifflin, 3rd edn, 1987), X.28, 24–5.
18 Mary Carruthers, *The Experience of Beauty in the Middle Ages* (Oxford: Oxford University Press, 2013), p. 53.
19 Carruthers, *The Experience of Beauty*, p. 171.
20 Carruthers, *The Experience of Beauty*, p. 54.
21 Any number of scholars have commented on this scribal desire for completion. See, for instance, Simon Horobin, 'Compiling the *Canterbury Tales* in fifteenth-century manuscripts', *Chaucer Review*, 47 (2013), 372–89 (p. 384); Thomas A. Prendergast, *Chaucer's Dead Body: From Corpse to Corpus* (New York: Routledge, 2004), p. 103.
22 This line from fol. 60*v* of Princeton, Firestone Library MS 100. Five manuscripts have this kind of notation (He; Nl; Cambridge, University Library MS DD.4.24 [Dd]; Oxford, New College MS D.314 [Ne], and London, Royal College of Physicians MS 388 [Py]). The lines from Landsdowne appear on fol. 87*r*.
23 Thomas A. Prendergast, 'Revenant Chaucer: early modern celebrity', in Isabel Davis and Catherine Nall (eds), *Chaucer and Fame: Reputation and Reception* (Cambridge: D. S. Brewer, 2015), pp. 185–99 (pp. 186–9).
24 Horobin, 'Compiling the *Canterbury Tales*', p. 388. For an earlier, if offhand, suggestion that the links were on separate sheets, see Pearsall, *The Canterbury Tales*, p. 18.
25 Carruthers, *The Experience of Beauty*, p. 54.
26 Daniel Wakelin, *Scribal Correction and Literary Craft: English Manuscripts 1375–1510* (Cambridge: Cambridge University Press, 2014), p. 155.
27 D. Vance Smith is quoting Maurice Blanchot here in 'The inhumane wonder of the book', *Chaucer Review*, 47 (2013), 361–71 (p. 362).
28 Wakelin, *Scribal Correction*, p. 305.
29 John Burrow attempts to make the case that 'many earlier English poets had composed in the same mix of six- and seven-beat lines'; see 'The *Tale of Beryn*: an appreciation', *Chaucer Review*, 49 (2015), 499–511 (p. 500). Most notably, the *Tale of Gamelyn*, which appears as the *Cook's Tale* in no less than twenty-seven manuscript copies of the *Tales*, employs 'the characteristic loose long line of Middle English, the septenary/Alexandrine'; see Derek Pearsall, *Old and Middle English Poetry* (London: Routledge, 1977), p. 289. Yet *Gamelyn* doesn't appear in either He or Nl, so there's no evidence that the *Beryn*-scribe would have seen anything attributed to Chaucer with the same metre.
30 Northumberland MS 455, fol. 237*r*.
31 London, British Library, Additional MS 5140; Oxford, Christ Church MS 152; London, British Library, MS Egerton 2864; Austin, Harry Ransom Center MS 143 (Cardigan MS, Manly and Rickert Cn).

32 Egerton MS 2864, fol. 292v.
33 Trigg, *Congenial Souls*, p. 96.
34 London, British Library, MS Royal 18 D II, fol. 147v.
35 Alfred Hiatt, *The Making of Medieval Forgeries: False Documents in Fifteenth-Century England* (London: British Library; Toronto and Buffalo: University of Toronto Press, 2004), p. 158.
36 There is an apparent reference to the frame narrative near the beginning of *Beryn*:

> But yit the name is ever oon of Rome, as it was grounded
> After Romus and Romulus that first that ceté founded,
> That brithern weren both to, as old bookes writen.
> But of hir lyff and governaunce I wol nat nowe enditen,
> But of other mater that falleth to my mynde.
> Wherfor, gentill sirs, ye that beth behynde,
> Draweth somwhat nere, thikker to a route,
> That my wordes mowe soune to ech man aboute.
> After these too bretheren, Romulus and Romus,
> Julius Cezar was Emperour, that rightfull was of domus.
> (Bowers [ed.], *Canterbury Tales: Continuations*, p. 80, lines 757–66).

But, given the scribe's extensive alterations elsewhere in the manuscript, it very well could have been inserted by the scribe himself, as line 765 could easily follow line 760.

37 Elizabeth Allen, *False Fables and Exemplary Truth in Later Middle English Literature* (New York: Palgrave, 2015), p. 128.
38 See David Lorenzo Boyd, 'Social texts: Bodley 686 and the politics of the *Cook's Tale*', *Huntington Quarterly*, 58 (1995), 81–97 (p. 87), though later he asserts that readers probably thought it was Chaucer's tale (p. 90); Bowers (ed.), *Canterbury Tales: Continuations*, p. 34.
39 The *Cook's Tale* in Bowers (ed.), *Canterbury Tales: Continuations*, pp. 35–6, lines 12–31, italics indicate alterations.
40 Andrew Higl, *Playing the Canterbury Tales: The Continuations and Additions* (Burlington: Ashgate, 2012), p. 90.
41 D. H. Green, *The Beginnings of Medieval Romance: Fact and Fiction, 1150–1220* (Cambridge: Cambridge University Press, 2002), p. 11.
42 Green, *Beginnings of Medieval Romance*, p. 12.
43 See Ralph Hanna's review of *The London Chronicles of the Fifteenth Century: A Revolution in English Writing, with an Annotated Edition of Bradford, West Yorkshire Archives MS 32D86/42*: 'The scribe's texts show him to have been an innovative, not passive, copyist who "tailored" his works. He not only adds a series of alternative readings as an appendix to his *Prick*, but makes efforts to "complete" his Chaucers (adding 'Beryn' to *The Canterbury Tales* and, as he did with his *London Chronicle*, an intercalated lyric to "The Parliament")', *Reviews in History* (2003), www.history.ac.uk/reviews/review/340, accessed 4 May 2018.

9
Caxton in the middle of English
David Matthews

In 1988, when Stephanie Trigg was embarking on her career at the University of Melbourne, she presented a paper at a Deakin University conference which was the genesis of her book *Congenial Souls: Reading Chaucer from Medieval to Postmodern* (2002). I was present at the conference as a second-year doctoral candidate and was grateful to have been invited to speak also. My own contribution, probably my very first academic paper, outlined what became much later my book *The Making of Middle English, 1765–1910* (1999). In this chapter, I want to celebrate this congruence of disciplinary histories by revisiting the history of Middle English, returning not to the eighteenth- and nineteenth-century scene of my earlier work, but to the very beginning of the study of Middle English, as Trigg did in *Congenial Souls*.

My larger interest here, in the context of tracing the history of the reading of Middle English literature, is the question of self-consciousness, at the beginning of the early modern period, about medieval English, especially Middle English. My particular interest is in Middle English as a category of literature, rather than linguistic history, though obviously the two things can hardly be disentangled. To begin with we know of course that it is not strictly possible to speak of 'Middle English' before Grimm invented the concept of the middle phase of a language in 1822. But we can still ask about when, or whether, early modern people deemed there to have been a rupture with the literary or linguistic past. Today, after Grimm, we think that that break occurred some time around the end of the fifteenth century. But what did *they* think? Was there a sense of a linguistic break in addition to the other perceived ruptures of the late fifteenth and early sixteenth centuries, in religion and monarchical dynasty? Was there anything that matched the current consensus among historians of the language that the middle phase of English came to an end around the turn of the sixteenth century?

Helen Cooper argues that it is impossible to pinpoint a particular moment in the early Tudor period when a consciousness of medieval English developed. There is simply no trace of such linguistic self-consciousness:

> the term 'Middle English' was [not] available to the writers of the sixteenth and early seventeenth centuries, and it would not have made much sense to them if a single term had been coined. What we know as Middle English was for them the language of their recent forefathers, a language still recognizably spoken in parts of the country more distant from the capital.[1]

Nevertheless, there are traces of a self-consciousness about linguistic newness. John Skelton (c.1460–1529) projected the idea that he was doing something different from his predecessors Chaucer, Gower and Lydgate and doing so in a different linguistic phase. I have written elsewhere about how he and Stephen Hawes take an attitude to the literary past that suggests both reverence for their predecessors but also a sense that their work is now somewhat archaic, linguistically. Specifically, both poets address the charge that their predecessors' language is 'dark', that is, obscure. In *Phyllyp Sparowe*, in a section of the poem probably composed before 1505, Chaucer is referred to as a 'famus clerke', whose 'termes were not darke, / But pleasaunt, easy and playne; / Ne worde he wrote in vayne'.[2] Like Skelton, Hawes sees difficulty in the work of old poets, detecting the darkness inherent in old language. Poets write 'vnder cloudy fygures' with which they cover 'the trouthe of all theyr scryptures'.[3]

The apparent consciousness here, however, of the difficulty of old language is hard to take at face value. Each poet wishes to cement his association with his predecessors but each also wants to promote the newness of his own project. Skelton raises the 'darkness' or obscurity of Chaucer only in order to deny it (even if in a way that draws attention to that which is being denied); Hawes makes an argument that rhetorical obscurity is simply what poets do. Certainly as the sixteenth century goes on there is a growing sense that the language of the fourteenth and fifteenth centuries is, as George Puttenham put it, 'out of vse' with people of the present time.[4] But it is still difficult to judge the extent to which the difficulty is being exaggerated in order to enhance the prestige of Tudor literature. Nobody who comments on the fading into difficulty of medieval English does so without making it clear that, to him, this English is in fact 'pleasaunt, easy and playne', in Skelton's words. We are left with the paradox that those who comment on the archaism of the English of a century before do so in order to show their own easy mastery of the 'difficult' author in question.

In the context of these larger questions, in this chapter I am concerned not so much with Tudor England as with the role of William Caxton, a figure interstitial between the writers of the later fourteenth and early fifteenth centuries and the beginnings of the Tudor period. During Caxton's boyhood in the 1430s and 1440s, Lydgate was still active; Caxton's print output coincided, of course, with the early part of the reign of the first Tudor monarch. Caxton was certainly attentive to the language of the recent past. As Cooper writes, neither Caxton nor Wynkyn de Worde 'apologize[d] for any archaism in the language of the works they were printing that were already one or two centuries old'.[5] Caxton's concern, she continues, was chiefly with the synchronic aspect of language and the various dialects in different parts of Britain which hampered understanding. He had by contrast little to say about any problems in reading the language of authors who had been dead for fifty or a hundred years. Hence there is little sense in Caxton's writings of a break such as the nineteenth-century writers supplied, and this is not surprising given his commitment to the exemplarity of the history of the medieval past for the present.

Making a somewhat different argument, Tim Machan has stated that Caxton's own English at the time of his first *Canterbury Tales* edition would have been 'outmoded ... sharing as many of the habits of bygone poets like Hoccleve, Lydgate, and Chaucer as of modern speakers born in the last quarter of the fifteenth century'.[6] In its early days print, Machan argues, though innovative as a technology, established a conservative canon of Middle English and Caxton was not interested in innovation or new writers. Indeed, Caxton never printed any contemporary writers, a task only taken up by his successors Wynkyn de Worde and Richard Pynson.

Caxton was, nevertheless, hardly without a sense of diachrony in language. Seth Lerer describes the prologue to the *Eneydos* of 1490 (STC 24796)[7] as having 'vernacularity itself' as its subject, involving Caxton in 'a search for an English language among the welter of diachronic changes and synchronic variations'.[8] When Caxton printed poetical works such as those of Chaucer and Lydgate, his concern was to be seen as a philologist, printing with fidelity to the past on the basis of old manuscripts. The preface supplied to the second edition of the *Canterbury Tales* in 1483 is the most celebrated instance of this insistence on truth to an author's words, as Caxton recounts how one of the 'dyuerse gentyl men' who purchased the first edition approached him to say that the printing was not faithful to Chaucer's original writing and to tell him of a better book of Chaucer owned by his father. Caxton undertakes to print this version if the gentleman can procure it for him, 'trewe and correcte'.[9] The story projects an image of Caxton, the editor of Middle English verse, as being invested in fidelity to the literary-linguistic past. It has often been cited and, as has been pointed out, it perhaps represents a much-needed marketing ploy by which Caxton justifies the need for a new edition of the *Tales* not ten years after the first, in a context in which the 'reprint' or 'second edition' was something of an unknown quantity.

While I do not disagree with this position, I want to focus on the telling detail that, in order to make that ploy, Caxton has resorted to an idea of truth to the manuscript and the integrity of an author's words that must already have appealed to some kinds of readers. For James Simpson, Caxton here 'acts as philological editor' to an absent author and in that regard his approach sharply contrasts with that taken by such 'compiler-poets' as Hawes, for whom Chaucer is given the role of a kind of personal presence.[10] For this to function as a marketing strategy, there must already be a preparedness to see the work of a 'philological editor' as a worthwhile pursuit.

Yet, if Caxton locates himself as a philological editor where *verse* is concerned, this does not cover the full spectrum of his approaches to Middle English literature. Caxton takes a rather different approach when he prints Middle English *prose*: while still engaging with what might broadly be thought of as philological recovery, Caxton is far less concerned with authorial sovereignty and hence the notion of the 'trewe and correcte' original. To demonstrate this, I will consider Caxton's 1482 printing of John Trevisa's translation of Ranulph Higden's *Polychronicon* (STC 13438). This work is the largest he ever printed, and according to A. S. G. Edwards, it 'contains his most extensive discussion about his own understanding of the nature of historical writing'.[11] In addition, with this substantial work Caxton signals that he is far more prepared to interfere with the text he had inherited and to do so in a way that suggests a different relationship, on the part of a philological editor, to time and language from that signalled in the *Canterbury Tales* preface.

'To wryte fyrst ouer all': Caxton and Trevisa

Higden's *Polychronicon* circulated widely in manuscript in England in Trevisa's Middle English version and was one of those medieval works that made a smooth transition into the era of print. Caxton drew on the description of Britain in Book I, including it as part of the *Chronicles of England*, a version of the Prose *Brut*, which he printed in 1480 (STC 9991). He produced his full version of the *Polychronicon* in 1482 and Wynkyn de Worde printed it again in 1494 (STC 13439).[12] To prepare it for the 1480s, there was one obvious sense for Caxton in which the *Polychronicon* needed to be updated, and that was in its sequence of historical events. Trevisa's continuation of the *Polychronicon* had brought the history down to 1360 but, more than a century later, as Caxton notes, there was much to be added. Caxton, 'intent on moving history forward', as Edwards puts it, adds a 'Liber ultimus' which brings the history down to 1460.

For Caxton that was not quite the present day, but it was evidently a significant date, marking the accession of Edward IV, 'my most drad naturel and souerayne lord and moost cristen kynge'.[13] These words about King Edward might sound formulaic but they are more than mere ritual, as Caxton confirms elsewhere. In the second version of the *Chronicles of England*, printed in the same year as *Polychronicon*, Caxton emphatically ends the history with the accession of a king who has 'the hole possession of al the hole reame', bringing what we might think of as the Middle Ages to a close and ending with a prayer for Edward's wellbeing.[14] For the first English printer it is 1460 which provides a break with the past; the events of 1485, by contrast, would be not an ending for Caxton, but the beginning of potentially great difficulties.

Still discussing what as a printer he must add to Trevisa, Caxton goes on to state:

> I William Caxton a symple persone haue endeuoryed me to wryte fyrst ouer all the sayd book of proloconycon / and som what haue chaunged the rude and old englyssh / that is to wete certayn wordes / which in these dayes be neither vsyd ne vnderstanden / & furthermore haue put it in emprynte.[15]

With these words about 'rude and old englyssh' Caxton signals that he simply does not have the same respect for the English of Chaucer's near-contemporary Trevisa as he does for that of Chaucer himself. Whatever the motivation, there is here, by contrast with the *Canterbury Tales* edition, much more of a sense of a linguistic and historical break in Caxton's thinking and the possibility of the creation of a new kind of text.[16] Machan argues,

> By making such comparisons [as those between older and newer morphology, or rhyme] possible, early printers enabled the conceptualisation of medieval literature as a literary-linguistic category in a way not feasible theretofore. In effect, in their late fifteenth- and early sixteenth-century editions, these printers created a new genre – early modern Middle English – a genre with its own history, theoretical orientation, and ramifications for the English history of the book.[17]

Obviously this applies to the Chaucer editions, which enabled precisely such a comparison. But what Caxton did to Trevisa was rather different, changing the linguistic evidence so that what resulted was part Middle English, part the English of Caxton's day. This could be described as modernising, which in turn would suggest a distinct diachronic consciousness and a desire to forge something new out of what he quite clearly sees as Trevisa's 'old' English. As I shall elaborate, however, a great deal of caution is needed when it comes to the notion of modernising.

For now it can be asked: did Caxton feel more able to edit the text into a notion of conformity or modernity when it was prose rather than verse? Did he feel less respectful towards the clerkly translator Trevisa than he was towards the master poet Chaucer? Or was it the case that some genres demanded more respect than others? Might his motives have been a mixture of all of these? I will here present studies of particular instances, comparing Caxton's treatment of Trevisa with the way he deals with Chaucer, in order to gauge the extent to which Caxton forged a sense of 'medieval' English – long before the Middle Ages was a concept that could be thought.

Caxton as editor of Trevisa

It is not surprising that Caxton has been recognised as an interventionist editor of Trevisa. He notes it himself, in words already quoted about 'the rude and old englyssh' and the 'certayn wordes / which in these dayes be neither vsyd ne vnderstanden', and it seems to be implied in the somewhat ambiguous statement about the endeavour 'to wryte fyrst ouer all the sayd book'. The phrase suggests thoroughgoing intervention, and as such is a statement of editorial intent quite different from the commitment to fidelity to the original made two or three years later in the second edition of the *Canterbury Tales*.

Noting this passage in his Rolls Series edition of the *Polychronicon*, Churchill Babington clarifies Caxton's practice that 'Not only are certain words replaced by others, but the whole orthography is changed, so that the English is no longer the language of the 14th, but of the 15th century'. While this is in part simply because certain letters such as thorn are not used by Caxton, more importantly, Babington says, there are changes to vocabulary and to whole phrases. He then offers a useful table (though not the result of a complete collation) of 'certain words in Trevisa which Caxton *in general* (but not uniformly) replaces by others'.[18] For Babington these alterations bear 'considerable interest' in that they show 'what words and phrases were falling into desuetude in Caxton's time'.[19] Hence, for example, as Babington notes, Caxton often replaces Trevisa's noun *lore* with *doctryne*, and the verb *wonen* with *to dwell*. But was this because Trevisa's words were 'neither vsyd ne vnderstanden' in Caxton's time, or had 'fall[en] into desuetude'? That seems unlikely, as the original Middle English words were still to be found in late fifteenth-century English and beyond into the sixteenth century. The evidence of the *Oxford English Dictionary (OED)* suggests that even if both *lore* and *wonen* were giving way to replacements, it is unlikely that any well-read person of the Tudor period would have struggled to understand them. In 1610, for example, Philemon Holland was still using *woneth* in his translation of Camden's *Britannia*.[20] Perhaps the word had an antique feel by then; perhaps Holland intended that effect. But he was translating from Latin, and must have assumed that English-speaking readers would understand the term *woneth*.

The Chaucer editor Thomas Speght, at the end of the sixteenth century, found it necessary to gloss both *lore* and *wonen* in the list added to both his editions of the complete works of Chaucer, in 1598 and 1602, which he entitled 'The old and obscure words of Chaucer, explaned'. In 1598 Speght glossed *lore* as 'knowledge, or learning' and *wone, wones* and *wonning* as respectively 'dwelling place', 'dwelling' and 'dwelling'. In the more elaborate version of the glossary in 1602, which aimed to give the source languages of words, *lore* was glossed as '(*ratio*) regard, doctrine' and *wonneth* as '*d*. dwelleth', where the *d* indicates that the word was in Speght's opinion of Saxon origin.

These examples are nevertheless only equivocal evidence for a process of modernising on Caxton's part. They certainly suggest his sensitivity to linguistic trends but, as I aim to show, this need not be anything so simple as the substitution of plainly archaic terms with their modern replacements. In what follows I take this further by examining a small handful of words for what they tell us about Caxton's work on Trevisa. I have chosen words which are also common in Chaucer, so that Caxton's practice in relation to Trevisa can be compared with what he does to the Chaucerian text, and in turn with what happens to such instances in the sixteenth century and, in particular, how they are treated in Speght's glossary.

Beniman: this was certainly a form that became archaic in the sixteenth century, when Old English-derived forms of *niman* were replaced by Scandinavian-derived *take*. Trevisa uses this standard Middle English word but Caxton replaces it with 'take away' in his edition of *Polychronicon*. Trevisa's form, derived from Old English *niman*, was, like all such forms, in the process of being replaced by the Scandinavian-derived forms of 'to take'. Hence Caxton could be regarded as being up-to-the-minute in making the change, which could therefore be considered a modernisation showing Caxton's sensitivity to linguistic change. But evidence elsewhere in Caxton's own work at the same time suggests less concern about a supposed archaism. He uses *beniman* frequently in the second printing of the Prose *Brut* as the *Chronicles of England* in 1482 (STC 9992): the daughters of King Leyr, for example, 'bynome hym holy the royalme'.[21] Speght includes a form of the word in his glossary, giving 'benimmeth' correctly as 'bereaueth'. This is in line with the *OED*'s indications that *beniman* was archaic after about 1500. But Caxton's own evidence suggests it would be overstating to say that it was 'neither vsyd ne vnderstanden' in his day.

Shrew, shrewd, shrewednesse: this set of words offers a different example. They persisted in and beyond Caxton's time but of course had largely changed their senses by the late sixteenth century. For Chaucer, in whose work the expressions are common, a *shrew* is an ill-intentioned or wicked person, *shrewd* an adjective pertaining to the same quality of wickedness, and *shrewednesse* a noun referring to a wicked or accursed practice. Chaucer does not use this last word often and when he does it is generally in prose works: *Melibee*, *Boece*, the *Parson's Tale*. In Middle English, *shrew* had not yet been confined to a specific gender and indeed can clearly still be used of a man in the 1530s, as is seen in the 1538 edition of Thomas Elyot's *Dictionary*. But for Shakespeare, famously, a shrew has become more typically gender-specific and refers to an ill-intentioned woman. Shrewdness, meanwhile, had become relatively uncommon by the second half of the sixteenth century. By the time of *Antony and Cleopatra* around 1608, it had emerged with its meaning of 'sagacity', possibly reinvented given what was by then a new sense of the adjective *shrewd*, which had taken on its current sense of 'sagacious' by 1609, when it is found in Thomas Cooper's *The Churches Deliueraunce* (STC 5696).[22]

Higden, describing the Amazon women's practice of removing their daughters' breasts to facilitate archery, says that Hercules was the first to condemn this *feritas*, or rough or brutal practice. Trevisa, translating, refers to the Amazons' *schrewedness* while Caxton renders this as 'the ylle disposicion of these wommen'.[23] Clearly this set of words was not stable in meaning from the late fifteenth century onwards and that seems to be reflected in Caxton's decision in the *Polychronicon* to replace Trevisa's *schrewednesse* with a periphrasis. Given the near disappearance of this noun by the middle of the sixteenth century and its later reappearance with a different sense, Caxton could be seen here as modernising what was never a common word and which, by his time, was apparently becoming unfamiliar. The history of the word in the century after Caxton seems to support the notion of its semantic volatility.

Countering that suggestion, however, is the fact that Caxton is not consistent on this point. In his version of *Aesop's Fables* in 1484 (which he claims to have translated himself), Caxton refers to the 'shrewdnes and malyce of the dogge'.[24] And elsewhere he respects Chaucer's use of the word, even in prose contexts where the constraints of verse did not prevent him from altering it. Hence it is no surprise that the line in the *House of Fame*, 'Speke of hem harm and shrewednesse', is rendered by Caxton in his 1483 *Book of Fame* as: 'Speke of hem harme and shrewdnes'. The reference in the *Parson's Tale* to 'iniquitees and shrewednesses', where the prose theoretically allowed more latitude, is in Caxton's first *Canterbury Tales* edition of 1476 rendered as 'iniquyte & shreudnes'.[25] Both these usages, incidentally, persist in Speght's second complete Chaucer of 1602 and the word *shrewednesse*, notably, is not in Speght's glossary either in 1598 or 1602. This is despite the fact that it had become (as a noun) a rare word in written English in Speght's lifetime.

Hence although *shrewednesse* was possibly not a particularly common word in Caxton's time, it was certainly still being used in the Middle English sense in which Chaucer had employed it and, more than a century later, was apparently not deemed particularly difficult by a Chaucer editor. When Chaucer used it, Caxton did not alter it. But he felt no such constraint when printing Trevisa, and when he altered Trevisa's usage in the 1480s, it seems unlikely that it was simply in order to modernise for better comprehension. Perhaps Caxton was being particularly conservative, playing things safe so as not to leave an archaism in place. But if so, he was happy enough in other printings of the first half of the 1480s to preserve that same archaism. In all, then, it looks not as if Caxton were altering the word for fear of its not being understood, so much as if he was making a lexical choice which might have had something to do with the kind of readership Caxton was imagining for *Polychronicon*.

Finally, *clepen*: this verb is a very common one in late Middle English but was gradually being replaced by 'to call' in the course of the sixteenth century. Both in 1598 and 1602 the verb was included in Speght's glossary, suggesting it was thought to be 'old and obscure' by the editor. Despite that, it had been in use throughout the sixteenth century, and the past participle *yclept* was well known, even if chiefly as a literary archaism (in which role it continued in use until the nineteenth century). Spenser's use of the word is probably a deliberate archaism, but it is less clear that that is the case when Hamlet complains that the Danes' habit of 'wassail' leads people to 'clepe us drunkards' (*Hamlet* I.iv.18). Speght's glossing of it as a 'hard word', then, does not necessarily indicate that it really posed anyone any great difficulty in 1598. Instances such as these among Speght's 'hard words' suggest more that he is showing off his own diligence as a glossarist than that the word in question is so old and obscure as to be incomprehensible. Caxton routinely (but not exclusively) adjusted Trevisa's uses of *clepeth* and the past participle *yclept* to 'callith' and 'called' or 'named'. His inconsistency alone suggests that these Middle English words, like *shrewednesse*, were not entirely obscure to late fifteenth-century readers.

These, and many other instances too numerous to cover here, might suggest that what Caxton did to Trevisa in 1482 by way of updating lexical choices should be called 'modernising'. His practice could then be recognised as indicating a linguistic break that was actually occurring, by which what is now labelled Middle English was becoming early modern English. I want to resist that conclusion. While that process of transformation was taking place at the end of the fifteenth century and in the early sixteenth, there is no evidence that Caxton could truly detect it and act as its instrument. What Caxton did to Trevisa does not overall seem to have been essential to understanding the Middle English author. Instead, Caxton's approach to the language of *Polychronicon* seems to be of a piece with a larger attitude in that work. In *Polychronicon* (along with the 1480 print of the Prose *Brut* which clearly acted as a kind of rehearsal for the more comprehensive work) what was at stake was no less than the exemplarity of history itself. Caxton, for example, argues that history is of more value in a moral role than fiction; while he does not deny such a role to fiction it is historical truth that takes the paramount ethical role:

> And also yf the terryble feyned Fables of Poetes haue moche styred and moeued men to pyte / and conseruynge of Iustyce / How moche more is to be supposed / that Historye assertryce of veryte / and as moder of alle philosophye, moeuynge our maners to vertue / reformeth and reconcyleth nerhande alle thoos men / whiche thurgh the infyrmyte of oure mortal nature hath ledde the mooste parte of theyr lyf in Ocyosyte and myspended theyr tyme passed ryght soone oute of Remembraunce / Of whiche lyf and deth is egal oblyuyon.[26]

It seems possible that Caxton could have left his author alone without sacrificing understanding where a 1480s readership was concerned. As we have seen, in other texts of the same period Caxton was content with Middle English expressions he rejected in Trevisa – expressions which may have been natural to him, as his work as translator of *Aesop's Fables* suggests. Hence what Caxton did to Trevisa was perhaps less the result of an actual necessity to modernise the author, so much as the desire to make Trevisa *seem* more up to the minute, less like a clerk from the past. When Caxton brought Higden/Trevisa down to the threshold of his own era in 1460, he seems to have thought it appropriate to drag those authors out of their own eras at the same time. Certainly, Caxton shows a sensitivity to semantic changes which appear to have been going on at the time. Such a view would accord with those understandings of Caxton, like Seth Lerer's, which see his monumental history as reifying a monumentalised past, a past which before too long will be thought of as belonging to the Middle Ages.[27]

But (as Lerer also recognises), Caxton's approach to Chaucer exhibits the 'retrospective impulses of fifteenth-century Chaucerianism'.[28] Caxton was confident, when he wanted to be, that readers did *not* struggle with fourteenth-century English and that that past, in effect, was not as disconnected as the monumental histories suggest. As William Kuskin argues about print, its significance 'is less that it signals a fundamental break with the past than that it reasserts this past by transforming it, restating the symbolic basis for vernacular literary authority through material reproduction'.[29]

For many readers, much of what went on in *Polychronicon* must have been silent and unostentatious work. It is surely unlikely that many readers were comparing print and manuscript in a way which would have allowed them to see what Caxton had done – that is, doing precisely that kind of comparison which the anonymous 'gentyl' reader of Caxton's first Chaucer edition is supposed to have performed. Even if there were such readers, Caxton had provided himself some insurance against any accusations of philological bad faith by declaring, from the beginning, that Trevisa's 'rude and old englyssh' would get the updating it obviously needed because it was 'neither vsyd ne vnderstanden' in the 1480s. As ever, when anyone makes that claim, what he is really saying (like Skelton or Puttenham later on) is of course that *he* can fully understand this supposedly outmoded language. He is not offering a set of philological tools, as Speght would do in the 1590s, by which to read Middle English, but rather saying that the work of philology is to make the text completely transparent.

To say that Caxton modernises Trevisa (or anyone else) presupposes that we know what the modern is at the time the statement is made, as a norm in accordance with which Caxton works. But not only do we not know that, we have to allow for the fact that what Caxton does is, by its very existence, the modern. In a sense, Caxton cannot not be modern. He is a particularly good case study because, for a period of about fifteen years, he is almost the only person producing literature in print. If Caxton alters *yclept* to 'called' this may say nothing about how people in Westminster were actually speaking and a great deal about what the printer thought was good English, and what he wanted to be good English, in his time.

Caxton's alterations to Trevisa therefore do not show us the transformation of Middle English into something more modern. But they do show us a process which would be greatly intensified in the decades after Caxton's death as printed books proliferated. Perhaps that process is something akin, but inverse, to making antique furniture by adding a patina of age. Caxton makes his works look more up to date by adding the patina of modernity. While there was, presumably, some connection to spoken English we cannot reliably say what that connection was. As I have shown, words which Caxton, at least by implication, wanted to consign to the past still persisted more than a century later in the time of Speght, some of them not even requiring a gloss. For now, then, my conclusion is that in linguistic terms, Caxton was not a moderniser. But he was, certainly, engaged in the operation of fabricating the modern, or a modernity-effect, successfully enough that hindsight grants him a key role at the end of Middle English.

Notes

1 Helen Cooper, '"The most excellent creatures are not ever born perfect": early modern attitudes to Middle English', in Tim William Machan (ed.), *Imagining Medieval English: Language Structures and Theories, 500–1500* (Cambridge: Cambridge University Press, 2016), pp. 241–60 (p. 242).
2 David Matthews, 'The spectral past: medieval literature in the early modern period', in Robert DeMaria, Jr., Heesok Chang and Samantha Zacher (eds), *A Companion to British Literature, Vol. II: Early Modern Literature 1450–1660* (Malden MA and Oxford: Wiley-Blackwell, 2014), pp. 1–15; *Phyllyp Sparowe* in John Scattergood (ed.), *John Skelton: The Complete English Poems* (New Haven and London: Yale University Press, 1983), lines 801–3.
3 See Hawes's *The Conversion of Swearers* (1509) in Florence W. Gluck and Alice B. Morgan (eds), *The Minor Poems of Stephen Hawes*, EETS o.s. 271 (London: Oxford University Press, 1974).
4 George Puttenham, *The Arte of English Poesie Contriued into Three Bookes* (London, 1589, STC 20519.5), ch. 4; sig. r.iv*v*.
5 Cooper, '"The most excellent creatures"', p. 242.
6 Tim William Machan, 'Early modern Middle English', in William Kuskin (ed.), *Caxton's Trace: Studies in the History of English Printing* (Notre Dame: University of Notre Dame Press, 2006), pp. 299–322 (p. 299).
7 STC refers to A. W. Pollard and G. R. Redgrave (eds), *A short-title catalogue of books printed in England, Scotland and Ireland, and of English books printed abroad 1475–1640*, 2nd edn, revised and enlarged, begun by W. A. Jackson and F. S. Ferguson, completed by K. F. Pantzer, 3 vols, London: Bibliographical Society, 1976–91. References to early printed books in this chapter are followed by an STC number.
8 Seth Lerer, 'William Caxton', in David Wallace (ed.), *The Cambridge History of Medieval English Literature* (Cambridge: Cambridge University Press, 1999), pp. 720–38 (p. 737).
9 William Caxton, 'Prohemye' to the *Canterbury Tales* (Westminster, 1483, STC 5083), sig. A.iv*v*; see also Derek Brewer (ed.), *Chaucer: The*

Critical Heritage, 2 vols (London: Routledge and Kegan Paul, 1978), vol. 1, pp. 76–7.
10 James Simpson, 'Chaucer's presence and absence, 1400–1550', in Piero Boitani and Jill Mann (eds), *The Cambridge Companion to Chaucer* (Cambridge: Cambridge University Press, 2nd edn, 2003), pp. 251–69 (p. 253).
11 A. S. G. Edwards, 'History in print from Caxton to 1543', forthcoming. I am grateful to Professor Edwards for sharing this piece with me ahead of publication. On Caxton's treatment of Trevisa and intervention in historiography, see further Kathleen Tonry, 'Reading history in Caxton's *Polychronicon*', *Journal of English and Germanic Philology*, 111 (2012), 169–98.
12 On Caxton's histories of the early 1480s and their textual affiliations, see Lister M. Matheson, 'Printer and scribe: Caxton, the *Polychronicon*, and the *Brut*', *Speculum*, 60 (1985), 593–614.
13 Ranulph Higden, *Polychronicon*, trans. John Trevisa (Westminster, 1482, STC 13438), sig. A.iiiv.
14 William Caxton, *Chronicles of England* (Westminster, 1482, STC 9992), sig. y.ivr.
15 Higden, *Polychronicon*, fol. ccclxxxxr.
16 There is also perhaps a sense that the kind of writing Trevisa is engaged in is more open-ended, and *designed* to be supplemented as Edwards argues in 'History in print'. See further N. F. Blake, 'Caxton's language', in his *William Caxton and English Literary Culture* (London and Rio Grande: Hambledon Press, 1991), pp. 137–47, who argues that Caxton kept his language simple and as a translator did not seek to expand his vocabulary through contact with foreign works.
17 Machan, 'Early modern Middle English', p. 301.
18 Churchill Babington (ed.), *Polychronicon Ranulphi Higden, Monachi Cestrensis, Together with the English Translations of John Trevisa and of an Unknown Writer of the Fifteenth Century*, vol. 1 (London: Longman, Green, Longman, Roberts, and Green, 1865) p. lxiii; the table is on pp. lxiv–lxvi.
19 Babington (ed.), *Polychronicon Ranulphi Higden*, p. lxvii.
20 *OED* s.v. won | wone v. I.1.a.
21 Caxton, *Chronicles of England*, ch. xiii, sig. b.ir.
22 While the *OED* entry in question is an old one (first published in 1914) and not fully revised, after a search through *EEBO* I have not found anything to contradict it. The adjective *shrewed*, in its negative Middle English sense, is in regular use in incunables, and more common than the noun *shrewedness*. The latter first appears in print in Mirk's *Festial* in Pynson's 1493 text (STC 17960), where charity, it is said, 'worcheth no shrewedenesse'. But as the *EEBO* search confirms, *shrewedness* appears much less often and in the second half of the century, as the *OED* suggests, it becomes rare.

23 Babington (ed.), *Polychronicon Ranulphi Higden*, p. 153; Higden, *Polychronicon*, book 1, ch. 18, sig. xxii*v*.
24 Aesop, *Here begynneth the Book of the Subtyl Historyes and Fables of Esope* (Westminster, 1484, STC 175), fol. 104*r*.
25 Geoffrey Chaucer, *The Book of Fame made by G. Chaucer* (Westminster, 1483, STC 5087), sig. c.vi*v*; cf. *House of Fame*, line 1627 in *The Riverside Chaucer*, gen. ed. Larry D. Benson (Oxford: Oxford University Press, 3rd edn, 1988); *Parson's Tale*, fragment X, line 442, in *The Riverside Chaucer*.
26 Higden, *Polychronicon*, sig. A.ii*v*.
27 Lerer, 'William Caxton', esp. pp. 737–8. The first English use of 'Middle Age' in a chronological sense is attributed in the *OED* to the 1570 edition of Foxe's *Actes and Monuments* (s.v. middle age, 2.a); I think this is dubious, as I have discussed at greater length in 'Middle', in Elizabeth Emery and Richard Utz (eds), *Medievalism: Key Critical Terms* (Cambridge: D. S. Brewer, 2014), pp. 141–7. But there is no doubt that, as the headnote to the *OED* entry shows, the concept of a 'middle time', in various Latin phrases, was commonplace from the middle of the fifteenth century onwards.
28 Lerer, 'William Caxton', p. 723.
29 William Kuskin, *Symbolic Caxton: Literary Culture and Print Capitalism* (Notre Dame: University of Notre Dame Press, 2008), pp. 4–5.

10
'Hail graybeard bard': Chaucer in the nineteenth-century popular consciousness
Stephen Knight

Mass-mediating medievalism

Chaucerians have long perceived and applauded the return that the poet enjoyed in the nineteenth century from a period of extra-canonical positioning, and three scholars have most notably gathered and commented on the available material: Caroline Spurgeon, Derek Brewer and Stephanie Trigg. Thanks to modern mechanisation, this chapter can explore the foothills, even the arid plains, of nineteenth-century Chaucerian reception through the range of magazines and newspapers that have become electronically accessible in recent years. There are now available – from Portland, Oregon, to Dundee, Scotland, and at many points in between – statements, reviews and reports of lectures or events not to be found in Spurgeon's extensive index, or considered by previous commentators. This material often offers multi-level confirmation of known patterns of Chaucer reception – notably of him as a natural and national figure appealing to contemporary Romanticism and patriotism, as well as providing a medium for both young people's education and scholarly self-realisation. But this survey's new revelations also offer a range of curiosities and contradictions, along with elaborations of, and exceptions to, existing knowledge – as well as a few entertainments: even a victorious Victorian racehorse named Chaucer.

National Chaucer

Helen Phillips sees the late Romantic, and long continuing, interest in Chaucer as poet of the past and the natural world as based on 'the era's own anxious and conflicted responses to rapid urbanisation', whereas Charlotte Morse describes the key quality Chaucer offered the late Romantics and the subsequent Chaucer popularisers as 'the new valuation of sincerity, the overriding (and complex) virtue that emerges during the shift from the aristocratic, universalist, pro-French culture of the earlier eighteenth century to the middle class, nationalist, and determinedly native culture of the early nineteenth century'.[1]

While such strong foci can be found in the media-based Chaucer references, many of them are more simply historical, patriotic or even random in their transmission of poetic prestige. In 1806–07 Thomas Stothard, a well-known painter and Royal Academy Librarian, not only produced his painting of *The Pilgrimage to Canterbury* (see plate 6), which appears to have been inspired by, while structurally reversing, Blake's own early version of the scene (see plate 7), and in its engraved form sold many copies – Scott had one at Abbotsford[2] – but he also presented to the Prince of Wales a 'little Cabinet Picture' on the same topic. *The Times* reported that the Prince admired it enough to accept graciously its dedication to him.[3] Conservative as this event is, it at least has some sense of historicity, unlike the idealistic antiquity identified by Professor Silliman, who was reported in Washington DC in 1820 as having seen at the British Museum 'an Egyptian pebble, which, being broken, discovered, on both faces of the fracture, a striking likeness of the poet Chaucer'.[4]

At a socially different level, Chaucerian references can apparently relate to the radical politics of the time, as with an anonymous letter of 1820 to the *Morning Chronicle* that recommends Hazlitt's suggestion that Chaucer be reworked in a modern context, and proposes someone do this with the Summoner, to reveal modern elements of 'persecution and intimidation'.[5] Contacts with the traditions of an earlier period continued, and the substantially enlarged range of Chaucer's 'works' from that time could still operate. A thoughtful anonymous essay on 'Chaucer, and his testament of love' appeared in the *Edinburgh Magazine* in 1826, and *The Floure and the Leafe* was included in the influential collection *The Riches of Chaucer* (1835): Phillips comments on 'the extraordinary esteem' of this poem through the period.[6]

Some early references to Chaucer offer a bland version of the Romantic response, like the short essay reprinted in Calcutta's *Oriental Observer* in 1833 from the *New Monthly Magazine*'s 'Chat upon men and books' series, which celebrates the clerk as an Oxbridge-type scholar and suggests Chaucer also went to college, as he is 'a great bookworm'.[7] Other responses can be more fully developed, at least in terms of history: the 'Geoffrey Chaucer' essay by W. H. Forman in the 1840 series, 'Lives of the British poets', is quite scholarly, though as usual at this time it spells his contemporary's name as 'Wickliffe' and dates Chaucer's birth to 1328 – and makes almost no reference to the poetry.[8]

In her account of this period, Morse focuses on a friend of Keats and Hunt, Charles Cowden Clarke, and his avatars Charles Knight and John Saunders. They all worked in publishing, but also at Mechanics' Institutes and for the newly formed Society for the Diffusion of Useful Knowledge (SDUK). Morse sees them as 'reformist bourgeois popularizers' who were 'situated between the aristocracy and its cultivation of chivalry and extravagant gothic revivalism, on one side, and a radical and potentially violent industrialized working class, on the other'.[9] As part of the liberal SDUK project, Clarke produced in 1833 *Tales from Chaucer in Prose: Designed Chiefly for the Use of Young Persons*. This bold venture into Chaucer for the young seems to have been unduly early: it was some forty years before much headway was gained in this direction. The difficulty of the fourteenth-century language was a recurring issue at the time: 'rude as it now appears', to quote J. H. Hippisley's rather scholarly *Chapters on Early English Literature* of 1837.[10] Such problems were avoided by translation in Clarke's *Tales from Chaucer* and in his next collection, a major feature of this group's work, the modernised collection *The Riches of Chaucer* (1835) – the title seems to imply modern economic prestige. Offering a full range of texts, volume 1 provided the *General Prologue* and eleven *Canterbury Tales* (not the vulgar ones, but including the anti-clerical *Friar's Tale*), while volume 2 contained *Troilus and Criseyde*, the *Legend of Good Women*, the dream poems and lyrics, as well as *The Romaunt of the Rose* and, once again, *The Floure and the Leafe*.

The subtitle to *The Riches of Chaucer* proclaims: *In Which His Impurities Have Been Expunged and His Spelling Modernised; His Rhythm Accentuated; and His Obsolete Terms Explained*. Forbidding as that might sound, it is in fact much like a twentieth-century school edition, with spelling modernised where that was easy, e.g. 'heart' for 'herte'; final -e syllables are marked with an accent when modern readers would miss them; and both glosses and explanatory comments appear on the page. There is a Romantic element in this edition when the 'Life', drawing heavily on William Godwin, turns to the poetry and identifies Chaucer's 'native feeling' and his 'sweet and earnest sincerity'.[11] The review in the *Examiner*, pursuing idealism rather than history, said: 'We have much pleasure in welcoming this book, because we think it likely to produce, in many excellent quarters, a taste for one of the greatest of English poets, whose writings are as real as truth, and deserve to be universal.'[12]

Clarke's initiative had impact, and was followed in 1840 by *The Poems of Geoffrey Chaucer, modernized*, edited by Richard Hengist Horne, poet and journalist (he had changed his second name from Henry in medievalist enthusiasm), who later spent nearly twenty years in Australia, from the gold rush onward. Here, too, 'modernized' meant re-spelling and occasional verbal substitutions, rather than full-scale translation or adaptation. A review in the *Illustrated London News* found in the book Chaucer's 'magic eloquence', but also linked his work to many classical references.[13] Elsewhere, Horne's Chaucer was seen as culturally patriotic, being celebrated in seasonal terms on New Year's Day 1841 in the *Court Magazine* as resembling 'Old-English sirloin, lately smoking at the Christmas board'.[14] Not everyone was so positive about modernising Chaucer: in 1845, the *Penny Satirist* reported, presumably unsatirically, that Samuel Boyce, author of the poem 'The Deity', was employed to translate Chaucer into modern English, 'which he did with great spirit, at the rate of threepence a line' – but was 'at last found famished to death with a pen in his hand'.[15]

As is suggested by the *Court Magazine* review, Chaucer's socially medial values did not make him inaccessible higher up. The *Morning Post*, in May 1842, printed two stanzas, signed with the initials R. M. M. and entitled 'The poet Chaucer to Prince Albert at the Bal Costumé' – though Chaucer did not actually speak:

> When Chaucer stood before Philippa's throne,
>   Wise Edward's brow was bent with glorious cares;
> And round the parents, like a halo, shone
>   The radiant deeds of England's Royal heirs.
> As is the Poet here before his time:
>   But thou, good Prince, will such a fault excuse.
> And let the homage of old English rhyme
>   Now rest prophetic for the later muse.[16]

The Bal Costumé must be that of 5 May 1842 when Victoria and Albert appeared in splendid fourteenth-century costumes with the arms of Edward III on the wall. Stephanie Trigg drew attention to Edwin Landseer's famous 1846 painting of the scene (see plate 8).[17] The link between Chaucer and Edward III was normal in the period, helped by the 1328 birthdate. The 'fault' of

'Hail graybeard bard'

line six remains obscure, as Chaucer in fact seems present after, not 'before', his time. Contemporaries also noticed problems: *The Times* received a letter from 'A Constant Reader' saying 'these stanzas I have read and re-read, without having been as yet able to form the most remote conception of their meaning or point'. The Editor replies: 'We confess ourselves altogether unable to give the explanation requested by our Correspondent.'[18]

Not only confused royalists engaged with the emergent national figure. Soon after its establishment in July 1841, *Punch* started its series on 'The old English poets' in early 1843 with the words, 'Chaucer is known as the father of English poetry, and seems to have left his offspring very shabbily off, if we are to judge by the mass of antiquated gammon he has bequeathed to posterity'.[19] This short essay raises Chaucer's political engagements (calling him 'a meddling old humbug'), and also his alleged debts. The Nun's Priest's farmyard cock and the Wife of Bath are admired, but the author complains it is not clear how closely the Reeve was in fact shaven.

Punch returned to the topic briefly at the end of 1843 when Chaucer was the first name offered in a series called 'Comicography, or the history of humorous writing': this first 'Jokewright' flourished 'towards the end of the fifteenth century' (possibly itself a joke), and mocked the church. The entry concludes with a new, robust, if metrically uncertain, parody:

> Whan that this Dan had romed atte his wille
> And gan speke on Tipperarie Hill
> And sayde thus: Herkeneth if you lest,
> Let see now who shal have the beste.
> And whan Saxon preeste demaund tithes
> Shall be ypaid with staffs and eke seythes,
> And crie Out and Harrow, for the Nones,
> So that ye may not paie, but brake bones;
> And for a geste ye make the preeste flie,
> To siten down myself *par compaignie*.[20]

Comic and satirical reference came together in 1847 with 'The Poleesemanne – an omitted character in Chaucer's Canterbury pilgrims', by 'The Man in the Moon', published in the *Illustrated London News* (the next item is an excerpt from the brand-new *Dombey and Son*). The fourteen-line passage concludes:

> With servaunt maydes wel liked hym to be,
> And eke for colde mete grete love hadde hee,

Hee loked grym, men shulde nat ate hym laughe,
And yn hys honde hee helde a sturdye staffe.[21]

A more serious and extended Chaucerian parallel was 'The pilgrims to Rome (after Chaucer)', which appeared in *Punch* in 1851 (curiously, the Great Exhibition issue) and rewrote the opening of the *General Prologue*, beginning 'Whanne that ye firste of April breedeth jokès' and gave entries for lord, squire and maid. The modern lord is not a warrior knight but an oppressive aristocrat: 'Him seemed it a sinne that pourè elves / Should thinken or should reden for themselvès'; he was a devout Catholic and 'His Hall, I wot, was sely Pugin's glory'. His son the squire was 'An Exquisite and a Young Englander' who was 'at parties serviceable' and also 'spent much time in the stable'. The modern maid only 'did much incline' to be a nun, 'And often, after Almacke's, down ye staires, / Came she at nine next morn for early prayères': more like the prioress, she 'entuned' the divine service in her nose, but now the effect is 'As don ye Highland bagpipes in ye strete'.[22]

While nineteenth-century Chaucer could be at times comic and satiric, the new thrust of national Chaucer was operating steadily, and growing in its extent. Though Clarke's 1833 attempt to include children seems to have been unrealistic, there were now editions for poorer and newer readers, as evinced by Clarke's colleague John Saunders in his still-modernised *Canterbury Tales from Chaucer* of 1847, which *The Economist*'s reviewer found 'neat, cheap, and well-edited'.[23]

As a result of this wider dissemination, the poet was also now found worth remembering properly in public. 'A Rambler among the Tombs' complained in *The Times* in 1845 about 'the present dilapidated state of Chaucer's tomb in Westminster Abbey' – the name being now very hard to read – and there should be a collection to restore it as there was in 1778 for Spenser. Others debated the validity of the tomb itself, as Thomas A. Prendergast has discussed in his analysis of 'the Chaucerian uncanny', but the writer in *The Times* connected the memorial with conscious feeling, saying that when it was restored he and others could 'point our children to the place where repose the ashes of our great English poet, whose lovely tale of the patience of Griselda has often drawn tears from our eyes'[24] – respect, medievalism and sentimentality combine. It is interesting that an 1850 scholarly report on 'The restoration of Chaucer's monument', then under way, appeared in the *Lady's Newspaper*.[25]

But the poet was not merely an honoured memory; matching his national and natural validity in the present could be his apparent foresight. Under the title 'Chaucer and the Exhibition', speaking of the stunning pavilion for the 1851 Great Exhibition, the *Liverpool Mercury* – quite likely drawing on another source, as was common – saw 'a prophetic faculty' in his prefiguration of this new 'Palace of Glass' in quotations from the *House of Fame*: 'the temple made of glass' with 'many a pilar Of metal' visited by a 'right great company' from 'sundry regions' of 'al kinds of conditions', and overall 'Such a great congregation Of folks as I saw roam about'.[26]

In general, the Chaucer of this early-to-mid-nineteenth-century re-imagination had a mobile multiplicity, past and modern, national and spiritual, learned and popular. Lawrence Horne summed it up in a poem published in the forward-looking *London Pioneer* in 1847 (formerly the *Penny Satirist*), seeming to provide a very English response to the coming year of revolution:

> To Chaucer
> Hail ! graybeard bard ! father of our land's lay !
>   Crowned with still circling centuries of years,
>   How reverend thy thought-visioned form appears,
> Germ of the mighty mind of modern day !
>   Who chased the soul's dense midnight gloom away !
>   Great harbinger of intellectual day,
>   Who wakened up to life the things of clay
>   With thine immortal melody, 'till they
> Become a spirit-moved, thought-uttering throng !
> Homer of our old Fatherland ! I see –
>   I picture how thy now quaint rhyme hath fired
>   Our rude forefathers, who their sons inspired
> With glowing thought that had its source in thee ![27]

Chaucerian scholarship and lectures

Though Catholicism might have passed, with what Horne here calls 'the soul's dense midnight gloom', forces were at work to make the understanding of Chaucer require longer and more scholarly hours, and that around the world. A strong early contender was the well-known poet and scholar James Russell Lowell, of Boston's Lowell Institute, founded by his own family, though he also had affiliation with Harvard. He gave, in 1855, a set of lectures on English poets, with Chaucer interestingly late at number five. Lowell set out Chaucer's well-known three literary periods

(French, Italian and English), still gave his birth as 1328 and used the spelling Wickcliffe. He found in Chaucer 'a sentiment of seclusion', presumably looking back to the Romantics' supra-social interests, but also saw him as a historical realist, who, attractively for the present, 'held up a mirror to contemporary life' – and yet his work was also gratifyingly idealistic: Chaucer 'quietly and naturally rises above the conventional into the universal'.[28]

Lowell was not alone in America in this interest. In November 1857, Henry Coppee, Professor of English Literature at the University of Pennsylvania, Philadelphia, made Chaucer the first of a set of literary lectures. Coppee was reported as having dealt with 'numerous facts from the history of the times' and 'especially from the reform movements in regard to religion, language and social institutions'; there also appeared 'graceful and impressive elocution' and 'numerous brilliant touches of wit and humor'; the next lecture was reported to be on 'Spencer'.[29]

In Britain, the academy was slower to engage, but there were other institutions. William Palmer gave a paper on the *Canterbury Tales* to the Leicester Literary and Philosophical Society in 1854. He focused on the *Knight's Tale* and stressed the 'poetic and dramatic bearing' of the tales, and their realism and humour, before discussing Chaucer's links to Boccaccio and Dante. He stated – the idea is quite common – that in a later period Chaucer would have been a playwright because of his capacity to create human voices interrelating. Palmer recommended using, as he did, a non-modernised edition like Thomas Wright's of 1847–51, 'the best now extant', insisting it was necessary for readers to overcome language problems: the man who proposed the vote of thanks, Mr Caillard, said he enjoyed the talk but could not understand the language of the old poetry.[30]

In much the same context, George Dawson in 1859 delivered two lectures on Chaucer at the Birmingham & Midland Institute, which at that time apparently focused on secondary education. In the second lecture, the one reported, he stressed Chaucer's power of realism – 'He showed Shakespeare how to depict'.[31] For Dawson, Chaucer was sincere, hearty, frank, jovial, a man who shared Wordsworth's love of nature, and it was important to do a little work and read him in the original. The next lecture, puzzlingly, was on Pepys.

A major English university response appears to be indicated by a report of a talk given at Woodstock, not far from Oxford, by the Rev. E. B. Jones in 1857, titled 'Chaucer and his connexion with Woodstock'.³² He linked the poet not only to Woodstock, but also to *The Cuckoo and the Nightingale*, which had in the past been accepted into the canon. However, the reverend was described as a 'Senior Proctor' at Oxford, which is a disciplinary rather than academic role – and the Woodstock connection, often discussed in this period, was later shown to be an error: in fact, Henry IV's queen in 1411 gave a Woodstock house to Thomas, Chaucer's son.

The more serious of these lecturers were now using a non-modernised Middle English text – sometimes from Tyrwhitt's frequently reprinted 1775 edition, but also from new non-modernised editions as the editorial element of the professionalisation of Chaucer's reception was developing. Thomas Wright's edition of 1847–51 had a substantial impact, then Robert Bell produced *The Poetical Works of Geoffrey Chaucer*, based on it, in 1854–56. The *Newcastle Courant* reviewed Bell's edition favourably, praising the 'purity of the text' and the stress on historical context. Wright's text was, as Thomas Ross explained, the first to use the new classics-oriented 'best text approach', which had become standard, but the text he chose as 'best' was the unreliable Harley 7334, subject to heavy, and pervasive, scribal editing. Its unduly persuasive power seems to have started because it belonged to an earl powerful in Urry's day and continued because it was later sold to the British Museum.³³

In 1864, Professor Hiram Corson produced in Philadelphia an edition of the *Legend of Good Women*, with on-page glossary and explanations. A reviewer felt the editor had 'a most scholarly manner', while also 'shaping his book to meet a popular want'.³⁴ As David Matthews has shown, the general public interest in Chaucer, from Godwin on, was now being supplemented, and in a way displaced, by a new scholarly rigour in editing.³⁵ This was indicated by a rather learned article on 'Chaucer and his editors' in a major London paper, the *Sunday Times*, in 1866, which identified Urry's work as 'execrable', and saw Wright and Bell as the best editors so far. In the following year, the *Examiner* saw more improvement on the way in the work of Richard Morris, 'our foremost scholar in Early English' – though for his edition he, like Wright and Bell, still used Harley 7334. The reviewer felt Morris's edition would 'give a new impulse to the exact study of the language', as well as stressing 'the essentially dramatic spirit' of the text: the Chaucer-as-early-Shakespeare argument is pressed.³⁶

While editing was making serious steps forward, biographical and historical scholarship on Chaucer was also moving from passing comment towards professional accuracy. Some of this was general and nationalistic, as in Henry Morley's *English Writers* volume 2 part 1, 'From Chaucer to Dunbar', which was favourably reviewed in the general periodical *John Bull*, commenting how the characters of the Italian story of the *Knight's Tale* were given 'totally new and English garb'.[37] Morley was Professor of English Literature at University College London, which was by now forty years old but distinctly modern in curriculum compared to Oxbridge. A more focused and influential scholarly source was Matthew Bourne's *Chaucer's England* (1867), reviews of which appeared across England in the *Manchester Courier*, the *Leeds Daily News* and, from London, the *Penny Illustrated Paper* and the *Morning Post*. In a notably long and expert analysis, the *Sunday Times* found the criticism 'free, subtle and filled with spirit' and summed up the book as 'one that all readers of English literature should possess'.[38]

Professional scholarship had a new focus when F. J. Furnivall founded the Chaucer Society in 1868 – funds were provided by the major American scholar, F. J. Child, who was keen to see a reliable edition of Chaucer. Defeating, by omission, the influence of the unreliable Harley 7334, the imposing *Six-Text Print of Chaucer's Canterbury Tales* was edited by Furnivall; however, the volatile Harley manuscript was one of the two later added to make the *Eight-Text* edition on which Skeat worked. As Trigg has outlined, Furnivall deliberately chose three sources in public hands, as well as three still privately owned, as a sign of his insistence on broad public access to Chaucer – and to other cultures, past and present.[39] The *Six-Text* set of principal manuscripts – not itself an edition for readers but for scholarly use – appeared in 1868–71 and was given a learned and approving welcome in the *Pall Mall Gazette* in 1871. Its 'Temporary preface', published in 1871, was analysed in the *Examiner*'s round-up of other more general Chaucer editions in 1872, where Furnivall's insistence on the birthdate of 1340 was noted, though with some scepticism.[40] The *Six-Text* edition had worldwide impact, being soon reviewed in favourable and scholarly terms in Milwaukee's *Daily Sentinel*, reprinting the piece from *Macmillan's Magazine of London*.[41]

This new turn towards the scholarly and professional reading of Chaucer did not mean the influence of the Romantics was forgotten. National and natural continuity appeared in an essay by A. Smith in the *Cheltenham Chronicle* in 1870, summing up both the nationalist Chaucer – he wrote, 'when the Saxon and Norman race had become fused' – and the natural poet of the Romantics, who was as 'fresh, charming, fanciful as the springtime itself' and, like any contemporary writer, was 'half humorous, half melancholy'.[42] The *Chronicle* continued in the following year with an essay praising Chaucer's 'native energy' and 'unformed, unique language', especially admiring the way in which 'the limped [*sic*] fountain' of his work had influence on 'the spiritual part of our being'.[43] This tradition was also found in the Rev. H. D. Atkinson's 1869 talk in the *Churchman's Shilling Magazine*, 'Stray thoughts about old Chaucer', which summed up by saying that Chaucer's work was 'neglected out of all reason' and urging a new edition of Clarke's 1835 generalist edition.[44]

The physical memorabilia of Chaucer were increasingly prominent. He was a 'New Addition' to Madame Tussaud's increasingly celebrated waxworks – along with William Caxton, the *Sunday Times* noted in 1862.[45] In 1868, the *Morning Post* reported the establishment of a Chaucer window near his Westminster Abbey tomb 'to embody his intellectual labours and his position among his contemporaries'.[46] In 1869, the London *Daily News* reported that the threat from 1867 to pull down the Tabard Inn had been defeated; but then, in 1873, a report came from America that it had now been sold to be demolished.[47] A fuller, less volatile account of the locations of 'the tenants of Chaucer's London' was provided in Walter Thornbury's *Old and New London* (1874), approvingly reviewed in the *Manchester Times*.[48]

The comic possibilities of Chaucer had not quite been swamped in scholarly seriousness. The *Milwaukee Daily Sentinel*, which would soon admire the work of Furnivall, reported in 1866 the opinion of American humourist Artemus Ward that 'It is a pity that Chaucer, who has genius, was so uneducated. He is the wuss speller I know of'.[49] The same spirit, evinced in 'The Poleesemanne' from 1847 (possibly the source), seems behind 'The policeman's tale', published in the London *Punch* competitor, *Fun*, in 1875, where several police bash a man lying in the 'Haimaurkette' (London's dubious Haymarket), who has in fact been dead for two days – so revealing 'what doltes are in auctoritie'.[50] A lighter version of the popular festive spirit may have been behind the naming of the racehorse Chaucer, which won the Glasgow Stakes at Doncaster, England, in 1870.[51]

Chaucer scholarship had flourished in the mid-nineteenth century, but the general popular connection to the medieval poet, itself an inheritance of Romantic and liberal traditions, was not overwhelmed by that academicisation. In the remainder of the century, the scholars would continue to thrive in their Chaucerian activities, but a wider audience would be assembled for the poet, notably among younger people and those who tended and educated them, primarily women.

Women and children and Chaucer

Engagement with Chaucer by scholarly women increased from the middle of the century. Morse notes that Clarke's wife, Maria Victoria Novello, a Shakespeare scholar, published an essay on Griselda in 1853 in the *Ladies' Companion*.[52] An 1857 issue of the *Englishwoman's Review and Drawing Room Journal* included, under the title 'Chaucer in a new dress', a review of a French translation of *The Floure and the Leafe* by the Chevalier de Chatelain, followed by 'Le cri des enfants', his translation of 'The cry of the children', an anti-child-labour poem by Elizabeth Barrett Browning.[53] There seems a clear connection with the large numbers of well-bred and well-educated women who read French: a review by Basil Pickering, offering both general comment and a detailed analysis of the translator's treatment of the *Tales*' opening, appeared in the *Englishwoman's Review and Drawing Room Journal*; and a review of de Chatelain's work also appeared in the *Lady's Newspaper* – though it was also noted in the generally cultured the *Sunday Times* and the distinctly radical *Reynolds' Magazine*: the editor G. W. M. Reynolds's strong interest in France probably led to the last connection.[54]

When *Beeton's Christmas Annual* for 1869 offered 'Modern Canterbury Tales', the *Englishwomen's Domestic Magazine* responded favourably, saying 'The men and women of the world are the same'.[55] There may be an implied interest in using this popular annual with children, and that idea was evidently behind the first re-issuing since 1833, in time for Christmas 1870, of Clarke's *Tales from Chaucer in Prose and Verse, Designed Chiefly for Young Persons*.[56] In 1876, *Chaucer for Children* – with, as Phillips notes, some stress on 'natural Chaucer', arranged and illustrated by Mary Haweis[57] – was reviewed among 'Christmas books' by London's *Graphic*, while the essay on 'The father of English poetry' in *Aunt Judy's Magazine* of 1879 started by addressing 'our young friends'.[58] 'Peeps at the poets' in *Kind Words for Young Friends* of 1879 offered a lively account of Chaucer, though some tales were avoided as 'unfortunately bespattered by the coarseness of the age'.[59] 'The children's column' in the *Leeds Mercury* of 1880 was about

Chaucer's knight; there was a short biography and description of Chaucer in the *Young Folks' Paper* in 1885;[60] Griselda was the main figure in the Chaucer-focused 'Types of virtue, or ideal heroines of English writers' in *Girls' Own Paper* in 1888; and Mrs Hamilton King wrote a fifteen-page essay on Chaucer in the first 'Studies of great English poets' in *Every Girl's Annual* for 1891.[61]

There were also events for the young focusing on Chaucer. Mary Haweis appeared again, this time organising a 'Chaucer ball' for children at Christmas 1881, where a major scholar attended – the report in *Funny Folks*, a magazine with pictures aimed at the young, said he gave 'Furnivall-uable services'.[62] At Hartington village school in Derbyshire, in 1893, a series of 'tableaux vivants' focusing, once again, on 'Pacient Griselda' was much admired by the local newspaper.[63] In 1895 a more elaborate 'Chaucer pageant' was organised at a fine house at Otterspool, Liverpool, by a ladies' charity for 'young girls in peril'; the entertainment included a play entitled 'A Riddle', based on the *Wife of Bath's Tale*, written by Walter Raleigh, Professor of English at Cambridge.[64]

Late nineteenth-century Chaucer

While the young were being included in the overall reception of Chaucer, earlier traditions continued. Clarke's original, modernised and adapted edition from 1835, *The Riches of Chaucer*, was reprinted, with over six hundred pages, in 1870, and welcomed in *John Bull*.[65] A contemporary version of Romantic Chaucer could still appear: in 1875, the essay 'Chaucer as the spring-poet' stressed his 'quaint and musical beauty', but opened by noting that the country where the essay was directed lacked that kind of spring – it appeared in the *Friend of India*.[66] Continuities could be more convincing: the *Monthly Packet of Evening Readings for Members of the English Church*, founded in 1851 to counter the Catholicising forces of the Oxford Movement, was later in the century attracted to Chaucer as a less-than-mystical medieval figure. A. Weber wrote on the 'Good counsel of Chaucer' in 1879, stressing the author's 'intense humanity'; in 1889, Eva Knatchbull-Hugessen discussed with some authority the *General Prologue* and the *Clerk's Tale*. The magazine was also open to scholarship: the previous monthly issue discussed Chaucer's 'Language and versification', while a later issue offered a knowledgeable essay on 'Chaucer's England'.[67]

Humour also survived. The *Los Angeles Times*, in 1882, offered a short story from 'The modern Canterbury Tales': a doctor advises a mean patient from Sacramento to rub turpentine on his skin; the doctor hopes the pain will make him pay his bill. The verse was modern and the author was appropriately named 'A. Doggrell Jr'.[68] A less negative updating appeared in the ultra-modern pages of *Cycling*, which offered a poem in good Middle English, with comic illustrations of knights and pilgrims on bicycles: the knight (riding a fine Beeston Humber) 'ypunctured privilie with sharpe sper ye Miller's tyer' (see plate 9).[69]

But the dominant form of Chaucerian reception in the later nineteenth century was the growing range and strengthening weight of scholarly analysis of the poet and his context. In 1883, a firm letter by T. H. W. to *The Times* dismissed the connection of Chaucer to Woodstock, observing that it was his son Thomas who had the house there, and noting that Godwin first disseminated this mistake.[70] Other contributions were made at a high level: Arthur Gilman's scholarly essay on 'Chaucer's religious sympathies', arguing for the poet's proto-reformation position, appeared in the *Churchman* in 1878 and was reported in San Francisco's *Daily Evening Bulletin*.[71] In 1883, the *Graphic* printed M. G. Watkins's full and intelligent account of 'Chaucer's birds'.[72]

Public lectures continued to be publicised on both sides of the Atlantic. A striking example was by Harriet Monroe, rising poet and future founder of the important American *Poetry* magazine, who spoke in 1894 at the Newberry Library, a grand public institution established in 1887 in Chicago, arguing in highly modern terms that, in his own century, Chaucer worked 'to strengthen national pride and vitalize national character'.[73] Even Oxford finally contributed: William Courthope, Professor of Poetry 1895–1901 (then, as now, a short-term elected position) decided to orate before retiring on 'Law in taste', and in one lecture in the series used Chaucer as an archetype of 'the creation of harmonious ideas out of contrary qualities'. Apart from this idealist manoeuvre, Courthope asserted that Chaucer was still the father of the poets and 'everything in English poetry was the product of the Anglo-Saxon genius' – it and Chaucer had now gained an Oxonian gloss.[74]

Chaucer could also be seen as the equal of the most serious of modern thinkers: Arthur Galton wrote in 1885 in the *Dundee Evening Telegraph* how his work was parallel in weight and narrative richness to that of William Morris. But he could also still be part of modern folly: the same paper would, in 1898, print 'Chaucer a cockney', a paragraph from its 'London Correspondent' reporting that 'Mr Gollancz', no doubt the major Shakespearean and medieval scholar Israel Gollancz, though not known as a Chaucerian, had said Chaucer lived in Wallbrook, with William Langland as a near neighbour at Aldgate (Chaucer's actual address).[75]

Such distractions aside, the weight of the press references at the century's end was towards sound study and scholarly understanding of the great poet, now publicly disseminated in 'Home study' pages and publications like A. J. Wyatt's offering on the *Canterbury Tales* in the University Tutorial Series, covering the *General Prologue* and the *Man of Law's Tale*, which the *Morning Post* in 1897 found 'most serviceable'.[76] A transatlantic parallel was the *Oregonian*'s 'Home study circle popular studies in literature' of 1899, which had, as its first item, Morris Francis Egan's interesting and learned account of Chaucer himself.[77]

The author surpassed and patronised in the eighteenth century had returned, like other medieval formations, notably in architecture and art, to be a central imaginative force by the mid-nineteenth century, and would later solidify his position, especially in educational terms. The major London publisher and bookseller, Routledge, reported in mid-1885 sales figures for British poets in the previous year. The stars had sold around or above two thousand copies in a year: Byron, Burns, Milton, Scott, Shakespeare and, to modern people perhaps surprisingly, Moore; also close to two thousand was Felicia Hemans, the now quite uncanonical Welsh Romantic. Chaucer was in the second group, selling under a thousand – but the other poets in his category were more recent: Cowper, Hood, Pope, Shelley. Chaucer was by now a strong, steady seller, in many editions and showing varied medievalist powers, including at times rarity: a first edition of Caxton's *Canterbury Tales* sold at Sotheby's in 1897 for £1020.[78]

As school and university curricula bore down on the graybeard bard, he retained what would prove a broad and fertile range of possibilities for admiration and reinterpretation as a result of what nineteenth-century readers and writers, as reported across the now recoverable mass media of the time, had found in the depths of what Horne's poem called Chaucer's 'thought-visioned form'.

Notes

I thank very much Anna Kay, whose electronic expertise was the prime source for the range of new citations in this essay; poetic justice is involved, as she was employed with research funds made available to me during tenure of a Vice-Chancellor's Fellowship at the University of Melbourne, a position for which Stephanie Trigg was a major supporter. It is to be regretted that some of the electronic-sourced references do not offer page numbers.

1 Helen Phillips, 'Chaucer and the nineteenth-century city', in Ardis Butterfield (ed.), *Chaucer and the City*, Chaucer Studies XXXVII (Cambridge: D. S. Brewer, 2006), pp. 193–210 (p. 193); Charlotte C. Morse, 'Popularizing Chaucer in the nineteenth century', *Chaucer Review*, 38 (2003), 99–125 (p. 101).
2 Caroline Spurgeon, *Five Hundred Years of Chaucer Criticism and Allusion: 1357–1900*, 3 vols (Cambridge: Cambridge University Press, 1925), vol. 2, pp. 164–5.
3 'Thomas Stothard, fine arts, Chaucer's pilgrims', *The Times* (21 March 1807), p. 2.
4 'Professor Silliman saw in the British Museum "an Egyptian pebble"', *Daily National Intelligencer* (25 August 1820), n.p.
5 'Letter to the Editor', *Morning Chronicle* (6 December 1820), n.p.
6 'Chaucer and his testament of love', *Edinburgh Magazine and Literary Miscellany* (1 June 1826), pp. 664–5; Phillips, 'Chaucer and the nineteenth-century city', p. 194.
7 'Chaucer's scholar', *Oriental Observer* [Calcutta] (8 June 1833), p. 269.
8 W. H. Forman, 'Lives of the British poets: Geoffrey Chaucer', *Odd Fellow* (22 February 1840), n.p.
9 Morse, 'Popularizing Chaucer', p. 102.
10 J. H. Hippisley, *Chapters on Early English Literature* (London: Moxon, 1837), p. 79.
11 John Cowden Clarke (ed.), *The Riches of Chaucer*, 2 vols (London: Effingham Wilson, 1835), vol. 1, p. 47.
12 'Review of *The Riches of Chaucer*', *Examiner* (4 January 1835), n.p.
13 'Review of *The Poems of Chaucer*, ed. Richard Hengist Horne', *Illustrated London News* (5 November 1842), p. 410.
14 *Court Magazine and Monthly Critic* (1 January 1841), p. 58.
15 'Starved with a pen in his hand', *Penny Satirist* (19 July 1845), p. 1.
16 'The poet Chaucer to Prince Albert', *Morning Post* (13 May 1842), p. 3.
17 Trigg's observation was made at one of the University of Melbourne's Medieval Round Table seminars on 13 November 2017.
18 'Chaucer and Prince Albert', *The Times* (26 May 1842), p. 6.
19 'The old English poets, no. I – Chaucer', *Punch* (4 January 1843), p. 30.
20 'Comicography, or the history of humorous writing', *Punch* (5 December 1843), p. 239.
21 'The Poleesemanne', *Illustrated London News* (2 October 1847), p. 219.

22 'The pilgrims to Rome (after Chaucer)', *Punch* (20 October 1851), p. 230.
23 'Review of *The Canterbury Tales from Chaucer*, ed. John Saunders', *The Economist* (1 May 1847), p. 507.
24 Thomas A. Prendergast, 'Nineteenth-century necronationalism and the Chaucerian uncanny', in Prendergast, *Chaucer's Dead Body: From Corpse to Corpus* (New York: Routledge, 2004), pp. 71–84; 'The tomb of Chaucer', *The Times* (25 August 1845), p. 6.
25 'The restoration of Chaucer's monument', *Lady's Newspaper* (29 June 1850), p. 359.
26 'Chaucer and the Exhibition', *Liverpool Mercury* (14 June 1851), n.p.
27 Lawrence Horne, 'To Chaucer', *London Pioneer* (23 September 1847), p. 361.
28 James Russell Lowell, 'Chaucer', *Boston Daily Advertiser* (24 January 1855), n.p.
29 'Prof. Coppee's lectures', *North American and United States Gazette* [Philadelphia] (11 November 1857), p. 170.
30 'Woodstock', *Leicester Chronicle, or Commercial and Agricultural Advertiser* (15 April 1854), n.p.
31 'Mr Dawson's second lecture on "Chaucer"', *Birmingham Daily Post* (1 June 1859), n.p.
32 'Chaucer and his connexion with Woodstock', *Jackson's Oxford Journal* (31 January 1857), n.p.
33 'Review of *The Poetical Works of Geoffrey Chaucer*', *Newcastle Courant* (16 February 1855), n. p.; see also Thomas Ross, 'Thomas Wright', in Paul G. Ruggiers (ed.), *Editing Chaucer: The Great Tradition* (Norman: Pilgrim, 1984), pp. 145–56 (pp. 148–9).
34 'Literary notices', *North American and United States Gazette* [Philadelphia] (22 January 1864), p. 691.
35 David Matthews, 'Speaking to Chaucer: the poet and the nineteenth-century academy', in David Metzger, Kathleen Verduin and Leslie J. Workman (eds), *Studies in Medievalism IX: Medievalism and the Academy I* (Woodbridge: D. S. Brewer, 1997), pp. 5–25 (pp. 8–11).
36 'Review of *The Works of Geoffrey Chaucer*', *Examiner* (12 January 1867), n.p.
37 'English writers', *John Bull* (6 July 1867), p. 48.
38 *Manchester Courier* (17 March 1869), p. 3; *Penny Illustrated Paper* (17 April 1869), p. 251; *Leeds Daily News* (12 April 1869); *Morning Post* (17 May 1869), p. 3; *Sunday Times* (28 March 1869), n.p.
39 Stephanie Trigg, *Congenial Souls: Reading Chaucer from Medieval to Postmodern* (Minneapolis: University of Minnesota Press, 2002), pp. 160–73.
40 'The Chaucer Society's *Six-Text Edition* of *The Canterbury Tales*', in the *Pall Mall Gazette* (13 October 1871), n.p.; 'Chaucer', *Examiner* (10 August 1872), n.p.

41 'The Chaucer Society and its work', *Milwaukee Daily Sentinel* (2 May 1873), p. 3.
42 A. Smith, 'Chaucer', *Cheltenham Chronicle and Parish Register and General Advertiser for Gloucester* (6 September 1870), p. 2.
43 'Chaucer', *Cheltenham Chronicle and Parish Register and General Advertiser for Gloucester* (18 April 1871), p. 5.
44 Rev. H. D. Atkinson, 'Stray thoughts about old Chaucer', *Churchman's Shilling Magazine*, reported in 'Gossip about books and the arts', *Northampton Mercury* (6 February 1869), p. 3.
45 'Madame Tussaud's wax work exhibition', *Sunday Times* (28 December 1862), p. 3.
46 'The Chaucer window, Westminster Abbey', *Morning Post* (12 December 1868), p. 2.
47 'The old inns of Southwark', *Daily News* (6 February 1869), n.p.; 'An ancient inn', *Daily Evening Bulletin* [San Francisco] (24 July 1873), n.p.
48 'Review of Walter Thornbury, *Old and New London*', *Manchester Times* (7 March 1874), n.p.
49 Artemus Ward, *Milwaukee Daily Sentinel* (20 October 1866), n.p.
50 'The policeman's tale', *Fun* (26 June 1875), p. 267.
51 'Sporting intelligence', *Leeds Times* (17 September 1870), p. 8.
52 Morse, 'Popularizing Chaucer', p. 103, n. 24.
53 'Chaucer in a new dress', *Englishwoman's Review and Drawing Room Journal* (11 July 1857), p. 4.
54 'Review of *Contes de Canterbury*, trans. Chevalier de Chatelain', *Englishwoman's Review and Drawing Room Journal* (22 August 1857), p. 1; *Lady's Newspaper* (10 April 1858), p. 236; *Sunday Times* (2 August 1857), p. 2; *Reynolds's Magazine* (11 April 1858), n.p.
55 'Modern Canterbury Tales', *Englishwomen's Domestic Magazine* (1 October 1869), p. 191.
56 'Review of *Tales from Chaucer in Prose and Verse, Designed Chiefly for Young Persons*', *Western Times* (13 December 1870), p. 7.
57 Phillips, 'Chaucer and the nineteenth-century city', p. 202; Mary Flowers Braswell, *The Forgotten Chaucer Scholarship of Mary Eliza Haweis, 1848–1898* (London: Taylor & Francis, 2016).
58 'Christmas books', *Graphic* (2 December 1876), n.p.; 'The father of English poetry', in H. K. F. Gatty (ed.), *Aunt Judy's Christmas Volume* (London: Bell, 1879), p. 654.
59 'Peeps at the poets', *Kind Words for Young Friends* (1 April 1879), pp. 118–19.
60 'The children's column', *Leeds Mercury* (10 January 1880), n.p.; 'Geoffrey Chaucer', *Young Folks' Paper* (31 October 1885), p. 288.
61 Mrs Harriet Hamilton King, 'Studies of great English poets', *Every Girl's Annual* (London: Routledge, 1891), p. 1; 'Types of virtue, or ideal heroines of English writers', *Girls' Own Paper* (27 October 1888), p. 52.

62 'Chaucer ball', *Funny Folks* [London] (28 January 1882), p. 27.
63 'Tableaux vivants', *Derbyshire Times and Chesterfield Herald* (11 February 1893), p. 8.
64 'Chaucer pageant at Otterspool', *Liverpool Mercury* (20 June 1895), n.p.
65 'Review of *The Riches of Chaucer*', *John Bull* (17 December 1870), p. 872.
66 'Chaucer as the spring-poet', *Friend of India* [Calcutta] (12 June 1875), pp. 522–3.
67 A. Weber, 'Good counsel of Chaucer', *Monthly Packet* (1 September 1879), p. 219; Eva Knatchbull-Hugessen, 'Papers on English literature VIII: Chaucer: Prologue and Clerk's Tale', *Monthly Packet* (1 March 1889), pp. 278–90; 'Papers on English literature VII: Chaucer: language and versification', *Monthly Packet* (1 February 1889), pp. 178–89; 'Chaucer's England', *Monthly Packet* (1 November 1896), pp. 519–26.
68 'The modern Canterbury Tales', *Los Angeles Times* (3 October 1882), n.p.
69 'Ye Canterburie pilgrymage (ye real thynge)', *Cycling* [London] (10 April 1897), pp. 287–8.
70 'Letter', *The Times* (27 June 1883), p. 6.
71 'Chaucer's religious sympathies', *Daily Evening Bulletin* [San Francisco] (10 August 1878), n.p.
72 'Chaucer's birds', *Graphic* (30 September 1882), n.p.
73 'Poetry of Chaucer', *Daily Inter Ocean* [Chicago] (9 February 1894), p. 4.
74 'Professor Courthope on Chaucer', *The Times* (5 June 1899), p. 6.
75 Arthur Galton, 'Morris and Chaucer', *Evening Telegraph* [Dundee] (11 September 1885), p. 4; 'Chaucer a cockney', *Evening Telegraph* [Dundee] (2 June 1898), p. 3.
76 'University tutorial series: Chaucer, *The Canterbury Tales*', *Morning Post* (28 July 1897), n.p.
77 'The *Oregonian*'s home study circle', *Morning Oregonian* (4 April 1899), p. 9.
78 'The national taste in poets', *Evening Telegraph* [Dundee] (20 November 1885), p. 3; 'A great price', *Denver Evening Post* (27 February 1896), p. 3.

11
Chaucer as Catholic child in nineteenth-century English reception

Andrew Lynch

'A Catholic, but not very keen'

In *The Poet Chaucer*, first published in 1949, Nevill Coghill applied to Chaucer's religious outlook something once said to him by 'a Swiss cathedral organist': '"*Oui, je suis catholique, mais pas très aigu*"' ('Yes, I'm a Catholic, but not very keen').[1] Coghill's comment may be said to reflect the mainstream view of Chaucer's religion in critical reception throughout much of the twentieth century, picking up a mood that had been established by 1900. The nineteenth century was the period in which 'the Father of English poetry' changed from being a satirist of universal character types to a figure of 'simple' and sincere piety, and then to a subtle secularist with agnostic tendencies. Linda Georgianna's survey of critics as diverse as George Lounsbury, E. Talbot Donaldson and Derek Pearsall argues that the 'Protestant' Chaucer of the sixteenth-century Reformers strangely survived into late modernity. She identifies a shared critical assumption that Chaucer could not possibly have accepted many aspects of medieval Catholicism at face value, including the apparent outlook and discourse of his religious tales, that his 'attitude toward prevailing religious values is most basically one of protest against a controlling, inquisitorial Church, or against a credulous, sensual piety', and that in various ways the mainstream of modern criticism 'presupposes Chaucer's privileging of rational [what she calls 'Protestant'] religion over "simplicity of belief"'.[2]

There is no need to go all the way back to the Reformation to find the basis for views of this kind. Rarely did critics of the long nineteenth century read Chaucer 'straight' as a medieval Catholic poet. Instead, there grew up a wide range of critical strategies to put Chaucer off-side with medieval Catholicism, creating interpretations in which he features in almost every conceivable non-orthodox role: zealous proto-Protestant; undoctrinal nature-worshipper;

trifler in belief; 'manly' figure of English liberty, with a religion independent of the institutional church of the day; Laodicean; and a 'child' at heart.

In what follows here, while risking over-simplification, I suggest a common element in these strategies: it was simply too hard, and generally unpalatable, in the nineteenth-century English cultural climate to credit the 'Father of English poetry' with a sincere medieval Catholicism. To identify Chaucer as an adult Catholic with a strong religious allegiance would have meant for most readers branding him as fundamentally un-'English' – subservient, superstitious and illiberal, rather than the manly, sensible, tolerant fellow most of them desired. The problem was not simply fear of the Church as 'a totalitarian, foreign power, a "feline" institution', although those sentiments continued to play a large part.[3] More generally, conventional English historiography represented religious reform, linguistic maturation, Enlightenment and the rise of state institutions as adult developments which had left behind the nation's medieval childhood, and especially its medieval religion, in an inevitable course. The Middle Ages could be somewhat forgiven when regarded as part of the 'infancy' of the race and the nation, but for those desiring to make Chaucer an honorary modern Englishman, or a timeless English 'classic', the worst way to achieve that purpose would have been to read him as a mainstream mature Catholic.

The ensuing relative neglect of religion in modern Chaucer studies has been one of the longest-lived elements of what Jeff Espie calls 'Chaucer's interpretive baggage': 'various paradigms of reception – vocabularies to describe his poetic accomplishments and techniques to imagine a relationship with him'.[4] Nineteenth-century reception of Chaucer both reacted to continuing pressures from previous centuries and did much to shape ideas of the secular poet that readers have mainly encountered ever since. Despite the greater recent interest in reading Chaucer within medieval religious culture, Nicholas Watson observes that

> In the area of religion, it seems that Chaucer still retains his traditional privilege (one no longer extended to any of his contemporaries) to be read as though his experimentalism must by definition baffle our attempts to situate him.[5]

Watson's comment acknowledges yet another iteration of the critical tendency to grant Chaucer a religious exceptionality within his own times. To be himself, as required, Chaucer must always somehow escape the limits of being medieval, whatever the conditions for that escape may be.

'Something ... childlike or childish'

Earlier nineteenth-century readings of Chaucer see him as a satirist of religious abuses, a visionary of the Reformation, a cheerful connoisseur of character and a poet of Nature. Even when it was acknowledged, as it is by Blake, that 'it appears in all the writings of Chaucer, and particularly in his Canterbury Tales, that he was very devout, and paid respect to true enthusiastic superstition',[6] the main emphasis remains on his depiction of 'the physiognomies or lineaments of universal life, beyond which Nature never steps.... As Newton numbered the stars and as Linnaeus numbered the plants, so Chaucer numbered the classes of men'.[7]

Derek Brewer sums up the nineteenth-century view of Chaucer and religion as 'related to a view of his personal temperament'; 'the general opinion ... tends to see him as something of a rationalist and therefore somewhat lukewarm in religion and not a reformer'.[8] This change partly happened because some more radical Protestant works previously wrongly attributed to Chaucer were slowly removed from the canon,[9] and his repentant 'Retraction' made its way into editions after centuries of exclusion. The long suppression of the very Catholic 'Retraction' 'suggests why the Protestantization of Chaucer's reputation encountered less resistance than it might have otherwise' and also how 'his presence as a national poet was emphasized, and the *Canterbury Tales*, in particular, came to be celebrated as his major work'.[10] Improved knowledge of Chaucer's life and works slowly made it harder to accept him as a proto-Protestant, although that belief died very hard, as I shall indicate. More generally, I suggest, the change to the 'lukewarm' Chaucer that Brewer notes occurred because the idea of him as a medieval Catholic religious poet clashed badly with the growing desire to treat him as the first and quintessentially 'English' poet, and as a much more modern and immediate presence than he had been in the eighteenth century, which emphasised his antiquity and obscurity. How was this problem to be solved by Chaucerians? One way was to keep asserting his credentials as religious reformer. Another was to make him a secularist at heart, as Brewer remarks. Another still, and the one I examine most closely here, was by stressing the sublime simplicity and child-likeness of his world-outlook, including his religion.

The 'real' Chaucer available to much of the nineteenth century was different in many ways from the one known today. Until the late 1800s, the Chaucer canon might still include Usk's *Testament of Love*, lending the poet the potential appearance of one who suffered for his religious adherence. To John Saunders in 1845 he is 'their great religious Reformer – the literary Titan who could at once pull down and build up with equal power and skill',[11] anticipating the Reformation, seen as 'one of the greatest epochs in the history of intellectual independence'.[12] Chaucer had

> set up for the guidance of his countrymen, a light, that did not shine merely to bring *them* forward, but that remains to this day, so far in advance of all that we have yet achieved, that it may serve, if we will, to bring forward ourselves, and our children ... to the remotest generations.[13]

Henry Innes maintains that 'Chaucer was a church reformer and espoused the principles of John WICKLIFFE', as shown by the fact that he 'thrashed a Friar in Fleet Street'.[14] Thomas Arnold distinguishes Wyclif and Chaucer as 'two literary movements', but pairs them in spirit: 'Admirable as Chaucer was, it must not be forgotten that Wyclif was yet more in the thick of the intellectual strife of the period than he'.[15] Less carefully, and still following William Godwin's very inaccurate but influential *Life* (1804),[16] 'H. W. D.' could write as late as 1881 that Chaucer 'took part in the great religious controversy of his time as a Wycliffite and a partisan of John of Gaunt, and suffered exile and imprisonment', spending three years in the Tower.[17] As with many such claims, the writer's respect for Chaucer as an 'Englishman' living under Edward III, 'a thoroughly English king', seems to demand no less zeal, and looks forward to an even brighter English age:

> To Shakespeare he [Chaucer] may be likened in the sturdy manliness of his religious belief – his honest reverence for all things truly sacred and holy, with an outspoken contempt for counterfeits and hypocrisy.[18]

In the same year, in one of several editions she made for children and schools, Mrs Haweis writes that the *Parson's Tale* is 'full of Wickliffism and true Protestant feeling' and that Chaucer had 'striven ... to propagate with his pen the pith of the new religious views ... long before Luther sounded the note of victory'.[19] Chaucer's anti-Catholicism, seen as vouched for by his clever satire of church abuses, if nothing else, is made a matter of the national character as much as his own, and a forecast of its great future development. Later Victorian intellectuals like Matthew Arnold would enlist literary classics to perform the moral, cultural and social labour, the 'criticism of life', traditionally undertaken by religion,[20] but it is clear that in other circles literary criticism still closely followed confessional lines.

The continuing widespread belief that Chaucer was born in 1328 helped make the author of the *Canterbury Tales*, which were dated to the end of his life, continue to seem 'old Chaucer'. (By contrast Godwin had dated *Troilus and Criseyde* to the poet's supposed student days at Oxford, helping to divert more attention to the *Canterbury Tales* as a mature work.[21]) But 'Old Chaucer' was changing its force. It had earlier stood for a widespread view that the poetry's archaic language and 'rough unequal verse' would inevitably keep it at a great distance from modern taste: 'His tuneless numbers hardly now survive, / As ruins of a dark and gothic age'.[22] As a growing reaction set in, first against Dryden's and Pope's versions and later against all substantial translation, the difficulties of reading the medieval text began to be played down considerably. Moreover, 'Old Chaucer' began increasingly to stand less for a book and more for an authorial personality, a man,[23] even when he was offered in translation or prose retellings. A 'Life' of Chaucer was usually included with the 'Works' or 'Selections', often with considerable detail of the poet's 'Times'. In these books, the strategic critical articulation of a historical Chaucer responded inventively in various ways to solve the continuing problem of his medieval religion.

In the process, Chaucer's Englishness could be invoked in his favour as a feature that overrode other considerations. Within the context of what Henry Morley called the 'national biography ... the story of the English mind', Chaucer's medieval Catholicism would normally represent what England had had to escape from to gain 'the inheritance of an inalienable freedom'.[24] Yet by emphasising 'the spirit of Chaucer' – the 'cheerful', 'manly', 'shrewd', 'kindly' and 'just' qualities of the true Englishman[25] – rather than specific doctrinal or ecclesiastical topics, Morley makes Chaucer an already complete image of what the national character should aspire to be. His Chaucer is to be read as both a symptom and a continuing cause of national freedom. Chaucer's 'spirit' *is* England's history, in which his religious outlook is the result of benign racial miscegenation, combining 'the simple sturdiness of the dutiful God-seeking Saxon' with 'the social joyousness of Norman wit'. In this guise,

Morley allows Chaucer to write 'not less religiously' than Wyclif, Gower and Langland, and to be 'Earnest ..., disposed at times even to direct religious teaching'.[26] But Morley was highly unusual in his liking for pre-Chaucerian English literature and for the wider European and English range in which he views Chaucer. To him, Chaucer was no 'lone star' or 'spring day in the midst of winter',[27] but thoroughly of his own times and comfortable within them. The great majority of Chaucer's admirers, by contrast, wanted to disassociate him from the medieval.

In this context, one important strategy was to promote a non-controversial critical discourse in which the poet figured as 'Fresh Chaucer', 'Simple Chaucer' and 'Child Chaucer'. All these Chaucers strongly relate to each other and may be found together. They also relate to the continuing concept of 'Old Chaucer', and all have the capacity to situate him positively either within or beyond the dominant timeline of England's historical development. They did not provide a clear paradigm shift, or set up an uncontestable image of the poet. In fact, the image of Chaucer as child was unstable, and liable to varied and hostile readings and usages, as I aim to show. But Chaucer-as-child became an important motif in a changing but long-memoried critical climate, where the 'response to four centuries of Chaucerian mediation involve[d] not its complete elimination, nor its complete reproduction, but its strategic and silent reappropriation'.[28]

An early example associating Chaucer with childhood is provided by Wordsworth's Ecclesiastical Sonnet (1821–22) on Edward VI,[29] linking the young Tudor king with the little martyred schoolboy of the *Prioress's Tale*, which Wordsworth had translated twenty years before.[30] Through this reference, the figure of the praying child unites Chaucer, 'meek and simple' Edward, and the younger and older Wordsworth in a moment of piety and pathos. In the sonnet's opening line, 'Sweet is the holiness of youth', Wordsworth quotes his own translation of the tale. The line does not correspond with Chaucer's text at this point, but is still confidently attributed as 'felt' by 'Time-honoured Chaucer'. The link is emotional, not doctrinal. Through the complex sympathetic interaction centred on the praying child, Wordsworth, looking back, elides religious difference by imagining how inspired with hope Chaucer, looking forward, would have been had he foreseen young King Edward's humble Protestant simplicity, and, it seems fair to infer, foreseen the glorious realisation of his own poetic child as the nation's and church's leader in the reformed religion he desired, but whose form and ultimate success he could not know. Although Chaucer is credited with power to 'employ' '[t]he lucid shafts of *reason*' to '[p]ierc[e] ... the papal darkness from afar', the deeper communion that the poem imagines is through a bond of feeling for the angelic child–king that transfigures his own martyr and elevates the Marian piety of his poem onto a higher plane. Through the child Edward, placed between the two poets, and joining them 'from afar', Chaucer is claimed for 'universal Christendom' and consequently for England.

Childhood and youthfulness of spirit continued to help refashion Chaucer as the century progressed. Continuing appreciation of Chaucer's 'pathos' maintained his connection with childhood by highlighting intense parent–child relations in the *Canterbury Tales*:[31] the *Prioress's Tale*; Griselda and children in the *Clerk's Tale*; Constance and her baby in the *Man of Law's Tale*; Ugolino and his children in the *Monk's Tale*. In an associated discursive move, as Helen Phillips has noted, '"fresh"', along with '"healthy", "bright", "hale", "green", "manly"', became a favourite word for mid-century Chaucer critics, perhaps as 'a counter to the contemporary trauma of environmental damage'.[32] Yet it is not only the Chaucerian landscape that is felt to be young and 'fresh', but also the poetic sensibility. R. H. Horne's introduction to *The Poems of Geoffrey Chaucer, Modernized* (1841) gives many examples. Charmingly, Horne explains that Chaucer sometimes seems old because he repeats himself so much, but this was solely because in his 'period of religious and political controversies', 'fears of inability to communicate efficiently ... induced all sorts of repetitions in order to prevent misunderstandings'. Otherwise,

> in every other respect he is the most invariably fresh and youthful poet ever given to the world. His poetry not only has the freshness of morning in it, but gives the impression of the youngest heart enjoying that freshness.
> ...
> The green leaves of Chaucer are among the very greenest we ever saw, the coolest and freshest.
> ...
> The sun and the moon of Chaucer have in them all the wonder of our childhood. His mirth is ever youthful, his daisies and stars are those we first know.[33]

It becomes clear that 'freshness' and 'childhood' inevitably go together for Horne, in Wordsworthian fashion – his collection features two items by Wordsworth – and that together both themes support a version of 'simple Chaucer' which either keeps the poet below, or raises him above, the level of religious controversy: 'There is in Chaucer the strength of a giant combined with the simplicity of a child';[34] 'the profoundly simple-hearted old poet call[s] upon God, and upon Christ, through the voices of earth's many happy and many suffering children'.[35] Prepared by repetition of this language, the reader will not be surprised to hear that

> it is not to be inferred that he [Chaucer] was a practical reformer in religion, any more than in politics, or that he made any systematic attacks upon abuses of any kind in church or state.[36]

Horne presents Chaucer as neither alien Catholic nor Reformer *manqué* by making the potentially dangerous association of him with the childhood of the nation into an argument for his purity of 'heart'. 'Child' Chaucer ran the risk of exciting negative implications of the Middle Ages as an immature stage in England's history and literature, and in poetic terms of invoking Dryden's famous comment that Chaucer 'liv'd in the Infancy of our Poetry ... we must be Children before we grow Men'.[37] Daniel Scrymgeour's view (1860) was commonplace:

> From the lispings of a barbarous age, jejune often in thought, and meagre in expression, the English mind has reared a literature inferior to none in depth of thinking, splendour of originality, and dignity and harmony of language.[38]

Even later (1874), William Minto could quote a section of the *Knight's Tale* to assert that 'The archaic inflections and turn of language give this a quaint unction, as if it were the imperfect utterance of an astonished child'.[39] But Horne mounts a critique of 'quaint' as merely 'express[ing] ... the resentments of a modern ear'.[40] His preface offers readers a different kind of childhood in Chaucer, one that overrides historical and linguistic change and lets them share an ever-fresh timeless world with him – '*our* childhood', 'those *we* first knew'; 'the greenest *we* ever saw' – and they are assured that 'If the head be sometimes under an undue influence of time and place, the heart of his morality never errs'.[41] Rather than descend to religious controversy, Horne creates a Chaucer seeking for a vaguer and unchanging transcendent truth, 'the creative Principle, wherein alone it [his spirit] can find peace and repose'.[42]

Horne was not alone in his attitudes. For Elizabeth Barrett, writing in 1842, the genius of the poet shares the character of his position: he was made for an early poet, and the metaphors of dawn and spring doubly become him. A morning-star, a lark's exultation, cannot usher in a glory better. The 'cheerful morning face', 'the breezy call of incense-breathing morn',[43] you recognize in his countenance and voice. ... His senses are open and delicate, like a young child's – his sensibilities capacious of supersensual relations, like an experienced thinker's. Child-like, too, his tears and smiles lie at the edge of his eyes.[44]

In this common assessment of Chaucer as a poet of 'Nature', a term which had altered in meaning from Blake's idea of essential natural types to 'natural scenery',[45] everything associates him with an imagined childhood of the world. Barrett easily extended the idea to Chaucer's religion. In 1843, arguing that Christianity offers 'the highest and purest objects of contemplation', she writes:

> Chaucer, with all his jubilee of spirit and resounding laughter, had the name of Jesus Christ and God as frequently to familiarity on his lips as a child has its father's name.[46]

For Barrett, the relationship of intense poetic sensibility to religious piety is consummated in the 'young child', a figure whose thematics engage the idea of the Middle Ages as the nation's infancy in a positive sense – the unspoiled 'morning' of the day, the year, of life and of English history. The 'mist' and 'darkness' of the medieval, in which Chaucer alone sees clearly or shines light, was a theme sustained from Philip Sidney to Wordsworth and still highly current.[47] Barrett, like Horne, replaces it by an identification of Chaucer with bright dawn and daylight itself, a purer, healthier version of the 'present day'.

Among many more instances of a 'morning' Chaucer that might be given, John Ruskin's use of the phrase stands out for combining an April morning with essential Englishness. Chaucer, 'the perfect type of a true English mind in its best possible temper ... is for the most part full of thoughts of beauty, pure and wild like that of an April morning'.[48] The opening of the *General Prologue* had indelibly identified Chaucer with April. Ruskin's 'April *morning*' and 'wild' add something more, vouching for the essential purity and unsophisticated nature of the mind behind the writing. Nevertheless, the context of the remark shows Ruskin wishing to probe Englishness further, especially in his view that 'there is one strange, but quite essential character in us ...: a delight in the forms of burlesque which are connected in some degree with the foulness in evil'. In Chaucer's case this quirk 'renders some of quite the greatest, wisest and most moral of English writers now almost useless for our youth'. There is nothing 'strange' or child-like about Chaucer in Ruskin's view. He is in essentials ('mind', 'thoughts') a model English (male) adult, but the problem is that the English themselves are 'strange' in one respect, which partly disqualifies him from being a good model for them to follow. Ruskin then turns to Chaucer as his first example to explain why 'we [the English] shall never be successful in the highest fields of ideal or theological art', through the national failure to meet 'the first necessity for the doing of any great work in ideal art', which is 'to look ... upon all foulness with horror, as a contemptible though dreadful enemy'.[49] That failure 'precludes them from that speciality of art which is properly called sublime'. Chaucer and Shakespeare lack Dante's sublimity for this reason. Even Milton fails in the attempt.[50]

I have lingered on Ruskin's views for some time here because of their similarities and contrasts with another reading of Chaucer, a decade later, that they readily bring to mind. Matthew Arnold's comment that Chaucer lacked 'high seriousness' had been anticipated by Ruskin,[51] though on rather different grounds. In a comparison between them, a muted uneasiness with Chaucer's religion, quite absent in Ruskin, becomes apparent in Arnold, who is more concerned with a historical view of English national and cultural development. I shall suggest that Arnold's uneasiness relates to aspects of the complex critical tradition in which the English Middle Ages were constructed as a kind of childhood, within a progressivist cultural nationalism which Arnold seems to share with other writers on Chaucer around this time.

In his essay, Arnold famously singles out one line, 'O martyr souded [fixed fast] in virginitee', referring to the little schoolboy of the *Prioress's Tale*, as characterising in itself 'the charm of Chaucer's verse', and, perhaps not coincidentally, he argues in the same breath that Chaucer's poetry lacks 'the high seriousness which comes from absolute sincerity', such as he found in 'the first great classic of Christendom ... Dante'. It is striking, yet very conventional, that out of all Chaucer Arnold should have chosen the *Prioress's Tale* as his test case. It was a tale that Wordsworth had made prominent through his modernised version, and was much noted by critics for its 'pathos' and 'tenderness'. Arnold takes the opportunity to remark that Wordsworth's translation completely loses Chaucer's 'charm',[52] but in other respects his concentration on this passage shows the influence of the older writer, who is much praised in the same volume where Arnold later concluded his essay in 1885.

Despite Arnold's aim in this work to find the 'best' poetry wherever it occurs, he sets up Chaucer, for all his 'charm' and affability – his 'large, free, simple, clear yet kindly view of human life' – as a figure liable to be over-rated through a 'historical fallacy' that mistakes the great interest of medieval writing as a 'stage' in 'the course of development of a nation's language, thought, and poetry' for a sign of classic greatness. Arnold asserts that '[Chaucer's] poetical importance does not need the assistance of the historic estimate; it is real',[53] and yet it is he who hints that there may be a tendency to over-rate it on historical grounds, prefiguring his own judgement that Chaucer is still not one of the 'great classics'. The discussion is prefaced by warnings against misguided over-estimates of medieval 'romance' literature: the *Chanson de Roland* and Chrétien de Troyes. The statement that Chaucer's poetry 'transcends and *effaces* all the romance-poetry of Catholic Christendom [and] all the English poetry contemporary with it' speaks for Arnold's generally low view of the Middle Ages, and is typical of much Victorian (and earlier) criticism where the status accorded to Chaucer as 'spring time' and 'morning star' denies value to anything else in medieval English literature.

It may be significant, in this context, to note what is missing in Arnold's praise of Chaucer's 'substance' and 'truth', 'his large, free, sound representation of things',[54] and of his 'style': the 'virtue of manner and movement',[55] 'his divine liquidness of diction, his divine fluidity of movement'.[56] These are strong terms of praise for Arnold, but one cannot relate them to religious culture or thought, even though he cites only the *Prioress's Tale* (why not the *Knight's Tale*?). In the process of substituting poetic classics for religion in order 'to interpret life for us, to console us, to sustain us',[57] and choosing Dante for the purpose, Arnold seems not to have considered Chaucer as a religious writer, or at least not a deeply 'serious' or 'sincere' one. In that, his view may be aligned with others of the period which saw medieval English Catholicism as symptomatic of an immature stage in the life of the race. For Wordsworth, the image of the child merged Chaucer's religious outlook with the 'meek' sincerity of early Protestant piety. For Horne and Barrett, it made Chaucer 'simple-hearted', beyond questions of confessional allegiance. For Arnold, arguably, it is negatively present as a silent influence that keeps Chaucer from recognition as possessing 'seriousness' as a mature writer engaging readers in the highest concerns. Where for Ruskin it was Chaucer's occasional obscenity that disabled him as a poet of the 'theological' and 'ideal', for Arnold, it is something vaguer, the want of an 'accent', which 'It may be said ... was *necessarily* out of the reach of any poet in the England *of that stage of growth*'.[58] The 'historic' evaluation enters in force here, but as a supporting argument, not a 'fallacy'. Given that Arnold has spoken so highly of Chaucerian 'style' and 'liquidity', the 'stage of growth' he refers to can hardly be linguistic or stylistic.

I may seem to be overstating a case that Arnold treats Chaucer, on veiled historical grounds, as something less than a full adult because he belongs to the English Middle Ages, but his cultural attitudes do seem in line with a work like Adolphus William Ward's volume on Chaucer in *English Men of Letters* (1879), published only a year before Arnold's essay. Ward's comments on the lack of 'seriousness' in medieval English religion and outlook raise several concerns similar to Arnold's, though in a different idiom:

> About our national life in this period, both in its virtues and in its vices, there is something – it matters little whether we call it – childlike or childish. It lacks the seriousness belonging to men and to generations, who have learnt to control themselves, instead of relying on the control of others.
>
> ...
>
> the nation was in that stage of its existence when the innocence of the child was fast losing itself, without the self-control of the man having yet taken its place.
>
> ...
>
> noticeable shortcomings by no means uncommon in the case of undeveloped civilisations (as for instance among the most typically childish or childlike nationalities of the Europe of our own day).[59]

It seems clear from other comments Ward makes that by 'childish and childlike nationalities' he means specifically Catholic regions, where what he calls 'the great movement that was to form the [English] national character', and of which Chaucer 'displays no serious foreknowledge', has not taken hold.[60] Wanting to claim Chaucer as English, which means disavowing his religion, Ward constructs him as a hybrid figure of cultural 'transition':

> in him the mixture of Frenchman and Englishman is still in a sense incomplete, as that of their language is in the diction of his poems. His gaiety of heart is hardly English; nor is his willing (though, to

be sure, not invariably unquestioning) acceptance of forms into the inner meaning of which he does not greatly vex his soul by entering; nor his airy way of ridiculing what he has no intention of helping to overthrow; nor his light unconcern in the question whether he is, or is not, an immoral writer. ... But he IS English in his freedom and frankness of spirit; in his manliness of mind; in his preference for the good in things as they are to the good in things as they might be; in his loyalty, his piety, his truthfulness.[61]

This is cultural criticism by means of racial and religious profiling. Chaucer's religion and its practices are made foreign and immature, sharply distinguished from his 'manly' Englishness. Chaucer must become a trifling modern Frenchman in matters of religion, because if he were thought to have been a serious medieval Catholic he could not be considered truly English in other ways. It is notable that to French critics, Chaucer was no child or beginner, but a late follower in French tradition; they did not have the English religio-national timeline in their heads, and so had no need to work around it.[62] But Ward, like Arnold, has French literary criticism in his sights,[63] and Chaucer is caught in the crossfire. In nationalist assessments like Ward's, demanding 'manliness' and denigrating pre-Reformation and pre-Enlightenment submission to 'the control of others', child-likeness could be no advantage, and that guise for Chaucer seems to have faded in criticism by 1900, despite the continued growth of versions for children and schools.[64] Child Chaucer, in turn, may be seen as mainly a Romantic motif.[65]

One longer-term outcome of *not* calling Chaucer a child in religion can be seen in a slightly later critic, J. S. P. Tatlock, who argued in 1916 that the poet must have been aware of and sympathetic to Wyclif's views, and so concludes 'he was not such stuff as martyrs are made of but something of a Laodicean'.[66] Tatlock was agreeing, on better-informed grounds, with an assessment made in 1869 by Matthew Browne, to whom Chaucer was 'a man incapable of such high degrees of faith and moral steadfastness as we must inevitably associate with ... Wickliffe'.[67] Tatlock, like Lounsbury, did not have Browne's investment in Protestant historiography, but his comment shows the limiting influence of that tradition in shaping the kind of religious poet that Chaucer was now much less able to be, a committed anti-establishment religious campaigner. If he was *not* that, but still recognisably a Catholic rather than an honorary modern secularist, then to match the new mainstream critical mood he needed to become Coghill's 'not very keen'

Catholic, who can be read as a product of conflicting tendencies in Chaucer's nineteenth-century reception history.

Notes

1. Nevill Coghill, *The Poet Chaucer* (London: Oxford University Press, 2nd edn, 1967), p. 134.
2. See Linda Georgianna, 'The Protestant Chaucer', in C. David Benson and Elizabeth Robertson (eds), *Chaucer's Religious Tales* (Cambridge: Boydell & Brewer, 1990), pp. 55–69 (pp. 55–6 and 65).
3. Georgianna, 'The Protestant Chaucer', p. 60, quoting George Lounsbury, *Studies in Chaucer: His Life and Writings*, vol. 2 (New York: Harper, 1892), p. 505.
4. Jeff Espie, 'Wordsworth's Chaucer: mediation and transformation in English literary history', *Philological Quarterly*, 94:4 (2015), 377–403 (pp. 379–80).
5. Nicholas Watson, 'Chaucer's public Christianity', *Religion and Literature*, 37:2 (2005), 99–114 (p. 100).
6. Geoffrey Keynes (ed.), *The Complete Writings of William Blake: With All the Variant Readings* (London: Nonesuch Press, 1957), p. 575.
7. Keynes (ed.), *The Complete Writings of William Blake*, p. 567.
8. D. S. Brewer (ed.), *Chaucer: The Critical Heritage*, 2 vols (London: Routledge, 1978), vol. 2, pp. 7–8.
9. Brewer (ed.), *Chaucer: The Critical Heritage*, vol. 2, p. 19.
10. Megan L. Cook, '"Here taketh the makere of this book his leve": the *Retraction* and Chaucer's works in Tudor England', *Studies in Philology*, 113:1 (2016), 32–54 (p. 54).
11. John Saunders, *Chaucer's Canterbury Tales and Sketches*, 3 vols in 1 (London: Charles Knight, 1845), pp. 273–4.
12. John Saunders, *Cabinet Pictures of English Life: Chaucer* (London: Charles Knight, 1845), p. 149.
13. Saunders, *Cabinet Pictures of English Life*, p. 150.
14. Henry Innes, *A Lecture on the Genius of Chaucer* (Malta, 1851), p. x.
15. Thomas Arnold, *Chaucer to Wordsworth: A Short History of English Literature* (London: Thomas Murby, 1870), pp. 15–16.
16. William Godwin, *Life of Chaucer* (London: T. Davison, 1804).
17. H. W. D., *The Life of Geoffrey Chaucer: The Father of English Poetry* (London: Ward & Lock, 1881), p. 244.
18. H. W. D., *The Life of Geoffrey Chaucer*, p. 245.
19. Mrs H. R. Haweis [Mary Eliza], *Chaucer for Schools* (London: Chatto & Windus, 1881), p. x.
20. Matthew Arnold, 'General introduction', in T. H. Ward (ed.), *The English Poets, Selections, vol. 1: Chaucer to Donne* (London: Macmillan, 1880), p. xix.
21. Godwin, *Life of Chaucer*, chapter 14.

22 Hugh Dalrymple, *Woodstock Park: An Elegy* (London: D. Wilson, 1761), lines 169–70.
23 The classic study of this aspect of Chaucer reception is Stephanie Trigg, *Congenial Souls: Reading Chaucer from Medieval to Postmodern* (Minneapolis: University of Minnesota Press, 2002).
24 Henry Morley, *English Writers: From Chaucer to Dunbar* (London: Chapman & Hall, 1867), vol. 2, part 1, pp. vii, 2.
25 Morley, *English Writers*, vol. 2, part 1, p. 336.
26 Morley, *English Writers*, vol. 2, part 1, pp. 140–1.
27 Morley, *English Writers*, vol. 2, part 1, p. 140.
28 Espie, 'Wordsworth's Chaucer', p. 380.
29 William Wordsworth, *Ecclesiastical Sonnets* (New Haven: Yale University Press, 1922), p. 154.
30 For Wordsworth and Chaucer, see also Elizabeth Robertson, 'Chaucer and Wordsworth's vivid daisies', in Bettina Bildhauer and Chris Jones (eds), *The Middle Ages in the Modern World: Twenty-First Century Perspectives* (Oxford: British Academy, 2017), pp. 219–38.
31 See, for example, Charles Cowden Clarke, *The Riches of Chaucer*, 2 vols (London: Effingham Wilson, 1835), vol. 1, p. x: 'the sudden, and electrical pathos of old Chaucer'.
32 Helen Phillips, 'Chaucer and the nineteenth-century city', in Ardis Butterfield (ed.), *Chaucer and the City* (Cambridge: D. S. Brewer, 2006), pp. 193–210 (p. 194).
33 R. H. Horne (ed.), *The Poems of Geoffrey Chaucer, Modernized* (London: Whittaker, 1841), pp. xxxvi–xxxvii, xcvi, xcvii.
34 Horne (ed.), *The Poems of Geoffrey Chaucer*, pp. xiv–xv.
35 Horne (ed.), *The Poems of Geoffrey Chaucer*, p. civ.
36 Horne (ed.), *The Poems of Geoffrey Chaucer*, p. ciii.
37 John Dryden, *Fables Ancient and Modern* (London: Jacob Tonson, 1700), preface.
38 Daniel Scrymgeour, *The Poetry and Poets of Britain* (Edinburgh: Adam and Charles Black, 1860), p. viii.
39 William Minto, *Characteristics of English Poets: From Chaucer to Shirley* (London: William Blackwood, 1874), p. 35.
40 Horne (ed.), *The Poems of Geoffrey Chaucer*, p. xxxiv, n.
41 Horne (ed.), *The Poems of Geoffrey Chaucer*, pp. xcvii, xcvi, xcix.
42 Horne (ed.), *The Poems of Geoffrey Chaucer*, p. civ.
43 The reference is to Thomas Gray, 'Elegy written in a country churchyard'.
44 Elizabeth Barrett, 'The book of the poets', *The Athenæum*, 4 June 1842, p. 498.
45 See Brewer (ed.), *Chaucer: The Critical Heritage*, vol. 2, p. 9.
46 Elizabeth Barrett, 'Letter to John Kenyon, March 25 1843', in *The Letters of Elizabeth Barrett Browning*, vol. 1 (London: Smith Elder, 1897), p. 128.

47 Philip Sidney, *An Apology for Poetry (or The Defence of Poesy)*, ed. Geoffrey Shepherd, revd R. W. Maslen (Manchester: Manchester University Press, 2002), p. 110: 'Chaucer ..., of whom, truly, I know not whether to marvel more, either that he in that misty time could see so clearly, or that we in this clear age go so stumblingly after him.'
48 John Ruskin, *Lectures on Art* (Oxford: Clarendon Press, 1870), p. 15.
49 Ruskin, *Lectures on Art*, p. 15.
50 Ruskin, *Lectures on Art*, p. 16. For Swinburne also, arguing on other grounds, Chaucer had 'childlike manfulness of compassionate or joyous emotion', but lacked 'sublimity': Algernon Charles Swinburne, 'Wordsworth and Byron', in *Miscellanies* (New York: Worthington, 1886), p. 152.
51 Matthew Arnold, 'General introduction', p. xix. Later published as *Essays in Criticism*, 2nd series (London: Macmillan, 1885), p. 33.
52 Arnold, *Essays in Criticism*, pp. 29, 48, 32 and 30–1.
53 Arnold, *Essays in Criticism*, p. 27
54 Arnold, *Essays in Criticism*, p. 28.
55 Arnold, *Essays in Criticism*, p. 30.
56 Arnold, *Essays in Criticism*, p. 28.
57 Arnold, *Essays in Criticism*, p. 2.
58 Arnold, *Essays in Criticism*, p. 32, emphasis added.
59 Adolphus William Ward, *Chaucer*, English Men of Letters Series (London, 1879), pp. 41–2, 45, 42.
60 Ward, *Chaucer*, p. 46.
61 Ward, *Chaucer*, pp. 45–6.
62 See Stephanie Downes, 'Chaucer in nineteenth-century France', *Chaucer Review*, 49:3 (2015), 352–70.
63 Ward mentions 'a living French critic of high repute, according to whom the English, still weighted down by Teutonic phlegm, were drunken gluttons, agitated at intervals by poetic enthusiasm', and badly in need of Norman 'esprit' (*Chaucer*, pp. 20–1). The reference must be to Hippolyte Taine, *Histoire de la littérature anglaise*, vol. 1 (Paris: Hachette, 1863).
64 See Velma Bourgeois Richmond, *Chaucer as Children's Literature: Retellings from the Victorian and Edwardian Eras* (Jefferson NC: McFarland & Co., 2004).
65 Interestingly, Eve Salisbury revives a '"Child Chaucer"' as a strategy 'to offer a broader appreciation of the imaginative play at work in the Tales. ... By "Child Chaucer" I mean the component of mind that enables the poet to breathe life into his characters, speak in the voice of a child, and lure readers into his virtual worlds': *Chaucer and the Child* (New York: Palgrave Macmillan, 2017), p. 7.
66 Brewer (ed.), *Chaucer: The Critical Heritage*, p. 339.
67 Brewer (ed.), *Chaucer: The Critical Heritage*, p. 128.

12
Flesh and stone: William Morris's *News from Nowhere* and Chaucer's dream visions
John M. Ganim

Towards the end of William Morris's *News from Nowhere*, the narrator, a visitor to a future socialist society, takes a detour with Ellen, a charismatic and beautiful woman in this new society. In the midst of a dialogue about the importance of beauty in everyday life, they come upon a lovingly preserved old house dating from before the revolution (see plate 10):

> She led me up close to the house, and laid her shapely sun-browned hand and arm on the lichened wall as if to embrace it, and cried out, 'O me! O me! How I love the earth, and the seasons, and weather, and all things that deal with it, and all that grows out of it, – as this has done!'
>
> I could not answer her, or say a word. Her exultation and pleasure were so keen and exquisite, and her beauty, so delicate, yet so interfused with energy, expressed it so fully, that any added word would have been commonplace and futile. I dreaded lest the others should come in suddenly and break the spell she had cast about me; but we stood there a while by the corner of the big gable of the house, and no one came.[1]

This extraordinary scene more nearly resembles a passage from D. H. Lawrence than one we would identify as typical of Morris. The scene seems at first an exception or even a contradiction in a socialist utopia. But such a reaction unfairly limits what we can expect from Morris as a writer. One of the striking aspects of *News from Nowhere* is how prescient Morris is in his insistence that the personal is the political, a conviction that informed the key bohemian and countercultural movements of the nineteenth and twentieth centuries.

My choice of this passage is meant as a homage to Stephanie Trigg's recent work, especially her investment in the history of emotions on the one hand, and her arresting survey of bluestone cityscapes, monuments and relics in Melbourne and Victoria on the other.² Here, right before Morris's narrator must leave the perfect world, stones and emotions meet in an ecstatic union. This union, observed rather than experienced by the narrator, functions as a modernist/symbolist epiphany of Morris's many concerns: the relation between the past and the future, the healing and rejuvenating power of a lovingly built environment, the point at which nature and culture are one and the same. To disaggregate these connections, I am aided by Richard Sennett's book, *Flesh and Stone: The Body and the City in Western Civilization*.³ Sennett nowhere mentions Morris in this book, but his attention to the relation of the human body and its senses to an apparently inert landscape, opens an avenue to understanding a passage in *News from Nowhere* that at first glance seems a distraction from the novel's primary concerns.

Sennett rewrites the relation between cities and their inhabitants by emphasising the bodily, the sensory and the frankly sensual. He charts the tactile, aural, somatic and olfactory dimensions of cities and the costs of ignoring them in design. At times he describes a hostile, even violent relation between human bodies and needs and the way in which cities have been built. At other times, Sennett offers something close to an organic utopia as a solution to our urban failure, one which would recover the lost possibilities of what he takes to be classical Greece's frankness or medieval France's therapeutic ideals of urbanism. Of medieval Paris, although it was packed with strangers and 'its streets were rampant with gratuitous violence, its economy shuffled human beings from town to town as well as goods, the city could nonetheless be shaped into a moral geography'.⁴ Its gardens were planned as places of respite and privacy for those that had neither. In the end, Sennett allows that a perfect city is not possible because of our own divided and conflicted desires, between what Freud called the reality and pleasure principles. Sennett concludes that an urbanism that served all of its people would acknowledge its own limits and its own implication in perpetuating injustice and inequality. He argues for an aesthetic directly opposed to the sleek, interchangeable modules of our present-day global centres: 'This desire to free the body from resistance', he writes, 'is coupled with a fear of touching'.⁵

Whereas Sennett imagines a city dialectically engaged between conflicting forces, between, as it were, purity and danger, Morris produces a utopian solution that places such conflict in the past.⁶ In contrast to more recent urbanists such as Jane Jacobs, who argued against suburbanisation and urban renewal,⁷ the landscape and townscape of Morris's future have been forged by revolutionary violence and counter-revolutionary reaction, which, after the revolution, results in the 'rest' of Morris's little-noticed subtitle, 'An epoch of rest'.[8] Interestingly, the one exception is the place of sensuality and sexuality in a perfect future, both from the point of view of the visiting narrator, stifled by the mores of his own world – even though he is a radical reformer in the nineteenth century, as was Morris – and by the comrades of this imagined future.

Even Ellen, the ecstatic guide in the above scene, is aware of the danger of her own power. It has already had its effect on the narrator: 'Ellen's laugh, even amongst the others, was one of the pleasantest sounds I had ever heard'.[9] She was not only beautiful, but 'was in all ways strangely interesting'.[10] Ellen tells him that she has invited herself along for the pleasure of his company, but warns him that 'even amongst us, where there are so many beautiful women, I have often troubled men's minds disastrously'.[11] Even her courtesy has a double edge to it: 'This evening ... I shall make a proposal to you to do something which would please me very much, and I think would not hurt you'.[12] When she smiles, she smiles 'with pleasure' and her body, despite her obvious fitness and healthy suntanned complexion, is languorous in repose. We would suppose that her aura was the result of the narrator's male gaze, if she herself did not contribute to its explanation. And indeed her frankness, which causes embarrassment or uncertainty only to the narrator himself, is part and parcel of the sexual mores of Nowhere. We learn somewhat earlier that almost the only crimes that plague the utopian future are crimes of passion. A man, 'bitten with love-madness', pursues a woman who does not love him back, and attacks her successful lover with an axe, but in the ensuing struggle, the love-mad man is killed. His friends are now worried about the despair of the survivor after the manslaughter, concerned that he might take his own life, and plunge his beloved into a similar despair.[13] Part of the point of the story is the attempt by the community to regulate itself and care for the survivors, but also the awareness of all of the disruptive potential of passion. The narrator has earlier been told this story immediately after he has praised a woman who is guiding a horse: 'What a beautiful creature!' he exclaims to his guide, Dick, who asks him teasingly if he is referring to the horse.[14] We move from an adolescent remark by the narrator, to an indication that desire remains socially problematic in the new world, as it was in the nineteenth century, and in Morris's own troubled and complicated private life, which utopia cannot entirely exorcise.

At the same time, Ellen is her own woman, and her near-union with her beloved stones has echoes that run through the mid-nineteenth century. John Ruskin's *The Stones of Venice* tells a rather different story about gender and stones. It is possible to think of the scene as an implicit response to Ruskin, much as his 'Defence of Guenevere' is in dialogue with Tennyson's portrayals of Arthurian women. By now, it seems almost self-evident that Ruskin's narrative of a virtuous medieval Venice changed into a fallen Renaissance courtesan is based on autobiographical experience. Ruskin supposedly delayed the consummation of his marriage in order to complete the writing of his book. Richard Ellmann's elegant essays in *Golden Codgers* suppose that at the same time that Ruskin was defending his wife Effie's chastity in the face of her flirtatiousness and love of pleasure, he was projecting his anger on to the city of Venice itself. Renaissance Venice bears the brunt of Ruskin's internal rage, as he rails against the corruption of the purity and honesty of her former medieval form.[15] Morris's Ellen, however, embraces the authenticity of the stones of the old house, integrating them into an experience that is sensual, historical and ethical all at once. Unlike Ruskin, the narrator suspends judgment, and even enjoys Ellen's pleasure voyeuristically. Yet his paralysed response reveals that he is in some way a secret sharer of Ruskin's discomfort. The narrator's voyeuristic distance is a culmination of his puzzlement with the sexual and romantic arrangements of this future society as they are revealed to him up to this point, as well as his enthusiasm for the healthy attractiveness of the many female figures who appear with regularity in the landscape.

The passage has not gone unremarked in recent Morris studies, and some brilliant interpretations have been proposed. Béatrice Laurent reads the passage in terms of the dichotomy between Morris's Romanticism and his Marxism:

> Her semi-pantheistic, semi-orgasmic outcry makes Ellen more than a character of fiction, an allegory of Life. Through renunciation both of established politics and of religious dogma, the Nowherians seem to have regressed, in an historical perspective, to a pre-capitalist, even a pre-Christian era, indeed to the legendary period when the Western world was inhabited by humans and fairies living in harmony.[16]

Laurent suggests that Morris engages in a kind of word-painting of landscapes in the novel, akin to how the visual arts successfully merge the moral and the political qualities of buildings and landscapes. Nathaniel Gilbert interprets the scene as emphasising the relationship between humans, the built landscape and the natural world, following on the theory of landscape developed by W. J. T. Mitchell, Anne Bermingham and others.[17] As Florence Boos notes, 'Soon afterwards, however, the impossibly beautiful dream dissolves. Guest becomes aware that he has become a kind of spectral presence: his new friends at the harvest-festival no longer recognize him'.[18] For Boos, Ellen actually voices some of the positions of twentieth century neo-Marxism, from Ernst Bloch to Henri Lefebvre, rather than those of industrial-age Marxism. Boos points out that it is Guest who becomes a 'spectral presence' so that, I may add, the utopian future is more real than the nineteenth-century present.

A case could be made that the alienated narrator of *News from Nowhere* is a reflection of Morris's familiarity with the role of the narrator in the dream visions of Geoffrey Chaucer. Most readers familiar with Morris nowadays think of the Kelmscott Chaucer as the epitome of Morris's identification with Chaucer. However, despite the enormous iconic importance of the Kelmscott edition, Morris kept a surprising distance in his comments about Chaucer. Morris and Edward Burne-Jones, the illustrator of the Kelmscott Chaucer, were supposedly lifelong admirers of Chaucer, though J. W. Mackail, in the official biography, concludes that Morris read Chaucer only later in his education.[19] Morris seems to have gone out of his way to deny any obvious imitation of Chaucer. In 1895, for instance, he writes to a German student, Hans Ey, who told Morris of a thesis reporting minimal impact of Chaucer on Morris's style:

> I quite agree with your friend as to the resemblance of my work to Chaucer; it only comes of our both using the narrative method: and even then my turn is decidedly more to Romance than was Chaucer's. I admit that I have been a great admirer of Chaucer, and that his work has had, especially in early years much influence on me; but I think not much on my style.[20]

Indeed, despite Morris's admiration, Chaucer's influence remains an inspiration rather than an obvious model, and more evident in the visual arts than in prose or poetry. Nevertheless, Chaucer operates as something of a talisman for Morris throughout his life, helping him to negotiate the many contradictions and confusions that his personal life created for him.

I have described in a previously published article how, in the Kelmscott portrait of Chaucer, Burne-Jones melds traditional images of Chaucer with a portrait of Morris himself. Some of Morris's friends thought they resembled each other, and this resemblance is recorded in Mackail's biography, which notes that the 'resemblance even extended to physical features: the corpulent person, the demure smile, the "close, silent eye"'.[21] Burne-Jones's portraits of Chaucer in the Kelmscott edition are strangely solitary and detached, and even seem to age as the volume progresses.

Morris was extremely guarded about his inner life, in contrast to his exuberance about business, art or politics. His daughter, May Morris, wrote in her recollections that 'no glimpse of his inner life ... was ever vouchsafed even to his closest friends'.[22] At the same time, some of his poems have been read as obliquely autobiographical. *The Earthly Paradise*, inspired by Chaucer's framed story collections, may express a sense of longing, loss and regret for Jane: 'Can we regain what we have lost meanwhile?'[23] *The Defence of Guinevere,* written before Morris even met Jane, expressed a strangely sympathetic and prophetic understanding of the romantic triangle and its compromises: Guinevere seems to speak as much for the betrayed as for the betrayer. Morris and Jane Burden were married in 1861, but Dante Gabriel Rossetti and Jane carried on an affair for many years, and it was not to be Jane's last affair. The strange combination of sympathy, voyeurism and distraction that one can sense in Morris's private life is also evident in the mechanics of narration in *News from Nowhere*, and it is mediated by similar devices such as the narration of Chaucer's dream visions.[24]

The early twentieth century canonised a particular Chaucer: ironic, comic and realistic, most himself in the *Canterbury Tales*. In G. L. Kittredge's *Chaucer and his Poetry*, Chaucer becomes a sophisticated cosmopolitan, only pretending to be naive.[25] In *Congenial Souls*, Trigg has demonstrated the gender and class bias behind such an identification.[26] Morris, however, was attracted to Chaucer's dream visions, as well as the rich tradition of medieval dream poetry they depended on. The reaction of most readers is that the dream visions are more 'medieval', and so alert us to another Chaucer than the one who has been canonised in our recent literary history. Indeed, early-twentieth-century criticism read the dream visions as a phase that Chaucer matured from. We may continue to delight in the comic realism of the *Canterbury Tales*, but the dream visions and lyrics offer us very different sorts of effects, such as an interest in moral states, an openness to the vagaries and validity of psychological experience and fantasy.

They require a previous knowledge of highly conventional medieval forms or a willingness to engage the premises of those forms. Morris was sensitive and open to the effects of the dream vision, even if he viewed the form through the lens of Romanticism and neo-Romanticism.

What did Morris borrow from Chaucer's dream visions? Primarily, he employs the narrative stance that has been so debated in subsequent criticism. This is the 'Chaucer' found in the dream visions of the *Book of the Duchess*, the *House of Fame* and the *Parliament of Fowls*. Typically, the narrator is in the throes of insomnia and then finds himself in an enchanted landscape, filled with both manufactured and natural beauties. He begins a courteous dialogue with an interlocutor, who becomes a guide to this dream world. Sometimes, as in the case of the gigantic talkative eagle in the *House of Fame*, the effect is comic, as the eagle answers the predictable questions of the narrator at great length, while the narrator holds on for dear life as they ascend. In the *Book of the Duchess*, the narrator encounters a man dressed in black. A series of questions, answered metaphorically and indirectly until the end, results in the awareness that the man is in mourning for his beloved. As with the narrator of the *General Prologue*, the impression we have is of an inquisitive, if obtuse, and sometimes embarrassing observer of personal and social crises that he does not totally understand. As scholars have pointed out, Chaucer himself had considerable diplomatic and official experience, and could not have been as naive as his self-portrait.

Chaucer was writing in the tradition of late medieval dream visions. His French contemporary, Guillaume de Machaut, portrayed himself in an unflattering light, and dramatised his personal failures and incompetence. Dante, in the *Inferno*, has to be corrected constantly by his guide, Virgil. Critics such as Alfred David surmised that Chaucer may have fashioned this convention to suit his own situation as a poet and courtier of non-aristocratic origins writing for his social superiors, who may have been both charmed and flattered by an opening that alludes to their greater sophistication.[27] Chaucer may also have been distancing himself from potentially controversial content in his work. In the 'prologue' to the *Legend of Good Women*, he allows himself to be defended as ignorant of proper social niceties. That is, from a modern critical perspective, Chaucer is operating like one of Joseph Conrad's narrators, shaping the story with his own sometimes confused misunderstandings. We have had to learn to read his narrative persona as if he were a distinct fictional character, which criticism has come to call 'Chaucer-the-narrator' or 'Chaucer-the-pilgrim', especially in *Troilus and Criseyde* and the *Canterbury Tales*. But that persona is forged and perfected in the dream visions.

At the same time, *News from Nowhere*, and especially the scene I opened with, is more deeply personal than any of Chaucer's indirect and largely comical comments about his own life or marriage. The narrator stares in distant wonder at Ellen's ecstatic, almost polymorphously perverse, embrace of the wall of the ancient building. But that is not just any building: it is Kelmscott Manor, Morris's own home for a good part of his life. Her embrace includes Morris, and perhaps his narratorial stand-in 'William', in the form of the building. He is a spectator and her exclamation and action is a form of theatre, but it also symbolically enacts his own desires, both towards Ellen and towards the building itself. Ellen's sexualised response is in contrast with, but also consistent with, her natural confidence leading up to this point. Rather than being a contradiction, however, the moment encapsulates the peculiar place of sexuality in Morris's view of the future. Throughout *News from Nowhere*, and elsewhere in his work, he offers a defence of a Free Love that he is uncomfortable with.

Ellen is in a long line of attractive females, and males, that the narrator has noticed, and in whom temporality and sexuality are linked:

> I fairly felt as if I were alive in the fourteenth century; a sensation helped out by the costume of the people that we met or passed, in whose dress there was nothing 'modern'. Almost everybody was gaily dressed, but especially the women, who were so well-looking, or even so handsome, that I could scarcely refrain my tongue from calling my companion's attention to the fact.[28]

Many other such comments pepper the novel. On his first day, he notices the young women serving the meal: 'I naturally looked at them very attentively, and found them at least as good as the gardens, the architecture, and the male men'; they are frank and open, 'thoroughly healthy-looking and strong'.[29] Later, Dick, Guest's guide, encounters his ex-wife, and they are invited by an old man who is explaining the future to Guest, to disappear into the upstairs room, indicating the casual naturalness with which sex is treated in the future:

> 'Dick, my lad, and you, my dear Clara, I rather think that we two oldsters are in your way; for I think you will have plenty to say to

each other. You had better go into Nelson's room up above; I know he has gone out; and he has just been covering the walls all over with mediæval books, so it will be pretty enough even for you two and your renewed pleasure.'[30]

Guest, the narrator and stand in for Morris, is cut off from this ease, but at this point begins to develop the relationship with Ellen, who takes over from Dick and the old man in revealing human possibility to Guest. They talk rather than act, or, I should say, act out what they feel without actually acting upon it.

Significantly, the new Middle Ages of the future is pleasant and clean. Morris is countering a Victorian, and even Enlightenment, portrayal of the Middle Ages as dirty and diseased, one which persists to the present day. For instance, the International Health Exhibition was mounted in 1884 to celebrate devices, plans and structures to improve public and personal health, including clean and modern water facilities. But you entered through an 'Old London Street'. 'Old London' was meant to represent the crowded, unsafe and unhealthy past, and was even decorated with artificial dirt.[31] As opposed to the sounds and smells that animate the medieval cities that Sennett describes, Morris's future is an ecological as well as a social utopia, shaped by suburbanised, decentralised and local planning. The result is not noise and dirt but quite the opposite. What Morris is doing, as he is in responding to contemporary utopias, is emphasising the ugliness and dirtiness of modern London and equating the Middle Ages with a healthy, organic, holistic way of life. Behind this celebration of tidiness and cleanliness as almost sensual luxuries is a response to a much more common Victorian assumption about medieval life, one that associates the medieval with dirt, disgust and abjectness. But he is also doing something else: he is disassociating the connection made by puritanism and Victorianism between dirtiness and sexuality. Women are described, and even rendered desirable, by the same standards as buildings and ground, and men. Their frankness and ease (despite the fact that Morris assigns domestic tasks to the women of the future) attracts the narrator, although he appreciates them as he does the built environment, voyeuristically. Their health and heartiness, in reproach to the decadent past, or even the pre-Raphaelite past, is rendered attractive, and, as the novel proceeds, rendered erotically.

At the end of the nineteenth century and the beginning of the twentieth, bohemian circles espouse various extremes of the value of sexual experience. In America, certain directions in psychology and medicine seek to purge sexual desire as unhealthy. But new ideas from Germany and Scandinavia espouse an acceptance of the body and its desires as healthy and natural, eventually developing into a discourse of vitalism. Morris would have been aware of these ideas from circles in London, and it is possible, though not necessary to my argument, that they inform *News from Nowhere*. The most well-known of these circles is the Fellowship of the New Life, whose members advocated or explored free love, vegetarianism, animal rights, simple clothing and wholesome recreation, and an openness to exotic ideas from other cultures, as well as inspiration from Thoreau, Emerson and the American Transcendentalists. A stereotyping of the Fellowship of the New Life as having a largely ethical and personal agenda, akin to present-day New Age movements, has been questioned, and its socialist, materialist and political goals have been emphasised.[32] A surprising number of members or sympathisers would become famous figures in British culture, but the Fellowship is best remembered for the migration of many of its members into the Fabian Society, whose gradualist politics Morris rejected. Edward Carpenter, one of the founders of the group, and a socialist comrade of Morris, was one of the earliest champions of homosexual rights. Havelock Ellis became one of the leading figures in the emerging field of sexology. One member, Patrick Geddes, would become one of the founders of British town and regional planning.

In *News from Nowhere*, Morris imagines a rather limited and diluted version of these countercultural ideals. The men of the future are attractive and beautiful, but Morris's portrayal of them seems borrowed from Walt Whitman (also one of the heroes of the Fellowship of the New Life). The narrator describes innovative marriage and sexual arrangements, but is almost apologetic in describing them and voyeuristically distant in observing them. While women in the future are described as possessing agency and equal rights, they choose to continue to work in the same gender-specific fields that they do in patriarchal societies, such as food preparation, house care, domestic arrangements and so forth. Indeed, the perspectives of Morris-the-author and William-the-narrator are reversed here, since the narrator also finds this self-imposed limitation surprising. At the least, it has to be explained to him.

Returning to Ellen's ecstatic embrace of the old stones, we can now read the passage not so much as an exception, but as a doubly refracted image. Ellen's experience predicts what Serena Anderlini-D'Onofrio defines as ecosexuality, a polymorphously perverse erasure of the bounds of the human and the natural world.[33] For Morris, the old stones of Kelmscott are as close to natural creation as humans can attain. The scene thus encapsulates on a sexual and bodily level the paradoxes of Utopia, and perhaps of Morris's politics generally, in which, like Chaucer's dream narrators, he observes from a distance the passion and grief he has imagined as an author. The erotics of *News from Nowhere* constitute an allegorical emblem of its politics.

Notes

1. William Morris, *News from Nowhere*, in *Three Works by William Morris*, ed. A. L. Morton (London: Lawrence & Wishart, 1968), p. 391.
2. Stephanie Trigg, 'Bluestone and the city: writing an emotional history', *Melbourne Historical Journal*, 44:1 (2017), 41–53.
3. Richard Sennett, *Flesh and Stone: The Body and the City in Western Civilization* (New York: W. W. Norton & Company, 1996).
4. Sennett, *Flesh and Stone*, p. 159.
5. Sennett, *Flesh and Stone*, p. 18.
6. Fredric Jameson, *Archaeologies of the Future: The Desire Called Utopia and Other Science Fictions* (London: Verso, 2005).
7. See, especially, her seminal work in Jane Jacobs, *The Death and Life of Great American Cities* (New York: Random House, 1961).
8. Morris's goal of a frictionless future is the basis for Lionel Trilling's critique in 'Aggression and utopia: a note on William Morris's *News from Nowhere*', *Psychoanalytic Quarterly*, 42 (1972), 214–33.
9. Morris, *News from Nowhere*, p. 370.
10. Morris, *News from Nowhere*, p. 371.
11. Morris, *News from Nowhere*, p. 377.
12. Morris, *News from Nowhere*, p. 377.
13. Morris, *News from Nowhere*, p. 215.
14. Morris, *News from Nowhere*, p. 216.
15. Richard Ellmann, *Golden Codgers: Biographical Speculations* (London and New York: Oxford University Press, 1973).
16. Béatrice Laurent, 'The landscapes of Nowhere', *Journal of William Morris Studies*, 18:2 (2009), 52–64 (p. 57).
17. Nathaniel Gilbert, 'The landscape of resistance in Morris's *News from Nowhere*', *Journal of William Morris Studies*, 16:1 (2004), 22–37 (p. 23).
18. Florence Boos, 'The ideal of everyday life in William Morris' *News from Nowhere*', in Marguérite Corporaal and Evert Jan van Leeuwen

(eds), foreword by Peter Liebregts, *The Literary Utopias of Cultural Communities, 1790–1910* (Amsterdam: Rodopi, 2010), pp. 141–70 (p. 143). See also Jan Marsh 'Concerning love: *News from Nowhere* and gender', in Stephen Coleman and Paddy O'Sullivan (eds), *William Morris and 'News from Nowhere': A Vision for Our Time* (Bideford, Devon: Green Books, 1990), pp. 107–25. Boos and Marsh have written extensively and persuasively on gender in Morris.
19 J. W. Mackail, *The Life of William Morris*, vol. I (London: Longmans, 1901), p. 61.
20 William Morris, 'Letter 2427: "To Hans Ey"', in Norman Kelvin (ed.), *The Collected Letters of William Morris, vol. IV: 1893–1896* (Princeton: Princeton University Press, 1996), p. 338.
21 Mackail, *The Life of William Morris*, p. 214.
22 May Morris, *William Morris: Artist, Writer, Socialist*, vol. I (Oxford: Blackwell, 1936), p. 441.
23 William Morris, *The Earthly Paradise*, in May Morris (ed.), *The Collected Works of William Morris*, vols 3–6 (London: Longmans Green, 1910–15), 2.143. On the interplay between Morris's fiction and poetry, medieval romance and romance as a genre, with particular attention to *News from Nowhere*, see Amanda Hodgson, *The Romances of William Morris* (Cambridge: Cambridge University Press, 2011), pp. 127–33; Carole G. Silver, *The Romance of William Morris* (Athens OH: Ohio University Press, 1982), pp. 141–56; and Frederick Kirchhoff, *William Morris: The Construction of a Male Self, 1856–1872* (Athens OH: Ohio University Press, 1990), pp. 230–1.
24 David Matthews cites Ellen's ecstatic embrace of the wall as a possibly elegiac reference to his troubled marriage; see his important *Medievalism: A Critical History* (Cambridge: D. S. Brewer, 2015), p. 63.
25 George Lyman Kittredge, *Chaucer and His Poetry* (Cambridge MA: Harvard University Press, 1915).
26 Stephanie Trigg, *Congenial Souls: Reading Chaucer from Medieval to Postmodern* (Minneapolis: University of Minnesota Press, 2002), p. 33, *passim*.
27 Alfred David, *The Strumpet Muse: Art and Morals in Chaucer's Poetry* (Bloomington: Indiana University Press, 1976). On the history of scholarship of the dream visions, see John M. Ganim, 'The interpretation of dreams: Chaucer's early poems, literary criticism and literary theory', in William Quinn (ed.), *Chaucer's Dream Visions: A Casebook* (New York: Garland, 1999), pp. 463–76.
28 Morris, *News from Nowhere*, p. 203.
29 Morris, *News from Nowhere*, p. 193.
30 Morris, *News from Nowhere*, p. 234–5.
31 See the excellent account of the exhibition by Annmarie Adams, *Architecture in the Family Way: Doctors, Houses, and Women,*

1870–1900, McGill-Queen's/Hannah Institute Studies in the History of Medicine, Health, and Society (Montreal and London: McGill-Queen's University Press, 1996), pp. 9–35.

32 See Kevin Manton, 'The Fellowship of the New Life: English ethical socialism reconsidered', *History of Political Thought*, 24:2 (2003), 282–304.

33 Serena Anderlini-D'Onofrio, *Gaia and the New Politics of Love: Notes for a Poly Planet* (Berkeley: North Atlantic Books, 2010). See also Martin Delveaux, '"O me! O me! How I love the earth": William Morris's *News from Nowhere* and the birth of sustainable society', *Contemporary Justice Review*, 8:2 (2005), 131–46.

13
'In remembrance of his persone': transhistorical empathy and the Chaucerian face

Louise D'Arcens

From the earliest manuscript images through to cinematic depictions, Chaucer's face has been a key focus in the pursuit of transhistorical empathy – or, to use Stephanie Trigg's term, 'congeniality' – with the author. Along with the myriad translations, adaptations and continuations of his written works, Chaucer's face has been portrayed repeatedly across subsequent centuries, in an array of media: illuminations, paintings, etchings, sculpture, stained glass, animations, puppets and literary pen-portraits, as well as being brought to life in theatrical, televisual and cinematic performances. This chapter explores what Chaucer's 'persone', and especially his face, has come to mean to post-medieval audiences, and analyses why it has been such a significant part of what can be called his long 'empathic afterlife'.

The emergence of the field of emotions history has opened important inroads into understanding how affective experiences can be treated as substantially historical phenomena, or at least as experiences that are intelligible within the social and historical contexts within which they take place. One related area yet to receive as much attention in work from emotions historians is how we might understand the affective-experiential dimension of transhistorical contact. By this I mean how contact with the past evokes in the modern Western subject a range of feelings associated with the affective-imaginative experience of another time from their own; what I wish to call here *transhistorical feeling*. An interest in transhistorical feeling sits somewhat awkwardly alongside the field of emotions history. Prominent historians of emotion have cautioned against potentially reductionist accounts that do not sufficiently acknowledge the historically specific way in which emotions are elicited and understood. That position, which favours the focus on the social and historical contingencies of emotional life, is summed up by Barbara Rosenwein's argument that 'to assume that our emotions were also the emotions of the past is to be utterly unhistorical'.[1] Even if one accepts the argument for the historicity of emotions, an examination of transhistorical feeling must be able to accommodate the fact that however 'utterly unhistorical' such feelings in relation to the past might be, they are nevertheless regularly experienced. Some within medieval studies, such as Aranye Fradenburg, have pointed to the potential for approaches that move beyond an 'alterist' subscription to historical periodisation, in order to develop an 'epistemology of contact' between the Middle Ages and the present.[2] Fradenburg's call recalls earlier efforts within German hermeneutics to develop a conceptual vocabulary of transhistorical feeling, and in particular of transhistorical empathy, that could elucidate the non-positivistic means by which modern historians come to understand and interpret people of the past. It is on this vocabulary that I will draw to discuss transhistorical empathy within medievalism generally, and as it has been directed at Chaucer specifically.

A notion that is of particular interest from hermeneutic theory is *Einfühlung,* which has been translated into English as 'empathy' or 'empathic understanding', although it literally means 'feeling into'. The term is most closely associated with such late nineteenth- and early twentieth-century thinkers as Robert Vischer, Theodor Lipps and Wilhelm Dilthey. While most theorists used it to discuss aesthetic sensibility or a connection to nature, Dilthey is of interest to a consideration of medievalist empathy because he linked *Einfühlung* to its sister term *Verstehen,* a historical understanding based on a 'process by which we know something interior from signs given outwardly to the senses'.[3] These thinkers developed the idea from their reading of the early nineteenth-century thinker Friedrich Schleiermacher, who in turn derived it from the Romantic hermeneutics of Johann Gottfried Herder. It is not my purpose in this chapter to disentangle all the permutations of how *Einfühlung* and its related terms have been formulated by each of them;[4] rather I want to draw out the common aspects that are most suggestive for a consideration of empathic responses to Chaucer. First, all agree that this is a mode of understanding that emerges out of the exchange between a body and a perceived object (in the cases that will be examined later, Chaucer's face and body, as they have been represented); it emerges out of an attempt to 'feel into' the historical other's experience via analogy; it is experiential rather than abstract and documentary; and it permits, and admits to, an affective attachment to the experiences of past people.

Critics of *Einfühlung* as a mode of historical understanding, including Max Weber, Hans-Georg Gadamer and Jürgen Habermas, have argued that as a form of transhistorical empathy it is naively immersive and projective, imposing the perspective of the interpreter onto the historical object, and therefore too subjectivistic to provide genuine historical knowledge. Gadamer argued in *Truth and Method*, furthermore, that its grounding in Romantic hermeneutics means it 'takes no account of the historical nature of experience',[5] while Habermas dismissed it as a suspect and promiscuous belief in the possibility of 'submer[sion] ... in a subhistorical stream of life that allows a pleasurable identification of everyone with everyone else'.[6] They imputed to this a naive (what Rosenwein would later call 'utterly unhistorical') belief in the possibility of contemporaneity between the historian and her object – a position that they regarded as aesthetic rather than properly epistemic. A closer look at how the idea of transhistorical empathy has been formulated within Romantic and post-Romantic hermeneutics, however, throws this critique into question. Schleiermacher, for instance, probably the figure most criticised for his Romantic intuitionism, insists that the intuition should always be coupled with a clear recognition of the sociocultural context of the historical object or person; a point reiterated by Dilthey who insisted that *Einfühlung* and *Verstehen* are oriented towards the world and socio-historical processes rather than to psychological immersion in the worlds of past people.[7]

Although *Einfühlung* is the term most commonly associated with transhistorical empathy, Dilthey's favoured term for describing this process in his most-quoted work on this subject, *The Rise of Hermeneutics* (1900), is actually *Nachfühlen*. This can be glossed as a reflective 're-feeling' and 're-experiencing'; a reflective experiencing of secondary feeling that is not psychological but rather, in the words of Max Scheler, 'grasps experientially the quality of the [historical] other's feelings without these feelings ... stimulating similar actual feelings in us'.[8] These states of knowledge are not simply projective and immersive, resting on the assumption that the modern subject can identify emotionally with the medieval figure, but foreground instead a notion of transhistorical empathy that negotiates a dialectic of similitude and difference between the subject and object of empathy. These earlier theories correspond, moreover, with more recent formulations of empathy as a form of knowledge, such as philosopher Martha Nussbaum's well-known definition of it as 'a participatory enactment of the situation of [another] … but always combined with an awareness that one is not oneself [that person]'.[9]

Transhistorical empathy is not limited to medievalism; indeed, it is at the heart of our engagement with the past. But these ideas are particularly apt for capturing medievalism, which can avail itself of the diffuse feelings that underpin transhistorical modes of feeling. I believe this framework to have broad applicability to considerations of medievalism because the medieval is the historical era that attracts the most richly capacious and associative forms of apprehension, which cut across history, myth and fantasy. It also invites from modernity a uniquely empathic relationship based on what many have described as its contradictory dual positioning as both 'other' to the modern and the crucible of the modern. It is in this paradoxical imaginative space that is both premodern and proleptically modern that Chaucer can frequently be found. Embodying both remoteness and proximity, he stands out among authors from the Middle Ages, and certainly from the English Middle Ages, for his seemingly limitless capacity to elicit *Einfühlung* among later writers, artists and performers. In this chapter I cannot hope to offer a comprehensive account of Chaucer's emotional reception, which stretches across six centuries and straddles both scholarly and creative modes; rather I aim to consider the dominant tenor of the transhistorical empathy he has elicited, and to examine two recent performative examples that demonstrate the complexity and variety of his emotional legacy in the last half-century.

Since Caroline Spurgeon's pioneering work from over a century ago, Chaucer's long and proliferative afterlife has been a subject of recurrent analysis. In addition to many individual essays on the subject, the twenty-first century has alone produced several wide-ranging studies of Chaucer's reception: Steve Ellis's *Chaucer at Large: The Poet in the Modern Imagination* (2001); Stephanie Trigg's *Congenial Souls: Reading Chaucer from Medieval to Postmodern* (2002); Candace Barrington's *American Chaucers* (2007); Geoffrey W. Gust's *Constructing Chaucer: Author and Autofiction in the Critical Tradition* (2009); and Kathleen Forni's *Chaucer's Afterlife: Adaptations in Recent Popular Culture* (2013); as well as Kathleen Coyne Kelly and Tison Pugh's essay collection, *Chaucer on Screen: Absence, Presence, and Adapting the* Canterbury Tales (2016). Among these recent studies, which diagnose the cultural and ideological vicissitudes of the author's centuries-long reception, Trigg's stands out for its focus on the fundamentally affective impulse underlying this phenomenon across time.

Speaking of 'our unspoken and increasingly unspeakable desire to see and speak with Chaucer, to capture an elusive, virtually forbidden moment of authorial presence',[10] she locates this desire in the experience of *congeniality*, an idea she develops from John Dryden's claim in *Fables Ancient and Modern* (1700) that his own soul and Chaucer's were 'congenial'.[11] Lest this notion of congeniality seem to authorise the ahistorical 'pleasurable submersion' that Habermas rejects, Dryden actually invoked it, as Trigg points out, to license his modernising 'improvements' to Chaucer's work. It is, then, a kind of fellow feeling made up of both historical distance and emotional intimacy. Although Trigg does appeal to a generalised notion of identification when she describes 'the metaphysical fiction of authorial presence, sustained by the reader identifying with the author, the better to hear their words directly',[12] the impulse of congeniality that effects this fiction of presence rests on a sense of 'affiliation and affinity',[13] terms that bring her idea of congeniality much closer to the affective experience of *Einfühlung*.

Trigg's focus on affective reception in *Congenial Souls* enables her to demonstrate how Chaucer's writings have generated an abiding tendency to attribute to the author not only genius, originary linguistic paternity or (more amorphously) essential Englishness, but also, significantly, an emotional disposition which is deemed to animate his work and in turn to inspire fellow feeling in his readers across time. Unsurprisingly, the quality deemed to solicit congeniality is Chaucerian geniality, a quality which inheres in him both as author and as character in his works, especially in the *Canterbury Tales*: 'the convivial Chaucerian personality eases such identifications.... Chaucer is less the solitary bookish figure than the jovial companion on pilgrimage'.[14] Although commentators do attend to the melancholy and restless lover–dreamer *personae* of his dream visions, across hundreds of years of reception the emotions imputed to Chaucer have clustered more insistently around the joyful end of the affective spectrum.

For some within this sometimes densely reiterative tradition, the Chaucerian temperament is abidingly serene; even those who portray the *Canterbury Tales* as a penetrating exposé of folly tend to ascribe a wise and equable benignity to the author's satiric vision. Among the majority of commentators, though, Chaucer is overwhelmingly associated with a more sociable mode of good cheer, characterised by joviality, affability and geniality. Among the many examples that could be cited here are John Dart's largely imaginative biographical account (revised by William Thomas) which appeared in John Urry's edition of Chaucer's works (1721–22) and emphasised Chaucer's 'learning, wit, amorous disposition, gay humour, and gallantry',[15] and later, G. K. Chesterton's allusion to the popular idea of the author as 'a stout and genial gentleman'.[16] For Ellis it is this jovial persona that makes possible the *Einfühlung* readers experience when reading Chaucer's work – a 'feeling into' that recognises the specificity of the author's historical and linguistic context (Dart's biography, for instance, suggests that the Ricardian court, with its 'perpetual Mirth, Tilts, and Tournaments', was the perfect environment for Chaucer) even as it responds to a perceived invitation to shared sociability. The result of Chaucerian geniality, he claims, is that 'Across the tantalizing space that separates him from the general reader there is every enticement to build bridges'.[17] Ellis emphasises in his study that in the twentieth century this hearty joviality becomes an attribute of a manly healthiness that subsumes and neutralises the author's formerly troubling association with the bawdy. The meaning of the joviality shifts, but it remains stable as a perceived attribute of both the author and the man.

One striking feature of the long history of Chaucerian *Einfühlung* is the extent to which empathic responses have been inspired by apprehensions of the author's physical being – his 'persone', as his devoted follower Thomas Hoccleve put it, referring to the now-iconic 'liknesse' of Chaucer in the margin of his *Regiment of Princes* (see plate 11).[18] This interest in Chaucer's 'persone' corresponds, and may even partly be due, to the fact that the text of the *Canterbury Tales* itself solicits a sense of physical familiarity through its inclusion of details about the pilgrim-narrator Chaucer's appearance – the famous thick 'waast', the smallness, the eyes staring at the ground, and the 'elvyssh' expression – in the prologue to the tale of *Sir Thopas*. But the longstanding preoccupation with Chaucer's face, which forms its own subgenre of reception, moves well beyond Chaucer's own piecemeal description, elaborating notions of the author as an affective subject in a way that reflects an abiding sense of empathic affiliation with him.

It should not be surprising that the author's face would be a locus of intersubjective affinity for those who claim to have a transhistorical empathic encounter with him. Many who work on the intersubjective experience of encountering the face cite Emmanuel Levinas's quasi-theological account in *Totality and Infinity* of the ethical demand made by the face of the Other and its ineluctable alterity, which compels a response that transcends one's own subjectivity.[19] But the post-phenomenological nature of Levinas's account means that it does not necessarily illuminate the transhistorical affinity I am discussing here; his account of ethical responsibility has little to do with the affective experiences of empathy, affinity or sociability. Moreover, Levinas's suspicion of representation makes his account difficult to apply to responses to a face that is produced by a long history of visual and verbal depictions. More conducive, and more closely consonant with Trigg's exploration of transhistorical congeniality, is Shaun Gallagher's account of the embodied and affective experience of encountering faces, which confirms but modifies Levinas's account by combining phenomenology and enactive cognitivist approaches. Although Gallagher agrees with Levinas that 'the transcendence at stake' in face-to-face encounters 'involves one's capacity to perceive in the other ... the potential to take one beyond oneself',[20] he grounds this intersubjective experience in cognitive perception and, importantly, in affective response which 'involves complex interactive behavioral and response patterns arising out of ... the recognition of emotions', both in the other and in oneself.[21] In arguing, furthermore, that facial encounters

> rely on a variety of bodily aspects in social interaction – posture, movement, gesture ... – as well as communicative and narrative practices, place-related and contextual factors, background knowledge about the person, etc. and our own prior experience,[22]

Gallagher characterises these encounters as complex phenomenological, affective and social experiences. His conclusion, *contra* Levinas, that rather than the face being a site of pure alterity, '[there is nothing] like a complete alterity of the other that is not already mediated in interaction',[23] also confirms the extent to which the facial encounter is a hermeneutic exchange in which the experience of the interpreter is deeply involved. Although Gallagher does not deal with transhistorical encounters, his phenomenological-enactivist account implicitly accommodates them, providing a helpful frame for thinking about the complex phenomenon of *Einfühlung* that has been occasioned by Chaucer's face.

This subgenre of 'facial reception' in Chaucer's afterlife comprises, most obviously, visual representations stretching forward from the Hoccleve image and the equally famous miniature of Chaucer on horseback in the Ellesmere manuscript. Together these influenced portraiture across the centuries, with versions appearing, to offer just a few examples, in the author portraits in the 1698 Speght and 1721 Urry editions, the sixteenth-century Plimpton Portrait, the image of Chaucer in the 1747 engraving of The Death of Alexander Pope in William Mason's *Musæus*, the central figure of Ford Madox Brown's monumental painting *Chaucer at the Court of Edward III* (1847–51) and even the Chaucer puppet narrating Jonathan Myerson's 1998 BBC animated adaptation of the *Canterbury Tales*.[24] But these images have not circulated independently; rather, they have existed alongside an abundance of written interpretations of Chaucer's countenance, which in some cases respond to the portraits but elsewhere elaborate accounts of the author's face with little or no reference to any visual depictions. Unlike the relative stability of depiction across many of the visual portraits, which largely revisit the Ellesmere–Hoccleve three-quarter profile image of Chaucer as a man of mature years with light skin and a neat forked beard, wearing a hood and a dark robe, the written reception varies widely in its rendering of Chaucer's visage. While the early pen portraits concerned only with physical description tend to reiterate the key details of the portrait tradition, with occasional minor variations in which the author's complexion is either pale or ruddy and his hair either silver or gold,[25] Ellis and Forni both document that his move into being a novelistic character introduced new and sometimes anomalous detail. This ranges from the indeterminate handsomeness of Emily Riching's 1902 novel *In Chaucer's Maytime* to the eye bags and double chins in Garry O'Connor's 2007 mystery novel *Chaucer's Triumph*, in which the poet is a slobbish philanderer.[26]

If variation came late to the descriptive tradition, it is an abiding characteristic of the textual genre that focuses on the Chaucerian face as a sign of the author's emotional essence. Despite the visual portrait tradition's more consistent depiction of Chaucer with a demeanour that is mild and composed, neither smiling nor frowning – a demeanour that is repeated even in William Blake's and Thomas Stothard's more 'sociable' depictions of him riding among the other pilgrims (see plates 7 and 6) – in textual accounts his expression ranges widely. This instability is present even within single accounts. In Leigh Hunt's 1846 study, *Wit and Humour, Selections from the English Poets*, Chaucer's face looks down meditatively (in the style of the Thopas prologue), chuckles heartily and becomes tearful all in the space of one paragraph; its changeability sketched as a manifestation of the poet's deep responsiveness and sympathy. The emotional range apparent in Algernon Charles Swinburne's depiction of Chaucer in his 1884 poem 'On a country road' is more typical in that while it is limited to the genial affects, it spans from earnest serenity through to mischievous cheer. While Chaucer's 'glad grave eyes' reinforce the familiar composed expression of the best-known portraits, as well as a long textual tradition emphasising Chaucerian serenity, Swinburne also bestows upon 'father Chaucer' an unambiguously merry countenance, with a 'smile that warmed the world with benison'.[27] This trope of the poet's smiling face, whether explicitly described as such or implied through allusions to merriness or jocosity, is repeated throughout Chaucer's afterlife, dating from at least *c.*1592, in the depiction of his 'countenance blithe and merry' in the pen portrait by Robert Greene, which Helen Cooper surmises could be working from the (now lost) tomb portrait.[28] The extent to which this smiling convention strays from, and even strains against, the Ellesmere–Hoccleve pictorial tradition is captured in Ellis's amusement at W. H. Thompson 'persuading himself that he could see the characteristic of "mischievous merriment" in the Hoccleve portrait' in his 1936 biography *Chaucer and his Times*.[29]

The prologue to the tale of *Sir Thopas* and the Ellesmere miniature are both salutary reminders that from the outset Chaucer's face was not apprehended separately from his body. Almost as persistently present as his face in both pictorial and textual portrayals is a generously proportioned midsection. With the exception of only a handful of lean Chaucers, he is described variously from the eighteenth century on as 'plump', 'stout', 'inclined to corpulence' or, more plainly, 'fat'. I wish to suggest that this bodily plumpness does not draw attention away from Chaucer's face but instead operates in a metonymic pairing with it, as another manifestation of his English cheerfulness. This metonymic relationship is most immediately apparent in Thomas Hearnes's 1711 portrait, where body and countenance are fused in the image of Chaucer's 'fleshie' face and his 'plump and ruddy' lips;[30] but even when it is more loosely articulated, the collocation of girth, face and geniality is nevertheless a commonplace of Chaucer's long empathic reception.

What is fascinating in the case of Chaucer reception is the extent to which the tendency to intersubjective and transhistorical affinity has led to a merging of the poet's face with that of his interpreters. In the medium of pictorial reception this has led to some famous instances in which another's face is inserted into a recognisable Ellesmere–Hoccleve figure. The best known examples of this are Ford Madox Brown's use of both his own face and that of his friend Dante Gabriel Rossetti for his portrayal of the declaiming poet in

Chaucer at the Court of Edward III, and Edward Burne-Jones's drawing of his own lean self into the figure of Chaucer in the Kelmscott Chaucer, which Velma Bourgeois Richmond calls 'a sign of the empathy he felt as artist'.[31] In the domain of performance it has led to others actually expressing affinity through the act of incarnating the poet. Performance is a particularly apposite form for thinking about Chaucerian *Einfühlung* because the 'feeling-into' it requires is not psychological identification but rather a physical embodying of a Chaucerian habitus. The body of the performer is crucial to the historically empathic performance. From John Gay's ill-fated play *The Wife of Bath*, in which Chaucer was played by Drury Lane heart-throb Robert Wilks, to Paul Bettany's lauded turn in Brian Helgeland's *A Knight's Tale* (2001), where he plays Chaucer as a charming young grifter, a performative tradition has run parallel, albeit in a more discontinuous pattern, to the portrait tradition and the descriptive textual discourse.[32] In order to explore Chaucerian performance as a complex form of *Einfühlung*, for the remainder of this chapter I will look at two examples from within the last half-century: Italian filmmaker Pier Paolo Pasolini's performance of Chaucer in *I Racconti di Canterbury* (1972) and British comedian Bill Bailey's stand-up performance as a Chaucerian narrator in the skit 'Pubbe gagge' from his *Bewilderness* tour (2001). Pasolini and Bailey embody both Chaucerian pilgrim and narrator *personae* in ways that prove the physical and affective, rather than psychological, basis of the transhistorical congeniality extended to Chaucer by those after him.

As a key part of their transhistorical empathy, both performances are invested, like many of the earlier interpretations discussed above, in Chaucer's status within a long comic inheritance. Pasolini's opening scene, set in the inn yard of the Tabard, features an exchange between the pilgrim Chaucer and the Cook (played by the infamous 'tattooed man', Jacobus Van Dyn) whose speech to Chaucer, 'between jokes and banter, great truths can be spoken' (tra scherzi e giochi grandi verità si possono dire), not only frames the film as satiric in intent, but reinforces Pasolini's own status as a filmmaker and writer committed to exposing the state of the world.[33] This frame would appear to be belied by much of what follows: the comedy of most of the film's selected tales is actually focused on sexual and scatological farce (*Merchant's Tale, Reeve's Tale, Miller's Tale, Cook's Tale, Wife of Bath's Prologue, Summoner's Tale*) rather than on social or political satire. But the film is returned to the realm of grim anticlerical satire by the introduction of Pasolini's own original 'Tale', which depicts male homosexual activity being spied on and then punished by immolation at the hands of ecclesiastical authorities, and by the film's concluding scene, an explicit depiction of the scene of hell in the *Summoner's Prologue* in which friars are expelled from Satan's anus.

Pasolini's physical appearance as Geoffrey Chaucer, pilgrim and author, was not his first as a medieval figure. Just a year earlier, in another gesture of transhistorical affinity, he had played a student of the Italian painter Giotto in his version of Boccaccio's *Il Decamerone*, empathically channelling the combination of realism and humility associated with Giotto the man and the artist. But while his wiry, workman-like persona in *Il Decamerone* is an anonymous Italian forbear, his embodiment of the English poet would seem to go completely against the grain of Chaucer's longstanding portrayal. Pasolini's wiry frame, frequently shown at full length or in medium close up, defies the convention of Chaucer's rotund 'waast', and places Pasolini–Chaucer in the select company of Edward Burne-Jones's elegant Kelmscott figure and Paul Bettany's gangly ectomorph in *A Knight's Tale*. Although Chaucer's full body has been part of the pictorial tradition as far back as the Ellesmere miniature, Pasolini introduces extrapolated scenes of the poet's corporeal life, showing him variously in his undergarments, sleeping at his desk with a cat curled in his lap, bumping his head (twice) and sitting fidgeting with his feet.

Even more arrestingly, the blunt, olive-skinned handsomeness of the filmmaker's face, which is frequently featured in close-ups, goes against the fair and rosy Chaucer of pictorial tradition and anglophone textual reception. Yet despite the stark departure from dominant conventions of how the author's face has been represented, Pasolini–Chaucer's facial expression of quiet mirth throughout the film can be described as conspicuously 'feeling into' and reinforcing the trope of merry Chaucer. The viewer first sees Pasolini–Chaucer smiling to himself in the opening Southwark sequence as he eavesdrops on the other pilgrims talking to one another about themselves (using dialogue derived from their prologues and from the *General Prologue*). This same smile of inward amusement returns in scenes when he takes up his pen to write down their tales. One of these writerly scenes takes place on pilgrimage, as Chaucer genially studies his slumbering companions, the camera tracking his gaze, and begins his notes toward the *Cook's Tale*. The other scenes are extradiegetic ones featuring

Chaucer in his study, the well-lit and well-appointed interior of which alludes closely to fourteenth- and fifteenth-century portraits of authors at their desks. It is in this environment that the viewer witnesses the steady smile erupting into a single instance of hearty laughter, as Pasolini–Chaucer reads *Il Decamerone*, doubling over with mirth before hiding the book deep into a pile on the floor. Like Pasolini's bold 'Italianising' of the Chaucerian face, this sequence exposes the Italian influence in a number of Chaucer's (and hence the film's) tales, but succinctly alludes to the masking of that influence by nationalist tropes of Chaucer as literary and linguistic originator – the 'morning star of English' and the 'well of English undefiled'.

The dominance of English, which Pasolini regarded as the homogenising language of global commerce that had its crucible in the bourgeois world of Chaucer, is also cleverly rebutted in the only two moments in the film when Pasolini–Chaucer speaks. These scenes rely heavily on Pasolini's re-envisioned Chaucerian face: both times we see the lips of the actor–director in medium close-up forming words in English, but hear those words dubbed into the Neapolitan dialect. In his opening exchange with the Cook, moreover, Pasolini–Chaucer speaks in English, dubbed into Neapolitan, plus his hand covers his lower face (the narrative reason being that he has bumped his nose on the Cook's head). The film's playfully defamiliarised Chaucer reflects Pasolini's idiosyncratic *Einfühlung*, his empathy with Chaucer as an observer and satirist, but also the limits of that empathy, given the Marxist director inserts Chaucer into a bourgeois cultural lineage – a lineage expressed in the rich, voluminous robes he wears, which closely echo those of the early manuscript images of the medieval poet.

Bill Bailey's performance of the Chaucerian 'persone' in 'Pubbe gagge', a forty-four-line comic tale of a drunken lads' night out, is remarkable in a way that is the opposite of Pasolini's performance. For while Pasolini overtly embodies 'Geoffrey Chaucer' while deviating audaciously from representational conventions, Bailey's own physical resemblance to early images of the poet serendipitously links him back to these very conventions even though he does not actually claim to be playing Chaucer. At the beginning of the two most widely circulated versions of 'Pubbe gagge', he tells his audiences that his jokes are about to 'enter the realm of Geoffrey Chaucer', and be told 'in the style of Geoffrey Chaucer'.[34] He presents himself not *as* Chaucer, but as the inheritor of a specifically British pub gag genre that links him to Chaucer across six centuries, via the *Dick Emery Show* of the 1970s, which he mentions in the gag. By mentioning the 'lewdness and debaucherie' of Emery's very politically incorrect sketches, Bailey playfully suggests that they contribute, like his and Chaucer's tales, to a continuous comic tradition portraying a long-thriving ritual of British life.

Although Bailey merely presents himself as telling a 'very old pub joke' that is simultaneously both his and Chaucer's inheritance and creation, as soon as he begins telling the gag, words fuse with image and his resemblance to the medieval poet becomes difficult to deny. Beginning with the lines

> Three fellowes wenten into a pubb<u>e</u>
> And gleefullye their handes did rubb<u>e</u>
> In expectatione of revelri<u>e</u>
> For 'twas the houre that is called happy<u>e</u>

Bailey's enunciation of the skit's (mostly) decasyllabic rhyming couplets, with their heavy comic emphasis on the final -e, is reinforced visually by the 'Chaucerian' combination of his fair skin, his trim beard, his round face and his thick waist, all of which closely echo the key features of the Ellesmere–Hoccleve image.[35] For viewers of the video recordings of the 2001 *Bewilderness* tour, there is the further coincidence of Bailey standing in the same three-quarter profile as seen in the Ellesmere and Hoccleve miniatures (see plates 11 and 12). In the live theatre recording, moreover, Bailey repeatedly points his index finger in a way that strongly (though probably accidentally) recalls the pictorial tradition of Chaucer pointing, which developed out of the early images. Bailey's English-speaking filmed audiences are familiar enough with Chaucer's verse, or at least with the cultural valency of Chaucer, to respond with laughter to his *faux* Middle English fusion of the pub gag with grotesque medievalism. Although it cannot be assumed that this familiarity extends to the author's appearance, the recirculation of the Ellesmere–Hoccleve image of Chaucer via Jonathan Myerson's 1998 animated version of the *Canterbury Tales* on the BBC could have prompted a readier recognition of Bailey's resemblance to the medieval author.

Bailey–Chaucer's face also differs from Pasolini–Chaucer's face insofar as it is a constantly mobile face, the expressions of which modulate as he narrates his tale. What the two faces have in common, however, is their expression of suppressed conspiratorial mirth. In Pasolini's case the expression is directed inward, with the viewer looking on; in Bailey's case it is addressed genially to the audience. There are aspects of Bailey's appearance that would appear to disrupt the Chaucer-effect, in particular the long, light brown hair that flows back from his receding hairline. This, along with his modern attire, moves him away from the respectably dressed and hooded Chaucer of the Ellesmere–Hoccleve lineage, as well as from Pasolini, who is never without at least a linen coif at home, and a pilgrim's broad-brimmed hat when in public. But if we consider the content of Bailey's gag, his long wispy hair in fact deepens the Chaucerian nature of his performance. On more than one occasion, Bailey's tale uses phrases taken from the *Pardoner's Tale*. His lines 'well we know that gluttonye / stoketh the fire of lecherye', for instance, is a close inversion of the Pardoner's lines 'To kyndle and blowe the fyr of lecherye, / That is annexed unto glotonye' (VI.481–2), while his phrase 'stinking, foul corruption' condenses 'O wombe, O bely! O stynkyng cod! / Fulfilled of dong and of corrupcioun!' (VI.534–5).[36] Bailey's tale about 'three fellowes' in a pub, then, fuses the 'three men' gag trope with the Pardoner's tale of 'riotoures thre' (VI.661), although the fates of the men are very different in each tale. Taking this into account, one is put in mind of the famous description of the Pardoner's hair in the *General Prologue* to the *Tales*:

> This Pardoner hadde heer as yelow as wex
> But smothe it heeng as dooth a strike of flex;
> By ounces henge his lokkes that he hadde,
> And therwith he his shuldres overspradde;
> But thynne it lay, by colpons oon and oon. (I.675–9)

In a corporeal equivalent to Chaucer's ventriloquising of the Pardoner's voice, Bailey becomes a hybrid Chaucer-face with Pardoner-hair, fusing their attributes into a single comic 'persone' that embodies the continuing malleability of 'merry Chaucer'.

Trigg and co-author Stephanie Downes have recently argued for the importance of recognising the historicity of the face as a key site of human emotion.[37] Analysing representations of Chaucer's face through time reveals the extent to which faces also have *transhistoricity*. It is true that the transhistorical story of Chaucer's face is notable for being characterised by variations within a larger arc of hermeneutic stability. But the persistence with which his face has remained cheerful across the centuries need not be read as testament to the timelessness of his face, or the universality of facial expression. Rather, it discloses how Chaucer has elicited a long cumulative emotional afterlife, driven not just (or even primarily) by an informed understanding of his writings, but by an 'utterly unhistorical' yet powerful apprehension of him as an emotional being.

Notes

1. Jan Plamper, 'The history of emotions: an interview with William Reddy, Barbara Rosenwein, and Peter Stearns', *History and Theory*, 49 (2010), 237–65 (p. 253).
2. Aranye Fradenburg, 'Going mental', *postmedieval*, 3:3 (2012), 361–72 (p. 369).
3. W. Dilthey, 'Die Entstehung der Hermeneutik', in G. Misch (ed.), *Wilhelm Dilthey: Gesammelte Schriften V* (Stuttgart: B. G. Teubner, 1924), pp. 318/236; translation in Austin Harrington, 'Dilthey, empathy, and *Verstehen*: a contemporary reappraisal', *European Journal of Social Theory*, 4:3 (2001), 311–29 (p. 317).
4. For a good overview, see Magdalena Nowak, 'The complicated history of *Einfühlung*', *Argument*, 1:2 (2011), 301–26; and Harrington, 'Dilthey, empathy, and *Verstehen*', pp. 311–29.
5. Hans-Georg Gadamer, *Truth and Method*, trans. J. Weinsheimer and D. G. Marshall (London and New York: Continuum, 2nd edn, 2004), p. 233.
6. Jürgen Habermas, *Knowledge and Human Interests*, trans. J. J. Shapiro (London: Heinemann, 1972), p. 181.
7. Nowak, 'The complicated history of *Einfühlung*', pp. 309–11.
8. Max Scheler, *The Nature of Sympathy*, quoted in Harrington, 'Dilthey, empathy, and *Verstehen*', p. 319.
9. Martha Nussbaum, *Upheavals of Thought: The Intelligence of Emotion* (Cambridge: Cambridge University Press, 2001), p. 327.
10. Stephanie Trigg, *Congenial Souls: Reading Chaucer from Medieval to Postmodern* (Minneapolis: University of Minnesota Press, 2002), p. xv.
11. Trigg, *Congenial Souls*, pp. xix–xx.
12. Trigg, *Congenial Souls*, p. xviii.
13. Trigg, *Congenial Souls*, p. xvii.
14. Trigg, *Congenial Souls*, p. xx.
15. John Dart, 'Life of Chaucer', revd William Thomas, in Derek Brewer (ed.), *Geoffrey Chaucer: The Critical Heritage*, vol. 1 (New York: Routledge, 1995), pp. 176–86 (p. 177).
16. G. K. Chesterton, *The Collected Works of G. K. Chesterton*, vol. 18, ed. and intro. Russell Kirk (San Francisco: Ignatius Press, 1991), p. 214.
17. Steve Ellis, *Chaucer at Large: The Poet in the Modern Imagination* (Minneapolis: University of Minnesota Press, 2000), p. 20.
18. London, British Library Harley MS 4866, fol. 88r. On Hoccleve's claims concerning the portrait's verisimilitude, see David Carlson,

'Thomas Hoccleve and the Chaucer portrait', *Huntington Library Quarterly*, 54:4 (1991), 283–300.
19 See for instance Michael Edward Moore, 'Meditations on the face in the Middle Ages (with Levinas and Picard)', *Literature and Theology*, 24:1 (2010), 19–37.
20 Shaun Gallagher, 'In your face: transcendence in embodied interaction', *Frontiers in Human Neuroscience*, 8 (2014), 1–7 (p. 1).
21 Gallagher, 'In your face', p. 3.
22 Gallagher, 'In your face', p. 3.
23 Gallagher, 'In your face', p. 5.
24 A selection of scholarship on the portraits includes William K. Finley and Joseph Rosenblum, *Chaucer Illustrated: Five Hundred Years of The Canterbury Tales in Pictures* (New Castle DE and London: Old Knoll Press and the British Library, 2003); Derek Pearsall, *The Life of Geoffrey Chaucer: A Critical Biography* (Oxford: Blackwell, 1992), pp. 285–305; Alice Miskimin, 'The illustrated eighteenth-century Chaucer', *Modern Philology*, 77:1 (1979), 26–55; and Alan T. Gaylord, 'Portrait of a poet', in Martin Stevens and Daniel Woodward (eds), *The Ellesmere Chaucer: Essays in Interpretation* (San Marino CA: Huntington Library, 1995), pp. 121–42.
25 See, for instance, Thomas Brown's 1704 'Letters from the Dead to the Living' in which Chaucer regards himself in the mould of the 'Jolly well complexion'd Englishman', in James Drake (ed.), *The Works of Mr Thomas Brown*, vol. 2 (London: Sam Briscoe, 1707), p. 207.
26 Novels cited in Kathleen Forni, *Chaucer's Afterlife: Adaptations in Recent Popular Culture* (Jefferson NC and London: McFarland & Co., 2013) p. 74.
27 Algernon Charles Swinburne, *A Midsummer Holiday and Other Poems* (Piccadilly [London]: Chatto & Windus, 1884), pp. 9–11.
28 Helen Cooper, 'I. Chaucerian representation', in Robert G. Benson and Susan J. Ridyard (eds), *New Readings of Chaucer's Poetry*, Chaucer Studies XXXI (Woodbridge: Boydell & Brewer, 2003), pp. 7–30 (p. 18).
29 Ellis, *Chaucer at Large*, p. 23.
30 Thomas Hearne, 'Extracts from his diary, April 28 (Sat) 1711', in *Remarks and Collections of Thomas Hearne*, vol. 3, ed. C. E. Doble (Oxford Hist. Society: 1711), p. 155.
31 Velma Bourgeois Richmond, 'Edward Burne-Jones's Chaucer portraits in the Kelmscott *Chaucer*', *Chaucer Review*, 40:1 (2005), pp. 1–38 (p. 7). For an account of Ford Madox Brown, see also Richmond, 'Ford Madox Brown's medievalism: Chaucer and Wycliffe', *Christianity and Literature*, 54:3 (2005), 363–92.
32 For a discussion of Gay's play, see Calhoun Winton, *John Gay and the London Theatre* (Lexington: University of Kentucky Press, 1993), pp. 30–1. See also Brian Helgeland (dir.), *A Knight's Tale* (Black and Blu Entertainment, Columbia Pictures: 2001).

33 Pier Paolo Pasolini (dir.), *The Canterbury Tales / I Racconti di Canterbury* (Les Productions Artistes Associés, Produzione Europee Associati: 1972). For selected scholarly accounts of the film, see Agnes Blandeau, *Pasolini, Chaucer, and Boccaccio: Two Medieval Texts and their Translation to Film* (Jefferson NC and London: McFarland & Co., 2006); Kathleen Forni, 'A "cinema of poetry": what Pasolini did to Chaucer's *Canterbury Tales*', *Literature/Film Quarterly*, 30:4 (2002), 256–63; and Tison Pugh, 'Chaucerian fabliaux, cinematic fabliau: Pier Paolo Pasolini's *I racconti di Canterbury*', *Literature/Film Quarterly*, 32:3 (2004), 199–206.

34 The two versions discussed here are the live theatre version recorded in Bill Bailey, 'Pubbe gagge', *Bewilderness* (Talent Television, 2001) and the live TV studio version available at www.youtube.com/watch?v=mNEWatD0viw&t=11s, accessed 6 May 2018. For another discussion of this skit, see Louise D'Arcens, 'You had to be there: anachronism and the limits of laughing at the Middle Ages', *postmedieval*, 5:2 (2014), 140–53.

35 In her keynote address at the 2016 Congress of the New Chaucer Society, Trigg remarked that her experience of prosopagnosia (facial blindness) affects her assessment of whether Bailey actually resembles Chaucer, or whether the perceived resemblance is due to his parodic Chaucerian performance. As I argue here, the resemblance is performative, physical, and produced by the similar framing of the author's and comedian's bodies. See Stephanie Trigg, 'Chaucer's silent discourse', *Studies in the Age of Chaucer*, 39 (2017), 33–56.

36 All quotations of Chaucer's poetry refer to *The Riverside Chaucer*, gen. ed. Larry D. Benson (Oxford: Oxford University Press, 3rd edn, 1988) and are cited by fragment and line number.

37 Stephanie Downes and Stephanie Trigg, 'Editors' introduction: facing up to the history of emotions', *postmedieval*, 8:1 (2017), 3–11.

14
Textual face: cognition as recognition
James Simpson

When university presidents defend the humanities, they do so in the same way they defend the sciences: as *discovery* of knowledge. That may be true of the sciences, but in this short chapter I want to persuade you that there is a distinctive form of thinking in the humanities. Thinking in the humanities is more a matter of *re*covery than *dis*covery. Moments of revelation in the humanities are more inventions in the older sense (finding the already known) than scientific inventions in the newer sense (discovering the never previously known). To know in the humanities is 'to recover what has been lost / And found and lost again and again'.[1]

What I have to present is less a compact, self-enclosed essay, than a set of feelers into a world view – a world view we have forgotten or which, for historically intelligible reasons, has been repudiated. I hope, for reasons that should become clear, that my project is not at all original, but rather a way of connecting with, or recovering, that world view. I'll be practising what might be called 'cultural etymology' – an intellectual practice that assumes that truth is in here rather than out there, immanent rather than transcendent, visible and radiant despite repeated use and usage; and where recovery of truth is all the more intense for having been known already.

Our language for the truths of literature is (in universities, at any rate) reformist and nominalist; our experience of reading is, by contrast, habitual and idealist. Contrary to the way we talk about what kind of new, liberatory truths literature expresses, our reading practice itself is grounded in long-standing forms of recognition. Every time we interpret, we recall deep-seated, ingrained and circular protocols that give us access to truths immanent within the separate realms of literary experience. As interpreters, we depend on *préjugés* that produce recognition of already existing truths.[2]

Such, at any rate, is the thesis of this chapter. That literary knowledge is thus Janus-faced, looking resolutely forward even as it draws deep on a backward gaze, is in no way contradictory or disabling. The deepest posture of Anglo-American literary pedagogy is grounded, rightly, on the conviction that literature liberates. We prize what is new, what destabilises the solidities of official culture, and what points to liberation from the strictures of the norm. We also prize the individuality of each work, partly because we prize individuality and partly because we need the business: as long as each work and, more recently, each material text of each work, is distinct, there's work in it for us. My chapter is in no way designed to undo these Enlightenment-derived convictions about liberation from the past, or to question these perfectly reasonable business necessities for the research university.

I am, however, concerned to show that our reading practice is differently grounded, on opposed premises. Our reading practice, that is, depends on deeply instilled norms, and begins by assuming that every work in a certain genre is the 'same' work, a work that we 'knew' before we began reading the 'new' work. Literary knowledge, that is, is dependent on recognition. We know because we knew. Literary cognition is fundamentally a matter of re-cognition.

This default position for reading is certainly at odds with any revolutionary pedagogic programme that prizes originality and pure novelty, wholly freed from the strictures of the past. The default practice of 'recognitional' reading proposed here is not, however, at odds with a reformist and a nominalist interpretation of a work, since the recognitions of literary experience are not instances of *mere* repetition; on the contrary, the literary recognitions we care about are memorable because we see a truth – we know the place, we see a face – as if for the first time, and as unique. The recognition is old and general; the force of the recognition is reformist and very particular.

The old, the dying and the general are, that is, the very conditions of the revivification, the reform and unique application. An abiding literary canon is never therefore obsolete, since it remains fresh for every generation of new readers. Informed conversation with a recognised past, central to the entire tradition of liberal education since Antiquity – and, in my view, for our undergraduate pedagogy (as distinct from our research operation) – is the condition of reformist movement into the future.

My central hermeneutic perception for knowledge in the humanities is as follows: that cognition is re-cognition (a word with exactly parallel formations in a variety of European languages, dead and alive, such as *recognitio, reconnaissance, riconoscenza, Wiedererkennung, anagnorisis*). Before we can know, we must already have known. I will adumbrate that paradox in three ways: (i) with reference to examples of facial recognition; (ii) with a connection between facial recognition represented in literature and what I call textual face (and here I apply the lessons we learn from facial recognition to textual recognition), or the whole text as a kind of face; and (iii) finally, I answer some possible objections to the paradox.

Face to face

'Make It New' enjoined Ezra Pound in 1935, two years after he met Mussolini, expressing the essence of a long and still vibrant revolutionary tradition of originality in which Pound, as committed fascist, himself actively participated.[3]

The injunction to make it new flies in the face, however, of something that Pound as poet and Samuel Beckett as playwright knew better: they knew that it's the old, *known* poetic faces that evoke the most intense responses – these are the faces, that is, that impress us emotionally even as they save us. In fact they save us *by* impressing us emotionally; Pound and Beckett knew that we need to re-encounter the old in the shadows before we can re-emerge to see the stars afresh again: what Beckett says of the old questions and answers in *Endgame* is no less true of the old faces: 'Ah, the *old* questions, the *old* answers, *there's nothing like them*!'[4]

There's 'nothing like them', nothing like these old faces (except, apparently, themselves of course): only the old faces, the recovered faces, have the power to move us to novelty. But precisely as they move to reform us, they become new and unlike anything else – there is, indeed, 'nothing like them'. Only the old faces can produce magnetic, transformative beauty in the darkness; they are 'like a jewel hung in ghastly night', making 'black night beauteous and her old face new'.[5]

Let me give some examples from within literary texts.[6] In Book 4 of the *Aeneid*, Dido confesses to her sister Anna that she is falling in love, again. She knows it's new because it's old. About Aeneas, she says:

> solus hic inflexit sensus animumque labantem
> impulit. agnosco veteris vestigia flammae.[7]
>
> (He alone has swayed my will and overthrown my tottering soul. I recognise the trace of that former flame.)

The metaphor Dido uses for recognition is not the face, but the footstep (*vestigium*). The footstep is not that of Aeneas, but rather of an experience itself – the flame of falling in love, the 'old flame', as we still say. She sees and is mesmerised by the potentially destructive path of that life-changing flame, but what moves her is, of course, the face that she has fallen in love with – the face of Aeneas. The experience of that face is not itself, however, a direct one – Dido has been taught to fall in love with that face by re-cognising it already: Venus has Cupid simulate Aeneas's son Ascanius, and assume that boy's face, in order to beguile Dido:

> tu *faciem* illius noctem non amplius unam
> falle dolo, et notos pueri puer indue *vultus* (1.683–4, my emphases)
>
> (for but a single night, feign by craft his form and, boy that you are, don the boy's familiar face)

Because Ascanius looks like his father, Dido is being trained to learn Aeneas's face via Cupid, via Ascanius, and via the experience of having fallen in love already. It's the compacted experience of already seen and now recognised faces that produces the life changing force of the encounter with Aeneas: 'animum ... labantem / impulit'. By the time Dido cognises the face of Aeneas, along with everyone else in the Carthaginian hall,[8] she, unlike everyone else, recognises it. She's been taught to see it afresh by past experience.

The reader of the *Aeneid* has been attuned to the emotional force of recognition through art in Book 1. There Aeneas's response to the mural of the Trojan War he sees in Carthage is all the more intense because he recognises the scene of Trojan disaster represented before him, including Priam imploring him with empty hands, and including himself among the attacking Greeks: 'se quoque principibus permixtum agnovit Achivis' (1.488) (himself, too, in close combat with the Achaean chiefs, he recognised). Like Dido, however, he has been taught previously, by experience, to see the event afresh, and therefore to see it with so much more intensity: 'sic ait, atque animum pictura pascit inani / multa gemens, largoque umectat flumine vultum' (1.464–5) (so he speaks, and feasts his soul on the insubstantial portraiture, sighing oft, and his face wet with a flood of tears). None of the key sightings is a new one: they are profoundly mediated, profoundly moving. Aeneas sees and understands the work of art because he's seen it all before. Like Dido's recognition, it's new and moving because it's old and painful.

Of course, Dido's Book 2 recognition is disastrous for Dido, and, ultimately, profoundly painful for Aeneas. But the way out of self-destruction for Dido, and the way into self-reform for Aeneas, is also along the vestigial path of facial recognitions. For in Book 6 of the *Aeneid*, Aeneas must descend into the underworld in order to regain the dynamism for forward movement: across the entire breadth of the *Aeneid* the pattern of going backward to the old in order to move forward to the new is replicated in large and small.

Aeneas's visit to the underworld, there to encounter the shades of the dead, is the largest example of the generative pattern. The key moments are, however, facial recognitions. Aeneas sees Dido in the Campi Lugentes, in conditions of diminished light that sharpens cognitive apprehension: he sees Dido as one might see under a new moon: 'qualem primo qui surgere mense / aut videt aut vidisse putat per nubila lunam' (6.453–4) (even as, in the early month, one sees or fancies he has seen the moon rise amid the clouds). Aeneas is stopped in his tracks and recognises her: 'ut primum iuxta stetit agnovitque per umbras / obscuram' (6.452–3) (and as soon as the Trojan hero stood near and knew her, a dim form amid the shadows). Dido, however, repays Aeneas's earlier insult to her by refusing to look at him, keeping her gaze fixed firmly on the ground ('solo fixos oculos aversa tenebat') (6.469) (kept her looks fixed on the ground). Aeneas, *percussus* (6.475), moves on, next to meet a ghastly face that underscores the Trojan shame: he meets Priam's son Deiphobus, who had taken Helen as wife after the death of Paris; now Aeneas meets him with ears torn off, nostrils cut off and a 'face cruelly lacerated' (lacerum crudeliter ora) (6.495).

These shame-filled facial recognitions having been made, these narrative debts having been paid in the pain of facial recognition, Aeneas can now move forward, once again by first moving backward: he moves to the blissful groves to meet his father who will direct and inspire him to his proto-imperial destiny. Aeneas recurs to the past in order to move forward to the future (again); the pivot is a facial recognition of the already known, the *nota*. In this meeting, the first passionate claim of recognition is from father to son: 'datur ora tueri, / nate, et tua et notas audire et reddere voces?' (6.688–9) (is it given me to see your face, my son, and hear and utter familiar tones?). The second claim is from son to father: a weeping Aeneas thrice seeks vainly to throw his arms around the neck of his father's empty shade:

> ter conatus ibi collo dare braccia circum,
> ter frustra comprensa manus effugit imago
> par levibus ventis volucrique simillima somno (6.700–2)
>
> (thrice there he strove to throw his arms about his neck; thrice the form, vainly clasped, fled from his hands, even as the light winds, and most like a winged dream)

The old, the known and the loved move us more passionately than anything else – there's nothing like them. That said, there's also nothing there; the reformist novelty is produced out of pain for the fugitive, loved past.[9]

Textual face

In *Aeneid* 1–6, then, facial recognition serves many cardinal functions: readiness to follow fire (Dido); rebuke for the shameful deeds of the past (the underworld encounters of Aeneas with Dido and Deiphobus); and energy for the future (Aeneas and Anchises). The movements of world history are generated by profoundly moving emotional facial encounters. Each encounter centrally involves cognition – something understood; but my main point is that the lesson of this *cognitum* is powerful and unavoidable because it is in each case grounded on a *re-cognitum*: it's known profoundly now because it's been known before.

How might we move from understanding recognition *in* texts to understanding recognition *of* texts? What consequences might recognition thus defined have for literary pedagogy? I'll broach that in the first instance by looking to the way in which Dante models the function of literary pedagogy in his ethical education in *Inferno* and *Purgatorio*. For here, too, facial recognition is decisive, but the facial recognitions are profoundly embedded in *literary* recognitions by the reader. To cognise Dante's poem we must recognise Virgil's. We as readers must have '*fore*suffered all, / Enacted on this same' landscape of suffering in order to understand it.[10] The fact that it's happened before is essential to the force of its meaning.

We can broach this topic first by looking to a facial encounter of great force in the *Divine Comedy*. At the summit of Purgatory, Dante first catches sight of Beatrice thus:

> e lo spirito mio, che già cotanto
> tempo era stato, che a la sua presenza
> non era di stupor, tremando, affranto,
> sanza de li occhi aver più conoscenza,
> per occulta virtù che da lei mosse,
> d'antico amor sentì la gran potenza.[11]

> (And my spirit, which for such a long time had not been shaking and overcome in her presence, without further cognisance of those eyes felt, through hidden power that moved from within her, the mighty force of a deep love.)

Experiences of cognition and presentness are centrally involved here – they are precisely the rhyme words used by Dante: *presenza*, *conoscenza*. But that new cognition is produced through facial re-cognition: one glance at Beatrice's eyes suffices to provoke memories of the 'old love'. 'Antico amor' might suggest Virgil's 'antica[e] flamma[e]', as might the verb Dante uses to express the immense force of the recognition of Beatrice, *percosse*: 'Tosto che ne la vista mi percosse / l'alta virtù' (30.40–1): Aeneas, we remember, was *percussus* by Dido's refusal to look at him in the underworld.

Those suggestive echoes of Virgil become inescapably explicit within a few lines: Dante runs to Virgil as a child to a protective mother, crying in pain that 'conosco i segni dell'antica fiamma' (30.48) (I recognise the signs of the ancient flame), which is, I need hardly say, a direct translation of Dido's line from *Aeneid* 4 cited earlier.[12] The poetic recognition of Virgil is all the more moving here, since this is precisely the moment in which Virgil vanishes from the narrative: he's no longer there, as he gives way to Beatrice as guide. As, that is, Virgil's ultimate limitations as a pagan are reached, Dante draws precisely on Virgil's poetry to signal his profound love for the ancient poet.

The literary history is of course subjected to the emotional ethical encounter between Dante and Beatrice – the *antica fiamma* is Dante's adolescent love for Beatrice. The representation of a human encounter in the now of the poem is of course more urgently experienced than a literary historical narrative about Dante's poetic dependence on Virgil. The essential point is, however, that these two narratives are in fact indistinguishable. Just as Dido's love for Aeneas was profoundly mediated by prior visions, so too is Dante's recognition of Beatrice mediated and magnified by the reader's literary experience: the cognition of the potentially self-destroying, potentially redemptive love, is grounded in recognition. Dante cognises Beatrice all the more forcibly in part because he recognises the experience. And he recognises that experience, just as we do, from reading Virgil.

By the account of both Virgil and Dante, then, to know profoundly, we must have known profoundly first. The experience will be life-changing only if we've had it before. The life-changing event is less a discovery, that is, than a recovery. Let me offer one more example from a Chaucerian locus before addressing objections you might have to the understanding of re-cognition I am proposing.

In Robert Henryson's *Testament of Cresseid* (*c*.1475), Troilus rides, by chance, across a group of lepers begging by the road. Cresseid is among the begging lepers. The moment of facial recognition runs as follows:

> Than vpon him scho kest up baith hir ene
> And with ane blenk it come into his thocht
> That he sumtime hir face befoir had sene
> Bot scho was in sic plye he knew hir nocht,
> ȝit than hir luik into his mynd it brocht
> The sweit visage and amorous blenking
> Of fair Cresseid, sumtyme his awin darling.[13]

Troilus does not fully recognise Cresseid here, but is somehow prompted to remember her, and so throws a bag of gold coins into Cresseid's lap. Cresseid, for her part, does not recognise Troilus at all. This shocking failure of recognition fulfils, I think, a prophecy made by Troilus in Book V of *Troilus and Criseyde*: 'whan ye next upon me se, / So lost have I myn hele and ek myn hewe, / Criseyde shal nought konne knowen me'.[14] All Cresseid can ask is what lord it was that has done such 'great humanitie' (535).

There are unavoidably two kinds of recognition at issue in this scene: recognition represented *in* the text, and the recognition *of* the text. They work in similar ways. The recognitions in the text (Troilus's and Criseyde's) must contend with radically new circumstances. Troilus and Criseyde contend with terrible obstacles in recognising each other. Those eyes that look up to Troilus have been cursed by disease: 'Thy cristall ene mingit with blude I mak' (37), to cite the moon's definitive sentence on Cresseid. Some inkling of the former Criseyde is, however, retraceable since, as we remember from Book I of Chaucer's poem, Troilus's first encounter with Criseyde is by a similarly chance meeting. Then, Troilus's eye 'percede, and so depe it wente, / Til on Criseyde it smot, and ther it stente' (I.272–3). Because Love has his dwelling in 'the subtile stremes of hire yen', Troilus 'felte dyen, / Right with hire look, the spirit in his herte' (I.305–7). It's that deepest of impressions that is activated in the Henryson moment, despite all the terrible obstacles, since 'The idole of ane thing in cace may be / Sa deip imprentit in the fantasy / That it deludes the wittis outwardly' (508–10). The effect of Cresseid's leper face on Troilus is profound and draining – without knowing why, he feels 'reddie to expyre' (515).

The effect on Cresseid is no less profound, once she understands who it was who passed by (after having, shockingly, failed to recognise Troilus). She delivers the second inset speech about her condition in the poem. In the first, she blames fortune in a magnificently rhetorical complaint (407–69); in the second, she accuses, without convicting, herself in bluntly plain address: 'Nane but my self as now I will accuse' (574).

The representation of recognition *within* the text parallels our recognition as readers *of* the text. Our view, too, of Criseyde must negotiate the intimacy of our relation with her – the moment when we first saw her 'somdel deignous' facial expression (I.290); the moment when she passes over to the Greek camp in Book V, chosen by the illuminator of the frontispiece to Cambridge, Corpus Christi College, MS 61;[15] and the moment soon after that passing, when we are told 'That Paradis stood formed in hire yën' (V.817).

The backward look is painful, but reformist: Chaucer had simply seen Criseyde diminish and disappear, and Henryson's leper Cresseid herself would *not* be seen – 'I wald not be kend' (380), she says. Henryson himself, however, brings her back for a revisionist account of our entire reading experience, to see Cresseid accuse (not convict) herself. Henryson attempts the near impossible of rescuing Chaucer's *Troilus and Criseyde* from being a tragedy. Whatever the success of Henryson's generic rescue mission, the key point I want to emphasise here is that the literary issue devolves on recognition as much as the ethical issue does. Both are concentrated in a moment of intense physical, facial re-cognition. We can 'see' Cresseid anew, and attempt to see the *Testament of Cresseid* as a whole, only because we have seen Cresseid before, and then only because we have ourselves seen the book that the narrator re-reads at the start of the *Testament* – the 'quair ... / Writtin be worthie Chaucer glorious' (40–1); cognition is recognition.

The moments of facial recognition so subtly delineated by Stephanie Trigg in her magnificent 2016 Biennial New Chaucer Society lecture point in different directions from the facial recognitions, or failed facial recognitions, to which I point here.[16] Trigg analyses those moments where the face speaks, as it were, in syntactic units. I am focusing on moments where the face unlocks the recovered presence of the whole person. Trigg's brilliant discussion of instances of the speaking face do, however, contribute to the specifically literary questions prompted by moments of recognition, since some of her cases of the speaking face translate the face into text: the moment of trying to 'read' the face (as we still say) is simultaneously a textual moment. Thus, Troilus's comment in Book III, when he looks into Criseyde's eyes, underlines the ways in which specifically literary understanding is inherently bound up with emotional encounter: 'Though ther be mercy writen in youre cheere, / God woot, the text ful hard is, soth, to fynde!' (III.1356–7).

Henryson himself prompts us, indeed, to understand Cresseid as a specifically textual, or literary critical, challenge. We are asked, that is, to define the genre of the poem, or what I am calling its textual 'face'. The poet himself calls his poem a 'tragedie' in line 4, but the text embeds another document (a last testament, or will) that underlines Cresseid's legacy beyond tragedy. The earliest recorded title of the entire poem (*The Testament of Creseyde*) is drawn, after all, from that documentary form represented within the poem – the 'testament' composed not, in the poem's fiction, by Henryson but by Cresseid herself.[17]

Is recognition only conservative? platonistic? unacceptably paradoxical?

My account of reading recovery might prompt objections. In the first place, it sounds as if it might be deeply conservative (the key act of knowing has already happened). Secondly, it also sounds as if it might be, not to put too fine a point on it, deeply improbable: if we can only know what we've already known, we are either Platonists who believe in anamnesis, or we can't give any account of how we came to know anything; we're either Platonists, that is, or we're talking nonsense. And finally, it sounds deeply paradoxical (we can only know what we've known).

I'll deal with each of these objections briefly in turn.

The conservative objection

The deepest posture of Anglo-American literary pedagogy is, as I have said, rightly grounded on the conviction that literature liberates. We prize what is new, what destabilises the solidities of official culture, and what points to liberation from the strictures of the norm. In my view, the notion that cognition is recognition is consonant with this liberatory conviction.

For, the surprise of this kind of literary understanding is never one of simply recovering the old and the known. It is, instead, more like astonishment at the recovery of an old now become wholly surprising and liberating; it is more like greeting a long-lost parent, or child, or friend, or lover, or teacher, or student – what you will – and being captured by wonder at the force of the recognition in new circumstances, as under the new moon. Recognition-derived perception does not, that is, provide original experience. It is not revolutionary. On the contrary, its recoveries radiate the exquisite pleasure of knowledge that illuminates precisely because it is *not* original. It offers deeply illuminating repetition in fresh circumstance.

I offer just one more facial recognition in Dante to buttress this point. In Canto 15 of *Inferno*, Dante meets his former teacher, now punished in the circle of the sodomites. Virgil and Dante first encounter a group of shades, each of whom 'ci riguardava come suol di sera / guardare un altro sotto nuova luna' (15.18–19) (scrutinised us as one does at evening under a new moon). One in particular recognises Dante and cries out 'Qual maraviglia!' (what a marvel!), which provokes Dante's own recognitional response:

> E io, quando 'l suo braccio a me distese,
> Ficcai li occhi per lo cotto aspetto,
> Sì che 'l viso abbruciato non difese
> La conoscenza sua al mio intelletto;
> E chinando la mano a la sua faccia,
> Rispuosi 'Siete voi qui, ser Brunetto?' (15.26–30)

> (and I, when he reached toward me, fixed my eyes on his baked face so intently that its burnt surface did not block recognition; and, bending my hand toward his face, replied: 'Are you here, Master Brunetto?')

Brunetto's marvel is all the greater given the cognitive difficulty of perception (the diminished light); and Dante's sympathetic

Textual face: cognition as recognition

response to his teacher, his 'cara e buona imagine paterna' (15.83) (his beloved and good paternal image) is all the greater given his cognitive challenge of looking, as we all look when looking into the past, through the 'cotto aspetto' of his interlocutor. This moment of astonished recognition is the prelude to Brunetto's prophecy, in the manner of Anchises to Aeneas, of Dante's own proximate future, and Dante's implicit challenge to the appalling divine judgment under which Brunetto suffers, when Brunetto runs back to catch up with his group of fellow sufferers, and 'parve di costoro / quelli che vince, non colui che perde' (15.123–4) (seemed like one of those who win, not like one who loses). The intense, astonished, affectionate recognition of the old is the prelude to, and prompt for, reform of the present and understanding of the future. Like each of the intense facial recognitions considered in this chapter, this one transforms the present and points to a reformed future.

The improbability objection

We do not need to evoke the ontological improbabilities of Platonism to buy into the idea that we need to have known once already in order to know fully again. All we need to do is to accept the pedagogic praxis built into great literary texts themselves. That pedagogic praxis is grounded in recognition.

Every work of art wants to be understood. As we try to understand it, we begin by recognising what we are familiar with in order to understand what's new. Our reading practice, that is, depends on deeply instilled norms, and begins by assuming that every work in a certain genre is the 'same' work, a work that we 'knew' before we began reading the 'new' work. Our hard-wired habit is to look first to the face for what we know, and so we might say that we treat the work of art as if it were itself a face. We're looking to its known features, the better to understand its unknown features. With that posture in focus, we suddenly notice that the fundamental analytical tools at our disposal for the analysis of literary texts are features of repetition. This is no less true of large-scale categories such as genre (the most evident analogue with a known 'face') than it is of medium-scale features of narrative (e.g. recapitulation, *in medias res* narrative order), or than it is of much smaller features of style. Many separate figures of speech in a text point us backward: the very etymology of 'verse' turns us backwards, just as rhyme, alliteration, anaphora and chiasmus, are, for example, all figures of repetition, turning us back even as we move forward.

Each invites cognition through recognition; each offers forms of recapitulation.[18]

As we read, we are always looking for the familiar face or feature, or topos (i.e. commonplace) from the past. Anagnorisis – re-cognition – is the master topos. To read any work well, we need to understand how such works operate, what kinds of meaning they habitually offer and what kinds of meaning they habitually do *not* offer. We need, it might be said, to recognise their 'face'. Our recognition of genre above all might involve analytical observation of these separate figures and features, but the moment of generic recognition, which is simultaneously the moment in which we recognise the reformist novelty of a text, tends to be a moment: it is sudden, synthetic, transformative and pleasurable rather than incremental, analytic, sequential and arduous. Such understanding does not attempt to stand outside the object of enquiry, as scientific experimental protocols would have us do. On the contrary, recognitional understanding works on the assumption that knowledge (of this kind, at any rate) is immanent, or remaining within, buried beneath and within the 'cotto aspetto', rather than discovered outside the pale of the previously known.

Our texts, that is, train us how to read and recognise them. What in an earlier critical idiom we might have called intertextual allusion, we might now call cognitive cues.

The paradox objection

We can only know what we re-know. This apparently nonsensical paradox is less nonsensical, then, if we take into account the pragmatic way art teaches us through repetition to make recognitions. The apparently nonsensical paradox dissolves altogether once we widen our purview from literary perception and consider our own hard-wired forms of cognition and perception through each sense.

All our senses organise and make sense of the world through recognitions. This is clearly a huge topic, so let one beautifully succinct example suffice to point us towards our broader perceptual habits (see plate 13). The key features of our psychological response to this amusing and classic image are as follows: we cannot see lively duck and humble rabbit simultaneously; it's we who decide what to see; and, as we decide what to see on the basis of our own, produced recognition of duck or rabbit, we organise our perception differently.[19] The eye remains an eye as the focus of our recognition (and it is of course no accident that the eye is the locus around which we organise perception), but every other principal mark serves different purposes according to the viewer's decision. Rabbit's ears become duck's beak according to what we decide to recognise, and what features we decide to demote.[20] We also experience this same psychological phenomenon whenever we unsuccessfully look for something with the wrong mental image: if we look for the book with the green spine using the mistaken mental image that the spine in question is blue, we can 'see' the green-spined book any number of times without recognising that this is the book for which we are in fact looking. We truly see only what we recognise. Perception is preception.

Recognition, then, characterises literary interpretation no less than the very much wider fields of linguistic and sense-derived interpretation generally. Despite that fact, at least three influential discursive fields in Western culture must, with powerful reason, maintain the fiction that recognition has no part to play in reading and perception. These fields must maintain the fiction of positivism, that the real-world datum comes first and that the real-world datum is the only source of truth, from which follows understanding. Such powerful currents, which are understood as the default, common-sense position of our society, must therefore continue to describe the action of interpretive recognition pejoratively, as prejudice.

Those three fields are as follows: Protestant biblical interpretation; scientific enquiry; and constitutional interpretation in revolutionary societies grounded on a written constitution. Each of these fields must strictly deny, by positing logically unmotivated meanings, that an interpreter should recognise the truths of the object of enquiry. Each field must instead posit (in the textual examples) that the entire meaning of a text is contained in its words, or (in the case of science) that the entire meaning of a natural object derives from the object itself. Such fields therefore maintain that we should restrict ourselves to those meanings derived wholly from the words on the page, or from the object under enquiry. To engage dialectically in the production of meaning is, for each of these traditions, to exercise prejudice. Each will also, not co-incidentally, actively posit that there is such a thing as the literal sense, and each will repudiate figural, or tropical, language of any kind.[21]

So, far from being unusual or exceptional, then, the paradox of recognitional knowledge is our cognitive default position.

In conclusion we can say that, in contrast with the textual default positions of revolutionary cultures and their attendant empiricism, literary knowledge must entertain *préjugés*. It must involve circularity. Understanding text is dependent on recognition of the text's long pre-history, compacted into the deep coding of genre. At the heart of our reading practice, that is, stands not the revolutionary discovery of the never-before-known, but rather the reformist recovery of the, somehow, already-known. That recovery always feels new; it has the capacity to bathe the reader in the sense of a freshly discovered perception so as to produce a sense of intense, refreshed wonder. That recovery itself is best described as a re-cognition, a marvellous uncovering of the immanent and already there. Meet the new face, to be sure; but we only do that by recognising the old face.

Notes

I dedicate this essay to my much admired friend of long standing, Stephanie Trigg, whose stylish, radiant optimism and intellectual initiative, not to speak of her mighty generosity and energy, has revivified the study of early English literatures in Australian universities.

1 T. S. Eliot, 'East Coker', in *Collected Poems 1909–1962* (London: Faber & Faber, 1963), section 5, p. 203.
2 My central case here and throughout the essay is inspired by the project of Hans-Georg Gadamer, *Truth and Method*, trans. Joel Weinsheimer and Donald G. Marshall (London: Sheed & Ward, 2nd edn, 1989; first published in German, 1960).
3 Ezra Pound, *Make It New* (New Haven: Yale University Press, 1935). For the ancient Chinese source of the citation, Pound's discovery of it in 1913 and his use of it in specifically fascist contexts, see Michael North, *Novelty: A History of the New* (Chicago and London: University of Chicago Press, 2013), pp. 162–9.
4 Samuel Beckett, *Endgame*, in *The Complete Dramatic Works* (London: Faber & Faber, 1986), pp. 92–134 (p. 110, my emphases).
5 William Shakespeare, 'Sonnet 27', in Stephen Greenblatt *et al.* (eds), *The Norton Shakespeare*, 2 vols (New York: W. W. Norton & Co., 2nd edn, 2008), line 12.
6 For the theme of recognition in literary texts, from Antiquity to the twentieth century, see the excellent study by Terence Cave, *Recognitions: A Study in Poetics* (Oxford: Clarendon Press, 1988).
7 The text and translations of Virgil's *Aeneid* are drawn from *Virgil: Eclogues, Georgics, Aeneid*, ed. and trans. H. R. Fairclough, revd G. P. Goold, 2 vols (Cambridge MA: Harvard University Press, 1999), 4.22–3. Further references are made in the text, cited by book and line number.
8 'Conticuere omnes intentique ora tenebant' (*Aeneid* 2.1) (all were hushed, and kept their rapt gaze upon him).

9 A point discussed in greater depth in James Simpson, 'Cognition is recognition: literary knowledge and textual "face"', *New Literary History,* 44 (2013), 25–44.
10 Eliot, *The Wasteland*: 'The Fire Sermon', in *Collected Poems*, line 243.
11 Dante Alighieri, *La Divina Commedia,* ed. Fredi Chiappelli (Milan: Mursia, 1965), *Purgatorio* 30.34–9. All further references are from this edition, and cited by canto and line number.
12 For which network of allusions, see Piero Boitani, *Ri-scritture* (Turin: Einaudi, 2014), chapter 8, 'Riconoscere è un dio'. Published in English as *The Bible and its Rewritings* (Oxford: Oxford University Press, 1999).
13 Robert Henryson, *The Testament of Cresseid,* in *The Poems of Robert Henryson,* ed. Denton Fox (Oxford: Clarendon Press, 1981), p. 127, lines 498–504. Further references are made in the text, cited by line number.
14 Geoffrey Chaucer, *Troilus and Criseyde*, in *The Riverside Chaucer*, gen. ed. Larry D. Benson (Oxford: Oxford University Press, 3rd edn, 1988), V.1402–4. Further references are made in the text, cited by book and line number. See *The Poems of Robert Henryson*, ed. Fox, p. 378 for previous accounts of why Cresseid does not recognise Troilus. This passage is discussed in Boitani, *Ri-scritture*, pp. 361–3.
15 For Cambridge, Corpus Christi College MS 61, see https://parker.stanford.edu/parker/catalog/dh967mz5785, accessed 6 May 2018.
16 For which now see Stephanie Trigg, 'Chaucer's silent discourse', *Studies in the Age of Chaucer*, 39 (2017), 33–56.
17 Geoffrey Chaucer, *The Workes of Geffray Chaucer newly printed*, ed. William Thynne (London: Thomas Godfray, 1532), fol. 219*r*.
18 Much more fully argued in Simpson, 'Cognition is recognition'.
19 See plate 13 for the image; for further information about the first appearance of this image, see http://en.wikipedia.org/wiki/Rabbit%E2%80%93duck_illusion, accessed 6 May 2018.
20 The point is proved by the amusing experiment in which viewers are directed to look for something but miss the anomalous gorilla. See www.theinvisiblegorilla.com/gorilla_experiment.html, accessed 6 May 2018.
21 Again, much more fully argued in Simpson, 'Cognition is recognition'.

Bibliography

Manuscripts

Alnwick Castle, Northumberland MS 455
Austin, Harry Ransom Center MS 143
Cambridge, Corpus Christi College MS 61
Cambridge, University Library MS DD.4.24
Copenhagen, Royal Danish Library (Det Kongelige Bibliotek) MS NkS 218 4°
London, British Library Additional MS 5140
London, British Library MS Egerton 2864
London, British Library MS Harley 4866
London, British Library Lansdowne MS 851
London, British Library MS Royal 18 D II
London, British Library MS Yates Thompson 19
London, Royal College of Physicians MS 388
Oxford, Bodleian Library MS Arch. Selden B. 14
Oxford, Bodleian Library MS Bodl. 686
Oxford, Christ Church MS 152
Oxford, New College MS D.314
Princeton, Firestone Library MS 100 (the Helmingham MS)

Published primary sources and secondary criticism

STC numbers refer to A. W. Pollard and G. R. Redgrave (eds), *A short-title catalogue of books printed in England, Scotland and Ireland, and of English books printed abroad 1475–1640*, 2nd edn, London: Bibliographical Society, 1976–91.

Adams, Annmarie, *Architecture in the Family Way: Doctors, Houses, and Women, 1870–1900*, McGill-Queen's/Hannah Institute Studies in the History of Medicine, Health, and Society, Montreal and London: McGill-Queen's University Press, 1996.

Adams, Jenny, *Power Play: The Literature and Politics of Chess in the Late Middle Ages*, Philadelphia: University of Pennsylvania Press, 2006.

Aers, David, 'Masculine identity in the courtly community: the self loving in *Troilus and Criseyde*', in *Community, Gender and Individual Identity: English Writing, 1360–1430*, London: Routledge, 1988, pp. 117–52.

Aesop, *Here begynneth the Book of the Subtyl Historyes and Fables of Esope*, Westminster, 1484, STC 175.

Ahmed, Sara, 'Happy objects', in Melissa Gregg and Gregory J. Seigworth (eds), *The Affect Theory Reader*, Durham NC: Duke University Press, 2010, pp. 29–51.

Akbari, Suzanne Conklin, *Idols in the East: European Representations of Islam and the Orient, 1100–1450*, Ithaca: Cornell University Press, 2009.

Akbari, Suzanne Conklin, *Seeing Through the Veil: Optical Theory and Medieval Allegory*, Toronto: University of Toronto Press, 2004.

Alaimo, Stacy, *Bodily Natures: Science, Environment, and the Material Self*, Bloomington: Indiana University Press, 2010.

Alighieri, Dante, *La Divina Commedia*, ed. Fredi Chiappelli, Milan: Mursia, 1965.

Allen, Elizabeth, *False Fables and Exemplary Truth in Later Middle English Literature*, New York: Palgrave, 2015.

Allen, Valerie, 'Waxing red: shame and the body, shame and the soul', in Lisa Perfetti (ed.), *The Representation of Women's Emotions in Medieval and Early Modern Culture*, Gainsville: University of Florida Press, 2005, pp. 191–210.

'An ancient inn', *Daily Evening Bulletin* [San Francisco] (24 July 1873).

Ancrene Wisse, ed. Bella Millett, EETS o.s. 325, Oxford: Oxford University Press, 2005.

Anderlini-D'Onofrio, Serena, *Gaia and the New Politics of Love: Notes for a Poly Planet*, Berkeley: North Atlantic Books, 2010.

Arnold, Matthew, *Essays in Criticism*, 2nd series, London: Macmillan, 1885.

Arnold, Matthew, 'General introduction', in T. H. Ward (ed.), *The English Poets, Selections, vol. 1: Chaucer to Donne*, London: Macmillan, 1880.

Arnold, Thomas, *Chaucer to Wordsworth: A Short History of English Literature*, London: Thomas Murby, 1870.

Atkinson, Rev. H. D., 'Stray thoughts about old Chaucer', *The Churchman's Shilling Magazine*, reported in 'Gossip about books and the arts', *Northampton Mercury* (6 February 1869), p. 3.

Babington, Churchill (ed.), *Polychronicon Ranulphi Higden, Monachi Cestrensis, Together with the English Translations of John Trevisa and of an Unknown Writer of the Fifteenth Century*, vol. 1, London: Longman, Green, Longman, Roberts & Green, 1865.

Bailey, Bill, 'Pubbe gagge', in *Bewilderness*, Talent Television, 2001; 'Pubbe gagge', www.youtube.com/watch?v=mNEWatD0viw&t=11s.

Bakhtin, M. M., *The Dialogic Imagination: Four Essays*, ed. Michael Holquist, trans. Caryl Emerson and Michael Holquist, Austin: University of Texas Press, 1981.

Barrett, Elizabeth, 'The book of the poets', *The Athenæum* (4 June 1842), pp. 497–9.
Barrett, Elizabeth, 'Letter to John Kenyon, March 25 1843', in *The Letters of Elizabeth Barrett Browning*, vol. 1, London: Smith Elder, 1897.
Barrington, Candace and Jonathan Hsy (eds), *Global Chaucers: Online Archive and Community for post-1945, non-Anglophone Chauceriana*, https://globalchaucers.wordpress.com.
Bartels, Andreas and Semir Zeki, 'The neural basis of romantic love', *NeuroReport*, 11:17 (2000), 3829–34.
Bartlett, Robert, *The Natural and the Supernatural in the Middle Ages*, Cambridge: Cambridge University Press, 2008.
Bechstein, Reinhold, '*Der Heliand* und seine künstlerische Form', *Jahrbuch des Vereins für Niederdeutsche Sprachforschung*, 10 (1885), 133–48.
Beckett, Samuel, *Endgame*, in *The Complete Dramatic Works*, London: Faber & Faber, 1986.
Beidler, Peter G., 'The *Reeve's Tale*', in Robert M. Correale and Mary Hamel (eds), *Sources and Analogues of the Canterbury Tales*, vol. 1, Woodbridge: D. S. Brewer, 2002, pp. 23–74.
Berry, Reginald, 'Chaucer's eagle and the element air', *University of Toronto Quarterly*, 43:3 (1974), 285–97.
Blake, N. F., 'Caxton's language', in *William Caxton and English Literary Culture*, London and Rio Grande: Hambledon Press, 1991, pp. 137–47.
Blandeau, Agnes, *Pasolini, Chaucer, and Boccaccio: Two Medieval Texts and their Translation to Film*, Jefferson NC and London: McFarland & Co., 2006.
Boitani, Piero, *Ri-scritture*, Turin: Einaudi, 2014.
Bolens, Guillemette, 'La narration des émotions et la réactivité du destinataire dans *Les contes de Canterbury*', *Médiévales*, 61 (2011), 97–118.
Boos, Florence, 'The ideal of everyday life in William Morris' *News from Nowhere*', in Marguérite Corporaal and Evert Jan van Leeuwen (eds), foreword by Peter Liebregts, *The Literary Utopias of Cultural Communities, 1790–1910*, Amsterdam: Rodopi, 2010, pp. 141–70.
Borroff, Marie, '*Sir Gawain and the Green Knight*: the passing of judgment', in Christopher Baswell and William Sharpe (eds), *The Passing of Arthur: New Essays in Arthurian Tradition*, New York: Garland, 1988, pp. 105–28.
Bowers, John M. (ed.), *The Canterbury Tales: Fifteenth-Century Continuations and Additions*, TEAMS Middle English Text Series, Kalamazoo: Western Michigan University, 1992.
Boyd, David Lorenzo, 'Social texts: Bodley 686 and the politics of the *Cook's Tale*', *Huntington Quarterly*, 58 (1995), 81–97.
Braswell, Mary Flowers, *The Forgotten Chaucer Scholarship of Mary Eliza Haweis, 1848–1898*, London: Taylor & Francis, 2016.
Brewer, Derek (ed.), *Chaucer: The Critical Heritage*, 2 vols, London: Routledge & Kegan Paul, 1978.

Brown, Peter, *Chaucer and the Making of Optical Space*, Bern: Peter Lang, 2007.
Brown, Peter, 'Journey's end: the prologue to *The Tale of Beryn*', in Julia Boffey and Janet Cowen (eds), *Chaucer and Fifteenth-Century Poetry*, London: King's College Centre for Late Antique and Medieval Studies, 1991, pp. 143–74.
Brown, Thomas, 'Letters from the dead to the living' in *The Works of Mr Thomas Brown*, vol. 2, ed. James Drake, London: Sam Briscoe, 1707.
Burnett, Dean, 'Why do relationship breakups hurt so much?', *Guardian* (16 February 2016).
Burrow, J. A., *Gestures and Looks in Medieval Narrative*, Cambridge: Cambridge University Press, 2002.
Burrow, John, 'The *Tale of Beryn*: an appreciation', *The Chaucer Review*, 49 (2015), 499–511.
Butterfield, Ardis, *The Familiar Enemy: Chaucer, Language, and Nation in the Hundred Years War*, Oxford: Oxford University Press, 2009.
Cadden, Joan, *Meanings of Sex Difference in the Middle Ages: Medicine, Science, and Culture*, Cambridge: Cambridge University Press, 1993.
Cannon, Harry Sharp, *Sudermann's Treatment of Verse*, Tübingen: Laupp, 1922.
Carlson, David, 'Thomas Hoccleve and the Chaucer portrait', *Huntington Library Quarterly*, 54:4 (1991), 283–300.
Carruthers, Mary, *The Experience of Beauty in the Middle Ages*, Oxford: Oxford University Press, 2013.
Carruthers, Mary, 'Virtue, intention and the mind's eye in *Troilus and Criseyde*', in Charlotte Brewer and Barry Windeatt (eds), *Traditions and Innovations in the Study of Middle English Literature: The Influence of Derek Brewer*, Cambridge: D. S. Brewer, 2013, pp. 73–87.
Cave, Terence, *Recognitions: A Study in Poetics*, Oxford: Clarendon Press, 1988.
Caviness, Madeline, *Visualizing Women in the Middle Ages: Sight, Spectacle, and Scopic Economy*, Philadelphia: University of Pennsylvania Press, 2001.
Caxton, William, *Chronicles of England*, Westminster, 1482, STC 9992.
Caxton, William, 'Prohemye' to the *Canterbury Tales*, Westminster, 1483, STC 5083.
Chaucer, Geoffrey, *The Book of Fame made by G. Chaucer*, Westminster, 1483, STC 5087.
Chaucer, Geoffrey, *The Riverside Chaucer*, gen. ed. Larry D. Benson, 3rd edn, Oxford: Oxford University Press, 1988; Boston: Houghton Mifflin, 1987, 2008.
Chaucer, Geoffrey, *The Workes of Geffray Chaucer newly printed*, ed. William Thynne, London: Thomas Godfray, 1532.
'Chaucer', *Cheltenham Chronicle and Parish Register and General Advertiser for Gloucester* (18 April 1871), p. 5.

'Chaucer', *Examiner* (10 August 1872).
'Chaucer a cockney', *Evening Telegraph* [Dundee] (2 June 1898), p. 3.
'Chaucer and his connexion with Woodstock', *Jackson's Oxford Journal* (31 January 1857).
'Chaucer and his testament of love', *Edinburgh Magazine and Literary Miscellany* (1 June 1826), pp. 664–5.
'Chaucer and Prince Albert', *The Times* (26 May 1842), p. 6.
'Chaucer and the Exhibition', *Liverpool Mercury* (14 June 1851).
'Chaucer as the spring-poet', *Friend of India* [Calcutta] (12 June 1875), pp. 522–3.
'Chaucer ball', *Funny Folks* [London] (28 January 1882), p. 27.
'Chaucer in a new dress', *Englishwoman's Review and Drawing Room Journal* (11 July 1857), p. 4.
'Chaucer pageant at Otterspool', *Liverpool Mercury* (20 June 1895).
'Chaucer's birds', *Graphic* (30 September 1882).
'Chaucer's England', *Monthly Packet* (1 November 1896), pp. 519–26.
'The Chaucer Society and its work', *Milwaukee Daily Sentinel* (2 May 1873), p. 3.
'The Chaucer Society's *Six-Text Edition* of *The Canterbury Tales*', in *Pall Mall Gazette* (13 October 1871).
'Chaucer's religious sympathies', *Daily Evening Bulletin* [San Francisco] (10 August 1878).
'Chaucer's scholar', *Oriental Observer* [Calcutta] (8 June 1833), p. 269.
'The Chaucer window, Westminster Abbey', *Morning Post* (12 December 1868), p. 2.
Chesterton, G. K., *The Collected Works of G. K. Chesterton*, vol. 18, ed. and intro. Russell Kirk, San Francisco: Ignatius Press, 1991.
'The children's column', *Leeds Mercury* (10 January 1880).
Chrétien de Troyes, *Le conte du Graal (Perceval)*, in *Les romans de Chrétien de Troyes*, vol. V, ed. Félix Lecoy, Paris: Honoré Champion, 1972–75.
'Christmas books', *Graphic* (2 December 1876).
Clarke, Charles Cowden (ed.), *The Riches of Chaucer*, 2 vols, London: Effingham Wilson, 1835.
Coghill, Nevill, *The Poet Chaucer*, 2nd edn, London: Oxford University Press, 1967.
Cohen, Jeffrey Jerome, 'The sea above', in Cohen and Lowell Duckert (eds), *Elemental Ecocriticism: Thinking with Earth, Air, Water, and Fire*, Minneapolis: University of Minnesota Press, 2015, pp. 105–33.
Cohen, Jeffrey Jerome and Lindy Elkins-Tanton, *Earth*, London: Bloomsbury, 2017.
Cohen, Jeffrey Jerome and Stephanie Trigg, 'Fire', *postmedieval*, 4:1 (2013), 80–92.
Colby, Alice M., *The Portrait in Twelfth-Century French Literature: An Example of the Stylistic Originality of Chrétien de Troyes*, Geneva: Droz, 1965.

Cole, Kristin Lynn, 'Chaucer's metrical landscape', in Clíodhna Carney and Frances McCormack (eds), *Chaucer's Poetry: Words, Authority and Ethics*, Dublin: Four Courts Press, 2013, pp. 92–106.
'Comicography, or the history of humorous writing', *Punch* (5 December 1843), p. 239.
Conlee, John W., 'The meaning of Troilus' ascension to the eighth sphere', *Chaucer Review*, 7 (1972–73), 27–36.
Cook, Megan L., '"Here taketh the makere of this book his leve": the *Retraction* and Chaucer's works in Tudor England', *Studies in Philology*, 113:1 (2016), 32–54.
Cooper, Helen, 'I. Chaucerian representation', in Robert G. Benson and Susan J. Ridyard (eds), *New Readings of Chaucer's Poetry*, Chaucer Studies XXXI, Woodbridge: Boydell & Brewer, 2003, pp. 7–30.
Cooper, Helen, '"The most excellent creatures are not ever born perfect": early modern attitudes to Middle English', in Tim William Machan (ed.), *Imagining Medieval English: Language Structures and Theories 500–1500*, Cambridge: Cambridge University Press, 2016, pp. 241–60.
Cooper, Helen, 'Passionate, eloquent and determined: heroines' tales and feminine poetics', Sir Israel Gollancz Memorial Lecture, *Journal of the British Academy*, 4 (2016), 221–44, www.britac.ac.uk/publications/pas sionate-eloquent-and-determined-heroines-tales-and-feminine-poetics.
Cooper, Helen, *Shakespeare and the Medieval World*, London: Methuen, 2010.
Cordaro, D. T. et al., 'The great expressions debate', *Emotion Researcher: The Official Newsletter of the International Society for Research on Emotion*, Special Issue (2015), http://emotionresearcher.com/the-great-expressions-debate/.
Correale, Robert M. and Mary Hamel (eds), *Sources and Analogues of the Canterbury Tales*, vol. 2, Cambridge: D. S. Brewer, 2005.
Court Magazine and Monthly Critic (1 January 1841), p. 58.
Crane, Susan, *The Performance of Self: Ritual, Clothing, and Identity During the Hundred Years War*, Philadelphia: University of Pennsylvania Press, 2002.
Crocker, Holly A., *Chaucer's Visions of Manhood*, New York: Palgrave Macmillan, 2007.
Crocker, Holly A., 'Medieval affects now', *Exemplaria*, 29:1 (2017), 82–98.
Curdy, Albert Eugene (ed.), *La Folie Tristan: An Anglo-Norman Poem*, Baltimore: John Murphy, 1903.
Cushman, Stephen et al. (eds), *The Princeton Encyclopedia of Poetry and Poetics*, 4th edn, Princeton: Princeton University Press, 2012.
Dalrymple, Hugh, *Woodstock Park: An Elegy*, London: D. Wilson, 1761.
D'Arcens, Louise, 'You had to be there: anachronism and the limits of laughing at the Middle Ages', *postmedieval*, 5:2 (2014), 140–53.

Dart, John, 'Life of Chaucer', revd William Thomas, in Derek Brewer (ed.), *Geoffrey Chaucer: The Critical Heritage*, vol. 1, New York: Routledge, 1995, pp. 176–86.

David, Alfred, *The Strumpet Muse: Art and Morals in Chaucer's Poetry*, Bloomington: Indiana University Press, 1976.

Delveaux, Martin, '"O me! O me! How I love the earth": William Morris's *News from Nowhere* and the birth of sustainable society', *Contemporary Justice Review*, 8:2 (2005), 131–46.

Dilthey, W., 'Die Entstehung der Hermeneutik', in G. Misch (ed.), *Wilhelm Dilthey: Gesammelte Schriften V*, Stuttgart: B. G. Teubner, 1924.

Dinshaw, Carolyn, 'Pale faces: race, religion and affect in Chaucer's texts and their readers', *Studies in the Age of Chaucer*, 23 (2001), 19–41.

Dodman, Trevor, 'Hunting to teach: class, pedagogy, and maleness in *The Master of Game* and *Sir Gawain and the Green Knight*', *Exemplaria*, 17:2 (2005), 413–44.

Donaldson, E. Talbot, *Speaking of Chaucer*, London: Athlone Press, 1979.

Downes, Stephanie, 'Chaucer in nineteenth-century France', *Chaucer Review*, 49:3 (2015), 352–70.

Downes, Stephanie and Rebecca F. McNamara, 'Middle English literature and the history of emotions', *Literature Compass*, 13:6 (2016), 444–56.

Downes, Stephanie and Stephanie Trigg, 'Editors' introduction: facing up to the history of emotions', *postmedieval*, 8:1 (2017), 3–11.

Dryden, John, *Fables Ancient and Modern*, London: Jacob Tonson, 1700.

Duggan, Joseph J., *The Romances of Chrétien de Troyes*, New Haven: Yale University Press, 2001.

Eliot, T. S., 'East Coker', in *Collected Poems 1909–1962*, London: Faber & Faber, 1963.

Eliot, T. S., *The Wasteland*: 'The Fire Sermon', in *Collected Poems 1909–1962*, London: Faber & Faber, 1963.

Ellis, Steve, *Chaucer at Large: The Poet in the Modern Imagination*, Minneapolis: University of Minnesota Press, 2000.

Ellmann, Richard, *Golden Codgers: Biographical Speculations*, London and New York: Oxford University Press, 1973.

'English writers', *John Bull* (6 July 1867), p. 48.

Espie, Jeff, 'Wordsworth's Chaucer: mediation and transformation in English literary history', *Philological Quarterly*, 94:4 (2015), 377–403.

'The father of English poetry', in H. K. F. Gatty (ed.), *Aunt Judy's Christmas Volume*, London: Bell, 1879, p. 654.

Feerick, Jean and Vin Nardizzi (eds), *The Indistinct Human in Renaissance Literature*, New York: Palgrave Macmillan, 2012.

Fernández-Dols, José-Miguel and James A. Russell (eds), *The Science of Facial Expression*, Oxford: Oxford University Press, 2017.

Finley, William K. and Joseph Rosenblum, *Chaucer Illustrated: Five Hundred Years of The Canterbury Tales in Pictures*, New Castle DE: Oak Knoll Press; London: British Library, 2003.

Flannery, Mary C., 'A bloody shame: Chaucer's honourable women', *Review of English Studies*, 62 (2011), 337–57.
Flannery, Mary C., 'The concept of shame in late medieval English literature', *Literature Compass*, 9:2 (2012), 166–82.
Fleming, John, 'Deiphoebus betrayed: Virgilian decorum, Chaucerian feminism', *Chaucer Review*, 21:2 (1986), 182–99.
Floyd-Wilson, Mary, *English Ethnicity and Race in Early Modern Drama*, Cambridge: Cambridge University Press, 2003.
Forman, W. H., 'Lives of the British poets: Geoffrey Chaucer', *Odd Fellow* (22 February 1840).
Forni, Kathleen, *Chaucer's Afterlife: Adaptations in Recent Popular Culture*, Jefferson NC and London: McFarland & Co., 2013.
Forni, Kathleen, 'A "cinema of poetry": what Pasolini did to Chaucer's *Canterbury Tales*', *Literature/Film Quarterly*, 30:4 (2002), 256–63.
Foucault, Michel, 'What is an author? (1969)', in *Essential Works of Foucault 1954–1984, Vol. 2: Aesthetics, Method, and Epistemology*, ed. James D. Faubion, trans. Robert Hurley *et al.*, New York: New Press, 1998, pp. 205–22.
Fradenburg, Aranye, 'Going mental', *postmedieval*, 3:3 (2012), 361–72.
Fradenburg, L. O. Aranye, *Sacrifice Your Love: Psychoanalysis, Historicism, Chaucer*, Minneapolis: University of Minnesota Press, 2002.
Frappier, Jean, 'La brisure du couplet dans *Érec et Énide*', *Romania*, 86 (1965), 1–21.
Freud, Sigmund, 'The ego and the id', in James Strachey (gen. ed.), *The Standard Edition of the Complete Psychological Works of Sigmund Freud*, vol. 19, in collaboration with Anna Freud, assisted by Alix Strachey and Alan Tyson, London: Hogarth Press, 1961.
Friedlander, Carolynn VanDyke, 'Early Middle English accentual verse', *Modern Philology*, 76:3 (1979), 219–30.
Froissart, Jean, *Le Paradis d'amour; L'Orloge amoureus*, ed. Peter F. Dembowski, Textes littéraires français 339, Geneva: Droz, 1986.
Gadamer, Hans-Georg, *Truth and Method*, trans. J. Weinsheimer and D. G. Marshall, 2nd edn, London: Sheed & Ward, 1989; London and New York: Continuum, 2004.
Gallagher, Shaun, 'In your face: transcendence in embodied interaction', *Frontiers in Human Neuroscience*, 8 (2014), 1–7.
Galton, Arthur, 'Morris and Chaucer', *Evening Telegraph* [Dundee] (11 September 1885), p. 4.
Ganim, John M., 'The interpretation of dreams: Chaucer's early poems, literary criticism and literary theory', in William Quinn (ed.), *Chaucer's Dream Visions: A Casebook*, New York: Garland, 1999, pp. 463–76.
Gaylord, Alan T., 'Portrait of a poet', in Martin Stevens and Daniel Woodward (eds), *The Ellesmere Chaucer: Essays in Interpretation*, San Marino CA: Huntington Library, 1995, pp. 121–42.

'Geoffrey Chaucer', *Young Folks' Paper* (31 October 1885), p. 288.
Geoffrey of Vinsauf, *Poetria Nova*, in E. Faral (ed.), *Les arts poétiques du XIIe et du XIIIe siècle*, Paris: Champion, 1924.
Georgianna, Linda, 'The Protestant Chaucer', in C. David Benson and Elizabeth Robertson (eds), *Chaucer's Religious Tales*, Cambridge: Boydell & Brewer, 1990, pp. 55–69.
Gilbert, Nathaniel, 'The landscape of resistance in Morris's *News from Nowhere*', *Journal of William Morris Studies*, 16:1 (2004), 22–37.
Gilles, Sealy, 'Love and disease in Chaucer's *Troilus and Criseyde*', *Studies in the Age of Chaucer*, 25 (2003), 157–97.
Glöde, Otto, 'Die Reimbrechung in Gottfried von Straßburgs *Tristan* und den Werken seiner hervorragendsten Schüler', *Germania*, 33 (1888), 357–70.
Godwin, William, *Life of Chaucer*, London: T. Davison, 1804.
Gower, John, *Confessio Amantis*, in *The Complete Works of John Gower*, ed. G. C. Macaulay, Oxford: Clarendon Press, 1899–1902; Oxford Text Archive and Corpus of Middle English Prose and Verse (1993), http://name.umdl.umich.edu/Confessio.
Gower, John, *Confessio Amantis: Volume 2*, ed. Russell A. Peck, trans. Andrew Galloway, Kalamazoo: Medieval Institute Publications, 2013.
Grady, Frank, 'Seigneurial poetics, or the poacher, the *prikasour*, the hunt and its oeuvre', in Frank Grady and Andrew Galloway (eds), *Answerable Style: The Idea of the Literary in Medieval England*, Columbus: Ohio State University Press, 2013, pp. 195–213.
'A great price', *Denver Evening Post* (27 February 1896), p. 3.
Green, D. H., *The Beginnings of Medieval Romance: Fact and Fiction, 1150–1220*, Cambridge: Cambridge University Press, 2002.
Grimm, Jakob and Wilhelm Grimm, *Altdeutsche Wälder*, 3 vols, Cassel: Thurneissen, 1813–16.
Guillaume de Lorris and Jean de Meun, *Le Roman de la Rose*, ed. and trans. Armand Strubel, Lettres Gothiques, Paris: Le Livre de Poche, 1992.
Habermas, Jürgen, *Knowledge and Human Interests*, trans. J. J. Shapiro, London: Heinemann, 1972.
Hanna, Ralph, 'Review of *The London Chronicles of the Fifteenth Century: A Revolution in English Writing, with an Annotated Edition of Bradford, West Yorkshire Archives MS 32D86/42*' [review no. 340], *Reviews in History*, London: University of London Institute of Historical Research (2003), www.history.ac.uk/reviews/review/340.
Harrington, Austin, 'Dilthey, empathy, and *Verstehen*: a contemporary reappraisal', *European Journal of Social Theory*, 4:3 (2001), 311–29.
Haweis, Mrs H. R. [Mary Eliza], *Chaucer for Schools*, London: Chatto & Windus, 1881.
Hawes, Stephen, *The Conversion of Swearers*, in *The Minor Poems of Stephen Hawes*, ed. Florence W. Gluck and Alice B. Morgan, EETS o.s. 271, London: Oxford University Press, 1974.

Hearne, Thomas, 'Extracts from his diary, April 28 (Sat) 1711', in *Remarks and Collections of Thomas Hearne*, vol. 3, ed. C. E. Doble, Oxford: Oxford Historical Society, 1711.

Heffernen, Carol F., 'Chaucer's *Troilus and Criseyde*: the disease of love and courtly love', *Neophilologus*, 74:2 (1990), 294–309.

Helgeland, Brian (dir.), *A Knight's Tale*, Black and Blu Entertainment, Columbia Pictures: 2001.

Heng, Geraldine, 'A woman wants: the lady, *Gawain*, and the forms of seduction', *Yale Journal of Criticism*, 5:3 (1992), 101–34.

Henryson, Robert, *The Testament of Cresseid*, in *The Poems of Robert Henryson*, ed. Denton Fox, Oxford: Clarendon Press, 1981.

Hiatt, Alfred, *The Making of Medieval Forgeries: False Documents in Fifteenth-Century England*, London: British Library; Toronto and Buffalo: University of Toronto Press, 2004.

Higden, Ranulph, *Polychronicon*, trans. John Trevisa, Westminster, 1482, STC 13438.

Higl, Andrew, *Playing the Canterbury Tales: The Continuations and Additions*, Burlington VT: Ashgate, 2012.

Hippisley, J. H., *Chapters on Early English Literature*, London: Moxon, 1837.

Hodgson, Amanda, *The Romances of William Morris*, Cambridge: Cambridge University Press, 2011.

Holland, Peter (ed.), *A Midsummer Night's Dream*, Oxford: Oxford University Press, 1995.

Horn Childe and Maiden Rimnild, ed. Maldwyn Mills, Heidelberg: Carl Winter, 1988.

Horne, Lawrence, 'To Chaucer', *London Pioneer* (23 September 1847), p. 361.

Horne, R. H. (ed.), *The Poems of Geoffrey Chaucer, Modernized*, London: Whittaker, 1841.

Horobin, Simon, 'Compiling the *Canterbury Tales* in fifteenth-century manuscripts', *Chaucer Review*, 47 (2013), 372–89.

Houdenc, Raoul de, *La Vengeance Raguidel*, ed. Matthias Friedwagner, Halle: Niemeyer, 1909.

Hunt, Tony, *Miraculous Rhymes: The Writing of Gautier de Coinci*, Cambridge: D. S. Brewer, 2007.

H. W. D., *The Life of Geoffrey Chaucer: The Father of English Poetry*, London: Ward & Lock, 1881.

Ingarden, Roman, *The Literary Work of Art,* trans. George G. Grabowicz, Evanston IL: Northwestern University Press, 1973.

Ingledew, Francis, *Sir Gawain and the Green Knight and the Order of the Garter*, Notre Dame: University of Notre Dame Press, 2006.

Innes, Henry, *A Lecture on the Genius of Chaucer*, Malta, 1851.

Ipomadon, ed. Rhiannon Purdie, EETS o.s. 316, Oxford: Oxford University Press, 2001.

Ipomedon: poème de Hue de Rotelande (fin du XIIe siècle), ed. A. J. Holden, Paris: Klincksieck, 1979.

Iser, Wolfgang, 'The reading process: a phenomenological approach', in *The Implied Reader: Patterns of Communication in Prose Fiction from Bunyan to Beckett*, Baltimore: Johns Hopkins University Press, 1974, pp. 274–94.

Ito, Masayoshi, 'Gower's use of *rime riche* in *Confessio Amantis*: as compared with his practice in *Mirour de l'Omme* and with the case of Chaucer', *Studies in English Literature* [English Literature Society of Japan], 46 (1969), 29–44.

Jacobs, Jane, *The Death and Life of Great American Cities*, New York: Random House, 1961.

Jakobson, Roman, 'Closing statement: linguistics and poetics', in Thomas A. Sebeok (ed.), *Style in Language*, Cambridge MA: MIT Press, 1960, pp. 350–77.

Jameson, Fredric, *Archaeologies of the Future: The Desire Called Utopia and Other Science Fictions*, London: Verso, 2005.

Jarvis, Simon, 'For a poetics of verse', *Proceedings of the Modern Language Association*, 125:4 (2010), 931–5.

Jarvis, Simon, 'The melodics of long poems', *Textual Practice*, 24:4 (2010), 607–21.

Johnson, Eleanor, *Practicing Literary Theory in the Middle Ages: Ethics and the Mixed Form in Chaucer, Gower, Usk, and Hoccleve*, Chicago: University of Chicago Press, 2013.

Kaluza, Max, *A Short History of English Versification from the Earliest Times to the Present Day*, trans. A. C. Dunstan, London: George Allen & Co., 1911.

Keats, John, *The Letters of John Keats: 1814–1818*, vol. 1, ed. Hyder Edward Rollins, Cambridge MA: Harvard University Press, 1958.

Kelly, Douglas, 'The art of description', in Norris J. Lacy, Kelly and Keith Busby (eds), *The Legacy of Chrétien de Troyes*, vol. 1, Amsterdam: Rodopi, 1987, pp. 191–223.

Keynes, Geoffrey (ed.), *The Complete Writings of William Blake: With all the Variant Readings*, London: Nonesuch Press, 1957.

King, Mrs Harriet Hamilton, 'Studies of great English poets', *Every Girl's Annual*, London: Routledge, 1891.

King Horn, in Jennifer Fellows (ed.), *Of Love and Chivalry: An Anthology of Middle English Romance*, London: J. M. Dent, 1993.

Kirchhoff, Frederick, *William Morris: The Construction of a Male Self, 1856–1872*, Athens OH: Ohio University Press, 1990.

Kittredge, George Lyman, *Chaucer and His Poetry*, Cambridge MA: Harvard University Press, 1915.

Kittredge, G. L., 'Guillaume de Machaut and *The Book of the Duchess*', *Proceedings of the Modern Language Association*, 30:1 (1915), 1–24.

Knapp, Ethan, 'Faciality and ekphrasis in late medieval England', in Andrew James Johnston, Knapp and Margitta Rouse (eds), *The Art of*

Vision: Ekphrasis in Medieval Literature and Culture, Columbus: Ohio State University Press, 2015, pp. 209–23.
Knatchbull-Hugessen, Eva, 'Papers on English literature VIII: Chaucer: Prologue and Clerk's Tale', *Monthly Packet* (1 March 1889), pp. 278–90.
Knight, Stephen, *The Poetry of the Canterbury Tales*, Sydney: Angus & Robertson, 1973.
Knight, Stephen, *Rymyng Craftily: Meaning in Chaucer's Poetry*, Sydney: Angus & Robertson, 1973.
Knight, Stephen and Thomas Ohlgren, 'Introduction', *The Tale of Gamelyn*, in Knight and Ohlgren (eds), *Robin Hood and Other Outlaw Tales*, TEAMS Middle English Texts Series, Kalamazoo: Medieval Institute Publications, 1997, pp. 184–91.
Kolve, V. A., *Chaucer and the Imagery of Narrative: The First Five Canterbury Tales*, Stanford: Stanford University Press, 1984.
Kuskin, William, *Symbolic Caxton: Literary Culture and Print Capitalism*, Notre Dame: University of Notre Dame Press, 2008.
Latini, Brunetto, *The Book of the Treasure (Li Livres dou Tresor)*, trans. Paul Barrette and Spurgeon Baldwin, New York: Routledge, 2013.
Laurent, Béatrice, 'The landscapes of Nowhere', *Journal of William Morris Studies*, 18:2 (2009), 52–64.
Lawton, David, 'Larger patterns of syntax in Middle English unrhymed alliterative verse', *Neophilologus*, 64:4 (1980), 604–18.
Lawton, David, 'Titus goes hunting and hawking: the poetics of recreation and revenge in *The Siege of Jerusalem*', in O. S. Pickering (ed.), *Individuality and Achievement in Middle English Poetry*, Woodbridge: D. S. Brewer, 1997, pp. 105–17.
Lerer, Seth, 'William Caxton', in David Wallace (ed.), *The Cambridge History of Medieval English Literature*, Cambridge: Cambridge University Press, 1999, pp. 720–38.
'Letter', *The Times* (27 June 1883), p. 6.
'Letter to the Editor', *Morning Chronicle* (6 December 1820).
Levine, Caroline, *Forms: Whole, Rhythm, Hierarchy, Network*, Princeton: Princeton University Press, 2015.
Leyerle, Blake, 'John Chrysostom on the gaze', *Journal of Early Christian Studies*, 1:2, Summer (1993), 159–74; doi: 10.1353/earl.0.0116.
Lindberg, David C., *Theories of Vision from al-Kindi to Kepler*, Chicago: University of Chicago Press, 1976.
'Literary notices', *North American and United States Gazette* (22 January 1864), p. 691.
Lochrie, Karma, *Nowhere in the Middle Ages*, Philadelphia: University of Pennsylvania Press, 2016.
Loomis, Roger S., 'Review of *Der Mittelenglische Versroman über Richard Löwenherz, vol. XLII*, ed. Karl Brunner', *Journal of English and Germanic Philology*, 15:3 (1916), 455–66.

Lote, Georges, *Histoire du vers français, Tome 1, Première partie: Le Moyen Âge*, Paris: Boivin, 1949.

Lounsbury, George, *Studies in Chaucer: His Life and Writings*, vol. 2, New York: Harper, 1892.

Lowell, James Russell, 'Chaucer', *Boston Daily Advertiser* (24 January 1855).

Lybeaus Desconus, ed. Maldwyn Mills, EETS o.s. 261, London and New York: Oxford University Press, 1969.

Lydgate, John, *The Fall of Princes*, 4 vols, ed. Henry Bergen, EETS e.s. 121–4, London: Oxford University Press, 1924.

Lynch, Andrew, '"With face pale": melancholy violence in John Lydgate's Troy and Thebes', in Joanna Bellis and Laura Slater (eds), *Representing War and Violence: 1250–1600*, Woodbridge: Boydell & Brewer, 2016, pp. 79–94.

Machan, Tim William, 'Early modern Middle English', in William Kuskin (ed.), *Caxton's Trace: Studies in the History of English Printing*, Notre Dame: University of Notre Dame Press, 2006, pp. 299–322.

Machaut, Guillaume de, *Les œuvres de Guillaume de Machaut*, ed. P. Tarbé, Collection des poètes de Champagne antérieurs au XVIe siècle 3, Reims: Regnier, 1849.

Machaut, Guillaume de, *Poésies lyriques*, vol. 1, ed. V. Chichmaref, Paris: Champion, 1909; repr. Geneva: Droz, 1973.

Mackail, J. W., *The Life of William Morris*, vol. I, London: Longmans, 1901.

Macrobius, *Commentarii in somnium Scipionis*, ed. James Willis, Leipzig: B. G. Teubner, 1970.

'Madame Tussaud's wax work exhibition', *Sunday Times* (28 December 1862), p. 3.

Maddern, Philippa, 'Reading faces: how did late medieval Europeans interpret emotions in faces?', *postmedieval*, 8:1 (2017), 12–34.

Manly, J. M. and E. Rickert (eds), *The Text of the Canterbury Tales*, vol. 1, Chicago: Chicago University Press, 1940.

Mann, Jill, *Chaucer and Medieval Estates Satire*, Cambridge: Cambridge University Press, 1973.

Mann, Jill, 'Shakespeare and Chaucer: "what is Criseyde worth?"', *Cambridge Quarterly*, 18:2 (1989), 109–28.

Manton, Kevin, 'The Fellowship of the New Life: English ethical socialism reconsidered', *History of Political Thought*, 24:2 (2003), pp. 282–304.

Marsh, Jan, 'Concerning love: *News from Nowhere* and gender', in Stephen Coleman and Paddy O'Sullivan (eds), *William Morris and 'News from Nowhere': A Vision for Our Time*, Bideford, Devon: Green Books, 1990, pp. 107–25.

Marshall, Simone Celine, 'The 1807 edition of the poetical works of Geoffrey Chaucer', *Notes and Queries*, 57:2 (2011), pp. 183–6.

Marvin, William Perry, *Hunting Law and Ritual in Medieval English Literature*, Cambridge: D. S. Brewer, 2006.

Massumi, Brian, *Politics of Affect*, Cambridge: Polity Press, 2015.
Matheson, Lister M., 'Printer and scribe: Caxton, the *Polychronicon*, and the *Brut*', *Speculum*, 60 (1985), 593–614.
Matthews, David, *Medievalism: A Critical History*, Cambridge: D. S. Brewer, 2015.
Matthews, David, 'Middle', in Elizabeth Emery and Richard Utz (eds), *Medievalism: Key Critical Terms*, Cambridge: D. S. Brewer, 2014, pp. 141–7.
Matthews, David, 'Speaking to Chaucer: the poet and the nineteenth-century academy', in David Metzger, Kathleen Verduin and Leslie J. Workman (eds), *Studies in Medievalism IX: Medievalism and the Academy I*, Woodbridge: D. S. Brewer, 1997, pp. 5–25.
Matthews, David, 'The spectral past: medieval literature in the early modern period', in Robert DeMaria, Jr., Heesok Chang and Samantha Zacher (eds), *A Companion to British Literature, Vol. II: Early Modern Literature 1450–1660*, Malden MA and Oxford: Wiley-Blackwell, 2014, pp. 1–15.
Maurer, Friedrich, 'Über Langzeilen und Langzeilenstrophen in der ältesten deutschen Dichtung', in Karl Friedrich Müller (ed.), *Beiträge zur Sprachwissenschaft und Volkskunde: Festschrift für Ernst Ochs zum 60 Geburtstag*, Lahr: Schauenburg, 1951, pp. 31–52.
McClellan, William, 'Full pale face: Agamben's biopolitical theory and the sovereign subject in Chaucer's *Clerk's Tale*', *Exemplaria*, 17 (2005), 103–34.
McClellan, William, *Reading Chaucer After Auschwitz: Sovereign Power and Bare Life*, New York: Palgrave Macmillan, 2016.
McNamara, Rebecca F., 'Wearing your heart on your face: reading love-sickness and the suicidal impulse in Chaucer', *Literature and Medicine*, 33:2 (2015), 258–78.
McNamer, Sarah, *Affective Meditation and the Invention of Medieval Compassion*, Philadelphia: University of Pennsylvania Press, 2010.
McNamer, Sarah, 'Feeling', in Paul Strohm (ed.), *Oxford Twenty-First Century Approaches to Literature: Middle English*, Oxford: Oxford University Press, 2007, pp. 241–57.
Menely, Tobias, 'Anthropocene air', *Minnesota Review*, 83 (2014), 93–101.
Mentz, Steve, 'A poetics of nothing: air in the early modern imagination', *postmedieval*, 4.1 (2013), 30–41.
Meyer, Paul, 'Le couplet de deux vers', *Romania*, 23 (1894), 1–35.
Middle English Dictionary, available at https://quod.lib.umich.edu/m/med/.
Miles, Margaret, 'Vision: The eye of the body and the eye of the mind in Saint Augustine's "De Trinitate" and "Confessions"', *Journal of Religion*, 63:2 (1983), 125–42.
Miller, Mark, 'The ends of excitement in *Sir Gawain and the Green Knight*: teleology, ethics, and the death drive', *Studies in the Age of Chaucer*, 32 (2010), 215–56.

Miller, Nelson, 'Basic sonnet forms', *Sonnet Central*, www.sonnets.org/basicforms.htm.
Minis, Cola, 'Zum Problem der frühmittelhochdeutschen Langzeilen', in *Zur Vergegenwärtigung vergangener philologischer Nächte*, Amsterdam: Rodopi, 1981, pp. 310–32.
Minnis, A. J., with V. J. Scattergood and J. J. Smith, *Oxford Guides to Chaucer: The Shorter Poems*, Oxford: Clarendon, 1995.
Minto, William, *Characteristics of English Poets: From Chaucer to Shirley*, London: William Blackwood, 1874.
Miskimin, Alice, 'The illustrated eighteenth-century Chaucer', *Modern Philology*, 77:1 (1979), 26–55.
Mitchell, J. Allan, *Becoming Human: The Matter of the Medieval Child*, Minneapolis: University of Minnesota Press, 2014.
'Modern Canterbury Tales', *Englishwomen's Domestic Magazine* (1 October 1869), p. 191.
'The modern Canterbury Tales', *Los Angeles Times* (3 October 1882).
Moore, Michael Edward, 'Meditations on the face in the Middle Ages (with Levinas and Picard)', *Literature and Theology*, 24:1 (2010), 19–37.
Morley, Henry, *English Writers: From Chaucer to Dunbar*, London: Chapman & Hall, 1867.
Morris, May, *William Morris: Artist, Writer, Socialist*, vol. I, Oxford: Blackwell, 1936.
Morris, William, *The Collected Letters of William Morris, vol. IV: 1893–1896*, ed. Norman Kelvin, Princeton: Princeton University Press, 1996.
Morris, William, *The Earthly Paradise*, in *The Collected Works of William Morris*, vols 3–6, ed. May Morris, London: Longmans Green, 1910–15.
Morris, William, *News from Nowhere*, in *Three Works by William Morris*, ed. A. L. Morton, London: Lawrence & Wishart, 1968.
Morse, Charlotte C., 'Popularizing Chaucer in the nineteenth century', *Chaucer Review*, 38 (2003), 99–125.
Mosser, Daniel W. and Linne R. Mooney, 'More manuscripts by the Beryn scribe and his cohort', *Chaucer Review*, 49 (2014), 39–76.
Mott, Lewis Freeman, *The System of Courtly Love Studied as an Introduction to the* Vita Nuova *of Dante*, Boston and London: Athenaeum, 1896.
'Mr Dawson's second lecture on "Chaucer"', *Birmingham Daily Post* (1 June 1859).
Mulvey, Laura, 'Visual pleasure and narrative cinema', *Screen*, 16 (1975), 6–18.
'The national taste in poets', *Evening Telegraph* [Dundee] (20 November 1885), p. 3.
Newman, Barbara, 'What did it mean to say "I saw"?: the clash between theory and practice in medieval visionary culture', *Speculum*, 80:1 (2005), 1–43.
North, Michael, *Novelty: A History of the New*, Chicago and London: University of Chicago Press, 2013.

Nowak, Magdalena, 'The complicated history of *Einfühlung*', *Argument*, 1:2 (2011), 301–26.
Nussbaum, Martha, *Upheavals of Thought: The Intelligence of Emotion*, Cambridge: Cambridge University Press, 2001.
'The old English poets, no. I – Chaucer', *Punch* (4 January 1843), p. 30.
'The old inns of Southwark', *Daily News* (6 February 1869).
On the Properties of Things, John Trevisa's Translation of Bartholomaeus Anglicus De Proprietatibus Rerum, a Critical Text, 3 vols, ed. M. C. Seymour et al., Oxford: Clarendon, 1975–88.
'The *Oregonian*'s home study circle', *Morning Oregonian* (4 April 1899), p. 9.
'Papers on English literature VII: Chaucer: language and versification', *Monthly Packet* (1 February 1889), pp. 178–89.
The Parlement of the Thre Ages, ed. M. Y. Offord, EETS o.s. 246, London: Oxford University Press, 1959.
Pasolini, Pier Paolo (dir.), *The Canterbury Tales / I Racconti di Canterbury*, Les Productions Artistes Associés, Produzione Europee Associati: 1972.
Paster, Gail Kern, *The Body Embarrassed: Drama and the Disciplines of Shame in Early Modern England*, Ithaca: Cornell University Press, 1993.
Paster, Gail Kern, *Humoring the Body: Emotions and the Shakespearean Stage*, Chicago: University of Chicago Press, 2004.
Pearsall, Derek, *The Canterbury Tales*, Winchester: Allen & Unwin, 1985.
Pearsall, Derek, *The Life of Geoffrey Chaucer: A Critical Biography*, Oxford: Blackwell, 1992.
Pearsall, Derek, *Old and Middle English Poetry*, London: Routledge, 1977.
'Peeps at the poets', *Kind Words for Young Friends* (1 April 1879), pp. 118–19.
Perler, Dominik, 'Perception in medieval philosophy', in Mohan Matthen (ed.), *The Oxford Handbook of Philosophy of Perception*, Oxford: Oxford University Press, 2015, pp. 51–65.
Phillips, Helen, 'Auchinleck and Chaucer', in Susanna Fein (ed.), *The Auchinleck Manuscript: New Perspectives*, Woodbridge: Boydell & Brewer for York Medieval Press, 2016, pp. 139–55.
Phillips, Helen, 'Chaucer and the nineteenth-century city', in Ardis Butterfield (ed.), *Chaucer and the City*, Cambridge: D. S. Brewer, 2006, pp. 193–210.
Phillips, Helen, 'Fortune and the lady: Machaut, Chaucer, and the intertextual "dit"', *Nottingham French Studies*, 38:2 (1999), 120–36.
'The pilgrims to Rome (after Chaucer)', *Punch* (20 October 1851), p. 230.
Plamper, Jan, 'The history of emotions: an interview with William Reddy, Barbara Rosenwein, and Peter Stearns', *History and Theory*, 49 (2010), 237–65.
'The poet Chaucer to Prince Albert', *Morning Post* (13 May 1842), p. 3.
'Poetry of Chaucer', *Daily Inter Ocean* [Chicago] (9 February 1894), p. 4.

'The Poleesemanne', *Illustrated London News* (2 October 1847), p. 219.
'The policeman's tale', *Fun* (26 June 1875), p. 267.
Pollard, A. W. and G. R. Redgrave (eds), *A short-title catalogue of books printed in England, Scotland and Ireland, and of English books printed abroad 1475–1640*, 2nd edn, revised and enlarged, begun by W. A. Jackson and F. S. Ferguson, completed by K. F. Pantzer, 3 vols, London: Bibliographical Society, 1976–91.
Pound, Ezra, *Make It New*, New Haven: Yale University Press, 1935.
Prendergast, Thomas A., *Chaucer's Dead Body: From Corpse to Corpus*, New York: Routledge, 2004.
Prendergast, Thomas A., 'Revenant Chaucer: early modern celebrity', in Isabel Davis and Catherine Nall (eds), *Chaucer and Fame: Reputation and Reception*, Cambridge: D. S. Brewer, 2015, pp. 185–99.
Prendergast, Thomas A. and Stephanie Trigg, *Affective Medievalism: Love, Abjection and Discontent*, Manchester: Manchester University Press, 2018.
'Prof. Coppee's lectures', *North American and United States Gazette* [Philadelphia] (11 November 1857), p. 170.
'Professor Courthope on Chaucer', *The Times* (5 June 1899), p. 6.
'Professor Silliman saw in the British Museum "an Egyptian pebble"', *Daily National Intelligencer* (25 August 1820).
The Prologue and the Tale of Beryn, in John M. Bowers (ed.), *The Canterbury Tales: Fifteenth-Century Continuations and Additions*, TEAMS Middle English Texts Series, Kalamazoo: Medieval Institute Publications, 1992.
Pugh, Tison, 'Chaucerian fabliaux, cinematic fabliau: Pier Paolo Pasolini's *I racconti di Canterbury*', *Literature/Film Quarterly*, 32:3 (2004), 199–206.
Purdie, Rhiannon, *Anglicising Romance: Tail-rhyme and Genre in Medieval English Literature*, Cambridge: D. S. Brewer, 2008.
Puttenham, George, *The Arte of English Poesie Contriued into Three Bookes*, London, 1589, STC 20519.5.
Rachel, Max, *Reimbrechung und Dreireim im Drama des Hans Sachs und andrer gleichzeitiger Dramatiker*, Freiberg: Gerlach, 1870.
'The restoration of Chaucer's monument', *Lady's Newspaper* (29 June 1850), p. 359.
'Review of *Chaucer's England*', *Sunday Times* (28 March 1869).
'Review of *Contes de Canterbury*, trans. Chevalier de Chatelain', *Englishwoman's Review and Drawing Room Journal* (22 August 1857), p. 1.
'Review of *Contes de Canterbury*, trans. Chevalier de Chatelain', *Lady's Newspaper* (10 April 1858), p. 236.
'Review of *Contes de Canterbury*, trans. Chevalier de Chatelain', *Reynolds' Magazine* (11 April 1858).
'Review of *Contes de Canterbury*, trans. Chevalier de Chatelain', *Sunday Times* (2 August 1857), p. 2.

'Review of *Tales from Chaucer in Prose and Verse, Designed Chiefly for Young Persons*', *Western Times* (13 December 1870), p. 7.
'Review of *The Canterbury Tales from Chaucer*, ed. John Saunders', *The Economist* (1 May 1847), p. 507.
'Review of *The Poems of Chaucer*, ed. Richard Hengist Horne', *Illustrated London News* (5 November 1842), p. 410.
'Review of *The Poetical Works of Geoffrey Chaucer*', *Newcastle Courant* (16 February 1855).
'Review of *The Riches of Chaucer*', *John Bull* (17 December 1870), p. 872.
'Review of *The Riches of Chaucer*', *Examiner* (4 January 1835).
'Review of *The Works of Geoffrey Chaucer*', *Examiner* (12 January 1867).
'Review of Walter Thornbury, *Old and New London*', *Manchester Times* (7 March 1874).
Richmond, Velma Bourgeois, *Chaucer as Children's Literature: Retellings from the Victorian and Edwardian Eras*, Jefferson NC: McFarland & Co., 2004.
Richmond, Velma Bourgeois, 'Edward Burne-Jones's Chaucer portraits in the Kelmscott *Chaucer*', *Chaucer Review*, 40:1 (2005), pp. 1–38.
Richmond, Velma Bourgeois, 'Ford Madox Brown's protestant medievalism: Chaucer and Wycliffe', *Christianity and Literature*, 54:3 (2005), 363–92.
Rickert, Edith, comp., *Chaucer's World*, ed. Clair C. Olson and Martin M. Crow, New York: Columbia University Press, 1948.
Robertson, D. W., 'Chaucerian tragedy', *English Literary History*, 19 (1952), 1–37.
Robertson, Elizabeth, 'Chaucer and Wordsworth's vivid daisies', in Bettina Bildhauer and Chris Jones (eds), *The Middle Ages in the Modern World: Twenty-First Century Perspectives*, Oxford: British Academy, 2017, pp. 219–38.
Robertson, Kellie, 'Exemplary rocks', in Jeffrey Jerome Cohen (ed.), *Animal, Vegetable, Mineral: Ethics and Objects*, Washington DC: Oliphaunt, 2011, pp. 91–121.
The Romance of Guy of Warwick: From the Auchinleck ms. in the Advocates' Libr., Edinburgh and from ms. 107 in Caius College, Cambridge, ed. Julius Zupitza, EETS e.s. 42, London: Oxford University Press, 1883, repr. 1966.
The Romance of Sir Beues of Hamtoun, ed. Eugen Kölbing, EETS e.s. 46, London: Trübner, 1885; Millwood NY: Kraus Reprint, 1978.
Rooney, Anne, *Hunting in Middle English Literature*, Cambridge: D. S. Brewer, 1993.
Rooney, Anne, 'The hunts in *Sir Gawain and the Green Knight*', in Derek Brewer and Jonathan Gibson (eds), *A Companion to the Gawain-poet*, Woodbridge: Boydell & Brewer, 1997, pp. 157–64.
Ross, Thomas, 'Thomas Wright', in Paul G. Ruggiers (ed.), *Editing Chaucer: The Great Tradition*, Norman OK: Pilgrim, 1984, pp. 145–56.

Rush, Rebecca M., 'Licentious rhymers: John Donne and the late-Elizabethan couplet revival', *ELH*, 84:3 (2017), 529–58.

Ruskin, John, *Lectures on Art*, Oxford: Clarendon Press, 1870.

Salisbury, Eve, *Chaucer and the Child*, New York: Palgrave Macmillan, 2017.

Saunders, John, *Cabinet Pictures of English Life: Chaucer*, London: Charles Knight, 1845.

Saunders, John, *Chaucer's Canterbury Tales and Sketches*, 3 vols in 1, London: Charles Knight, 1845.

Scala, Elizabeth, *Absent Narratives: Manuscript, Textuality, and Literary Structure in Late Medieval England*, New York: Palgrave, 2002.

Schiff, Randy, *Revivalist Fantasy: Alliterative Verse and Nationalist Literary History*, Columbus: Ohio State University Press, 2011.

Schipper, Jakob, *A History of English Versification*, Oxford: Clarendon Press, 1910.

Schultz, James A., *Courtly Love, the Love of Courtliness, and the History of Sexuality*, Chicago: University of Chicago Press, 2006.

Scott-McNabb, David, 'A re-examination of Octovyen's hunt in *The Book of the Duchess*', *Medium Ævum*, 56 (1987), 183–99.

Scrymgeour, Daniel, *The Poetry and Poets of Britain*, Edinburgh: Adam and Charles Black, 1860.

Sennett, Richard, *Flesh and Stone: The Body and the City in Western Civilization*, New York: W. W. Norton & Co., 1996.

Shakespeare, William, 'Sonnet 27', in Stephen Greenblatt *et al.* (eds), *The Norton Shakespeare*, 2 vols, 2nd edn, New York: W. W. Norton & Co., 2008.

Shakespeare, William, 'Venus and Adonis', in *The Poems*, ed. John Roe, Cambridge: Cambridge University Press, 1992.

Sidney, Philip, *An Apology for Poetry (or The Defence of Poesy)*, ed. Geoffrey Shepherd, revd R. W. Maslen, Manchester: Manchester University Press, 2002.

Sieburg, Heinz, *Literatur des Mittelalters*, Berlin: Akademie Verlag, 2010.

Silver, Carole G., *The Romance of William Morris*, Athens OH: Ohio University Press, 1982.

Simpson, James, 'Chaucer's presence and absence, 1400–1550', in Piero Boitani and Jill Mann (eds), *The Cambridge Companion to Chaucer*, 2nd edn, Cambridge: Cambridge University Press, 2003, pp. 251–69.

Simpson, James, 'Cognition is recognition: literary knowledge and textual "face"', *New Literary History*, 44 (2013), 25–44.

Sir Bevis of Hampton, ed. Jennifer Fellows, EETS o.s. 349–50, Oxford: Oxford University Press, 2017.

Sir Gawain and the Green Knight, in Malcolm Andrew and Ronald Waldron (eds), *The Poems of the Pearl Manuscript*, Berkeley: University of California Press, 1978.

Sir Percyvell of Gales in Ywain and Gawain, Sir Percyvell of Gales, The Anturs of Arther, ed. Maldwyn Mills, London: J. M. Dent, 1992.

Skelton, John, Phyllyp Sparowe, in John Skelton: The Complete English Poems, ed. John Scattergood, New Haven and London: Yale University Press, 1983.

Smith, A., 'Chaucer', Cheltenham Chronicle and Parish Register and General Advertiser for Gloucester (6 September 1870), p. 2.

Smith, A. Mark, 'Getting the big picture in perspectivist optics', Isis: A Journal of the History of Science, 72 (1981), 568–89.

Smith, A. Mark, 'Perception', in Robert Pasnau and Christina Van Dyke (eds), The Cambridge History of Medieval Philosophy, Cambridge: Cambridge University Press, 2014, pp. 334–45.

Smith, D. Vance, 'The inhumane wonder of the book', Chaucer Review, 47 (2013), 361–71.

Smith, D. Vance, 'Plague, panic space, and the tragic medieval household', South Atlantic Quarterly, 98:3 (1999), 367–414.

Somerset, Fiona, Feeling Like Saints: Lollard Writings After Wyclif, Ithaca: Cornell University Press, 2015.

Spenser, Edmund, The Faerie Queene, ed. A. C. Hamilton, 2nd edn, Harlow: Longman, 2001.

Spitzer, Leo, 'Anglo-French etymologies', Philological Quarterly, 24 (1945), 20–32.

'Sporting intelligence', Leeds Times (17 September 1870), p. 8.

Spurgeon, Caroline, Five Hundred Years of Chaucer Criticism and Allusion: 1357–1900, 3 vols, Cambridge: Cambridge University Press, 1925.

Stahl, Karl, 'Die Reimbrechung bei Hartmann von Aue', PhD dissertation, Rostock, 1888.

Stanbury, Sarah, 'The lover's gaze in Troilus and Criseyde', in R. A. Shoaf (ed.), Chaucer's Troilus and Criseyde, 'Subgit to alle Poesye': Essays in Criticism, Binghamton NY: Medieval and Renaissance Texts and Studies, 1992, pp. 224–38.

Stanbury, Sarah, Seeing the Gawain Poet: Description and the Art of Perception, Philadelphia: University of Pennsylvania Press, 1991.

Stanbury, Sarah, 'The voyeur and the private life in Troilus and Criseyde', Studies in the Age of Chaucer, 13 (1991), 141–58.

'Starved with a pen in his hand', Penny Satirist (19 July 1845), p. 1.

Steadman, John M., Disembodied Laughter: Troilus and the Apotheosis Tradition – A Reexamination of Narrative and Thematic Contexts, Berkeley and Los Angeles: University of California Press, 1972.

Strohm, Paul, The Poet's Tale: Chaucer and the Year that Made the Canterbury Tales, London: Profile, 2015.

Strohm, Paul, Politique: Languages of Statecraft between Chaucer and Shakespeare, Notre Dame: Notre Dame University Press, 2005.

Strohm, Paul, Social Chaucer, Cambridge MA: Harvard University Press, 1989.

Swinburne, Algernon Charles, *A Midsummer Holiday and Other Poems*, Piccadilly [London]: Chatto & Windus, 1884.

Swinburne, Algernon Charles, 'Wordsworth and Byron', in *Miscellanies*, New York: Worthington, 1886.

'Tableaux vivants', *Derbyshire Times and Chesterfield Herald* (11 February 1893), p. 8.

Taine, Hippolyte, *Histoire de la littérature anglaise*, vol. 1, Paris: Hachette, 1863.

The Tale of Beryn, with a Prologue of the Merry Adventure of the Pardoner with a Tapster at Canterbury, ed. F. J. Furnivall and W. G. Stone, London: N. Trübner & Co. for the Chaucer Society, 1887.

Taylor, Jesse Oak, *The Sky of Our Manufacture: The London Fog in British Fiction from Dickens to Woolf*, Charlottesville: University of Virginia Press, 2016.

'Thomas Stothard, fine arts, Chaucer's pilgrims', *The Times* (21 March 1807), p. 2.

'The tomb of Chaucer', *The Times* (25 August 1845), p. 6.

Tonry, Kathleen, 'Reading history in Caxton's *Polychronicon*', *Journal of English and Germanic Philology*, 111 (2012), 169–98.

Travis, Peter W., 'White', *Studies in the Age of Chaucer*, 22 (2000), 1–66.

Trigg, Stephanie, 'Affect theory', in Susan Broomhall (ed.), *Early Modern Emotions: An Introduction*, New York: Routledge, 2017, pp. 10–13.

Trigg, Stephanie, 'Bluestone and the city: writing an emotional history', *Melbourne Historical Journal*, 44:1 (2017), 41–53.

Trigg, Stephanie, 'Chaucer's silent discourse', *Studies in the Age of Chaucer*, 39 (2017), 33–56.

Trigg, Stephanie, *Congenial Souls: Reading Chaucer from Medieval to Postmodern*, Minneapolis: University of Minnesota Press, 2002.

Trigg, Stephanie, 'Faces that speak: a little emotion machine in the novels of Jane Austen', in Susan Broomhall (ed.), *Spaces for Feeling: Emotions and Sociabilities in Britain, 1650–1850*, London and New York: Routledge, 2015, pp. 185–201.

Trigg, Stephanie, 'Introduction: emotional histories – beyond the personalization of the past and the abstraction of affect theory', *Exemplaria*, 26:1 (2014), 3–15.

Trigg, Stephanie, 'Langland's tears: poetry, emotion and mouvance', *Yearbook of Langland Studies*, 26 (2012), 27–48.

Trigg, Stephanie, '"Language in her eye": the expressive face of Criseyde/Cressida', in Andrew James Johnston, Russell West-Pavlov and Elisabeth Kempf (eds), *Love, History and Emotion in Chaucer and Shakespeare:* Troilus and Criseyde *and* Troilus and Cressida, Manchester: Manchester University Press, 2016, pp. 94–108.

Trigg, Stephanie (ed.), *Medievalism and the Gothic in Australian Culture*, Carlton: Melbourne University Publishing, 2006.

Trigg, Stephanie, 'The romance of exchange: *Sir Gawain and the Green Knight*', *Viator*, 22 (1991), 251–66.
Trigg, Stephanie, *Shame and Honor: A Vulgar History of the Order of the Garter*, Philadelphia: University of Pennsylvania Press, 2012.
Trigg, Stephanie, 'Vitreous archives: fire and transfigured objects', in Grace Moore (ed.), *On Fire*, Brooklyn: Punctum Books, forthcoming.
Trigg, Stephanie, 'What does normal look like?', *TEDxSydney*, 21 May 2015, www.youtube.com/watch?v=tHlh5v5erWA.
Trigg, Stephanie (ed.), *Wynnere and Wastoure*, EETS o.s. 297, London: Oxford University Press, 1990.
Trilling, Lionel, 'Aggression and utopia: a note on William Morris's *News from Nowhere*', *Psychoanalytic Quarterly*, 42 (1972), 214–33.
'Types of virtue, or ideal heroines of English writers', *Girls' Own Paper* (27 October 1888), p. 52.
Tyrwhitt, Thomas, *The Canterbury Tales of Chaucer, to which are added an essay upon his language and versification; an introductory discourse; and notes*, vol. 1, London: T. Payne & Son, 1775.
'University tutorial series: Chaucer, *The Canterbury Tales*', *Morning Post* (28 July 1897).
Urry, John, *The works of Geoffrey Chaucer, compared with the former editions, and many valuable mss. out of which, three tales are added which were never before printed; by John Urry, student of Christ-Church, Oxon. deceased: together with a glossary by a student of the same college*, London, 1721.
van den Berg, Evert, 'Évolution de la versification des adaptations des chansons de geste en moyen néerlandais', in *Au Carrefour des routes d'Europe: la chanson de geste*, vol. 2, Aix-en-Provence: Presses universitaires de Provence, 1987.
van den Berg, Evert and Bart Besamusca, 'Middle Dutch Charlemagne romances and the oral tradition of the *chansons de geste*', in Erik Kooper (ed.), *Medieval Dutch Literature in its European Context*, Cambridge: Cambridge University Press, 1994, pp. 81–95.
Virgil, *Aeneid*, in *Virgil: Eclogues, Georgics, Aeneid*, 2 vols, ed. and trans. H. R. Fairclough, revd G. P. Goold, Cambridge MA: Harvard University Press, 1999.
von Eschenbach, Wolfram, *Parzival*, ed. Karl Lachmann, 6th edn, Berlin: Walter de Gruyter, 1926.
von Eschenbach, Wolfram, Parzival, *with* Titurel *and the Love-lyrics*, trans. Cyril Edwards, Cambridge: D. S. Brewer, 2004.
Vorstius, Joris, 'Die Reimbrechung im frühmittelhochdeutschen *Alexanderliede*', PhD dissertation, Marburg, 1917.
Wack, Mary F., 'Lovesickness in "Troilus"', *Pacific Coast Philology*, 19 (1984), 55–61.
Wackernagel, Wilhelm, *Geschichte der deutschen Literatur*, Basel: Schweighauser, 1848.

Wakelin, Daniel, *Scribal Correction and Literary Craft: English Manuscripts 1375–1510*, Cambridge: Cambridge University Press, 2014.
Ward, Adolphus William, *Chaucer*, English Men of Letters Series, London, 1879.
Ward, Artemus, *Milwaukee Daily Sentinel* (20 October 1866).
Warnke, Karl (ed.), *Die Fabeln der Marie de France*, Halle: Niemeyer, 1898.
Warren, F. M., 'Some features of style in early French narrative poetry (1150–70) – (Concluded)', *Modern Philology*, 4:4 (1907), 655–75.
Watson, Nicholas, 'Chaucer's public Christianity', *Religion and Literature*, 37:2 (2005), 99–114.
Weber, A., 'Good counsel of Chaucer', *Monthly Packet* (1 September 1879), p. 219.
Weiskott, Eric, 'Real formalism, real historicism', unpublished paper delivered at the MLA Annual Convention, Vancouver, January 2015.
Weiss, Judith, 'The wooing woman in Anglo-Norman romance', in Maldwyn Mills, Jennifer Fellows and Carol Meale (eds), *Romance in Medieval England*, Cambridge: D. S. Brewer, 1991, pp. 149–61.
Weissman, Hope Phyllis, 'Late gothic pathos in the *Man of Law's Tale*', *Journal of Medieval and Renaissance Studies*, 9 (1979), 133–54.
Whitaker, Cord, (ed.), 'Making race matter in the Middle Ages', special journal issue, *postmedieval*, 6:1 (2015).
Wimsatt, James, *Chaucer and the French Love Poets: The Literary Background of the Book of the Duchess*, Chapel Hill: University of North Carolina Press, 1968.
Windeatt, Barry, *Chaucer's Dream Poetry: Sources and Analogues*, Cambridge: D. S. Brewer, 1982.
Windeatt, Barry, 'Gesture in Chaucer', in Paul Maurice Clogan (ed.), *Medievalia et Humanistica 9: Studies in Medieval and Renaissance Culture*, Cambridge: Cambridge University Press, 1979, pp. 143–62.
Winton, Calhoun, *John Gay and the London Theatre*, Lexington: University of Kentucky Press, 1993.
'Woodstock', *Leicester Chronicle, or Commercial and Agricultural Advertiser* (15 April 1854).
Woolgar, C. M., *The Senses in Late Medieval England*, New Haven: Yale University Press, 2006.
Wordsworth, William, *Ecclesiastical Sonnets*, ed. Abbie Findlay Potts, New Haven: Yale University Press, 1922.
Wright, Thomas (ed.), *The Canterbury Tales of Geoffrey Chaucer*, London and Glasgow: R. Griffith, 1880.
'Ye Canterburie pilgrymage (ye real thynge)', *Cycling* [London] (10 April 1897), pp. 287–8.

Index

Aeneid see Virgil
Aesop's Fables 146, 148
affect 25, 207
   air as 93–6, 99
   Chaucerian pale faces as 74, 76, 83, 85–6, 89n.16
   in connecting with Chaucer 205–6, 208–10
   history and 201–4
   see also empathy; facial pallor
air 97–9
   broken (farting) 64–5
   stories within 91–6, 100
   see also atmosphere
Aldgate (Chaucer's residence) 21, 167
Alhazen 29, 31
Alighieri, Dante *see* Dante, Alighieri
aristocracy 63, 109–11, 113–20, 154, 155, 158
   see also courtly; Fortune; hunt, the
Arnold, Matthew 176, 181–4
atmosphere 91–9, 102, 104
Auchinleck manuscript 46, 47, 48–9
Augustine, St 24, 27, 28, 33, 35, 37
authorship 14–20, 125–7, 129–34, 141, 176
   see also editing

Babington, Churchill 144
Bacon, Roger 29–31, 36
Bailey, Bill 210, 212–14
Bailly (Bailey), Harry 15, 128
Bartholomeus Anglicus 30, 78
Beckett, Samuel 220
Beryn, Tale of 125–8
   Prologue to the 125–8, 130, 132
Beryn-scribe 126–9, 130–4
Beryn-writer 125–7, 130–1
Bevis of Hamtoun 46–8
Blake, William 154, 174, 180, 208
Boccaccio, Giovanni 32, 101, 103, 113, 160, 211, 212
bodies
   and death 75, 80, 83–6, 100–4, 116
   and desire 35, 44, 47–8, 51, 190, 197
   gendered 27–8, 30–1, 43, 52, 81–3, 86, 93, 94, 113, 122n.14, 145, 193, 197
   and soul 25, 29, 34–5, 37, 99, 103–4
   and transcorporeality 26, 91–3, 94–6, 99, 104, 189, 198, 202
   see also atmosphere; face; facial pallor; humours; senses, the
Boos, Florence 192
Brewer, Derek 153, 174
Brut, Prose 127, 142, 145, 148
Burne-Jones, Edward 192–3, 210, 211

Burrow, J. A. (John) 29, 31, 76, 131, 136n.29

Carruthers, Mary 34, 129
Caxton, William 140–50, 163, 167
  see also editing
chastity 43–4, 47, 50, 52, 191
Chaucer, Geoffrey
  father of English poetry 157, 159, 164, 166, 172, 173, 209
  hearing 32, 42, 65, 205
  images of 154, 192–3, 201, 202, 206, 207–10, 211–14
  as manly 173, 176, 178, 184
  voice of 15–16, 17–18, 187n.65
  working life 20–2, 51, 194–5
  see also dream visions; nineteenth-century Chaucer
Chaucer Society 126, 162
Chaucer the pilgrim 14–16, 42, 45, 52, 62–3, 195, 205–6
Chaucer's works
  Anelida and Arcite 84
  Boece 145
  Book of the Duchess 43, 65, 78, 84, 109–11, 114–15, 117–19, 194
  Canon's Yeoman's Tale 99, 128, 132
    Prologue 128
  Canterbury Tales 14–15, 17, 21, 51, 53, 59, 61, 64, 66, 75, 77, 84, 86, 125, 127–34, 140–1, 143, 144, 146, 155, 160, 162, 167, 174, 176, 178, 193, 195, 205–6, 208, 213–14
    Clerk's Tale 75, 79, 81, 85, 94, 158, 164–5, 178
    Cook's Tale 130, 133, 210, 211
    Franklin's Tale 43, 61, 75, 83
    Friar's Tale 155
    General Prologue 43–4, 59, 61, 63, 66, 77–8, 125, 128, 155, 158, 165, 167, 180, 194, 211, 214
    Knight's Tale 42, 75, 83, 102–4, 160, 162, 179, 182
    Man of Law's Tale 75, 80–3, 85–6, 129, 167, 178
    Manciple's Tale 84, 86, 129
      Prologue 75, 78, 135n.13
    Melibee, Tale of 15, 52–3, 145
    Merchant's Tale 42, 132–3, 210
    Miller's Tale 43, 64–5, 92, 210
    Monk's Tale 110, 113, 178
    Nun's Priest's Tale 83, 157
    Pardoner's Tale 75, 214
    Parson's Tale 145, 146, 175
      Prologue 128
    Physician's Tale 99
    Prioress's Tale 66, 75, 83, 177–8, 181–2
    Reeve's Tale 92–3, 157, 210
    Second Nun's Tale 127, 128
    Sir Thopas 42–53
      Prologue 206, 209
    Squire's Tale 43–4, 92, 129–30
    Summoner's Tale 64, 127, 154, 210
      Prologue 211
    Wife of Bath's Tale 64, 122n.13, 129, 157, 210
      Prologue 63–4, 210
  House of Fame 20–1, 65, 92, 101–2, 146, 159, 194
  Legend of Good Women 65, 155, 161, 194
  Parliament of Fowls 44, 117, 127, 194
  Romaunt of the Rose (Roman de la Rose) 85, 155
  Troilus and Criseyde 21, 24–37, 43, 66, 75, 78–9, 82, 84, 99–101, 103–4, 115, 155, 176, 195, 225–7

Index

Chaucerian community 67,
106n.20, 135n.5, 204–5,
214
identification with Chaucer
14–16, 18–19, 22, 126,
173, 180, 193, 210
see also Congenial Souls;
Einfühlung
Chrétien de Troyes 49, 56, 57, 60,
63–4, 182
Christ 20, 81–2, 179, 180
Christendom 178, 181–2
Christianity 45, 47, 81–3, 180
Clarke, Charles Cowden 155–6,
158, 163, 164, 165
see also editing
climate *see* air; atmosphere
cognition 24, 37, 94
re- 80, 219–32
Congenial Souls 14, 15, 67,
106n.20, 132, 138, 193,
205, 207
Cooper, Helen 139, 140, 209
courtly
practices 62, 117, 119–20
writing 60, 111, 116

Dante, Alighieri 181, 194, 223–5,
228–9
Divine Comedy 224
Dilthey, Wilhelm 202–3
dream
Dreamer 84, 110–11, 116, 117
as narrative framework 16, 52,
83–4, 193, 198
see also Dream of Scipio; dream
visions
Dream of Scipio 100–1, 103
dream visions 15–16, 192, 193–5,
205
Dryden, John 14, 176, 179, 205

editing 57
for 'good' English 142–50, 156
nineteenth-century 155–6, 160–3
philological 140–1, 149

scribal activity (fifteenth
century) as 125–34
see also Beryn-scribe; Caxton,
William
Edward III 69n.8, 119, 156, 175
Edward IV 142
Einfühlung 202–7, 210, 212
Ellesmere manuscript 110, 207,
209, 211, 213
Ellesmere-Hoccleve image 208–9,
213–14
embodiment
of Chaucer 163, 210–12, 214
and climate 91–3, 99
and emotions 79, 82, 207
medieval 83, 93, 118, 120
emotions
ambient 91, 94, 95
for Chaucer 158, 204–5, 207–8,
214–15
in encounter and recognition 24,
32, 220–1, 223–4, 227
history of 74, 76, 188, 201–2,
203
medieval representations of
25–6, 35, 54n.13, 74–87
see also affect; *Einfühlung;* love;
maidens
empathy
reading facial 76, 82, 86
transhistoric 201–4, 207, 210,
212
see also face

face
Chaucer's 201, 202, 206–9,
211–14
and recognition 219–32
speaking 40n.28, 40n.33, 76,
82–3
textual/hermeneutic guide 74,
76–81, 83, 86–7, 180, 208,
220, 227, 231
see also emotions; facial pallor;
gaze, the; recognition
facial pallor 74–87

fairies 42, 44, 52, 191
  see also Chaucer's works,
    Canterbury Tales, Sir
    Thopas
Fellowship of the New Life 197
Floure and the Leafe, The 154, 155, 164
Fortune 84, 104, 109–12, 113–16, 119–20
Freud, Sigmund 16–17, 189
Froissart, Jean 16, 65, 119
Furnivall, F. J. 126, 162, 163, 165

Gadamer, Hans-Georg 203, 232n.2
Gallagher, Shaun 207
Gamelyn, Tale of 68n.1, 125, 136n.29
Gawain-poet 39n.15, 113, 115, 117
gaze, the 26–32, 35, 36–7, 50, 79, 190, 211, 219, 222
  scopophilic 27–8, 34
  see also bodies, gendered;
    Chaucer's works, Troilus
    and Criseyde; snail-horn
    perception
gender see bodies, gendered
gestalt 18
gesture 29
  facial 77, 79, 81
  see also face
Godwin, William 155, 161, 166, 175, 176
Gower, John 91, 139, 177
  Confessio Amantis 85, 96–7
Guy of Warwick 45–6, 47, 50

Habermas, Jürgen 203, 205
Haweis, Mrs H. R. (Mary Eliza) 164–5, 175
Hawes, Stephen 139, 141
Henryson, Robert 225–7
Higden, Ranulph see Polychronicon
Hoccleve, Thomas 133, 140, 206, 207
  see also Ellesmere-Hoccleve
    image
Horn Childe and Maiden Rimnild
  (Romance of Horn) 47–8
  see also King Horn
Horne, Lawrence 159, 167
Horne, Richard Hengist 156, 178–80, 182
Hugh of St Victor 25, 29, 37
humanities 218, 220
humours, 77, 78, 79, 92–3, 94–5, 99
hunt, the 109–11, 115–17, 118–20
  see also Fortune; Sir Gawain and
    the Green Knight

Ingarden, Roman 18
intentio auctoris 129–31, 133–4
Ipomadon 49–52
Iser, Wolfgang 18

Keats, John 25, 33
Kelmscott
  Chaucer 192–3, 210, 211
  Manor 195, 198
  see also Burne-Jones, Edward;
    Morris, William
King Horn 47–8, 52
Kittredge, G. L. 65, 193
Knight, Stephen 56, 57, 61, 66
knights 158, 166
  and love 27, 46, 50
  see also Sir Gawain and the
    Green Knight
Knight's Tale, A 210, 211
knighthood 48, 49

Latini, Brunetto 98–9, 102–3
Levinas, Emmanuel 76, 80, 206–7
Levine, Caroline 57
love
  and the elements 98, 102, 107n.33, 160, 188
  encountering/falling in 24–5, 26, 38, 44, 46–7, 220–1

Index

free 195, 197
lovesickness 45, 48, 50, 52, 75, 83, 190
noble 118, 120
and recognition 223–6
sensual lust 34–6
and sleeplessness 43–4, 46
and the speaking face 27, 29, 30, 75, 78–9, 84, 86
see also Chaucer's works, *Troilus and Criseyde*
love-longing 44, 46, 48, 52
Lowell, James Russell 159–60
Lydgate, John 88n.14, 113, 127, 139, 140
Fall of Princes 114
Siege of Thebes 131–2

Machan, Tim 140, 143
Machaut, Guillaume de 16, 111, 122n.12, 194
Complainte 65
Dit dou lyon 65
Le jugement dou roy de Navarre 121n.6
Remede de fortune 118
McNamer, Sarah 25, 81
maidens
lovesick 44–5
mourning 42–3, 45–53
see also chastity; facial pallor; love
Malory, Sir Thomas 51, 115
manuscript
illustrations 89n.16, 98–9, 101, 110, 201, 207, 212
early print editions 140–4, 147, 148–9
scribal compilation (fifteenth century) 125–34
see also Beryn-scribe; editing; Middle English
Massumi, Brian 24, 35
medievalism 153, 158, 202, 204, 213

Middle English
language 44, 50, 91, 94, 118, 144–50, 166
literature 43, 47, 49, 57–8, 60, 74, 76, 110, 138–43, 182–3
romances 42, 44–7, 48–9, 52, 56, 67
see also editing; poetry; rhyme-breaking
Miles, Margaret 35
Mitchell, J. Allan 93, 96, 97
Morley, Henry 162, 176–7
Morris, William 166
News from Nowhere 188–98
see also dream visions
Morse, Charlotte 153, 155, 164

News from Nowhere see Morris, William
nineteenth-century Chaucer
Catholicism and 172–6, 182–5
English nationalism and 173–4, 176–7, 179–81, 182–4
English reception 153–9, 164–5, 173
scholarship 159–64, 166–7

object
of enquiry 180, 203, 230–1
of sight 27–8, 29–30, 35, 37, 202
subject– 17, 25
Ohlgren, Thomas 56, 57
optical theory (medieval) 26, 28–30, 34, 38n.1
see also vision

Parlement of the Thre Ages 51, 110, 119, 122n.13
parody 42–3, 44, 52, 53
see also Chaucer's works, *Canterbury Tales, Sir Thopas*
Pasolini, Pier Paolo 210, 211–14
Petrarch, Francesco 43, 45, 59, 83, 132

phenomenology 16, 18, 25, 207
Philippa Roet (Chaucer's wife) 20–1
Phillips, Helen 122n.12, 153, 154, 164, 178
Phyllyp Sparowe 139
pilgrims *see* Chaucer's works, *Canterbury Tales*
poetry (narrative)
   alliteration in 60, 85, 121n.3, 133, 229
   couplets in 47, 49, 56–61, 63–7, 213
   tail-rhyme 42, 47, 49, 52
   see also rhyme-breaking
Polychronicon 141–2, 146, 148
Pope, Alexander 167, 176, 208
Pound, Ezra 220
Prick of Conscience 127
'Protestant' Chaucer 172, 174–5, 177, 182, 184
Puttenham, George 68n.1, 69n.5, 139, 149

recognition
   of Chaucer 21–2, 183
   emotional 203, 207
   facial/textual 221–32
   literary/textual 80, 218–20
   see also cognition
Reimbrechung 59–60, 72n.24
   see also rhyme-breaking
religion
   and Chaucer 172–4, 176–7, 179–80, 181, 182–4
   see also nineteenth-century Chaucer, Chaucer's Catholicism
rhyme-breaking 56–67
Riches of Chaucer, The 154, 155, 165
Romantic
   Chaucer 153, 154, 155, 160, 162, 163, 165, 184
   hermeneutics 202–3
   Morris 191, 194
   post- 61, 129

Rosenwein, Barbara 201, 203
Rossetti, Dante Gabriel 193, 209
Ruskin, John 180–1, 183, 191

Saunders, John 155, 158, 175
Schipper, Jakob 58–9, 61, 68n.4
Sennett, Richard 189, 196
senses, the 25–6, 28–9, 33, 180, 189–90, 202
   encounter and 24–6, 30, 32–3, 34–8, 223, 230–1
   see also sight
sexuality 27, 44, 190, 195, 196, 198
   see also bodies
Shakespeare, William 33, 42, 52, 145–6, 160, 161, 167, 175, 181
shame 79, 85, 222–3
sight
   Augustine rays/*species* 28–31, 35
   first 24, 26–8, 32, 35–6, 43, 75, 81, 224
   sense of 25–6, 30, 33–4, 37
   see also gaze, the; optical theory; senses, the
Simpson, James 80, 141
Sir Gawain and the Green Knight 43, 109–17, 120, 122n.13
Sir Percyvell of Gales 45, 49
Skelton, John, 139–40, 149
snail-horn perception 24–5, 32–4, 36–7
species see sight
Speght, Thomas 144–5, 146–7, 149, 150, 208
Spenser, Edmund 44, 147, 158
Spurgeon, Caroline 153, 204
Stanbury, Sarah 28, 31, 36, 39n.15
Stothard, Thomas 154, 208
Swinburne, Algernon Charles 187n.50, 208–9

transcorporeality *see* bodies
Trevisa, John 91, 141–9

Trigg, Stephanie 42, 67, 153, 156, 162, 204
    on *Troilus and Criseyde* 31, 32, 36
    and the face 214, 227
    and history of emotions 25–6, 74, 76, 105n.10, 106n.20, 188, 204
    on *Sir Gawain and the Green Knight* 109, 114–15
    see also Congenial Souls
Troy 26, 101, 109, 113, 115, 117–18

Urry, John 125–6, 161, 206, 208

van den Berg, Evert 58
Verstehen 202, 203
Virgil 194, 220–5

vision 24, 28–30, 35, 37
    see also dream visions; sight; snail-horn perception

Ward, Adolphus William 183–4
Wordsworth, William 160, 177–9, 180, 181, 182
world
    bodies and 26, 94, 96
    human/physical 92, 95–104, 192, 198
    sensual encounter with 24–6, 30, 33–4, 35, 36–8, 223, 230–1
    underworld 222–4
    view (Chaucer) 18, 153, 174, 179–80, 187n.65
Wyclif, John 175, 177, 184

Lightning Source UK Ltd.
Milton Keynes UK
UKHW010112030719
345475UK00004B/182/P